BEHEMOTH

BEHEMOTH

Main Currents in the History and Theory of Political Sociology

Irving Louis HOROWITZ

Transaction Publishers
New Brunswick (U.S.A.) and London (U.K.)

Library of Congress Catalog Number: 98-45322
ISBN: 1-56000-410-X (cloth); 0-7658-0627-4 (paper)
Printed in the United States of America

Library of Congress Cataloging-in-Publication Data

Horowitz, Irving Louis.
    Behemoth : main currents in the history and theory of political sociology / Irving Louis Horowitz.
        p. cm.
    Includes bibliographical references and index.
    ISBN 1-56000-410-X (cloth: alk. paper).—ISBN 0-7658-0627-4 (pbk.: alk. paper)
    1. Political sociology—History. I. Title.
JA76.H66   1999
306.2'01—dc21   98-45322
                                                                          CIP

Neither anarchy nor tyranny, my people.
Worship the Mean, I urge you,
shore it up with reverence and never
banish terror from the gates, not outright,
Where is the righteous man who knows no fear?
The stronger your fear, your reverence for the just,
the stronger your country's wall and city's safety.

–Athena's instructions to the jury,
from Aeschylus' Oresteia

Contents

Acknowledgments

In recognizing the assistance provided by others, we tend to pay our respects to people who have had a hands-on connection with the particular manuscript at hand. But before I do so, it is only right and fair to point out to critical influences along the way and in diverse places whose own efforts at understanding the relationship of state and society played a part.

There were my wise teachers at the City College of the City University of New York, especially Samuel Hendel in political science, Henry Magid in philosophy, and Michael Krause in history, who held high the banner of liberal learning as well as objectivity in study. They did so against the tremendous rush of ideological extremism that was as pandemic in the 1940s as it was in the 1990s. The debt I owe to my mentor Abraham Edel is expressed in a festschrift whose title: *Ethics, Science, and Democracy* conveys much of what that mighty figure has contributed not just to me but to countless generations of CCNY and University of Pennsylvania students.

A quartet of figures at Columbia University followed my undergraduate years: Horace Friess in ethics, John Herman Randall in the history of philosophy, Joseph Blau in American Studies, and Paul Oskar Kristeller in Medieval and Renaissance Studies, and Herbert W. Schneider, the "most wordly philosopher" Columbia ever produced. More in retrospect than at the time, they gave philosophical meaning to wide-ranging social and political issues, and did so with a deep appreciation of history sorely lacking in purely normative studies of politics and social structure.

To this list must be added the extraordinary impact and
support of Gino Germani, Enrique Butelman, and Mario
Bunge of the University of Buenos Aires. Their work had a
freshness and solidity that derived not just from an empirical emphasis, but were examples of how unfettered minds
can come up with important new insights in looking at a
world much studied. They were also men in the world as
well as students of the world. Indeed, their work at Edito-
rial Paidos, and in assisting the birth of the University Press,
became part of a seamless effort at disseminating as well as
teaching social science. Their example in this connection
was not lost on me. My largest debt is to Mario Bunge, now
at McGill University in Canada, whose courageous political
observations perhaps equal his acumen in the philosophy
of science. It was an epistolary relationship during the dark
days of Peronism that brought to me to Buenos Aires in the
late 1950s on not much more than pure chance.

While my year at Brandeis University was not a simple
one, I again had the great good fortune of studying with
extraordinary individuals. Frank Manuel's rigorous sense
of staying close to the text; Paul Radin's naturalistic ability
to give meaning to sophisticated myths of primitive peoples;
Lewis A. Coser's vast and generous sense of the historical
mooring of social theory; Eugene V. Walter's pioneering
work in the anthropology of violence and state terror, made
a deep impression on me. I confess that such a cumulative
impact seems stronger in retrospect than it appeared at the
time. Without such figures, the world of learning would be
a barren place. The initial cohort assembled at the start-up
of Brandeis was something special.

In each institution of higher learning that I taught special individuals who were not only colleagues but also mentors entered my life, nearly all of whom had much to say
about the relationship of state and society in a variety of
guises. At Bard College there were Gerard DeGré and Frank
Riessman, occupying opposite ends of the political spec-

trum, but wise beyond their own years. I also had the chance to meet wonderful and enormously talented "literary" figures like Ralph Ellison whose booming voice lecturing on Russian classical literature was next door to my own class, and Eugene Goodheart, whose name tells it all.

At Hobart & William Smith, where I had my first taste in administering a department, I formed a special bond with Maynard Smith, whose quiet sense of America as a decent place because it is a decent polity finally penetrated my conscience. Without raising his voice above a whisper he managed to rattle my cage of political certitudes. Young C. Kim, who went on to found Asian Studies at Georgetown University, was a different sort of political scientist, but no less an impressive one. George Walsh in philosophy had a droll manner that could hardly disguise his erudition. That each of them went on to become Transaction authors indicates the strong and lasting impression these colleagues had on my own evolution.

There was a special interlude at the London School of Economics that had an impact on my work in political sociology far beyond the time there spent. In serving as an exchange professor with Ralph Miliband in 1961, I had the chance to meet with and learn from such extraordinary figures as Leonard Shapiro, Jacob Talmon, Richard Titmuss, and Michael Oakeshott. I came to understand that the "privilege of commons" was indeed a great deal more than teachers munching and lunching with each other.

At Washington University, where I spent the better part of the 1960s, there were so many important individuals who influenced my thinking in political sociology that I can barely keep the list down to appreciable levels. In sociology there was Gilbert Shapiro, Alvin W. Gouldner, Joseph A. Kahl, Robert Hamblin, Jules Henry, John W. Bennett (the sociology department was combined with anthropology at the time). In political science there was John W. Kautsky, Walter Dean Burnham, Merle Kling, and Michael Ledeen. Mike was actually in history, but his powerful concerns with the contrasting nature of political systems, made him in effect a political scientist without department portfolio. This was a brilliant cohort assembled at the right place in the right decade.

Having spent the past thirty years at Rutgers University, a time frame that dwarfs all the rest, it would be imprudent and indeed impossible to single out individuals who helped educate me. So I will refrain from "naming names." However, I will say that collectively, as well as individually, my colleagues at Rutgers have been uniformly helpful and giving of their time and effort. I realize, perhaps later than I should, that a good university is one in which faculty learn from one another, and not just a mechanical environment in which administrators, teachers, and students aspire to act in unadorned harmony. There are three people, two presidents and one dean: Mason W. Gross, Edward J. Bloustein, and Ernest A. Lynton, whose vision for Transaction as a significant voice for social science and social policy nearly equaled my own. These "administrators" were colleagues in the truest and best sense of the word.

Many of the aforementioned individuals have since passed away. They leave behind more than memories. The culture of learning which they inherited and in turn transmitted makes the world of scholarship an eternal flame as well as an immediate challenge. I am sure that I have left out of the mix many people who taught me many things. And at some point I will either remember or be reminded of my lapse in memory and hence my failings of sound judgment. But I did want to take this rare opportunity to acknowledge the guidance of those people, some who would have welcomed, others who would have frowned on my work on the Behemoth.

So I come now to an acknowledgment of those people who have kindly read critiques and where necessary corrected my manuscript. And here too it should be apparent that the world of learning is hardly confined to a small handful of places. I have been able to call upon dear friends and colleagues drawn from many institutions. Joseph Lopreato of the University of Texas, Paul Hollander of the University of Massachusetts, Daniel Mahoney of Assumption College, Peter Baehr of St. Johns University in Canada, David Marsland of Brunel University in the United Kingdom, and Richard Boyd, now of the University of Chicago, all read my effort with keen insight and skilled criticisms. By their detailed commentaries, they made my manuscript better. I want to take special note of the efforts by Richard Boyd. He was my last doctoral student prior to my reaching maturity, otherwise known as emeritus status. And I unabashedly declare him to be my best student over the years—and I take great pride in the accomplishments and brilliance of all my students. By the time his dissertation was completed, and his withering reading of my manuscript was a leitmotif along the way, I had become his student and colleague. This is another unique, if somewhat under appreciated blessing bestowed upon those who inhabit universities.

The staff at Transaction, starting first and foremost with Mary E. Curtis its president, was extraordinarily helpful at every stage of manuscript preparation. Donna Kronemeyer now of Princeton University Press was an excellent copy editor; Susan Hoffman not only typeset my manuscript in an attractive format but also slyly helped design the work along the way. Andrew McIntosh did far more than proofread the manuscript. He made changes that uniformly improved the final effort, and spared me some embarrassment at least. Laurence Mintz, our senior editor, is a secret weapon that makes any publishing house tick. He is a man of vast erudition, whose loving care, not just of my book but countless others made the difference for many scholars between acceptable levels of publication and outstanding final products.

The previous comments are more in the nature of appreciation rather than acknowledgement. But in three chapters, I drew upon materials previously published. And while in each case the changes made are sufficiently substantial to merit being called newly written, I do want to take note of these originating sources: On Hegel, *Foundations of Political Sociology,* Harper & Row. On Sorel, *Radicalism and the Revolt Against Reason,* Routledge & Kegan Paul. On Mills, *An American Utopian,* Macmillan-Free Press. I am grateful in each case to the original publishers for their reversion of rights.

I count my blessings that I can still go to work each day and number these people among my close associates. In the final instance, when push comes to shove, the manuscript is now published and in cold type before the reader. *Behemoth* represents my attempt to understand two big words, state and society—in historical context, theoretical richness, and emotional texture. It is not my only effort in such a quest, but I believe it to be my best effort. The history of ideas may be a dialogue with the dead, but I do not think it is a dialogue among the deaf. Were I unable to say this, the work would not merit publication. It remains for others to determine whether this is one in a series of archival relics or part of the living soul of our social world. It has been a difficult, sometimes even painful gamble, but one well worth taking. I started this process by trying to understand the historical antecedents of the current malaise in sociology, but I have ended with a far richer appreciation of what came out right in the magisterial field I have been privileged to be part of.

ILH

Introduction:
Main Currents in Political
Sociology, 1748–1998

"Anarchy: from the Greek *anarkhos*, without a chief; an instigator of anarchy, a leader of revolt.
Behemoth: from the Hebrew *Behemah*, a beast; an enormous creature, monstrously huge and vast"
—*The New Shorter Oxford English Dictionary on Historical Principles*[1]

I have come to believe that an introduction is a wonderful device that enables an author to cover his or her tracks; allowing one to admit to problems not actually solved in the text itself. In this regard, my opening remarks will not disappoint. For in reviewing the remarks received from colleagues and friends, and also reexamining the text itself, it is clear that some problems remain that at least merit self-awareness, if not resolution. How could a study of state and society be otherwise, given the magnitude and diverse meanings that attach to both words. Even in its restricted use, the state as the supreme public power or government within a given polity raises as many problems of definition as it answers. And the term society, the totality of social relationships among human beings, is hardly less porous. Indeed, recent researches indicate that societies exist as much in the animal kingdom as in so-called higher life forms.

It should be kept in mind that this is not so much a study of state and society as such, but rather how major analysts

of the past 250 years have interpreted these all-embracing
words. This is assuredly enough of a chore for any single
volume. Constructing a universe of major figures has itself
proven to be a daunting task. To start with, there is the question of where and with whom to start. Then there is a question of how the history of political sociology can be disen-
tangled from the history of political philosophy and
sociology. When these preliminary hurdles are cleared, or
at least thought to be cleared, there is the matter of national
pride and cultural limits. Why is there so heavy an emphasis on French and German and later American figures?
Would the issues look much different say with an emphasis
on British and Italian writers on the area? And even if my
bias in favor of French, German and American scholars is
accepted, critics have a perfect right to ask why so little attention to say Roberto Michels, Karl Mannheim, and Robert MacIver—to pull three figures at random—at the expense
of those high lighted for extended attention.

Let me admit to the vexing nature of such concerns. The
process of selection can indeed be arbitrary and capricious.
It might well be that a different choice of subjects would
have brought us to a different end point. But frankly, I doubt
it. Differences in nuance and style do not yet signify different outcomes. I prefer to think that the field now called
political sociology has a set of problems which it seeks to
address that give the field its substance as well as parameters. I also believe that the figures examined in depth have
given voice over time to these deeper empirical and theoretical considerations. The policy decisions and moral quan-
daries faced by past scholars differ far more in quantity than
in structure. It is for this reason that they can and are still
read. For were this not to be the case, this would be a quaint
text but not an especially significant one. Others will doubt-
less refine and revise the figures highlighted no less than
the themes examined. But I can hope and indeed do believe that *Behemoth* provides a starting point in the ever-con-

tinuing process of reconsideration the theoretical tools we carry about as well as the intellectual sources of our belief systems. My book is offered in that spirit of laying a foundation for a hyphenated field—political sociology—that refuses to pass quietly into the night of our intellectual discontent.

Another curious fact of scholarly writing, and for all that I know, of writing as such, is that the choice of title and subtitle appears at the start of a book, but often comes at the end of its creation. With regard to this particular book, this has certainly been the case. I settled on the word *Behemoth* with certain trepidation. For while it perfectly captures what the work is about, the word has been utilized in classical political writings since Thomas Hobbes, and more recently in a brilliant book by the late Franz Neumann (published in 1944) on the Nazi State: *Behemoth: The Structure and Practice of National Socialism.*[2] Neumann, a unique figure in the so-called Frankfurt School, never permitted his dedication to a socialist solution to deflect from his deep appreciation of the liberal and constitutional traditions of the West. In any case, and aside from being second to Neumann in the use of the work behemoth in a title, the two works are clearly so different in character and content that no confusion should result.

In electing to begin the sub-title with the words "Main Currents" I shamelessly draw upon the choice that was made by different sources of inspiration for my own work. I have in mind Vernon Parrington,[3] whose writings on American literature inspired a generation and elucidated the sources and inspiration of a national heritage that was quite different from the British tradition; and Raymond Aron, whose work on sociological thought served as a demonstration that the best of a discipline is universal in impact no less than in content.[4] However, I must confess that another reason for the choice of my sub-title was a reticence to employ a word that would convey the notion of a textbook, such as "Foundations," "Outlines of," "Essentials of," and so forth. I also

wanted to avoid the idea of a trade book, what I call the
"*Gone With the Wind* Syndrome": I wrote it, therefore it must
be a book for every man, woman and child walking the face
of the earth. *Main Currents* indicates a modest rather than
global characterization. And, indeed, I do want to emphasize
that the work is an effort at highlighting the main threads of
a discipline that arguably started with Montesquieu, and perhaps even more arguably is still in the process of evolution.

Permit me then to take a moment and explain what this
work is not. It is not intended to be an exploration into the
history of general sociology; we already have several fine
volumes in this area, above all, the work of Robert A. Nisbet
[5] and the aforementioned effort of Raymond Aron.[6] (I am
indebted to both of these pioneers for appreciating the extent to which the study of social science is a critical as well
as a constructive activity.) Nor is this book intended to be a
cultural study of the thought and ideas of the century, pos-
tulating a particular thesis. Again, in this area we have some
fine entries; perhaps the most outstanding of which is that
of William R. Everdell,[7] who declares that discontinuity is
the key to understanding modernity.

Rather, my work flows from a lifelong attachment to understanding the relationship of state and society, or more
accurately, the political system to the social order. This pursuit has taken me in diverse but hopefully not random path-
ways over the past forty-five years: covering the French Enlightenment, German Romanticism, the rise of socialism,
the emergence of a radicalism in revolt against reason (at
least against rationalist models of reason, through the European experience with fascism and communism, and the
ensuing exile and Diaspora of European intellectuals), and
finally to a study of American traditions—both nativist and
imported.

Along the way, curious phenomena of extraordinary proportions took place. The first of these was the emergence of
social science as the touchstone of the century, and the sec-

ond was the no less startling decomposition of several of its older branches, in particular sociology and anthropology.[8] Since my own concerns are in the former, I will restrict myself to noting the publication of major works in anthropology by figures such as Robin Fox[9] and John W. Bennett[10] that document parallels in other fields such as cultural anthropology.

In my book, *The Decomposition of Sociology*, I concentrated on contextual reasons for the rise of social science and the decline of sociology. Issues pertaining to the overall changes in American academic life were central, as were shifts in evaluative criteria from achievement factors of learning and education to ascriptive factors of race, class and gender. And while these seemed satisfactory at the start of the decade, I increasingly felt a serious gap in the intellectual sources of the discipline of sociology which made possible a desultory outcome against which nearly every other discipline—save again anthropology—seems to have been vaccinated if not immune.

Upon closer inspection, it became evident that sociology in practice gave strong attention to national conditions, but in theory continued to rest heavily on European antecedents. The field which at the start of the twentieth century hardly paid any attention to European thought—enmeshed as it was in a social work perspective rooted in religious values derived from various strands of Protestantism—by the close of the century boasted of its tremendous separation from social welfare and social work perspectives, and from "reformism" as a value. It also distanced itself from its roots in American Protestantism to such a point that the small sub-field of the sociology of religion gave more attention to marginal religious agencies than it did to established church denominations.

As a result, with sociology we have a field of study that spends a great deal of time inventing a tradition and thus creating a canon. But in doing so, the process of selection

becomes a critical variable in the study of the European
roots of the decomposition of sociology. The search for roots
took American sociology to Europe. The early, turn-of-the-
century Chicago types, such as Albion Small, embraced the
conflict school of Ludwig Gumplowicz and Gustav
Ratzenhofer, which seemed a suitable extension of Darwinian thought to the area of race and ethnic relations generally. The Harvard School, as exemplified by Parsons in the
post-World War One epoch, found an intellectual home in
Vilfredo Pareto and Gaetano Mosca. The Columbia group
preferred the functionalism of Herbert Spencer and even
more, Emile Durkheim.

The search for antecedents did not begin with the turn of
the century. It was clear even earlier that the work of Auguste
Comte, Saint-Simon, and Karl Marx would have to be addressed. Socialism of a left and right persuasion was in the
air, and sociology could hardly escape such new trends in
the social reconstruction of society. Indeed, it became a
weapon against "reformism," against the idea of meliorative approaches to social policy. In short, it provided the
intellectual rationale for the permanent separation of sociology from social work as well as the rationale for a durable
hostility to the political state as the repository of elitism,
the naked use of power, and other such presumed evils of
our age. But in this search for moral virtue, the field isolated itself from political life and its intellectual expression
in political science.

As a result, political sociology in the hands of sociologists
and political scientists grew in one-sided fashion. For sociologists and social welfare advocates it increasingly became
a vehicle to demonstrate how the good society could do battle
with and overcome the bad state. For political scientists and
public opinion researchers, the discipline was increasingly
reduced to political socialization, integrating behavior into
the political process. If sociology suffered from a moralism,
political science suffered the even greater sin of legalism,

and exhibited the belief that integrating individuals into the political process was more than a subject of ancillary and even marginal benefit. The "bottom up" faith of sociology in contrast to the "top down" emphasis of political science has led to a condition in which these two claimants to scientific status have become part of the problem no less than alternative frameworks for solutions.

These harsh points must be made since the formation of a political sociology has, since the time of Max Weber, become distended and distorted as the fields of sociology and political science pull in opposite directions, while utilizing the same rhetoric to express their basic tenets. I would be less than candid if I denied that a fundamental aim of my work is to bring both disciplines back to an earlier vision in which one could read the texts of George Sabine and Robert MacIver with equal joy and profit. For even if the fields are quite different from what they were in the halcyon days of the 1930s, the tasks remain the same: to provide a picture of human life that explains the place of the person in the larger scheme of social and political order.

An additional unpleasant theme that arises with increasing frequency in social research is the presumption of the moral superiority of social scientific judgment. This was the case with Comte, and it remained part of the emotional baggage of social theory throughout the twentieth century. Indeed, it is not sociologists alone who suffer from this conceit; even an outstanding psychiatrist like Carl Gustav Jung preached this theme.[11] Indeed, he criticized Freud and Adler for their one-sidedness, their efforts to construct a theory of human nature upon "drives," instead of addressing the gift of grace, that is "faith, hope, love and insight." Jung was too intelligent a scientist to think that the psychiatrist could provide the patient what the cleric could not provide his flock. But in an age that rejects the clergy as the source of resolving problems of spiritual suffering, the doctor can perform this role. "Healing psychic suffering," and not just recognizing the existence of material deprivation, becomes a task transferred from religion to the social and behavioral sciences. This is in the long tradition of Hegel, Marx, and Nietzsche.

Such intellectualism also permitted a closer tie of action-oriented social scientists to the world of professional distinction and scholarship. University language requirements and examinations for graduate degrees in the arts and sciences, when such things existed made sense only if such a university base were not only acknowledged but also promoted. Since the major language requirements were in German and French, other traditions were soon designated as "lesser" traditions, with a slight bow to Italian and Russian sources of sociology. In short, the invention, or as is now the linguistic fashion, the "construction" of political sociology proceeded in step with the discovery of Europe, in particular a canon rooted in the Old World.

It needs to be clearly stated that the invented canon is nonetheless real in its consequences. There emerged over time a genuine canonical set of works, ruefully or gratefully adhered to for theological if not sociological reasons. One could discard a bit or a piece of the canon, depending on one's own political or intellectual proclivities, but by the close of the twentieth century, the idea of the canon itself had been set in stone—with book after book acknowledging this reality. If race, class and gender were the triumphal trio of the field, Marx, Durkheim and Weber had become the essential Trinitarian source of the field. To call oneself a sociologist without at least having a cursory familiarity with these three (although hardly stopping there) was unthinkable. So-called examinations in "theory" were based on these three figures—often addressing these three themes.

To be sure, as Peter Baehr so wisely summed up matters: "the dispute around the canon is part of a larger struggle. Canon is a code word for a variety of concerns regarding the nature and purpose of a university education."[12] But that is the essential pitfall and weakness of canonical thought: it substitutes the academic ritual for the political reality. And while it remains a mechanism for establishing or inventing friends and enemies, its actual operational value is limited. Thus, it is of little consequence to have lengthy discourses on whether a canon exists, or who fits into a canonical mold. It is more important to know the trajectory of ideas and their human carriers. Rather than burden this effort with recitations on the commonplace, I want to emphasize the thread of basic theory in social research and what it adds up to. Of equal significance is to determine who becomes part of the canon and the relative weights assigned to the ante-cedent figures involved. Protean figures not only produce progeny, but also offspring that do not agree. Thus, as I have elsewhere noted, there is the Weber according to Par-sons, the Weber according to Merton, and the Weber ac-cording to Mills. Whatever else one can say in this connec-tion, whether one is enamored of a conservative, liberal, or radical reading of the canon, the steady point of light that emanates from a Weber must surely argue against a theo-logical view and for an operational view of the canon.

One reason for avoiding, better yet, overcoming, the im-pulse to a canonical view of political sociology is the pre-sumption in canonical thinking of intellectual history as some sort of stepping stone of a progressive sort. But to make of political sociology simply a theory of scientific progress is to deprive the field of the very dynamism that gives it a continuing appeal. I rather suspect that political sociology, and perhaps intellectual history as a whole, can best be read as a series of interconnected ribbons, much like the double helix system found in the construction of the human DNA system. This double interchange between state and society, between dictatorship and democracy in one part of the chain, and between the search for equity and liberty and the claims of altruism and egoism in the other part of the chain, make the study of this field difficult. But this double helix system of political sociology gives the field its vibrancy and its continuing fascination at the close of a century that has little time or patience with the trivial. So while I offer the reader something less than a canonical view of things, I also try to provide something more than a pasteboard rendition of serious, complex intertwined concerns.

What emerges in the history of political sociology is less a sense of progression than a feeling that one is in the presence of a social scientific equivalent of a double interchange system. On one side of this linked chain are figures like Montesquieu, Tocqueville, Durkheim and Weber. On the other side are Rousseau, Hegel, Marx, and Sorel. While there are differences between French, German and other national traditions, these tend to dissolve when considerations of an intellectual sort are accounted for. The paired polarities of objectivity-subjectivity, experience-intuition, empirical-metaphysical, and above all, scientific-ideological continue to serve as leit-motifs in both the creation of a canon and in the special forms of evolution in political sociology. I seriously doubt that the use of double helix as a metaphor for something as remote as political sociology will please seasoned veterans of biology and chemistry, but until our own science achieves a more advanced status, we have to take our metaphors wherever we can find them.

To study the European sources of the polarization of political sociology is also to study the European sources of the composition of society. The essence of my view is that the European "greats" were not only at odds with each other, but presented America with a double tradition: one emphasized experience, evidence and experimenting; a second offered ideology and theology wrapped in the cloth of science. The first sought after discovery; the second aimed at uncovering. The first sought to understand the world, the second attempted to change the world—essentially through arming men with the tools of social research sociology. As a result, it will be observed that a certain shift takes place in my efforts. The European contributions are almost uniformly described in terms of theoretical constructs offered, while the American contributions tend to examine in part at least the responses of outstanding analysts to conditions as they are found "on the ground."

These are not simply different visions of political sociology held by sociologists and political scientists; they more nearly represent a difference in the contexts and goals of research. I submit that this is of far greater importance than simply a difference of quantitative versus qualitative forms of work or, for that matter, a large-scale or small-group terrain of work. Upon locating the moral purpose of social research we are able to determine how, from the outset, sociology in particular was saddled with strongly different notions of the meliorative potential for social science. Sociology also identified the descriptive versus the prescriptive roots of sociology as a science and of sociology as an ideology.

The fortunes and fates of professional discipline rest ultimately on their capacity to reflect, anticipate, and predict events in the "real world." For my purposes, that world is essentially comprised of the structure of state and society, and their relation to each other. When the older disciplines were in tune with such real world events they were able to make immense contributions to the study of human associations. When they ignored or forgot those antecedents (as is now largely the case with the turn toward subjectivism, irrationalism and even solipsism), the worth of these disciplines shriveled.

What we have then in the study of the relationship of state and society is the essential source of the relationship of ideas to existence—and I feel more comfortable that my earlier diagnosis, while correct, needed this study of the anarch and the behemoth to cap the point. I started the journey with an effort to understand professional life as *sui generis*, as a thing in itself; it turns out that this is a mistaken way to go about the analysis of a material culture. It is indeed the case that there is a substructure as well as a super-structure—and heaven help those who would deny that which is self-evident to all but a small fraction of the intellectual class that continues to make a living off of the preaching of naked rulers.

Let me note that the book has few, if any, villains. What does take place in the writings of great, protean figures is not a subject for moral condemnation except on the part of the foolish and the arrogant (often one and the same). This does not cancel the need for sharp criticism when required. Whatever the status of the canon of political sociology, we know enough to appreciate its polarized character. However, the volume does have its heroes. They extend from Montesquieu through Tocqueville to Weber. They have in common a sense of the larger picture, but not at the expense of an accurate picture. And they have the courage of their convictions, but not at the expense of fabrication. That delicate balance of which Aristotle spoke—between reason and passion—is the task of all who aspire to greatness. I do hope that this volume contributes somewhat in making that balance less delicate and a little bit stronger.

Irving Louis Horowitz
Princeton, New Jersey
June 1998

Notes

1. Lesley Brown (editor), *The New Shorter Oxford English Dictionary on Historical Principles.* Oxford and New York: The Clarendon Press, Oxford University Press, 1993. pp. 73, 207.
2. Franz Neumann, *The Structure and Practice of National Socialism* (second edition). New York: Oxford University Press, 1944.
3. Vernon L. Parrington, *Main Currents in American Political Thought* (in 3 vols.).Norman, OK: University of Oklahoma Press, 1987. 454, 516, 476 pp.
4. Raymond Aron, *Main Currents in Sociological Thought* (in 2 vols.). New Brunswick and London: Transaction Publishers, 1996–1997. 374, 444 pp.

5. Robert A. Nisbet, *The Sociological Tradition*. New Brunswick and London: Transaction Publishers, 1993, 349 pp.
6. Raymond Aron, *Main Currents in Sociological Thought* (in 2 vols.). New Brunswick and London: Transaction Publishers, 1996–1997.
7. William R. Everdell, *The First Moderns: Profiles in the Origins of Twentieth Century Thought*. Chicago: The University of Chicago Press, 1997. 501 pp.
8. Irving Louis Horowitz, *The Decomposition of Sociology*. New York: Oxford University Press, 1993.
9. Robin Fox, *Conjectures and Confrontations: Science, Evolution, and Social Concern*. New Brunswick and London: Transaction Publishers, 1997. 238 pp. See also, Robin Fox, *The Challenge of Anthropology: Old Encounters and New Excursions*. New Brunswick and London: Transaction Publishers, 1994. 431 pp.
10. John W. Bennett, *Classic Anthropology: Critical Essays–1944–1996*. New Brunswick and London: Transaction Publishers, 1998. 425 pp.
11. Carl Gustav Jung, *Modern Man in Search of a Soul*. New York: Harcourt, Brace & World, 1933. pp. 221–244.
12. Peter Baehr and Mike O'Brien, "Founders, Classics and the Concept of a Canon", in *Current Sociology*. Volume 42, Number 1, Spring 1994, pp. 127–128.

1

Between Anarch and Behemoth:
The Spirit of Montesquieu

"There is one way in this country in which all men are created
equal—there is one human institution that makes a pauper the
equal of a Rockefeller, the stupid man the equal of an Einstein,
and the ignorant man the equal of any college president. That
institution, gentlemen, is a court.... I'm no idealist to believe firmly
in the integrity of our courts and in the jury system—that is no
ideal to me, it is a living, working reality. Gentlemen, a court is no
better than each man of you sitting before me on this jury. A court
is only as sound as the men who make it up."

—*Harper Lee (Atticus's Summation
from* To Kill a Mockingbird*)*[1]

This work is an effort to understand, if not entirely solve a
vexing problem: what is the relationship between state and
society in Western classical and modern theory? What is it
that makes these two gigantic entities function at loggerheads,
in much of the past at least, when addressing the problem of
social welfare and political order? Indeed, to even speak in
terms of welfare and order conjures up images of the good
society satisfying mass wants on one hand, and the evil state
keeping everyone in line on the other. That certainly was a
solid nineteenth-century vision of the situation.

To be sure, most reasonable people understand the need
for both ingredients. And yet uneasy hangs the relationship
of state and society within capitalist theory, socialist theory,
social welfare theory, and a welter of approaches that owe
their allegiance to feudalism no less than to post-modernism. In approaching matters in this way, I seek to take seriously the late Karl Popper's belief, expressed in his 1963
Harvard lecture, that science neither begins nor ends with
the collection of data and observation; rather, as he put
matters (and as Durkheim, Simmel, Weber and others did
before him), the issue of such a linkage starts and ends "with
the sensitive selection of a promising problem."[2] The problem of the actual and ideal relation of state to society strikes
me as at the core of the matter.

There is a sense in which we are concerned with a phenomenon—the state—as intrinsically a dual element: an instrument for the oppression of people and an agency for
their survival, if not salvation, through order. Of the former,
we know much: ranging from the Nazi state apparatus that
murdered millions and its counterpart, the Stalinist state
that likewise dealt in development through death—as if they
were organically and inseparably linked. These very regimes
cause us to think of anarchism in pleasantly romantic terms,
of a freewheeling disdain for authority. But as the twentieth
century rolls on, this romanticism produced one series of
nightmares after another: the Khmer Rouge murders of in-
nocent peasants, bands of Ugandan warlords kidnapping
and enslaving hundreds of children and making them part
of an army of nomads, the paramilitary troops of the Shining Path movement wreaking havoc on ordinary Peruvian
peasants. One of the more prominent nightmares produced
by this romanticism is a civil war of all against all in the
former Yugoslavia in which crosscutting bands of Moslems
and Christians, and Bosnians and Serbians slaughter one
another. One can go on at length in this hand-wringing fashion. What it comes down to is the absence of shared author-

ity, of law, of a sense of common destiny, in short the breakdown or absence of the state itself.

So before we simply adopt the position that all state authority is evil, or the high road to serfdom itself, it might be
worthwhile to step back and take a look at a universe in which
the state functions to prevent the sort of mayhem that is all
too commonplace the world over.[3] It might be pleasant to
contemplate a world in which all surrender of personal authority to an impersonal state is somehow an unmitigated
evil, a collapse of the individualism that made the ancients
self-reliant. But in the name of realism, unpleasant as that
name might be, we need to structure a world that takes seriously the existence of the state, not as a curse upon the poor
or a blessing upon them for that matter, but simply as that
agency which has come to dominate our age. And despite
the socialist calls to "smash state power," and the social democratic assurances that social welfare would accomplish precisely such ends, nothing of the kind has happened. Indeed,
it is evident that in all sorts of societies—democratic or totalitarian—the state, far from diminishing, is expanding. It is my
contention that society itself has come to be defined by the
state. The welfare societies of past decades and the warfare
states of past ages have merged to become one—the welfare
state. Indeed, the very concept has by now become a commonplace. Serious critics no longer speak in big terms about
smashing state power; they are content to consider ways in
which state power can be contained.

The state is, in short, a wondrous instrument. This medieval invention aimed at organizing and rationalizing the
secular society has survived, thrived and expanded despite
all sorts of vicissitudes and predictions of its imminent demise. It is almost as if the state is a realm apart—able to
overcome the intrigues of religious agencies, able to with-
stand the blandishments of "withering away" predicted by a
host of revolutionists, and above all, able to master the craft
of survival in the face of inventions and discoveries of oth-

erwise earth-shattering proportions. But before we proceed
too much further along this path, it is appropriate to admit
that this is not a work of social history. J.C.N. Raadschelders
has beautifully accomplished the task of delineating and
defining the history of the state.[4] In showing the medieval
origins of the state in the areas of general government and
finance, public order and safety, health and societal care,
education, trade and traffic, and finally public works in general, he has given us a descriptive narrative not soon or
easily to be replaced. However, missing from that sort of
study is whether the state must always be in charge of such
tasks and programs, or does so by default. Unless one is
prepared to believe in the myth of the "social contract," in
which individuals actually contract out large chunks of their
world to a thing called the state, it becomes evident that just
how the institutional formations between state and society
evolve is a problem, not a given.

The reader will also notice that the analysis of this problematic starts with theorists of the Enlightenment, rather than
with ancients like Plato the Greek, and post-Renaissance figures like Machiavelli the Italian and Hobbes the Englishman.
This is in no way to slight their contributions to the study of
the sate. Without their powerful intellects, the field of political studies would be barren. Rather, this is not aimed as pure
academic exercise or intellectual history, but the study of the
sate as something apart from rulers, from dynastic heads. And
it is this distinction between the study of, or advice to sovereigns and the study of sovereignty as such—that is the state as
an institution apart from the manipulation of the levers of
power—that one finds absent in the three major figures (Plato,
Machiavelli and Hobbes) who rightfully might be claimed as
the source of classical theories of those who rule. The great
Catholic theorist, Jacques Maritain, places these classical figures in the history of political philosophy, a *sapiential* knowledge directed to the ends of human conduct; whereas political sociology is concerned with the details of phenomena.[5]

While I would like to think that this volume crosses the bridge of politics and ethics, the fact remains that the sorts of special concerns of Machiavelli on the moral virtues belong to an earlier epoch, one that precedes the empirical study of the relation of state and society.

In his brilliant, if at times eccentric, reading of Plato, Machiavelli and Hobbes, Sheldon Wolin, in *Politics and Vision*, places the distinction between the medieval and the modern squarely: a failure to grasp the interconnection between social and political factors.[6] Modernity saw the emergence of the so-called popular classes as a critical pivot in all social analysis. For Plato, the idea of democracy was a violation of any serious study of both orderliness and goodness in human affairs. For Machiavelli, the popular masses could be a dangerous beast, the anarch itself, and a phenomenon that the sovereign had to manipulate and bridle—for the good of these self-same inchoate masses.[7] Nonetheless, Machiavelli fully understood that "the masses are more knowing and more constant than the Prince." This sense of tension between ruled and rulers preserves Machiavelli from converting national interest into a defense of reaction. For Hobbes, with a far deeper sense of political philosophy than political economy, the problem of rule was how to establish a theory of sate power in the absence of a theology that could sanction absolute obedience and mission.[8]

Ernest Cassirer, in his finely distilled observations on Machiavelli, pointed out that, "The State is entirely independent; but at the same time it is completely isolated." And he goes on to prophetically note: "The political world has lost its connection not only with religion or metaphysics but also with all other forms of man's ethical and cultural life. It [the State] stands alone—in an empty space."[9] Cassirer strikes an utterly modern note here. He does so with advice to rulers about the arts of war or connivance of diplomacy, but seeing the state as an object in itself, for itself, apart from specific rulers, becoming the essence of the modern political world. It is that world that confronts the other large-scale claimant to the attentions of the moderns, the society or the social system. It is this dialectic that my work seeks to address, rather than perhaps the most conventional political psychology that preceded in time and in depth modern political sociology.

In all candor my decision to commence the study of political sociology with Montesquieu rather than with Machiavelli does not receive universal approval. Perhaps the most serious challenge launched is that of Talcott Parsons and his colleagues who in their superb anthology on *Foundations of Modern Sociological Theory,* start with an extract from *The History of Florence.* Clearly, if Machiavelli is considered the staring point of sociology, my claim that he is the quintessential political theorist, without much concern for social considerations, is seriously weakened.[10] Indeed, other than Machiavelli's presumed attention to normative considerations from what Parsons calls "the actor's point of view," I fail to detect any rationale for assigning such a pivotal place to Machiavelli. It is fair enough to speak of him as one of the great political historians of all time, as well as a peerless analyst of political power. But I remain firm in viewing Montesquieu as the true starting point of modern political sociology. Indeed, Parsons would have been on firmer ground had he referenced the *Discourses* rather than *The History of Florence.*

Probably the most convincing reason for excluding Machiavelli from the canon of political sociology is provided by Harvey Mansfield, who in his outstanding translation of *The Prince,* points out that for Machiavelli, "politics is thought to be carried on for its own sake, unlimited to anything above it."[11] Mansfield goes on to point out that for Machiavelli politics is carried on for its own sake, with its own rules. In large measure, Machiavelli was concerned with the costs and benefits of winning and losing. In this, he was a shrewd advisor to rulers, not a servant to rulers as a special class of people. The need to come to grips with and resolve the placement of Machiavelli in the history of political sociology was an early wake-up call in the problem of selecting a proper starting point. It also alerted me to the difficulty of developing a canonical work, to know where to start as well as what to include. This was reinforced in the need to ask the identical question of the great Thomas Hobbes.

In this brief survey of the pre-history of political sociology an essential stopping point is the work of Thomas Hobbes and, in particular, his famed *Leviathan*. In this extraordinary work we are presented with a sense of the political as the dominant motif in all human existence. And whether this is viewed as a one-sided reading of society or a pure reflection of the realities of power, its essential vortex is not the relation between state and society, but the requirements and restraints of "office." The psychology behind the Hobbesian ruler is quite similar to the position taken by Machiavelli in *The Prince*: the acquisition of power is central and, in turn, appetites require a struggle for the acquisitions of still more power. There is no pure endpoint; or rather that endpoint of the terrorist state had not yet been reached in those earlier centuries. What did exist was desire mediated and tempered by a sense of duty. Indeed it has always been the aristocratic foil that their natural right of rule is underwritten by this sense of devotion to the whole and the duty to making that whole tranquil.

It was not just the French reformers who were suspicious of the state. The same could be said for the English liberal philosophers who came long after Montesquieu, Rousseau, and the Enlightenment tradition as a whole. But they did so in a somewhat more naive manner, what might be called the tradition of philosophical liberalism rather than legal liberalism. And since we will be concentrating on the continental founders of political sociology, it might be of some value to pause and consider the contributions of the British political philosophers of first rank. John Stuart Mill posed the human conscience in opposition to state power. The fabled essays *On Liberty* and *Utilitarianism*[12] both aim to show that the limits of the state reside in the individual and that any tendency to abrogate civil society is a threat imposed from the state. Mill was hardly consistent on this point, invoking the role of the state in the formation of British domestic and overseas policies alike, but he did set a tone of liberal discontent. The liberalism was predicated on the belief that the state was a necessary evil, and hence should be kept as small as possible.

Then came Herbert Spencer, who tried to replicate in politics what Adam Smith thought was the case for economics: the tendency toward equilibrium of a society if left undisturbed by bureaucratic authority. Spencer's theme articulated in *The Man Versus the State* is that, "there is in society that beautiful self-adjusting principle which will keep all its elements in equilibrium. The attempt to regulate all the actions of a community by legislation will entail little else but misery and compulsion."[13] Just as the struggle in nature arrives at some sort of equilibrium based on adaptation, so too Spencer, and much of nineteenth-century organic theory, presumes a similar process is at work in society. In this type of scenario, the state becomes an impediment to the normal relationships of people to one another. This sort of extrapolation was feasible only as long as analogical reasoning was permitted, and as long as individualistic doctrines of superiority and inferiority were held to be natural and part of the social order of things.

The twentieth century broke through such Spencerian myths, and did so on two fronts: the near universal acceptance of equity as a goal, if not a fact of society and the extraordinary breakthrough of technology that gave evidence that abundance was a possibility. The engineering of nature led to the notion of the engineering of the soul. And it is this huge leap that gave the state a regulatory role undreamed of even by its opponents in the past. Far from "withering away" on the left or "human self-adjustment" on the right, the state became the political equivalent of engineering and technology. The new century has witnessed the emergence of the assembly line, transistors, copiers, faxes, and memory chips. Technology has changed how we live, providing radio, television, air travel, household appliances, air conditioning, plastics, films, and compact discs. We have invented new forms of mass combat, from the nuclear weapon to rocketry and new forms of mass health, from antibiotics and birth control pills to body imaging. Rather than become the source of the diminution of the state, the reverse has taken place: the state has become the source of legitimization and permission for such new technologies to exist and to move forward. It stands in ever more fearsome involvement rather than splendid isolation.

The modern state embodies the principle of dualism—a realm of moral obligation standing side by side with a world of technological innovation. Yet they do interact, do cause each other to change, and compel us to examine the history of the relationship of state and society anew. It is not the purpose of this work to provide an all-inclusive history of the discipline of political sociology; we have fine works in this area already. Rather, my aim is to tease out the dorsal spine, the essential contradictions, that continue to permit the state to play a central role in the conduct of the social system—and when speaking of the social system, one must now include all of the wondrous developments in technology. At the same time, the society, as the source of energy and invention that offers a response to human needs and desires, is the drive shaft of that technology with which we have come to identify. Little wonder then that despite all sorts of changes and developments, the essential dialectic of the modern world, the contradictions between the state, and its embodiment of the principle of power, and society, and its embodiment of the principle of utility, continue to rival each other for attention and, to be sure, affection.

It is intriguing how many writers speak of the myth of the state when in fact they appear to be more concerned with the ephemeral nature of power. The liberal imagination is frustrated with the continued energy of the state, even as it realizes that the affection for the state on the part of broad masses is limited. Yet the liberal imagination cannot quite abandon the state as the force that imposes all good social changes, or better, all social goods. This is the reverse of the conservative imagination that sees in the state the source of moral order, the only curb against the natural, atavistic propensities of the common herd to take what it wants from society and the devil take the hindmost. Thus at its source, the struggle between statists and revolutionists is no less than the general struggle between conservative and liberal thought for pre-eminence in a changing social universe—one in which both statists and welfarists struggle not so much for the means of production as for the means of communication.

Before we leave Machiavelli too prematurely or dismissively, one is led to his letter of 1506, when he reminds his friend G.B. Soderini that, "to give reputation to a new ruler, cruelty, treachery and irreligion are enough in a province where humanity, loyalty and religion have for a long time been common. Yet in the same way humanity, loyalty and religion are sufficient where cruelty, treachery and irreligion have dominated for a time, because as bitter things disturb the taste and sweet ones cloy it, so men get bored with good and complain of ill." Here we have the source of discontent, but also the source of the dialectic between the evils of the state and the goods of society—and how very difficult it is to rid ourselves of the former or enmesh ourselves in the latter. The liberal imagination must confront the larger need for order, while the conservative imagination must confront the larger need for change. It is the task of the state to deliver both sets of social requirements and to do so in a convincing way, that is to say, a moral way. The burden of my work is to show how the major figures in political philosophy, and then political sociology, sought to establish a synthetic base for a world in which order and change can coexist. Montesquieu's checks and balances were the first principled effort at such a synthesis.

I want to emphasize that this placement on my part of the starting point of political sociology in the eighteenth century is in no way to slight the contributions of political philosophy. If anything the philosophical traditions are richer and more fruitful of genuine theory than what came later in sociology proper. But our concern here is not to place a moral valuation on previous traditions or even to develop a history of normative theory. Were that the case, the need to examine with care the work of not just Plato, Machiavelli, and Hobbes, but of such astounding figures as Thomas Aquinas, Augustine, and Spinoza would become manifest. Rather my task here is to establish the linkage of state and society within the modern social science tradition. That such a linkage must include the study of Rousseau and Hegel speaks to their unique ability to comprehend this dialectic of state and society as the core of human existence.

If political sociology must presume an appreciation of such major figures, or invent a canonical tradition, the honor of the actual start of the field goes to Charles Louis de Secondat, Baron de la Brede et de Montesquieu. This is the case despite the fact that Montesquieu does not seem to rate well in the contemporary era in the game of being canonized. Harold Bloom's effort to construct *The Western Canon,* for example, shows that Montesquieu does not even rate a mention, in contrast to the great essayist and moralist Montaigne.[14] Perhaps the very sense of Aristotelian balance which Montesquieu brought to the analytic table helps to explain the benign neglect of his work among some, although by no means all, contemporary students of political and social theory.

As his name clearly implies, Montesquieu was of noble provincial birth, but he chose a life of scholarship. His 1716 dissertation, delivered at the Academy in Bordeaux, was followed a year later by an academic discourse. Both his early work and mid-life efforts were dedicated to an understanding of the "causes and grandeur of the Roman Empire and its later decadence." That twenty-year focus of intellectual energies served as a driving force in a rather typical French pursuit: how to retain the grandeur but avoids the decadence. Specifically, it made him understand that to engage in empire building beyond the capacity to permit self-rule involves the imposition of tyranny. Further, tyranny involves the use of force, which in turn stimulates the desire for counter-force. It finally led Montesquieu to the painful conclusion that it was not some abstract set of historical forces, but the very human forces involved in decision-making that is the source of the problem, not progress, of social change. The opening of *The Spirit of the Laws* gives the unique quality of Montesquieu's inductive perspective: "I first examined men and I believed that in their infinite diversity of laws and customs they were not conducted solely by their caprice and fancy."[15] The late John Herman Randall profoundly understood Montesquieu as someone whose work has stood the test of time because "he alone saw farther the typical eighteenth century ideal and method of a social physics. He almost alone was so struck by the conception of a unified science of human society, and by the enormous amount of investigation necessary before such a science could hope to take form, that he spent more time in amassing facts than in formulating some systematic scheme in support of one or another program of action."[16]

Montesquieu was, from the viewpoint of the Enlightenment, a transitional thinker who stood apart from the great march of social progress and human liberation. He was declared a worthy aristocrat who came up to but never inside the democratic revolutionary period. But now that the Enlightenment itself is very much part of intellectual history, we are able to see the Baron in a sharper light, as "notre premier grand sociologue politique."[17] Indeed, in more general terms, he exemplified a liberality of spirit and a generosity of appreciation that is the hallmark of classical liberalism a solid century before such an ideology became fashionable.[18] The classic volume that commences our historical and theoretical study of the interrelation of state and society is *The Spirit of the Laws*. At the time of this writing, the work is precisely 250 years old. It is concerned with forms of government as well as the spirit of legal arrangements. In monarchical, republican, and despotic regimes there is a differential distribution of power and authority. As a consequence, the forms and nature of law are impacted. Hence, despotism in which resistance to the ruler is virtually nil and largely disallowed is a system characterized by a total concentration of power. Lacking the virtue that characterizes the republican form and honor, which is evident in monarchical form, we are left with fear as the ground of despotic rule.

Montesquieu formulated his approach to representative government in the specific setting of a France in which the monarchy was clearly obliged to recognize new secular forces at work in the economy and society. He held that the French Parliaments had never been a dependent creation of the monarchy, but quite the reverse—the crown was limited by legal accountability to legislative review. The Parliaments of each region served as arbiters of whether despotism threatened to overturn the delicate network of relationships between crown and princes. And, as Simon Schama has indicated: "this was not an esoteric view confined to antiquarian quibbles."[19] Drawing on previous historical work, Montesquieu's *De l'Esprit des Lois* lent it enormous political respectability and wide currency. Montesquieu was himself a president of the Parliament of Bordeaux, and at a time when Parliaments were claiming to protect the liberties of Frenchmen "from the tax policy of the crown, the book became an overnight best-seller." But no sooner had

Montesquieu staked out a position to mediate royal claims then the revolutionary forces that gathered just prior to 1789, were wary of the fact that his mid-way position was intended "to demonstrate the advantages of a government in which he occupied an advantageous place." It was the breakdown of the middle position, of the theory of political equilibrium Montesquieu sought to enshrine, that made the struggle for state power a direct struggle, rather than one mediated by the assumption of legislative power.

Montesquieu's concerns were less a matter of classification for its own sake than they were a search for sources of legitimization. Montesquieu was not concerned with sociological categories, but with political varieties that permit social order and political harmony. He does not, as the Encyclopedists were to do later in the century, presume a theory of progress, or even that varieties of political regimes involve any sort of evolution. Rather, like Machiavelli and Hobbes, Montesquieu treated moral considerations—virtue, honor, and fear—as properties of choice.[20] As a result, while the social structure might condition political outcomes, such outcomes are themselves often a function of personal qualities of leadership. It is important to recognize that Montesquieu had a moral objective to his thinking. He was concerned with freedom, but not as a function of the natural improvement of the species, rather as a consequence of the legal distribution of power. Checks and balances rather than grandiose notions of revolution and utopia characterized this scion of the aristocracy. He was the quintessential "outsider" or observer, not to be bridled to any doctrine or movement, but linked inextricably to the conditions under which the human species is given the broadest latitude for imagination.

While Montesquieu does not presume a theory of progress, like other Enlightenment figures, the transition from a world ruled by classical virtue (as defined by not especially virtuous or gifted monarchs) to one dominated by commerce stands at the cornerstone of his analysis. Christian morality and classical virtue yield hopeless division; whereas self-interest and commerce pave the way to a world in which human potential is realized. As a result, Montesquieu is not simply a theorist of constitutionalism. At least as important as political institutions or "states" in forging human character is the role of commerce: the sole force capable of attenuating the militaristic spirit and warrior ethos of the feudal epoch. This was to become a cardinal element in Darwinian thought. The rise of capitalism serves to both soften mores and polish manners. This point is significant not only in terms of the struggle between state and society, but it also gets to Montesquieu's modern concept of a society, namely the types of human relationships that are primary in holding individuals together in social life.

In his serious and profound appreciation of Montesquieu, Irving M. Zeitlin drew attention to the sociology of knowledge bases in his work: "How one views the customs and ideas of society depends on the social position one occupies and hence on the cultural perspective one adopts. That Montesquieu understood this is clear from the reactions of his Persian travelers. They begin to doubt their own customs and ideology as soon as they leave their own society; the longer they are in Europe, the less strange do the new customs appear. He posited the social genesis of ideas and the functional interdependence of social action and ideas; and while, many times, he invokes physical causes too, they are generally subordinate to socio-cultural conditions. He was more aware than most of his contemporaries of the human cultural variety."[21] These cultural varieties however are embedded in political systems. They are not free-floating nor are they simply evolutionary. This effort to integrate the social, political and cultural makes Montesquieu indeed not only the first great political sociologist in French history, but one of the earliest sociologists of knowledge.

It is Raymond Aron who uniquely appreciates the linkage of the social and the political. Indeed, he claims that Montesquieu's most important idea "is the connection established between the forms of government on one hand and the style of interpersonal relations on the other. Social life depends on the way in which power is exercised by the government, and vice versa. Such an idea lends itself admirably to a sociology of government. At the same time, it obviously raises a crucial question: to what extent are political regimes conceptually separable from the historical realities in which they are embodied?"[22] Aron goes on to say that Montesquieu found no solution to this problem, but that no one else has either. But my own view is that Aron overestimated Montesquieu's historicism and underestimated his voluntarism. For it is the task of the executive, legislative and judicial forms of authority to settle the question of political regimes. Precisely because he was free of any commitment to theological models that so impacted later sociology, Montesquieu was uniquely able to offer an empirical framework for describing the nascent new state and the moral framework for electing that system that is best suited to popular needs.

The balance of power, the peace achieved by the exchange between social groups, the actions and reactions of individuals, are definite characteristics of societies in transition. In a tradition that probably owes more to Aristotle than Locke, Montesquieu examined "influences" such as geography, physical milieu, economy, population, and religion. Again, it is the mixture rather than structures that require attention. All of these relatively randomized factors play their part in the relation of laws and manners, and as a result, we are confronted less with a deterministic framework than a voluntaristic one. As Aron properly concludes, from this sort of vision, all one can say is that there is a general spirit, often rooted in national and ethnic realities, that acquires a collective existence, an élan, over a period of time as a result of a variety of influences, but not as a consequence of an all-powerful cause, rather as the reality of quotidian activities of ordinary people.

It is fair to say that it was Montesquieu, in *The Spirit of the Laws,* who first understood the state as an object unto itself but not for itself. It must share its ultimate ends with the nation and the laws. And however conservative sounding a document Montesquieu wrote, its radical edge was a sense of the social organization of the people as a whole. For in that masterpiece, he is less concerned with the "spirit"—certainly in any Anglo sense—than with the flesh. That is to say, his interests were in the operations of government, and specifically, in the relationships people enter into with one another for both the manufacture and implementation of the laws of a land. In that supreme act of codification, the state was granted its legitimacy—properly understood as a de facto as well as a de jure entity—not as a function of power but as a system of obligations as well as rights over the nation and its people. While he held very definite views on political ruling classes, and indeed, was part of such a class, he functioned as a social scientist, a student of the social sources of power, and not a servant of power.

With Montesquieu we arrive at a decisive point—the termination of the aristocratic era and the first blush of a republican era. The rule of law was separated from the rule of men. And in this way, Montesquieu must be credited with having served as an inspiration for both the American and French revolutions that took place later in the century. Indeed, to read the American Constitution with any care (or for that matter, the *Federalist Papers)*, is to appreciate the large role of that extraordinary figure in the emergence of a political sociology as something apart from and different from a political psychology of rule. In addition, once this huge separation of laws from men was introduced, it was a short step away from a consideration of social forms of life: such as traditions, folkways, and the entire range of phenomena that are under the rubric of sociology.

It is also with Montesquieu that we observe another unique and perhaps less obvious characteristic—the assignment of an autonomous role of the political and the social processes with respect to the economy. The law makes it possible for both State and society to be observed as entities unto themselves and not just as a kind of subordinate clause that does the bidding of the national economy. That said, Montesquieu did not minimize or trivialize the place of the economy in the advanced nation. States may behave autonomously with respect to the creation of law, but they are structurally dependent on economic conditions. In post-Octavian Rome, prosperity without purpose breads luxury and decline. In the modern age, the national debt may constrain the actions of princes and legislatures—both for better and worse in terms of human liberty. It is a lesson that Karl Marx did not learn until close to the end of his life; in *The Critique of the Gotha Program*, in criticizing many of his own followers for being overly mechanical, he came to appreciate that the struggle for state power was a struggle that took place both within and apart from swings and curves in the economy. The longer run became even longer. The fact that nations share a common political economy is by no means a guarantor that they will have a common political sociology—a shared sense of what constitutes the proper relationship between the spirit of legislation, the character of the regime, and the performance of the economy.

The *Spirit of the Laws* is not an easy work to summarize. Indeed, there are about as many disputations about what the text signifies in content as in context. For example, Franz Neumann, one of the more sensible and more respectful of a classic tradition among the so-called Frankfurt School of Sociology, pointed out in his introduction to The *Spirit of the Laws*, that there is no prospect in making the work whole, or of making it any more than a set of essentially disparate and unrelated pieces: "If indeed *The Spirit of the Laws* has a structure it is very difficult to perceive."[23] But a less jaundiced reading, that of Émile Durkheim, claims that "it is Montesquieu who first laid down the fundamental principles of social science", specifically, "the ideas of *type* and *law*" [italics by Durkheim]. He goes on to critique Montesquieu on two counts: "First, he erroneously assumes that social forms are determined by the forms of sovereignty and can be defined accordingly. Second, he states that there is something intrinsically abnormal about one of the types he distinguishes, namely the despotic state."[24] My own view is that Durkheim was too intent in hitching Montesquieu to his own intellectual wagon of the organic society—that, in fact, Montesquieu had a determinism of his own, namely the legal bases of sovereignty. He understood quite well the "normalcy" of absolutist regimes. But he also appreciated the fragility of absolutism, the weakness and insolvency of all human relations based on master-servant contexts.

This legal determinism makes Montesquieu easy to understand but difficult to summarize. Indeed, the huge work (sometimes published as several volumes, other times in abbreviated form) is an explicit effort at macro-sociology, at understanding the social system as a whole. It is simply that the "base" for Montesquieu is the law, whereas the "superstructure" is the polity and the economy. In his view, civil society is a state of war, the state of nature, a state of weakness. Only with the infusion of law, "the necessary relations resulting from the nature of things," could one speak of that which is human in the human society.[25] There are *a priori* considerations introduced, since "relations of justice" are held to be antecedent to "positive law." It is precisely this element that permits Montesquieu to fashion a deterministic system of whole societies.

There are two types of laws: those of nations and those of civil society. Power resides in the one person or in many persons. Keep in mind Montesquieu's theory. The former is universal, but mischievous, since they are "not founded on true principles." But then one must turn to the polity, or "civil constitution," which Montesquieu considers identical, for 'no society can subsist without a form of government." This is the case since the aim: "is not to treat of laws, but of their spirit." And here he is using the term in its French *esprit* and German *Geist* meaning. It is not entity attached to an individual so much as to the collective will and passions as a whole. This permits him to develop a typology of political arrangements and, above all, to show how the legal order of things predisposes political regimes in either despotic or democratic goals.[26]

Living as he did in an age of absolute monarchs, Montesquieu was cautious about putting forth his ideas for a Republican form of government. He emphasized the "excellence" of monarchies with respect to the exercise of executive authority, personal decision-making, and over despotism of a conventional, traditional sort. There can be no doubt that his aim was to preserve the monarchy by distinguishing it as sharply as possible from feudal despotism. The bulk of the work is dedicated to that end. As a result, Montesquieu urges upon the monarch "elasticity," which turns out to be support for a separation of powers, a recognition of the independent role of legislative and judicial branches of government, and also an executive council that can make decisions or at least register opinions without fear of retribution or retaliation. Leniency and slight penalties for wrongdoing should be the hallmark of the good monarch.[27]

Montesquieu saw the sovereign as a linkage of "three powers": executive, legislative and judicial. Even if a monarch may serve in a legislative and executive capacity, dangerous but feasible, the judicial power needs to be separated. He recognized the risks for monarchs in a separation of powers, but he cited numerous historical examples, some hoary, some even thought fictitious, and others quite accurate to illustrate the enormous risks in a state without the distribution of power. All of this leads up to the twelfth book; for it is here that he makes it plain that the distribution of the three powers is not simply a matter of fairness, but of security. It is the delicate equilibrium of executive, legislative and judicial power that assures security to both the sovereign and the subject. "Philosophic liberty" consists in the free exercise of the will, which cannot be taken away from the subject save through death. But it is "political liberty" on which Montesquieu focuses, specifically the enjoyment of security that a legal order alone allow. He reminds the reader that constitutions may be perfectly designed instruments, but given the idiosyncrasies of sovereigns, subjects may still be abused. And it is here that *The Spirit of the Laws* shifts gears and focuses more on subjects than on sovereigns. The emphasis on well being is linked to a study of commerce in history. And throughout the preservation of the free market is seen as the essential succor for the preservation of the sovereign.[28]

The concluding segments of *The Spirit of the Laws* are the source of the sociological vision of Montesquieu. For it is in this volume that the sociological position is mapped out and the ideological proclivities laid bare. For example, he is adamant that there should be a limit to notions of perpetual inheritance through either primogeniture or tithing to Church lands. Montesquieu permits himself to say that any defense of inherited wealth at the expense of the state is so absurd that "he who should speak in their defense would be regarded as an idiot."[29] The volume is replete with preaching, delicately woven so as to ensure both the survival of the sovereign and the freedom of subjects. Like Machiavelli, he is appealing, albeit rather obliquely, to the best impulses of the monarch. But, unlike Machiavelli, he does not see such impulses as circumscribed by survival alone, and certainly not survival through any means available. So there are lengthy asides on the nature of matrimony, religious conversion, the trial system, and the limits of taxation—in short, all elements that goes into making up a society when seen from the viewpoint of the law, and no less the law dispenser.

The great work of Montesquieu concludes on a rather strange note: the end of the feudal system, its weaknesses, but also the transformation into the monarchical type of regime he both lived under and of which he approved.[30] The work seemed to tail off into a welter of indecision, of which Montesquieu himself gives substance by concluding a thousand pages of text with the words: "I finish my treatise of fiefs at a period where most authors commence theirs."[31] Being a cautious man, as well as a political actor in his own right, I suspect that Montesquieu ends his classic in an abrupt fashion in order to avoid drawing lessons for the mid-eighteenth century period in which he lived. His empiricism allowed for a conclusion that contained no explicit moral instruction to the rulers. But his methodological individualism allowed him to insinuate rather than assert a message concerning the limits of state power and the rights of the social subjects. Mark Hulliung in his fine contemporary study *Montesquieu and the Old Regime* captures this implicit sociological base of the political order—a base that the sovereign can ignore only at the risk of dismissing historical evidence no less than juridical classifications out of hand. "Society is more than a conglomerate of individuals, that the institutions have a life of their own, that the whole is greater than the sum of its parts. To be sure, Montesquieu upheld the sanctity of the individual and felt that institutions should serve humanitarian ends, but these were his moral postures, not his methodological premises. For purposes of empirical research and adequate explanation, society must be methodologically approached as a structural whole, the integrity of which is assured by the functions that institutions serve and the roles that individuals play."[32] In permitting history to draw the moral lessons for him, Montesquieu hoped to preserve the middle ground between the behemoth and the anarch. Clearly, in a French context over the next one hundred years, his monumental treatise on the spirit of the law did neither. There are limits to rationality after all.

Montesquieu was not only an analyst of the feudal past, but of its early democratic upsurges. He was therefore a product of competing intellectual traditions: the natural law school in which things emanate from first principles derived from eternal verities, and the empirical approach to the actual evolution of these things. This was to be a contradiction in intellectual history and the evolution of political sociology over the next 250 years. Contradictions notwithstanding, there is a long thin line from Montesquieu to Tocqueville to Weber that resisted the blandishments of ideology and utopianism alike. As a result, a tradition emerged that provides a canon within which political sociology could emerge. It is one purpose of this volume to show the binary character of the canon— one based on a belief in the primacy of observation, experience, and science; the other predicated on a primacy of action, the need to use social science to bring about desired social change. These are not clear lines of differentiation. The ideologists were often convinced that science itself vouchsafed certain lines of change. And the scientists were often convinced that certain hierarchies provided a better opportunity for law and order. Still, as in art so too in science, the lines between science for its own sake or for the sake of ameliorating historic injustices are clear and emotionally powerful. In every one of the past three centuries this struggle has been in evidence.

Notes

1. Harper Lee, *To Kill a Mockingbird.* New York: J.B. Lippincott, Company, 1960.
2. Karl R. Popper, *The Myth of the Framework: In Defense of Science and Rationality,* edited by M.A. Notturno. London and New York: Routledge Publishers, 1994, pp. 154-55.
3. Neil McInnes, "The Road Not Taken: Hayek's Slippery Slope to Serfdom," in *The National Interest.* Whole Number 51 (Spring) 1998, pp. 56-66.

4. Jos C.N. Raadschelders, *Handbook of Administrative History*. New Brunswick and London: Transaction Publishers, 1998, pp. 87–108.
5. Jacques Maritain, "The End of Machiavellianism," *The Social and Political Philosophy of Jacques Maritain*, edited by Joseph W. Evens and Leo R. Ward. New York: Charles Scribner's Sons, 1955, pp. 292–325.
6. Sheldon S. Wolin, *Politics and Vision: Continuity and Innovation in Western Political Thought*. Boston: Little Brown and Company, 1960, esp. pp. 195–285.
7. Niccolo Machiavelli, Letter to G.B. Soderini, between September 13–21, 1506 from Perugia. See *The Prince: Backgrounds and Interpretations*, edited by Robert M. Adams. New York: W.W. Norton & Company, 1977, pp. 127–128.
8. Thomas Hobbes, *The Leviathan*. New York: Penguin Books, 1982.
9. Ernest Cassirer, *The Myth of the State*. New Haven: Yale University Press, 1973. See in particular chapter XII on "Implications of the New Theory of the State: The Isolation of the State and Its Dangers," pp. 223–237.
10. Talcott Parsons, Edward Shils, Kaspar D. Naegele, and Jesse R. Pitts, editors. *Theories of Sociology: Foundations of Modern Sociological Theory*. New York: The Free Press of Glencoe, 1961. pp. 85–87, 98–99.
11. Harvey C. Mansfield, "Introduction," *The Prince* by Niccolo Machiavelli. Chicago and London: University of Chicago Press, 1998 (second edition), pp. vii–viii.
12. John Stuart Mill, *On Liberty*. New York: Penguin Books, 1982. See also John Stuart Mill's *Utilitarianism*. New York: Prometheus Books, 1980.
13. Herbert Spencer, *The Man versus the State: With Six Essays on Government, Society and Freedom*. Indianapolis: Liberty Fund, Inc., 1982. For an excellent statement on the statist revolt against classical liberalism in a British context, see Keith Windschuttle, "Liberalism and Imperialism", *The New Criterion*. Vol. 17, No.4, 1998. Pp. 4-14.
14. Harold Bloom, *The Western Canon: The Books and Schools of the Ages*. New York: Harcourt Brace & Co, 1994.
15. Charles de Montesquieu, *The Spirit of the Laws*. New York: Hafner Press/Macmillan Publishers, 1949, Preface.
16. John Herman Randall, *The Making of the Modern Mind: A Survey of the Intellectual Background of the Present Age*. Boston: Houghton Mifflin Co., 1926, pp. 319–320.
17. Xavier Darcos, *Histoire de la Litterature Francaise*. Paris: Hachette Education, 3, 1992, pp. 209–213. For a full-scale biography of Montesquieu, excellent in its narrative, but by self-decision, without an effort to examine the scientific and legal grounds of his work, see Robert Shackleton, *Montesquieu: A Critical Biography*. Oxford: Oxford University Press, 1961.
18. Thomas L. Pangle, *Montesquieu's Philosophy of Liberalism: A Commentary on the Spirit of the Laws*. Chicago: University of Chicago Press,

1989. The version used in this chapter is Charles de Montesquieu, *The Spirit of the Laws. (De l'Esprit des Lois).* New York: Hafner Press/ Macmillan Publishing Co., 1949. [1748].

19. Simon Schama, *Citizens: A Chronicle of the French Revolution.* New York: Alfred A. Knopf/Random House, 1989, pp. 107, 121.
20. Charles de Montesquieu, *Persian Letters.* New York: Penguin USA, 1977. See also the analysis and selections contained in Melvin Richter, *The Political Theory of Montesquieu.* Cambridge and New York: Cambridge University Press, 1977, esp. pp. 3–30.
21. Irving M. Zeitlin, *Ideology and the Development of Sociological Theory* (sixth edition) Upper Saddle River, NJ: Prentice-Hall, 1997, pp. 7–16.
22. Raymond Aron, *Main Currents in Sociological Thought.* New Brunswick and London, Transaction Publishers, 1998, pp. 13–63.
23. Franz Neumann, "Montesquieu," Introduction to *The Spirit of the Laws.* New York: Hafner Press/ Macmillan Publishing Co., 1949, p. x.
24. Émile Durkheim, *Montesquieu and Rousseau: Forerunners of Sociology.* Ann Arbor: The University of Michigan Press, 1960, pp. 61–62.
25. Charles de Montesquieu, *The Spirit of the Laws* (translated by Thomas Nugent). New York: Hafner Press/ Macmillan Publishing Co., 1949, pp. 1–2 (All references to the work are to the Nugent translation.)
26. Charles de Montesquieu, *The Spirit of the Laws,* (vol. 1), pp. 53–54.
27. Charles de Montesquieu, *The Spirit of the Laws* (vol. 1), pp. 83–64.
28. Charles de Montesquieu, *The Spirit of the Laws* (vol. 1), pp. 366–393.
29. Charles de Montesquieu, *The Spirit of the Laws* (vol. 2), pp. 49–55.
30. Charles de Montesquieu, *The Spirit of the Laws* (vol. 2), pp. 262–263.
31. Charles de Montesquieu, *The Spirit of the Laws* (vol. 2), p. 267.
32. Mark Hulliung, *Montesquieu and the Old Regime.* Berkeley: University of California Press, 1976, pp. 27–53.

2

Secularizing Society: Helvétius, Rousseau, and Comte

"There must be some private passageway to the heavenly throne, some strict backstairs entry that all the *Philosophes* know of, some door, closed to us, that will open to them when they give it a certain understood succession of raps. We should like to enter this door. We should really like to discover what it is that Jean Jacques Rousseau goes in search of when he wishes to know what God has said to him."

—Carl L. Becker[1]

The presumed "father of sociology," Auguste Comte, summarized the composition of sociology thus: "scientific men, ought in our day, to elevate politics to the rank of a science of observation. Such is the culminating and definitive point of view at which we should place ourselves."[2] In this way, Comte squarely placed himself and the science of sociology in the tradition of the Enlightenment. Here was to be a discipline that presumably did not augment metaphysics and religion, but was to replace these older forms of synthesis with nothing less than a new religion of positive science.

Whether the subject was the reorganization of society, the need for general education, or the reform of the work-

ing classes, Comte came at the subject with the inheritance—
some may less reverently call it the baggage—of the French
social contract tradition in which progress and security are
guaranteed by a rational ordering of society. Our first concern then is to examine the sources of this "new science of
man," the Enlightenment, in its optimistic or Voltairian form,
and no less, in its more cautious Rousseauian form.

By the final decade of the eighteenth century, the French
Enlightenment gripped all strata of the third estate. It was
converted into the philosophy of the Revolution of 1789.
Rarely has a doctrine been so integrated into a revolution.
In the latter part of the century, merchants, peasants, and
artisans all found their development hampered by the restrictions of the *ancien régime*. France was confronted with
political, religious, moral and philosophical problems, all
growing out of clashing economic interests. These problems
of a society in flux stimulated the educated sectors to think
of creating a mode of life in which everyone would be aware
of the possibilities inherent in social life.

The revolutionary nature of French eighteenth-century
thought was an accurate, albeit incomplete, reflection of
the social revolution then in progress. Enlightenment became the ideological justification of revolution. Unlike their
contemplative forebears, the *philosophes* believed that theory
becomes a genuine factor only when it propels elites into
action. Robert Nisbet summed up their legacy most accurately: "One and all, sociology, historiography, jurispru-
dence, moral philosophy, political science, found themselves
dealing with the issues raised dramatically by the Revolution: tradition versus reason and law, religion versus state,
the nature of property, the relation of social classes, administration, centralization, nationalism, and perhaps above all
others, egalitarianism."[3]

The fettered political position of the middle classes made
them antagonistic to the feudal regime and its religious and
philosophic traditions. The feudal system found its security

in looking to a bygone era when noblemen were truly noble. The merchant and industrial classes believed that the determinant of future progress rested upon the social universe and its variegated elements. The altered status of the urban bourgeoisie, their increased wealth and power, suggested endless social advances. This fostered the notion of progress as the central theme in the social essays. Unswerving faith in progress as secularization was the one point that the conflicting schools of Enlightenment thought held in common. Engels put it correctly when he wrote: "The conviction that humanity, at least at the present moment, moves on the whole in a progressive direction has absolutely nothing to do with the antithesis between materialism and idealism. The French materialists equally with the deists Voltaire and Rousseau held this conviction to an almost fanatical degree, and often made the greatest personal sacrifices for it."[4]

Ideas that in their content were products of the emergent bourgeoisie began to appear. In particular, the commercial classes applauded individual achievement and success. Individualism as a style became linked to urban life. What saved such individualism from egotism was utilitarianism, the presumed linkage of the person to the public good. Naturalism as a philosophy initiated the anthropocentric movement in modern social theory. The French Enlightenment appealed to the social world, the sensuous world, turning its back on the political conservatism fostered by idealism and supernaturalism. The ethics of the Middle Ages were determined to be contrary to emotional and rational elements in human experience. Feudal mores seemed bloodless and abstract. The color and imagery invested in the angels and saints faded considerably by the eighteenth century. The social standards of the new classes were held to correspond with the productive nature of man. For scholasticism, rational contemplation made great men. The encyclopedists were dedicated to the idea that great passions made great men. There was a powerful Enlightenment ten-

dency to interpret human passion in empirical terms of pleasure and pain, along with the characteristic bourgeois tang
of self-serving calculation.[5] All evidence indicates that the
source of utilitarianism's popularity during the eighteenth
century was its adaptability to newly introduced categories
of social exchange as measured by economic gains.

Criticism of the monarchy required moral justification.
The utilitarian doctrines provided just that sensibility. In
clear and measurable terms, the irrationality of decadent
feudal regimes was exposed, while ideas were put forth for
the formation of a more rational society based on personal
needs and interests. French utilitarianism did more than
argue for a society in which the happiness of the greatest
number would decide everything. It described the possibility of actualizing the potential of an environment through
education and legislation. These were to be the levers of
future progress. This double-edged sword of description and
prescription became the touchstone of all future political
and social theory.

In France, the Enlightenment received its most advanced
sociological expression because of the national passion for
learning and law. As the hub of eighteenth-century intellectual life, France provided such tenets of the Enlightenment
as the belief in the supremacy of science, human reason
and social progress. The Enlightenment was thus a movement with both national and personal features. It generated
and was in turn sustained by a rising middle-class European
culture. Yet the roots of the Enlightenment were so embedded in Christian imagery that it not only assumed different
national forms in France and Germany, but also developed
fundamental cleavages in the content of its social messages
to each of the contending social classes.

For all of its emphasis on equality, the Enlightenment
accepted for the natural stratification of men, and unhap-
pily admitted that divine appointment rather than the popular will remained the ultimate source of political power. Its

advocates insisted that democracy would bring on anarchy—
that is, the rule of the filthy mob and the uncultured money-
grubbing middle class. In the same Parisian *salons* that fostered the spirit of free discussion, the circulating library,
the popular newspaper, and the Society of Free Masons,
which provided channels for the flow of *philosophie democratique* to a wide audience, there was also to be found an
ideological sophistry amiable to the thought processes of
traditional social forces. Helvétius's theory of the equal capacities of man, an outlook that was to become the touchstone of democratic movements the world over and that was
to receive juridical recognition in the *Declaration of the Rights
of Man*, was rejected by some Enlightenment scholars because it exalted man at the expense of animals. It is not that
animals had "rights" but that men were animals at best, and
machines at worst. Enlightenment ideological currents revealed the bifurcation of French life in the eighteenth century. But they also anticipated the sort of dilemmas that
were later to plague sociological theory generally; to wit,
can the "people" in whose name all good things were advocated really be trusted? Jacob Talmon elucidated this dilemma of the age when he noted that "essential in the thinking of the early totalitarians was the refusal to take the people
as it was for granted. The aim of the Revolution and post-
revolutionary legislation was to give birth to the regener-
ated people, the true people, by the total elimination of the
unredeemable minority, and the proper education of the
remainder."[6]

The *philosophes* were not the first to conceive of the social
utility of ideas and their human carriers. They were however the first to elevate self-interest into the highest moral
precept. In this way, ideology was born. Ideas had a value
for action apart from their truth content. No longer were
intellectuals to be viewed as alienated from the mainstream
of social battles. The *philosophes* represented the role of the
intellectual as that of leader, responding to the demands of

the people. The defense made for the freedom of the press, the right of women and youth to a full measure of social power and responsibility and the need for a democratic re-organization of the educational system attested to the newfound self-consciousness of intellectuals as a social force. Knowledge was no longer viewed as a special province of the chosen few but as secular property and, hence, to some degree the right of all. This sort of analysis enabled the *philosophes* to become an organizing force for both social revolution and applied research.

Philosophes viewed themselves quite apart from the actual social status they occupied. Their moral dedication to "humanity" rather than to any particular class reflected the temporarily compatible relationship between all sectors allied against the aristocracy. They regarded the rise of technology, the natural and social sciences, and the crafts as powerful social weapons. They did not comprehend the shift in economic forces that made possible this expansion. This is revealed by their curious idea that they, the *philosophes*, and not any mere economic entity, were the repositories of the future of mankind, with a program of social reconstruction different from and superior to that of any other group in French life. This was the grand illusion harbored by the *lumieres*, an illusion bequeathed to the sociologists in later periods. They also firmly believed in a special, transcendent social mission, unbound by constraints of birth, breeding or bias.

This lack of class allegiance was a historical fact and not a personal failing. Certainly it in no way prevented the new philosophical leaders from playing a revolutionary role in helping to bring about the downfall of the *ancien régime*. Those who worked mainly with their heads overcame the supposed alienation of the intellectual from his fellowmen and joined in the struggles of the rest of humankind. Diderot emphasized that this was to be a contribution of the *Encyclopédie* to the common struggle. Reason, as codified in the sciences, arts and techniques of the age would provide the intellectual nourishment of progressive change. "Our philosophy is full of humanity. Civil society is, so to speak, a divinity for him on earth; he burns incense to it, he honors it by probity, by an exact attention to his duties, and by a sincere desire not to be a useless or embarrassing member of it. The sentiments of probity enter as much into the mechanical constitution of the philosophes as the illumination of the mind. The more you find reason in a man, the more you find in him probity."[7]

While Diderot was pointing out the necessary social duties of the intellectual, Helvétius was busy defining what these duties were. Throughout *Treatise on Man*, he showed that a *philosophe* plays a useful role only by criticizing despotic, corrupt and dying regimes while generating a love for truth, honesty and usefulness. "There are periods in every country when the word *prudent* bears the same meaning with *vile*; and when these productions are esteemed only for their sentiments, which are written in a style of servility. In all nations there are certain periods when the citizens, undetermined in what measures they ought to take, and remaining in a state of suspense between a good and bad government, are extremely desirous of instruction, and are disposed to receive it. At such a time, if a work of great merit makes its appearance, the happiest effects may be produced. But the moment it passes, the people, insensible to glory, are by the form of their government irresistibly inclined towards ignorance and baseness."[8]

One can see how far removed is Diderot's notion of philosophy from older traditions. With few exceptions, philosophies of classical antiquity and the Middle Ages were not concerned with the intricate relationship between philosophical theory and social practice. The contemplative attitude dominated from Plato and Aristotle to Bruno, Descartes and Spinoza. It had always been an accepted axiom that the highest philosophic activity is the "exercise of the mind," which served to justify the gulf between head and hand, mental and physical labor.

The pervasive animosity of the Enlightenment for philosophy as speculation stems from its understanding that philosophy lacked social compassion. By the same token, it can be seen how close the *philosophes* came to a pure theory of sociology—to a view of learning as linked to the presumed needs of the downtrodden. But in their contempt for the inability of the mass to rise above their station, the French tradition strangely avoided both the anti-intellectualism of modern pragmatism and the pseudo-populism of modern communism.

As Charles Frankel noted: "It lies in a new recognition that science and criticism have a social function even if the individual thinker is unaware of it. The *philosophes* were conscious that they were living through an intellectual revolution, a revolution among intellectuals, and they did not feel that the result of this revolution was simply that the man of books had come to be reminded that he had other obligations and that he also ought to be a man of action. Rather, the revolution lay in the discovery that when a man is properly intellectual he is in that way performing a social function and engaging in a species of social action."[9] One could hardly have a more apt description of the optimism that brought sociology into existence, and indeed permeated its message from Comte to Marx to Mannheim. The encyclopedists believed that by turning theory to the concrete needs of the age, it became at once both revolutionary and truthful. Again, we turn to Diderot, who spoke of the essence of an "honest man" as possessing a "love of society." Moreover, it is this "love" that permits philosophers to be kings and kings philosophers.[10]

The *philosophes* showed the middle class the value of science and the virtue of liberty. In this, they represented the philosophic spirit of the bourgeoisie, although they thought they represented the common spirit. The two "spirits" were harmonious because at this stage of French history the bourgeoisie was able to speak for "humanity" in general. The Enlightenment in France became a movement among intellectuals to assert themselves as a political force by introducing the significance of ideology as a decisive factor in human evolution.

The worldly philosophy of the French Enlightenment found its fulfillment in sociological concepts of equality and progress. And both of these were products of secularization as an end unto itself. Condorcet provided a forthright statement on this matter: "Our hopes, as to the future condition of the human species, may be reduced to three points: the destruction of inequality between different nations; the progress of equality in one and the same nation; and lastly, the real improvement of man."[11] Translating theory into social activity, the *philosophes* became the high priests of the democratic revolution. It was not for anything that the *philosophes* often compared themselves to the Old Testament prophets. They had the same revolutionary zeal, the same faith in the omnipotence of their message, the same hatred for oppressors. They had little theological use for the Bible, but they had valuation teachings that were calculated to root out the moneymakers and fear-makers from their feudal temples—the scientific theory of Newton and the social theory of Locke. The distinctive role played by the encyclopedists was to provide a moral basis for the French Revolution. The encyclopedists inherited from the past a desire to codify knowledge, to provide a taxonomy for the useful and a wastebasket for the useless.

But along with this broad-scaled effort at secularization there was an acceptance of fanaticism as well. The decline of the clerical was also a call for the blood letting of an enterprise that ended with Robespierre's terror. The *philosophes* lacked practical political skills. They became a class apart, aiding a restless bourgeois class with little or no practical experience in the art of governance. This combi-

nation of ideological purity and class aspiration is one of
the acute dangers inherent in canonical visions. People in
search of a canon, on which to base their actions are also
those impatient with the modest pace of political events taking, place in the real world. The new emphasis on the state
was a mechanism aimed to ensure social justice in a secular
world. Instead, it became an institution that ultimately was
to undermine the very emphasis on social justice that provided the original impetus for the Enlightenment.

Pierre Bayle's *Dictionnaire Historique et Critique* prefigured
the *Encyclopédie*. Bayle provided the notion that the past was
not only to be celebrated but also rejected on ethical
grounds.[12] Another indication of the "encyclopedic" approach was presaged in the works of Voltaire. The main difference between the works of Bayle and Voltaire on one side
and the *Encyclopédie* on the other was more in the organized
method of work than in the ideological thrust of their respective efforts. The *Encyclopédie* was a sociological undertaking in two basic aspects: it was an intellectual current in
which many thought streams were welded together, and these
views were advocated in common. Not only did the encyclopedists have a joint source of ideas, but also this very source
was the product of the interaction among these thinkers.

French revolutionary philosophy was not the world outlook of Fontenelle, Montesquieu, Condillac, Voltaire,
Rousseau, Diderot and Holbach, to name but a few of the
contributors, but a doctrine these people shared, out of discussions and criticisms resulting from intellectual cooperation. The encyclopedists shared with the physiocrats the idea
that social phenomena are governed, as are physical phenomena, by laws of nature, but they differed in emphasizing
the role of human intention. They held in common the goal
of freedom from sword and cloth, and to the actualization
of this goal they united in common endeavor.

Condorcet described the nature of this eighteenth-century vision of democracy: "The philosophers of different

nations, embracing in their meditations the entire interests of man, without distinction of country, of color, or of sect, formed a firm and united phalanx against every description of error and every species of tyranny."[13] But in rooting out "error" this vision led to the "terror"—the destruction of all whom would dare disagree with self-evident propositions of egalitarianism.

What welded the *philosophes* together more than abstract theoretical agreements were the tasks of writing and publishing a universal compendium of human knowledge that would lead to an unleashing of libertarian and true sentiments. They were, of course, the same. In the *Preliminary Discourse* of the *Encyclopédie*, d'Alembert indicated the dual purpose of this great venture in literature; it was to be a dictionary of the arts, sciences and crafts, expounding the basic premises of each in such a way as to "really reach the mind of a people rather than merely the surface."[14]

The *Encyclopédie* was to be a work aimed at exhibiting the order and connection of all human knowledge, "encompassing in a single system the infinitely varied branches of human science." The construction of the *Encyclopédie*, d'Alembert noted was actually begun when the contributors agreed to bypass inherited scholastic categories and "return to the origin and generation of our ideas," to nature. No one was more sensitive to the ideological needs of the day than was Denis Diderot, the guiding genius who conceived and edited the major portion of the *Encyclopédie*. He extended nature to include society. Free and disciplined criticism would be an antidote to the infections caused by church and state. Diderot hoped that his advanced views on human knowledge would become common currency among the readers of the *Encyclopédie*: "Truth is not for the philosophes a mistress who corrupts his imagination and whom he believes is to be found everywhere; he contents himself with being able to unravel it where he can perceive it. He does not confound it with probability; he takes for true what is true, for false what is false, for doubtful what is doubtful, and for the probable what is only probable. He does more when he has no reason by which to judge; he knows how to live in suspension of judgment. The philosophic spirit is, then, a spirit of observation and exactness."[15]

The *Encyclopédie* aimed at overthrowing the "edifice of mud" and putting in its place the "edifice of truth." The *Prospectus* prepared by Diderot reveals that he viewed this organ of liberal thought as more than a polished compendium of information that would disabuse men of their prejudices: "It is also an attempt to establish and exhibit the unity of science as a whole; the mutual help given by the individual sciences to one another; and the historic continuity of the scientific enterprise."[16] This sort of scientific rationalism was the political contagion of which Enlightenment impulses were the carrier.

The eighteenth century witnessed the sharp delineation of various disciplines. Just as it was the century of immensely important scientific discoveries, so, too, it was the century of new social theories. The *Encyclopédie* was conceived as the tool that would weave these intellectual advances into an integral whole. The *Encyclopédie* was the first unified social science movement. A statement by d'Alembert illustrates the temper of the age: "Our century has called itself the *philosophic century* par excellence. From the principles of the profane sciences to the foundations of revelation, from metaphysics to questions of taste, from music to morals, from the scholastic dispute of theologians to commercial affairs, from the rights of princes to those of peoples, from the natural law to the arbitrary law of nations, in a word, from the questions that affect us most to those that interest us least, everything has been discussed, analyzed and disputed."[17]

The *Encyclopédie* systematized the enthusiastic optimism of revolution and Enlightenment. Above all, agreement on dislikes made the encyclopedists the cohesive force they were. In positive theory there was a wide divergence between

Voltaire's skeptical deism and Diderot's physiological materialism, or d'Alembert's agnostic positivism and Helvétius's sociological materialism. Yet these scholars maintained the closest possible association throughout their lives. This philosophic front was made possible by the alignments of class forces. The forces of reaction, having not yet "discovered" the merits of British subjectivism, grouped about the philosophy of clerical idealism. The forces of progress were, in the main, grouped about sociological materialism and mechanical deism.

The encyclopedists were not "professional" philosophers. They were rather part of the intellectual class in the making. These people échoed the sentiments of the emerging economic classes: "free commerce, free industry and free men," but they also presaged an alignment in which intellectuals acted as a cohesive force in their own right. The theoretical precepts of the *philosophes* issued out of social problems and therefore were amenable to the classes in France that had the most to gain from the advocacy of new ideas. But they were themselves recruited from privileged groups and saw a budding science of society as a unique professional contribution to modernity.

Despite the practical harmony among the encyclopedists, there were persistent and significant differences reflected in their thinking. The same Rousseau who contributed brilliant studies to Diderot's *Encyclopédie* was not above attacking him, along with Grimm and Holbach, in the *Confessions*.[18] Divergences between the *philosophes* were one aspect of the social amalgamation that blended to overthrow the *ancien régime*. These classes exhibited marked ideological differences resulting from different levels of social maturity. There was a profound difference between the social role of a financier and that of a farmer producing for the urban market; a proletarian at work in a newly established machine industry or a collector of feudal tithes turned banker. Such a heterogeneous combination of classes, although united for the single purpose of destroying the dwindling power of the feudal classes, would naturally at the same time have certain independent aspirations. The *Cahiers de doleances*, which presented a list of grievances against the *ancien régime*, give an accurate picture not merely of the general antagonism between the *Tiers* and the old classes but also of specific class demands and levels of class-consciousness of each segment of the *Tiers*.

In a literal sense, the conscious defenders of the bourgeois interests—property interests—were with their limitations more sober in their appraisal of social conditions than were the more theoretically advanced *philosophes*. Voltaire, Rousseau and d'Alembert had an advantage over the radicals like Holbach, Helvétius and Diderot. The former trio knew, to a greater extent at any rate, the limited nature of the conflagrations in which they were entangled in, whereas the radical trio tended to arrive at utopian conclusions to absolve the harsh realities of political conflict. A deep contradiction between the two basic segments of the encyclopedic school showed that those dedicated to total liberation of humanity, though offering a more democratic and consistent doctrine, suffered under the illusion that the outcome of their struggles would end conflicts between men once and for all. Those who were clearly dedicated to the liberation of capital, though presenting a less enthusiastic outlook in its democratic implications, were not encumbered by hopes of apocalyptic utopianism. Therefore, those who were theoretically less consistent, were more consistent in relation to the needs and practices of the period. They also managed to avoid the problem of "totalitarian democracy" that was to have such a devastating impact on the French Revolution, and later to encumber radical sociological thought from Saint-Simon to Comte.

To Voltaire, Diderot and Holbach, social progress represented the political progress of all humanity. The encyclopedists, while admiring the benefits yielded by English constitutionalism, believed that a strong and intelligent monarch would be better able to achieve a smoother functioning state by eliminating the dilemmas inherent in a consensual, parliamentary system of government. The *philosophes* did not assume that parliamentary government was the same as democratic government. On the other hand, they were less concerned with individual safeguards against government. The social was everything. They had considerable respect for and defense of the rights of private property against both the "greed and envy" of the masses and "arbitrary confiscation" by a hereditary aristocracy. Voltaire, Diderot and Holbach were democrats who fought a two-sided battle. As long as the *ancien régime* remained in political power, the land-owning nobility and their compatriot, the Roman Catholic Church bore the brunt of their slicing attacks. But even before the Revolution of 1789, these *philosophes* held that their democratic and egalitarian goals were inaccessible to the ordinary people, who they imagined, were more cattle-like than human. Their attention was devoted to the possibilities for social order under a government operated by these troublesome beasts that were men.

Voltaire's intellectual development would indicate that his outlook was much more than a mirror-like idealization of English constitutional traditions. In emphasizing the necessity and advantages of an alliance between bourgeois and monarchical elements, his views were well adjusted to the realities of sociopolitical life in France. For a revealing insight into Voltaire's middle-class bias, we should recall his comment on equality in the *Philosophical Dictionary*: "The human race, such as it is, cannot subsist unless there is an infinity of useful men who possess nothing at all; for it is certain that if a man who is well off will not leave his own land to come to till yours; and if you have need of a pair of shoes, it is not the Secretary of the Privy Council who will make them for you. Equality is at once the most natural thing and the most fantastic."[19]

Voltaire continues with the statement that "all men have the right in the bottom of their hearts to think themselves entirely equal to other men: it does not follow from that the cardinal's cook should order his master to prepare him dinner."[20] Voltaire would allow men to *think* themselves equal as long as they did not try to put such thoughts into *practice*. Voltaire made use of the master-slave parable. A man may be enslaved to another materially, but he, in turn, holds the master captive in spirit. Because the master is dependent upon the slave for his wealth, he must always be a slave to the human slave's whims, fancies, desires and dreams. What this play on words always ignores is that the free spirit is free, precisely in his or her effort to engage in actions intended to implement new values into the body politic. The move from philosophy to sociology can well be described as a move from the cultural to the economic, or at least a shift in emphasis from consciousness to commerce as the essential base line for social analysis.

Bound to the ideology of aristocratic rule, Diderot started out by fulminating against the exploitation that personal wealth breeds, but remained in the end a firm adherent of the view that property rights are eternal rights. "It is property that makes the citizen; every man who has possessions in the State must have interest in the State, and whatever be the rank of that particular conventions may assign to him, it is always as a proprietor; it is by reason of his possessions that he ought to speak, and that he acquires the right of having himself represented."[21]

The logic, though not the sentiment, of the position developed by Voltaire and Diderot, was to make the fight for liberty equivalent to the struggle to broaden property rights in fact and in law. Holbach brushed aside proprietary claims as moral right. "True liberty consists in conforming to the laws which remedy the natural inequality of men, that is, which protect equally the rich and the poor, the great and the small, sovereigns and subjects. In a word, to be free is to obey only laws."[22] Holbach confused laws made by men, who have vested interests, with the laws of nature. Once again, we have the appearance of what we must term, for want of a better phrase, "spiritual egalitarianism." The propertyless peasant is little comforted to know that his nonexistent property will be given the same attention in "law" as that of the propertied squire. Holbach assumes that private-property relations are sacred.

Enlightenment theorists like Diderot and Voltaire began by indicating class iniquities and ended with appeals to the monarch for elevation of private property to a dignified and ranking social status. The struggle against the power of the old order did not readily translate into an assault on status hierarchy as such. Although figures like Diderot and Voltaire despised the exploitation caused by the *ancien régime*, they were unwilling to accept the bitter implications of expropriation. They accepted middle-class leadership because no other group in French society was in a position to exercise power democratically without destroying the status arrangements of the times. The revolutionary theorists made no demands beyond the needs of the peasantry, and the peasantry was first and foremost concerned with land ownership, with property rights. A strain of chiliastic fervor persisted in their writings. These *philosophes* did not accept Enlightenment despotism as a goal of social relations, but rather as an instrument, a means for reaching Thomas More's *Utopia*. The disparity between total liberation and total submission, that was to have such tragic consequences for the French Revolution, was to be avoided by walking this fine line between political freedom and economic entitlement.

The relation of Helvétius to his encyclopedist associates on the question of political power is two-fold. While paralleling their concept of the enlightened monarch as the dispenser of law and order, he disagreed with Voltaire's faith in the healing powers of economic classes. He developed his theory of political rule along the lines of the *Theses*

Democratique. He gave it a "proof" and a "popularity" it lacked
in the hands of Morelly, Mably and Argenson—namely, the
utilitarian motivation of individuals. If everyone is driven
to seek his own best interests, and those interests could only
be served in social intercourse, the monarch could really be
enlightened only if he served the interests of every man in
every class.

This broad utilitarianism differentiates Helvétius from his
colleagues. Legislation was to be in the name of all people,
without class prerogative. The criterion of the success of a
legislative program is the amount of happiness it brings each
and every person. This is the final test of political progress.
The monarch will be a good instrument for political advancement only as long as he abides by the dictums of utilitarianism. The test of his success is the mass of people—not a privileged class or sect, but the measurable wealth in the hands
of the producers. All rulers, all laws and all customs must
demonstrate their services to present needs. What fails in
this test should be discarded, without fanfare and certainly
without regrets.

Find out what people desire or need, and frame laws aimed
at securing just that—these were the elemental principles of
Helvétius's juridical and political reform program. It was
his deep-felt concern with the needs of the great mass of
society that prompted Helvétius to scorn the maze of juridical precepts and political edifices inherited from the old
order. These inherited evils, which both the adherents of a
bourgeois monarchy and a feudal monarchy would subtly
preserve, in effect only "preserve the errors accumulated
since the origin of the human race."[23] If the world had to be
made anew, let it allow for the happiness of all, not just for
the enjoyment of a new privileged class.

Helvétius's approach is at one and the same time an early
representation of sociological utopianism and a clear example of the collective aspirations of the radical forces which
seized control of the French Revolution. In his analysis of

past theories of politics, Helvétius sharply called to task the
a priori vision inherent in Plato's *Republic*, and Augustine's
City of God. They discussed what heaven ordained or what
should be divinely ordained, but they hardly took the trouble
to examine what *is*. Such political abstractions deal not with
real problems and real solutions, but with distant problems
and impossible solutions. "If there is a method to fix public
attention on the problem of an excellent legislation, it is by
rendering it simple and reducing it to two propositions."
Helvétius thought those propositions were of such a useful
nature that no person could fail to recognize their critical
significance: "The importance of the first should be the discovery of laws proper to render man as happy as possible,
and consequently to procure for them all the amusements
and pleasures compatible with the public welfare. The object of the second should be the discovery of means by which
a people may be made to pass insensibly from the state of
misery to one of happiness."[24]

Helvétius goes on to suggest that we should follow the
example of mathematicians to resolve the first proposition:
"When a complicated problem in mechanics is proposed to
them, what do they do? Simplify it; calculate the velocity of
moving bodies without regarding their destiny, the resistance
of fluids that surround them, their friction with other bodies, etc." In similar manner, to resolve the problem of excellent legislation, one should pay no regard to the prejudices
or friction caused by the contradictory interests, or to ossi-
fied mores, laws and customs: "The inquirer should act like
the founder of a religious order, who in dictating his monas-
tic laws has no regard to the habits and prejudices of his
future subjects."[25] Helvétius did not realize that he was setting a standard no less abstract and a priori than Plato. He,
too, was telling the "inquirer" to disregard the existing levels of human development and frame a perfect utilitarian
theory of legislation having no relation to historical reality.

To discover how people can pass from conditions of mis-

ery to those of happiness, Helvétius offered entirely different criteria: "It is not after our own conceptions, but from a
knowledge of the present laws and customs that we can determine the means of gradually changing those customs and
laws, and of making a people pass through by insensible
degrees, from their present legislation to the best possible
laws."[26] Thus, thesis two, unlike thesis one, was based completely on laws of history. Helvétius recognized that there
was an essential difference between these two propositions.
When the first, ahistorical proposition is resolved, its solution becomes general; the same for all peoples and nations,
while the resolution of the second differs widely according
to the form and level of social development of each people
and each nation. Satisfactorily overcoming the problems
generated by this contradictory but equally real proposition
will inevitably lead to political progress. They provide for
the universal happiness of people, while at the same time
taking into account basic differences between people.
Progress therefore has two elements: the transient forms
any search for happiness takes, and the universal desire of
all men for happiness as an end in itself.

In a series of "Questions on Legislation," Helvétius put
forth the essential features of his theory of legislation and
politics. The propositions are so worded that there is little
question he intended them not to raise doubt, but to demonstrate the absolute necessity for a conception of political
progress. He begins by claiming that in order to achieve
political progress; it behooves us first to understand the
motives that unite men in society. To this problem Helvétius
devoted much time. Society is formed when men realize that
the scourges of nature cannot be overcome singly, but only
by individuals banded together in shared interests. The necessities of material conditions force individuals to be essentially social in spite of their essentially egoistic, interest
driven natures. Mankind once *united against nature* becomes
divided against one another. The result is a division of labor,

an economically torn society. With the crystallization of these economic and social divisions, people are then "obligated to form conventions and give themselves laws." These laws have as their foundation "the common desire of securing their property, their lives, and their liberty, which, in an unsociable state, is exposed to the violence of the strongest."[27]

Helvétius likened the stage of savagery to modern despotism. Both had in common the destruction of all bonds of social union. Despotism, like its primitive ancestor, substituted might for right, the lash of the ruler for the law of people. He then suggested that a certain equilibrium of power among the different classes of citizens be introduced, as it was during the English revolutions of the preceding century. Once this relative harmony of social interests comes into existence during a revolution, the class and individual strife of those on the same side is minimized. After the revolution has achieved its aims, however, Helvétius noticed that there is a resurgence of the very social antagonisms that the revolution had sought to abolish. Just as prior to the revolution, so too, after the revolution, a polarization of class interests reemerges.

The despairing insight of Helvétius concerning the harmony and polarization of social and class interests led him to posit a social order that could finally end this cyclical path of development. His conception of the future society may best be characterized as sociological utopianism: "Does the man without property owe anything to the country where he possesses nothing? Must not the extremely indigent, being always in the pay of the rich and powerful, frequently favor their ambition? And lastly, have not the indigent too many wants to be virtuous? Could not the laws unite the interest of the majority of the inhabitants with that of their country by the subdivision of property? After the example of the Lacedaemonians, whose territory being divided into thirty-nine thousand lots, was distributed among thirty-nine thousand families, who formed the nation, might not, in case of too great an increase of inhabitants, a greater or less extent of land be assigned to each family, but still in proportion to the number who compose it?"[28]

Helvétius then discussed the development of the legal codes of a state, pointing out that a great number of involved legal statutes are not infrequently a maze of contradictions made useless by their abstraction from real-life situations. Helvétius indicated that such multiplicity of laws leads to ignorance and failure on the part of governing classes to execute the public will. The only purpose they serve is to institutionalize the oppression of the people and to confuse them concerning what their "true interests" actually are. "The multiplicity of laws, often contrary to each other, oblige nations to employ certain men and bodies of men to interpret them. May not these men or bodies of men, charged with their interpretation, insensibly change the laws and make them the instruments of their ambition? And lastly, does not experience teach us, that wherever there are many laws, there is little justice."[29] Therefore, in repressive governments, the laws serve directly as an instrument of oppression.

In a good society, one concerned with the welfare of the people, a small number of clear and self-evident laws are sufficient. Complicated laws that are interpreted and reinterpreted by elitist aspirations serve only to further political reaction. Where there are no private interests there will be no need for a complex legal scaffold to keep down the public will. Simple laws are sufficient to establish the simple goal of all humankind, happiness. Just as land should be divided up among all people for the purpose of doing away with conflicts between rulers and ruled, Helvétius advocated dividing up nations into small federations equal in size and political power. In this way, wars, national oppression and territorial aggrandizement could finally be abolished. "If a country as large as France were to be divided into thirty provinces or republics, and to each of them a territory nearly equal (in size) were to be assigned, and if each of these territories were circumscribed by immutable bounds, or its possession guaranteed by the other twenty-nine republics, is to be imagined that any one of those republics could enslave all the others, that is, that any one man could combat with advantage against twenty-nine men?"[30]

To prevent an aggressor nation from commencing warfare against a nation constituted in a democratic federation, Helvétius would impose certain safeguards. He acted on the supposition that these democratic republics "were governed by the same laws, where each of them took care of its interior police and the election of its magistrates, and reported its conduct to a superior council; or where the superior council composed of four deputies from each republic, and principally occupied with the affairs of war and politics, should be yet charged with observing that none of those republics changed its legislation without the consent of all the others: and where, moreover, the object of the laws should be to improve minds, exalt courage, and preserve an exact discipline in their armies. On such a supposition the whole body of the republics would be sufficiently powerful to oppose efficaciously any ambitious projects of their neighbors, or fellow-citizens."[31]

As long as the legislation of such a federated republic renders the greatest happiness to the greatest number of people, procuring for them all the pleasures compatible with public welfare, these republics could be sure of continued political progress. Helvétius's interest in peace and prosperity overshadowed his implicit utopianism.

Laws are good if they equalize the material basis of human welfare and extirpate all possibilities of special class interests and war of aggression. It was through peace and social equality that Helvétius saw the vast possibilities open for political progress. Legislation is moral if it secures peace and equality; it is immoral if it does not do so. "Whenever the public welfare is not the supreme law, and the first obligation of a citizen, does there still subsist a science of good

and evil; in short, is there any morality where the public
good is not the measure of reward and punishment, of the
esteem or contempt due to the actions of citizens?"[32]
Helvétius recognized that political progress is measured by
more than the democratization and equalization of the
material sources of pleasure. It is measured also in terms of
the ideals and attitudes it instills in people. Therefore, the
good society and good laws provide for emotional and psychological pleasures as well as for material goods. In fact, in
a quite real sense the ideas and opinions of people help
mold and shape the future course of civilization.

Helvétius's conception of development in the political and
legal structure of society, presented as it was in an epoch of
decomposition, cynicism and corruption of the *ancien régime*,
stood at the forefront in the cause of the rights and dignity
of man; but in his naturalized Platonism, such "rights" were
not to permit dissent, disagreement or loose morals. His
impatience in the face of questions concerning social evolution and revolution, the nature of historical change, revealed
his political philosophy to be one-sided and ultimately
flawed. In his view of history, he opposed God as a *deus ex
machina* only to substitute a divine monarch as the *deus ex
machina*. However useful this notion may have been in combating antiquated political dogmas, it had serious scientific
value only insofar as it attempted to explain the ideological
content of politics. Like other *philosophes*, Helvétius made a
remarkable effort in this direction only to end in failure. In
his view of political growth, Helvétius adopted a position
that culture—rather than social conditions—determines the
course of civilization. When empirical considerations forced
their way to the surface of Helvétius's thought, they did so
mechanistically and at the risk of destroying the spirit of his
efforts.

Social science and political goals found themselves divided
in his political outlook. When he concentrated on making
politics a science, he lost touch with the human participants

in the struggle for progress. When he concentrated on hu-
manizing politics, he lost touch with the actual roots of
progress. At one point, social consciousness becomes an
accidental response to atomic particles whirling about in the
mind, and at another, it becomes the prime mover. In the
first act, humanism battles cannibalism; in the second act,
science battles supernaturalism. But this doctrine never fin-
ishes the play because it never finds the proper resolution
and solution to the conflict posed.[33]

Typical of late eighteenth-century French thought,
Helvétius neither understood nor had patience with political theorists who were preoccupied with forms of government. In his view, governments were either good or evil, the
standard of judgment being their social utility. This view
presupposed yet another idea, which was to gain increasing
prominence in the nineteenth century, namely, that the *content* of society is its material resources—natural and human—
and that the *form* of society is in such a relation to the content as either to propel or retard the growth of the material
base of society. Since, in Helvétius's view, all previous forms
or stages of society rested on securing abundance for private selfish interests, a good (useful) economic and political
system was a thing of the future lacking any historical precedence. Helvétius's failure to concern himself with the political forms of government was part and parcel of a doctrinal
commitment to ends without discussion of means. His was a
rationalism in which history, culture, and institutions were
limiting conditions to be overcome, rather than agencies to
be managed.

The prime goal of man being happiness, all political institutions must be adapted to satisfy this aim. Political
progress is not the slow, gradual and haphazard adaptation
of old institutions to meet new situations, but their revolutionary transformation under the guidance of a providential monarch. As against Montesquieu, Helvétius thought
their veneration of ancient laws and credos were not only a

naive rejection of the requirements of the present but that they were also dangerous to an institutional comprehension of politics. For him, the individual alone is capable of determining his interest at any particular moment. The integration of these various individual interests into a common political organization makes possible a democratic society. It is this very meshing of individual interests that revealed to Helvétius the necessity of an equal distribution of wealth, labor, education and, above all, political control.

The desire to frame a democratic theory of politics rests on a comprehension that men must first change their environment if they are to bring about any profound change in their psychology. Materialism and causal determinism are the heart of the utilitarian science of morality. But this faith in the self-corrective powers of "man" went only so far. The utilitarians attributed to enlightened monarch powers of social change that are the sole property of society. This exaggeration in utilitarian political doctrine of the role played by a princely ruler stemmed from the almost sacred belief that, once enlightened, the ruler would be a dispassionate dispenser of law and justice, thereby becoming the prime agent of social progress. This view implies that a king does in relation to social institutions what a mechanic does in relation to a run-down machine, the separate parts of which can be reordered through purely external intervention. This is what the Russian Marxist George Plekhanov called "the transformation of a phenomenon into a fossilized thing by abstracting it from all the inner processes of life, the nature and connection of which it is impossible to understand."[34] The utilitarians were caught in a web of their own design. They developed a theory of politics that expressed democratic yearnings, but the theory remained tied to an authoritarian view of political progress, which rested on changing society through royal dictatorship. In the last analysis, equity was not so much achieved as imposed.

The contribution of Rousseau to a theory of political society is as great as those made by all other *philosophes* as a group to the sociology of politics. *A Discourse on the Origin of Inequality* occupies a place of honor in the historical genesis of political sociology. At the most general level, Rousseau succeeded in showing that the difference between the political society and the moral man, a distinction made by Plato and Aristotle, and one that has continued to grip thinkers in the vise of dualism, is largely fictitious. The political and the moral are equivalent; both are aspects of human socialization. Legal relationships are as binding or as limiting as moral persuasions permit; similarly, moral relationships are as binding or limiting as legal persuasions permit. The key to both is legitimacy; for authority to be made legitimate, all parties involved in a social contract must mutually agree upon a cluster of norms and values. The point is Rousseau's inability to move beyond the theory of the social contract and into a general theory of the history and evolution of political society.

The critical significance of Rousseau inheres, not in his idea of original goodness, which was, in the long run, but a ploy with which to beat back theological critics, but rather in his ideas that the human origins in an empirical context do not entail a settlement of the idea of original evils, but a settlement of actual interests. Indeed, his critique of Hobbes in *A Discourse on the Origin of Inequality* comes exceptionally close to a post-Enlightenment sensibility on this question: "Let us not conclude that because man has no idea of goodness, he must be naturally wicked; that he is vicious because he does not know virtue; that he always refuses to do his fellow-creatures services which he does not think they have a right to demand; or that by virtue of the right he truly claims everything he needs, he foolishly imagines himself the sole proprietor of the whole universe. Hobbes had seen clearly the defects of all the modern definitions of natural right: but the consequences, which he deduces from his, own show that he understands it in an equally false sense.

In reasoning on the principles he lays down, he ought to have said that the state of nature, being that in which the care for our own preservation is the least prejudicial to that of others, was consequently the best calculated to promote peace, and the most suitable for mankind."[35]

Rousseau believed that the primary human drives have little to do with the moral questions and a great deal to do with the social question—the question of survival. "Man's first feeling was that of his own existence, and his first care that of self-preservation. The produce of the earth furnished him with all he needed, and instinct told him how to use it. Hunger and other appetites made him at various times experience various modes of existence; and among these was one which urged him to propagate his species—a blind propensity that, having nothing to do with the heart, produced a merely animal act."[36]

Only when the long gestation period of human survival was resolved, then and only then did the period of social survival emerge. The act of people valuing each other created the conditions for human obligation to each other, and with that man moved on from the idea of society to that of polity or, civility. "As soon as men began to value one another, and the idea of consideration had got a footing in the mind, every one put in his claim to it, and it became impossible to refuse it to any with impunity. Hence arose the first obligations of civility even among savages; and every intended injury became an affront because, besides the hurt which might result from it, the party injured was certain to find in it a contempt for his person, which was often more insupportable than the hurt itself."[37]

Rousseau moved from this early recognition of the problems inherent in a sociological philosophy, to a unique denial of civil society. Whether as the pure theorist of participatory democracy or as the romantic individualist of the *Confessions* and *Diaries*, those partial attachments of religion, family, occupation, party, etc., get short shrift. Instead,

Rousseau inveighs against the bankruptcy of scientific progress and an irrational drive that leads to alienation. For Rousseau political men tend to perceive of the idea of liberty in precisely the same terms as philosophical men conceive the idea of nature. Just as there is no meaning to any notion of the "natural" propensity of men toward evil, so, too, there is correspondingly no basis to speak of the natural propensity of social man to a condition of slavery. "Politicians indulge in the same sophistry about the love of liberty as philosophers about the state of nature. They judge, by what they see, of very different things, which they have not seen; they attribute to man a natural propensity to servitude, because the slaves within their observation are seen to bear the yoke with patience; they fail to reflect that it is with liberty as with innocence and virtue; the value is known only to those who possess them, and the taste for them is forfeited when they are forfeited themselves."[38]

The idea of legitimacy serves to make men political as well as social. In the absence of legitimate authority, one has slavery. But that condition is not natural: It is a consequence of despotism and unfulfilled promises. It follows, then, that the emergence of inequality had nothing to do with the original state of human degradation or ignorance; rather, it was a direct consequence of imperfectly conceived political rule. In point of fact, the state encourages inequality precisely to the degree that it enshrines the social and economic inequalities found in a society. "If we follow the progress of inequality in these various revolutions, we shall find that the establishment of laws and of the right to property was its first term, the institution of magistracy the second, and the conversion of legitimate into arbitrary power the third and last. The condition of rich and poor was authorized by the first period; that of power and weakness by the second; and the third, that of master and slave. This condition is the last degree of inequality. The referential term to which all the rest remain. When a society goes that route, the government is either entirely dissolved by new revolutions or brought back to legitimacy by expelling the naked terms of inequality."[39]

Rousseau was unwilling to grant the possibility that it was in the very essence of the state to enshrine inequality through law. But he did get beyond the easy identification of progress with equity, of abundance with happiness and the other simple identifications that the men of the Enlightenment were, in fact, prone to make. If Voltaire and Diderot gave expression to a theory of progress, to the sociological imagination as such, then Rousseau, in his answer to this touching faith in measurable change, gave rise to the political imagination—to an appreciation of how human beings surrender their rights to society, only to find out that society then cedes its own rights to the state. Rousseau recognized that the impulse to examine antecedents is more profoundly an effort to know the future. Both historical and utopian longings stimulate discontent, but they can never be more than feelings. And sentiments can never really bring us back into the past. They can only be a stimulant to living in the present. Rousseau concluded the opening section on an optative note: the worth of looking backward and the necessity of going forward. Historicity plays a critical role in Rousseau's work.

Rousseau described backward conditions in terms of the savage man. The savage man, or the noble savage, is also an obvious fiction, and no one knew this better than Rousseau. However, out of that fictionalized and highly personalized account of what the savage man was supposed to be, came a probative line of theorizing. It should be added that the eighteenth century, the French Enlightenment in particular, stimulated all the *philosophes* to concern themselves with anthropology and to worry about the origins of man. This came about, in part, through the concern with the origins of nature as a source for overcoming theology. Many *philosophes* were concerned with the relationship of geological time to divine providential statements about the beginning of the world. This led to further inquiries into the origins of man, all of which were dedicated to one principle, the overthrow of divine truth. That is to say, Rousseau, along with the rest of the eighteenth-century Enlightenment, was interested in those subjects that would help overthrow organized religion. Toward this task geology and anthropology became important. That was the source of concern with the origins of man in his original form. And in his scientific pursuits, Rousseau was very much a man of his age.

Rousseau's concern was not with savage man as such, but with alienation in modern man. The wholeness of original man was being contrasted with the fragmented quality of modern man. This was the first inkling of the dialectician as a moral bookkeeper. At every advance in technological proficiency there is a loss of basic skills. The more one rides in an automobile, the less capable he is of walking. The more one uses electrical equipment, the less adept he becomes with mechanical skills. When there is a massive power failure, the social world grinds to a halt. Men stop. They have nothing at their disposal. Everything called "civilized" has in some sense become external to them, and their sheer physical prowess has become separated from themselves. Civility becomes an alienating experience. Men become alienated from their physical condition the less savage they are. The first premise of Rousseau's outlook was the notion of alienation in modern man, not in the form of the factory machine, not in the spiritual form of reasoning, but in the basic Spartan form of man's physical prowess separated from himself. In the schism between mind and body the origins of inequality are revealed. The struggle becomes the control not of the man, but of those forces external to man upon which he depends for his existence. The struggle for control is not for one's own body, but for the communication network, the electrical network, the mechanical apparatus. The forces of production and consumption, which are alien to men, become the essential focus of revolutionary struggle—although whatever interest group wins, man as a self-controlling force loses.

Original man, at least in terms of the presumed *Social Contract* entered into between man and society, is whole in that the individual controls his possessions; that which defines him is not isolated from what he uses. To that degree, he is able to say yes or no with relative free will, but the more civilized he becomes, the more the definition of civilization becomes the external relationship he has to the object. In effect, the individual contracts out freedom for safety.[40] The more an individual becomes brutalized, not simply in the sense of being incapable at the lower end of exercising free will, but incapable in the upper end of exercising considered judgment. In the effort to avoid the consequences of a Hobbesian war of all against all, the person loses his character as a free agent. The highly civilized man is not simply effete, though he may be worried about becoming effete; he is brutish in that he is without command over his free will. "The body of a savage being the only instrument he understands, he uses it for various purposes, of which ours, for want of practice, are incapable: for our industry deprives us of that force and agility which necessity obliges him to acquire. If he had an axe, would he have been able with his naked arm to break so large a branch from a tree? If he had a sling, would he have been able to throw a stone with so great velocity? If he had a ladder, would he have been so nimble in climbing a tree? If he had a horse, would he have been himself so swift of foot? Give civilized man time to gather all his machines about him, and he will no doubt easily beat the savage; but if you would see a still more unequal contest, set them together naked and unarmed, and you will soon see the advantage having all our forces constantly at our disposal, of being always prepared for every event, and of carrying one's self, as it were, perpetually whole and entire about one."[41] We tend to forget how involved earlier sociological discourse was with the question of civility and civilization. Much of those concerns involved precisely the Rousseauian belief that the relationship of man and society is part of an exchange relationship. Questioning the extent and character of that relationship became the task of Babeuf, Saint-Simon, and Comte—or the French connection in the evolution of early social science.

In the face of the celebration of progress, the legacy of Rousseau interjected a strongly cautionary note, pessimistic in its prospects. He turned to the subject that the entire eighteenth century was taken with, namely, reinvestigating the relations of reason and passion. In Diderot and Helvétius the passions and the reasons were in fine balance. Man is made up of some kind of mix between the two, and they had no doubt about the extent to which reason could curb the passions should the occasion arise. Rousseau issued a serious reminder that when societies unravel the potency of reason to curb the passions is precisely the definition of how far down the road to barbarism social systems have traveled. Rousseau interjected a reminder of the irreducible character of psychological propensities to violence in times of chaos.

Paradoxically, Rousseau argued that reason is not the enemy of the passions, but indebted to the passions. The notion of reason as the enemy of passions is overthrown; in order to have a reasoning being, one must have a passionate animal. Passion is the handmaiden of reason because the purpose of knowledge is never knowledge itself. It is instrumental in the person because it aids one to attain a personal sense of glory, satisfaction or happiness. Rousseau was not presenting a critique or ethic on the idea of reason, but was merely asserting that reason is related to the passions in such a way that both become essential for the survival of man. Indeed, his position is much like the twentieth-century notion of Schumpeter and Weber—that social science is not the enemy of ideology, but the handmaiden of ideology. But to speak thus is to speak of the end of science itself.

One of the problems Rousseau shared with his colleagues was the notion of a natural state or an original state. But while many of the *philosophes* were anti-religious in their ideology, Rousseau imbibed from classical Hebrew as well as Christian theology the notion of an original state not quite sinful, but a natural, in contrast to a social condition. That French social theory might argue whether the original state was good or bad, but that there was such a thing as a natural state was never doubted by Diderot or Rousseau. In part, one has to understand by the concept of the original state the parallel to natural law, the idea of some kind of sociological a priori, some kind of anchor point that is known to all men logically, something that is not merely empirically discovered, but is revealed to man. The function of the concept of the natural state was that it revealed to man his original condition.

In his discussion of Hobbes's ethics, Rousseau examines the idea that the natural state is a state of war. In effect, in response to the Hobbesian view, Rousseau argued that the natural state, far from being a state of war, is actually a state of peace. The arts of war are cultivated only when objects are alienated or externalized from man. Insofar as man is in self-possession and in self-command, his concerns are not so much fixed upon the liquidation of an enemy as upon his own survival. Hobbes was wrong, inductively, because a man does not attack another man simply to beat another man; he attacks him to gain something so that the death of the other man is an advantage for the killer. But if there are no objects externalized from the man, what advantage can there be? Only in a condition in which objects are possessed does killing become a premium and war a value, so that the deeper the alienation of the man from the objects of his life, the more likely the possibility of war.

Rousseau believed that depravity comes into being when there is something for which to be depraved, when there is an object of desire and when men falsely assume that force creates right, rather than assuming that free men exercise free choice. The nobility of the savage stems in part from his self-possession, his completeness as a person and, at the other end of the spectrum, from the absence of a need to agree because of his self-completeness. The notion of depravity comes into being only when objects of desire are restricted. Depravity existed for Rousseau, but only to the extent that man is not in control of his own personality, his own will.

Plenitude and abundance and the struggle over these, according to Rousseau, make for regional, national and international strife. For Rousseau, the revolution of pain could never be the liquidation of another person, but only self-improvement. There will never be sufficient material objects because "enough" is a thing that man, as a creature of passions, always pushes further and further away. Rights provide an infinite regress of desires. Within the framework of any situation, the character of the person determines the kind of behavioral system he or she will set forth.

The Rousseauian condition is a state of pure and perfect self-possession. To the extent that one needs objects and things, one is a slave of the passions. This is essentially a restatement of the Christian view of how one achieves a state of grace. Rousseau provided the inspiration for the transcendental movement was. His ideas were embellished with the idea of reason derived from the Hegelian world view, so that one lived not only in the state of nature but also in the state of grace purged of selfishness and greed. In all fairness to Rousseau, he alone amongst the *philosophes* understood that such a state is lodged in the power of the legal code, of a spiritual unity that enables human beings to overcome the vicissitudes of human affairs. As a result, and in sharp contradistinction to the utilitarian and materialist *philosophes*, Rousseau took seriously the moral basis of action and the normative framework for social contract. For this reason, Rousseau was able to rise above the cheap anti-religious rhetoric of the time, and the even more disastrous recourse to vilifying the Jewish people that was so endemic to the spirit of Voltaire and Holbach.[42]

As with his fellow *lumières*, Rousseau was faced with the question of egoism. Egoism is linked to society as the self-aggrandizement of men. This emphasis on self-respect is a Spartan notion, and Rousseau linked it to "nature." Nature provides self-respect; society provides self-aggrandizement. Asher Horowitz has called this the inverted parallelism of nature and society in Rousseau. For behind the ideal of conventional equality, expressed in political society and law, lie the true functions of state and law in bourgeois society: the perversion of natural equity and societal inequality. The context of the origins of inequality is in this dialectic of the displacement of the feeling of wholeness and totality one finds in nature over and against the egoistic feeling one finds prevalent in most societies. The tasks of the good state then become clear: the search for a supreme lawgiver to restore the natural wholeness to the social tasks. This became the leitmotif of all political writings of the nineteenth century—a task raised to the level of totalitarian practice.

Along with the birth of the sociological imagination within late eighteenth-century utilitarianism, there came about a disparity of libertarian social goals and totalitarian statist means. Implementing the brave new world of original goodness revealed a dark side of the birth of the sociological imagination—a contempt for the tragic potentials in social life and a denial that there were things on heaven and earth not subject to easy remedies and easier slogans. The age of enlightenment belonged to the optimists, to those who converted the study of society into a religion of society. Diderot managed to convince even such a skeptic as Rousseau that education and legislation would prevail, and that the march of progress, so admirably set forth in stages by Condorcet in the last decade of the eighteenth century, while paradoxical, was real, at least in its consequences.[44] Not even the terror of Robespierre could disabuse French social theory of its fundamental tenets. Henri Saint-Simon remained convinced that there was an automatic equivalence of egoism and sociality, of the advancement of the self with the advancement of every member of society. Just what happens when such a sociological "hidden hand" fails to operate was left to the discretion of those in charge of the state.[45]

The modern disaffected intellectual finds his inspiration in Rousseau and his followers. This tradition both feeds and motivates the modern passion for self-loathing on one side and self-loving on the other. Both tendencies have become a central part of the victimologists' tradition. Under his tutelage, the sociology of Comte and Saint-Simon becomes critical rather than constructive. A social world of original perfection, from which modern society is a contamination, becomes a norm that calls for the all-powerful state. With this device, the promise is held forth that the human race might once again become good, or better, that without the state we would be left to our egoistic devices.

On the opposite pole, the major figures of the Enlightenment brought with them a damnation of tradition and a celebration of the new. As key figures from Carl Becker to Frank Manuel have understood, the outer limits of French social theory, either in its Rousseauian or Voltairian forms, brought social theory to the edge of Statism. But to see how that ideology evolved we must move from French rationalism to German romanticism. The latter uniquely captured the full range of the nineteenth-century quest to capture state power and social progress in the same sociological bottle. German philosophy provided the notions of organicism and authority that brought social theory close to the edge of sociology—to a consideration of rights and obligations, and the recognition of order no less than the search for freedom. It is not that German social theorists rejected utilitarianism. Rather, they well understood the need to subsume it under a higher principle of human direction. Hegel was quite willing to admit,

indeed at times even defend the idea of Rousseau that behind every hidden hand was a nailed boot. The German State
delivered on the promises of French welfare theory. But it
did so without the benign rhetoric of egalitarianism or mythi-
cal appeals to a non-existent state of nature.

Notes

1. Carl L. Becker, *The Heavenly City of the Eighteenth-Century Philoso-
    phers.* New Haven: Yale University Press, 1932, p. 46
2. Auguste Comte, *Plan of the Scientific Operations Necessary for Reorga-
    nizing Society* (Third Essay, 1822). This work is contained in *Auguste
    Comte and Positivism: The Essential Writings*, edited with an introduc-
    tion by Gertrud Lenzer. New York: Harper & Row, Publishers, 1975,
    pp. 28–29. Professor Lenzer's opening essay on "Auguste Comte
    and Modern Positivism" is a masterful statement on how science
    and society are inextricably bound in Comte—and hence how the
    optimistic mood of sociology in its first blush got that way.
3. Robert A. Nisbet, *The Sociological Tradition.* New York: Basic Books,
    Inc., 1966, pp. 32–33.
4. Frederick Engels, *Ludwig Feuerbach and the Outcome of Classical Ger-
    man Philosophy.* New York: International Publishers, 1941, p. 31.
5. Mordecai Grossman, *The Philosophy of Helvétius.* New York: Colum-
    bia University-Teachers College Press, 1926, pp. 12–13.
6. Jacob L. Talmon, *The Origins of Totalitarian Democracy.* New York:
    Frederick A. Praeger Publishers, 1961, pp. 232–33.
7. Denis Diderot and J.L.R. d'Alembert, editors. *Encyclopédie, ou
    Dictionnaire raisonne des sciences, des arts et des metiers, par une societe
    de gens de lettres,* Volume 25, Geneva: J. Pellet, 1777–79, p.668. See
    Albert Soboul, "L'Encylopedie et le mouvement Encyclopediste."
    La Pensee. Whole No. 39, 1951, pp. 41–51.
8. Claude Adrien Helvétius, *A Treatise on Man, His Intellectual Faculties
    and His Education,* trans. W. Hooper, 2 vols. London: Vernor, Hood
    and Sharpe, 1810, pp. vii–viii.
9. Charles Frankel, *The Faith of Reason.* New York: King's Crown Press,
    1948, p.9.
10. Denis Diderot and J.L.R. d'Alembert, editors. *Encyclopédie, ou
    Dictionnaire raisonne des sciences, des arts et des metiers, par une societe
    de gens de lettres,* Volume 25, Geneva: J. Pellet, 1777–79, p. 669.
11. M.J. Condorcet, *Sketch for an Historical Picture of The Progress of the
    Human Mind.* New York: Noonday Press, 1955 (original publication,
    1796), p. 251.
12. Pierre Bayle, (1702) *Dictionnaire Historique et Critique,* 2nd ea., re-
    vised and augmented. Rotterdam: Reinier Leers, 1702 (original pub-
    lication, 1697).

13. M.J. Condorcet, *Sketch for an Historical Picture of The Progress of the Human Mind.* New York: Noonday Press, 1955 (original publication, 1796), p. 256.
14. Jean leRond d'Alembert, *Oeuvres*, Paris: A. Belin, 1821-22, volume 1, pp. 185-86.
15. Denis Diderot, *Oeuvres completes*, ed. J. Assezat. Paris: Gamier, 1875-77, volume 25, pp. 667-68.
16. Denis Diderot, *Supplement au voyage de Bougainville.* Geneva: Droz, 1955, pp. 122-37.
17. Jean leRond d'Alembert, *Oeuvres*, Paris: A. Belin, 1821-22, volume 1, pp. 185-86.
18. Jean-Jacques Rousseau, *The Confessions of Jean Jacques Rousseau*, translated by W.C. Mallard. New York: Tudor Publishing, 1928, book IX, pp. 623-762.
19. Francois M.A. Voltaire, *Philosophical Dictionary*, trans. H.I. Woolf, abridged edition. London: Allen & Unwin, 1945, p. 117.
20. Francois M.A. Voltaire, *Philosophical Dictionary*, trans. H.I. Woolf, abridged edition. London: Allen & Unwin, 1945, p. 118.
21. Denis Diderot, *Oeuvres completes*, ed. J. Assezat. Paris: Gamier, 1875-77, volume 17, pp. 15-16.
22. Paul Henri d'Holbach, *Systeme Social*, Paris: Niogret, 1822, volume 2, pp. 3-4.
23. Claude Adrien Helvétius, "Letter to Montesquieu," in *Oeuvres completes*, London: privately printed, 1818, volume 2, pp. 259-67.
24. Claude Adrien Helvétius, *Essays on the Mind*, translated by William Mumford. London: privately printed, 1809, pp. 123-27.
25. Claude Adrien Helvétius, *A Treatise on Man*, translated by William Hooper. London: privately printed, 1810, volume 2, p. 279.
26. Claude Adrien Helvétius, *A Treatise on Man*, translated by William Hooper. London: privately printed, 1810, volume 2, p. 280.
27. Claude Adrien Helvétius, *A Treatise on Man*, translated by William Hooper. London: privately printed, 1810, volume 2, p. 281.
28. Claude Adrien Helvétius, *A Treatise on Man*, translated by William Hooper. London: privately printed, 1810, volume 2, p. 283.
29. Claude Adrien Helvétius, *A Treatise on Man*, translated by William Hooper. London: privately printed, 1810, volume 2, pp. 284-85.
30. Claude Adrien Helvétius, *A Treatise on Man*, translated by William Hooper. London: privately printed, 1810, volume 2, pp. 285-86.
31. Claude Adrien Helvétius, *A Treatise on Man*, translated by William Hooper. London: privately printed, 1810, volume 2, p. 286.
32. Claude Adrien Helvétius, *A Treatise on Man*, translated by William Hooper. London: privately printed, 1810, volume 2, p. 288.
33. Peter Gay, *The Enlightenment: An Interpretation*, (volume 2: *The Science of Freedom.* New York: Knopf, 1969, pp. 522-29.
34. Georgi V. Plekhanov, *Essays in the History of Materialism*, translated by Ralph Fox. London: Bodley Head, 1934. p. 168.
35. Jean-Jacques Rousseau, *A Discourse on the Origin of Inequality*, trans-

lated and edited by G.D.H. Cole. New York: E.P. Dutton, 1950, p. 222.

36. Jean-Jacques Rousseau, *A Discourse on the Origin of Inequality*, translated and edited by G.D.H. Cole. New York: E.P. Dutton, 1950, p. 235.

37. Jean-Jacques Rousseau, *A Discourse on the Origin of Inequality*, translated and edited by G.D.H. Cole. New York: E.P. Dutton, 1950, p. 292.

38. Jean-Jacques Rousseau, *A Discourse on the Origin of Inequality*, translated and edited by G.D.H. Cole. New York: E.P. Dutton, 1950, p. 252.

39. Jean-Jacques Rousseau, *A Discourse on the Origin of Inequality*, translated and edited by G.D.H. Cole. New York: E.P. Dutton, 1950, p. 263.

40. Jean-Jacques Rousseau, *The Social Contract*, translated by G.D.H. Cole. New York: E.P. Dutton, 1913.

41. Jean-Jacques Rousseau, *A Discourse on the Origin of Inequality*, translated and edited by G.D.H. Cole. New York: E.P. Dutton, 1950, p. 201.

42. Frank E. Manuel, *The Broken Staff: Judaism Through Christian Eyes*. Cambridge, Mass.: Harvard University Press, 1992. pp. 192–221. This work contains undoubtedly the finest discussion of Rousseau's relations to the philosophes on the question of religious toleration as it was expressed in *Considerations on the Government of Poland*.

43. Asher Horowitz, *Rousseau, Nature and History*. Toronto: University of Toronto Press, 1987. pp. 115–119.

44. Henri Lefebvre, *Diderot*. Paris: Hier et Aujord huit, 1949.

45. Henri Saint-Simon, *Selected Writings on Science, Industry and Social Organisation*, translated with an introduction by Keith Taylor. New York: Holmes & Meier, Publishers, 1975, pp. 172–177.

3

Romancing the Organic State: Hegel

"It was in the State that Hegel's sharp sense of reality discerned the most powerful and efficacious, the all-pervasive factor in the history of the human race. Whatever his empiricism discerned, had to be sanctioned by his idealism. But then the soul of the State—*raison d'état* and the seed of Machiavelli's doctrine—had to be sanctioned also. And so something quite new and extraordinary occurred: Machiavellianism came to form an integral part in the complex of an idealist view of the universe, a view which at the same time embraced and confirmed all moral values—whereas in former times Machiavellianism had only been able to exist alongside the moral cosmos that had been built up. What happened now was almost like the legitimization of a bastard."

—*Friedrich Meinecke*[1]

It was a literary rather than sociological figure who best understood the fatal flaw in Rousseau's effort at creating a social science. Irving Babbit, in *Rousseau and Romanticism*, pointed out that the danger of Rousseauism and related Enlightenment currents was that they presented, as liberating and elevating currents, visions of life that reduced moral responsibilities to social norms. The flattering assessments of social life relieved the individual of the need for the discipline of the self.[2]

The task of Hegel, or at least one of his tasks, was to create a new synthesis that preserved the Rousseauian "general will," but placed it within a context of world systems and ideals. In a narrow sense, this was a debate between classicism and romanticism. But in a wider context, this was a struggle as to the true nature of the source of power in any society. Rousseau's soft sense of community came upon the flint-like object of Hegel's hard order. That conflict still exists within the social sciences, and is expressed as the struggle between the "field of social problems" and that of "political order." That no resolution has been brought about in more than a century of effort becomes an object of inquiry unto itself. But for now, it is critical to examine the politics of the statist, anti-sociologist Georg Wilhelm Friedrich Hegel.

Conventional sociology, at least in its Parsonian version, tends to assume that the state is part of the social system, and that a system of power operates only at some levels within the larger system. This is not the only possible, or for that matter, most plausible vision of human interaction. If the dialectical tradition culminating with Hegel did nothing else, it established the unique place of political theory in the study of culture. Hegel's analysis of freedom is distinguished by a firm separation of civil society from polity. His approach is legalistic in that throughout he is concerned with basic properties of social and political structures. Social phenomena are not viewed empirically as ongoing entities, but selectively, through logical, that is, dialectical distinctions. The Hegelian approach assumes completeness in that all relevant concepts and relations that would be required in empirical undertakings are worked out. This special sense of methodology as an ideal type should be kept in mind when examining Hegel. What we are provided with is a systems approach rather than empirical analysis.[3]

Few commentators have viewed the directly political and social writings of Hegel as an extension of his more abstract works. A British analytical philosopher has even suggested

that Hegel's *Philosophy of Right and Law*, in whom the social
and legal basis of political freedom is central, represent an
aberration, "a deep loss of integrity both in his character
and in his thinking."[4] It is the burden of this chapter to show
that his social writings are nothing of the sort. Rather, they
are a formal extension of his actual political beliefs and
dispositions.

Hegel shared with the post-Napoleonic intelligentsia a belief in the value of nation-building, and a parallel rejection of
class analysis, stimulated in large part by the excesses of the
French Revolution. It is precisely Hegel's effort to integrate
social and metaphysical thought that has come to dominate
current estimates of his worth. For in his emphasis on freedom as necessity, and order as the highest social expression
of human behavior, he set a tone as well as a standard for the
conservative rebellion against radical social theory. To be sure,
in Hegelian thought, the social and political issue of freedom
represents *die Weisheit*, the sociological expression of philosophic wisdom. So much that came after Hegel is a function
of this belief in freedom as order that any serious treatment
of the construction of sociology without an appraisal of his
impact would be woefully one-sided.

Hegel also shared with the *Sturm und Drang* movement
and its romantic aftermath dissatisfaction with the utilitarian impulse to define freedom in terms of a calculus of individual interests. Yet he was not willing to consider the notion of a crude *Volksgruppe* to be a replacement for a practical
theory of individual freedom and responsibility. Hegel's
contempt for abstract notions contrasts with Novalis, Muller,
Schleiermacher and other representatives of German romanticism during the Napoleonic era. In attempting to locate
the specific ethical coordinates of freedom, Hegel laid the
basis for a new view of social humanity.

Prussianism as a nineteenth-century ideology was quite
different from what it was to become during the age of National Socialism. In the years in which Hegel wrote Prussia

appeared as the least compromised part of Germany. Although defeated by the Napoleonic armies at Jena, Prussia retained a distinct moral advantage in the eyes of nationalists for having defended German interests. Other German states became French satellites in the Rhine Confederation. Austria capitulated to Napoleon through court maneuvers. Prussia alone remained an unwilling partner to the Continental System. The Prussianization of Germany was viewed by many of the intellectuals as the exclusive means for achieving the feeling, if not the fact, of sovereignty. The ultimate defeat of the Napoleonic forces served to enhance Prussian separatism. What should be appreciated is that the options for men like Fichte and Hegel were narrowed to Prussianism or Bonapartism. And whether Hegel was "pro-Bonaparte" or "pro-Prussian" represents an ideological irrelevance. The breakthrough of a democratic option did not take place in Germany until the second half of the nineteenth century, fifty years after Hegel died.[5]

Even if we are to consider Prussianism in its incipient forms as reactionary, it does not follow that the social thought of Hegel was proscribed by ultimate values about the *Volksgeist*. If it is proper to consider Hegel's ontology in terms of system and method, a position that Engels maintained,[6] it is no less the case that his social theory can be interpreted along similar lines. Hegel's concept of freedom was not simply an afterthought to his disaffection with Bonapartism. Its theoretical contribution was an effort to overcome the antinomies created first by Hobbes's mechanical rendering of the question of political power in an egocentric world, and second by Kant's abstract, rationalist approach to politics in a cosmopolitan, universalistic world. History became Hegel's way out of the dilemmas created by both mechanism and transcendentalism.

The problem of the scope and nature of political freedom occupies a technical status in Hegel's thought analogous to that of the issue of causality in natural philosophy.

Hegel was faced with the task of reestablishing the grounds of causality in order to make history scientific and to overcome the indeterminism of Locke's *Essay Concerning Human Understanding.* He confronted a similar problem in demonstrating that (contrary to theories based on custom and volition) freedom is inextricably tied to social necessity.

To demonstrate this, Hegel drew heavily upon the work of Aristotle, Spinoza and, to a lesser extent, Bacon. From Aristotle, Hegel learned that freedom is essentially social and political, rather than individual—freedom in the absence of organized social systems being a logical as well as an empirical contradiction for Aristotle. From Spinoza, he derived the determinist view of freedom as the comprehension of necessity—freedom being impossible in isolation from knowledge of the real and rational relations of human societies. From Bacon, Hegel derived the idea that there is a clear identification of positive freedom with the power to transform knowledge into social goods through the beneficent agent of science and experiment. These men clearly do not exhaust the philosophic influences that generated Hegel's desire to bring about an explicit context for discussing freedom. One would also have to reckon with the line of the German *Aufklärung* moving from Lessing to Kant. Nevertheless, the writings of Aristotle and Spinoza serve to indicate the intellectual network within which Hegel operated. More so than with most philosophers, the intellectual lineage of Hegel is of decisive importance; as his lectures in philosophic history make plain, he set himself the task of reconciling as well as comprehending the totality of the history of ideas.[7]

The romantic view of Hegel's doctrine of freedom was a caricature. In Germany, there were the well-known efforts by the monarchy to appropriate Hegel's theory of freedom by making it part of a system paying homage to the state. The writings of semiofficial ideologists such as F.J. Stahl are characteristic. They denounce Hegel only at those points when his writings serve no statist ends. There were the equally abstract efforts to make the Hegelian theory of freedom serve as a touchstone for a wholesale critique of German society. The work of the left-Hegelians, Bruno Bauer and Arnold Ruge, purged Hegel of his particular sociological message by reducing human emancipation to *political* emancipation.[8]

Outside Germany, Hegel's work underwent similar transformations. There were the feeble attempts of Anglo-American high culture to establish a simplistic formula: The free man is one who comprehends the necessary limits of history, nature and mind. Left as a formula, it is little wonder that Royce saw human freedom as circumscribed and defined in terms of the need for loyalty to the established social order.[9] This same formula led Bosanquet to implore man to suffer and be strong in the face of the higher necessity of preserving security and order.[10] The alternative to this somber synergy between freedom and the state was Kierkegaard's freedom from society, truth as subjectivity, the notion that man's abiding happiness is to be found in human freedom in conscious opposition to the physical world as such. The individual became the only reality, the only free entity.[11]

While the fragmentation of Hegelian social theory makes it plain that even the firmest edifice will crack with time and become obsolete under changing conditions, there remains the need to explore the rubble to see if there are any usable parts, and to understand what went wrong in the construction of the Hegelian social-philosophic system. The category of freedom pervades all areas of Hegel's philosophy. Every phase of life and logic is said to reveal the impulse toward freedom. In logic, which for Hegel encompasses the structure of the universe of mind and matter, the doctrine of notion, the core of his non-syllogistic logic, is equated with the necessity of development and self-development in the process of life. Freedom is knowledge, a symbol of "pure self-consciousness"—the absolute and unfettered awareness

of the logical relations underlying the generation and regeneration of life. Logic is considered as ontology, a description of a rational universe in motion. Further, this objective rationality is determinate because it is real.

The essence of social freedom is, by logical extension, a
derivative of state power, a comprehension of the forms of
actual development. The actuality of the state "consists in
the fact that the interest of the whole realizes itself through
the particular ends." In plain language, the guarantee of
property rights, protection from external coercion (such as
foreign invasions), and education are guarantees that the
citizen merits. But unlike Rousseau, Hegel argues that the
state's authority rather than the social contract is the sup-
plier of such guarantees. And as one scholar recently and
correctly noted, this was essentially a three-step ontology—
moving from society to the state to the ethical norms that
offer national cohesion.[12]

In Hegel's work, the expansion of freedom cannot happen
outside or in opposition to such a three-stage reality. To do so
is a violation of the purpose of philosophy, the cognitive search
for concrete truth. Hegel was compelled to satisfy the requirements of his idealism by ultimately conceiving of freedom
metaphysically, as "absolute self-security and self-repose."[13]
However, this does not alter the fact that he considered logic
to be a product of the free conscience, since only such a conscience is in a position to establish scientific truths. In *The
Science of Logic* we receive our first indication that Hegel's
view of freedom is not reducible to political totalitarianism
or to personal idiosyncrasy. An uncontrolled system of power,
like pure individualism, is irrational; by definition, that which
is irrational cannot be transformed into a mode for realizing
freedom. Husserl was to observe that Hegel, in his effort to
consecrate philosophy in the name of science, only succeeded
in falsifying its probabilistic characteristics.[14]

In *Phenomenology of Mind*, Hegel untangles the knot of
freedom in carefully evolved stages that demonstrate the

logical bases of consciousness. For Hegel, the evolution of human thought is no less an evolution in the positive freedom of civilization. Freedom comes through precision and exactitude. The social role of science, no less than its essential content, is the expansion of freedom through knowledge. This identification of philosophy with science provides mankind not only with a love of wisdom but also with wisdom as such. In the act of transforming potentiality into actuality, abstraction into specificity, man changes from a plaything of causality into its master. Freedom then, for Hegel, is emancipation through the "scientific" control of events—science not yet seen as differing from the ontological.

The *Phenomenology* offers an intensive description of the development of consciousness. The unfolding of ideas, true as well as false has its autonomous history. In Hegel, rational thought moves from the logical to the phenomenological—that is, from form to content. He is concerned with carrying the conclusions of the *Logic* to a higher stage, from a description of the forms of nature's laws to analysis of the content of thought. Consciousness is more than a quality of intellect; it is a category of society and its institutions. Freedom of spirit comes not by simple recognition of external objects as a mysterious event alien to thought; nor does freedom of spirit offer proclamations about personality development. Absolute knowledge is that which binds objectivity to subjectivity; it unfolds as law, ethics and religion—that is, knowledge as a social function.[15]

Hegel had an unyielding respect for this object-subject formula, considering such a relation more capable of yielding truth than either the individual or the group taken separately. He made the subordination of ordinary information to universal reason a guiding principle. As in his *Logic*, so, too, in his theory of science, what is important in the evolution of mankind is the concrete conditions of social life (especially its institutionalized forms), which give substance to the quest for freedom.

No sooner had *Phenomenology* been completed than a paradox revealed itself that relentlessly pursued Hegel. If the essence of freedom is the identification of individual reason with universal reason, the true realm of freedom is pure thought. Far from yielding freedom as concrete activity, freedom once more assumed the classic contemplative pose. Marx had to examine the core of this dilemma to arrive at an independent standpoint: "It is precisely abstract thinking from which these objects (Wealth, State, Power) are alienated and to which they stand opposed with their pretension of reality. The philosopher, who is himself an abstract form of alienated man, establishes himself as the yardstick of the alienated world. The history of estrangement, the reappropriation of this *Entausserung*, is therefore nothing more than the history of the production of abstract thinking, that is, absolute, logical, speculative thinking."[16]

Hegel grasped the *idea* of freedom. But since only the idea had reality, he effectively sealed himself off from a naturalist appraisal of degrees of human freedom. As a result, as Feuerbach expressed it, Hegel was led to convert freedom into a religious artifact by incorporating things into thoughts about existence.[17]

Since we have introduced the assessments of Feuerbach and Marx, it is worthwhile to show how historical sociology evolved in distinctive stages around the ideas of alienation. First, Hegel saw man as separated from reality, as the personal conscience is isolated from objective consciousness, or better, as ideas are separated from truths. Next, Feuerbach considered the alienation problem in so-called anthropological terms, that is, as man separated from his own biological nature, and in consequence, having no direct experience of nature *qua* nature. To overcome this alienated condition; man invents a religion in order to conquer nature artificially, and evolves a theology to justify this anthropomorphism. Finally, Marx examined alienation as an economic condition rather than a philosophical condition.

Alienation became a consequence of iniquitous, exploitative productive relations, man, the inventor of machines and/or laborsaving instruments, becomes captive to the machine. The problem becomes radically altered in modern psychoanalytical doctrine. To save labor time becomes a special case of the large-scale task of emancipating man. The intellectual movement from Hegel to Feuerbach to Marx can be described as a movement from a sociology of knowledge into a sociology of religion and finally into general sociology, or the criticism of social institutions as such.[18]

Our main concern is with how Hegel worked out his sociology of knowledge, or, for those who stoutly insist that sociology begin with Comte, with Hegel's phenomenology of freedom in society. Hegel was not unaware of the impasse into which his *Logic* and *Phenomenology* placed him. It was not just that he pictured freedom as the unity of thought and reality; Kant before him and Kierkegaard afterwards shared this belief. Hegel's real problem was his assumption that concrete reality is revealed through philosophic contemplation. This view left little room for social activity as a legitimate enterprise on the road to freedom. Hegel himself understood that metaphysical emancipation was not the same as emancipation from metaphysics. He attempted to overcome this paradox by retaining the belief that although logical and phenomenological forms delineate the foundations of freedom, the manifestations of freedom are social, economic and legal, and hence practical. The actual expression of Hegel's dilemma is that his attempt to develop a meaningful social statement came twenty years after his direct attention to political practice.

Hegel's *Philosophy of Right and Law* considers the problem of freedom in terms of social structure and historical process. In it, the individual is conceived of not only as consciousness, but also as economic, political and legal activity. The repository of human knowledge is the social institution, from kinship units to international relations. Making the thinking part of freedom philosophical and the practical part of freedom social bridged the resolution of the dilemma between thought and action. The trouble with this bridge lies in its faulty construction. Social phenomena were seen to supersede one another, rather than to coexist. Personal morality is "resolved" into the family, which in turn is "resolved" into civil society, which in turn is "resolved" into the state. The structure of society ultimately became its process. Once again, freedom became linked to the notion of metaphysical perfection.

Most evidence adduced to prove Hegel's attraction for statism is derived from the *Philosophy of Right*. In its uncritically high estimate of the German Reformation, its desperate efforts to give a philosophic basis to militarism with which to counter the effects of Kant's liberal pacifism, and its attempt to derive historically the necessity of nationalism with which to counter Rousseau's conventionalist idea of society, this work represents a classic defense of conservative political theory, overshadowing the less systematic efforts of Burke in England. Nevertheless, such a judgment, even granting its correctness, mistakes the political posture of Hegel with the quality and goals of his analysis.

In this work are to be found such cardinal concepts as the functional role of economy in the development of social systems, the conflict between economic and political interests in periods of crisis, and a precise description of the psychology of alienation. The work also provides clear distinctions between personal, primordial, sacral and civil. Throughout, Hegel offers a defense of private property guaranteed by the state and its laws. In the Preface to the work, which is said to stand as a monument to Hegel's unyielding reaction, he candidly declares that while the state is something rational in itself, such rationality is gained most readily by giving the person a chance to become a personality. Hegel rejects the Platonic critique of Greek democracy (and by extension all democracy) by declaring that his view led him to "violate most deeply the free and limitless personality."[19] Such a free personality is considered to be the basic direction and aim of social action. That this idea of the free personality is at variance with the ideal of the historical state should not prevent an acknowledgment that Hegel was concerned with how to gain concrete emancipation and to stipulate the conditions in society that would make this possible.

The *Philosophy of Right and Law* is divided into three parts. The first two deals with the nature of abstract right and morality, property and welfare "considered intrinsically." The third part, which has as its chief divisions the family, civil society and the state, is the core of the book. It traces the meaning of freedom in its "social forms."

Freedom is initially considered in its most cellular form as personal, undifferentiated caprice. Next, the individual is examined in terms of the forms of governing his relationships to other individuals, possession, property, contracts and moral obligation. From this, Hegel develops the idea of freedom in terms of law and ethics. The ethical life makes possible the socialization of the person in that it evaluates the notion of freedom to the forefront of self-consciousness. "Ethical life is the idea of freedom in that on the one hand it is the good becomes alive, the good endowed in self-consciousness with knowing the willing and actualized by self-conscious action—while on the other hand self-consciousness has in the ethical realm its absolute foundation and the end which actuates its effort. Thus ethical life is the concept of freedom developed into the existing world and the nature of self-consciousness."[20]

Hegel desires to move beyond personal freedom to universal freedom. He proceeds, via the dissolution of the family and community associations, to a consideration of freedom in terms of civil society and the political state which represents the social realization to rise above private interests and mediate conflicting private claims in terms of a larger national purpose. The idea of the rule of law, rather than men, did not, of course, originate with Hegel; it is a fundamental juridical principle of Western societies. What Hegel did do was convert this juridical principle into an ethical absolute. Law was provided with a mystique. Ethics was thereby to be codified like law. The sameness of law and ethics is not just a peculiarity of Hegel, but of the language as well. The word *Recht,* the German equivalent to *jus* in Latin, *droit* in French, or *derecho* in Spanish, can be translated as either "right" or "law." Hegel himself declares that by *Recht* he means not only civil law, but also morality, ethics, and at times, world history—that is, in the sense of the dialectical pattern of human growth.[21]

Throughout Hegel's *Philosophy of Right,* a deceptively commercial imagery is used to describe freedom. Individual freedom becomes the right to private ownership, use and exchange of property. Civil society has as its essential core "the protection of property by law."[22] Even the heralded state, which genetically displaces society, is said to have a middle-class basis. Indeed, "that this middle class be formed is a main interest to the State."[23] The structure of society is economy considered historically. This fact is central in understanding Hegel's social thought. He makes plain that whatever his reservations about the moneyed classes, he was never willing to adopt a nostalgic view of the German landed aristocracy. While Hegel mistrusted the *burgerliche Gesellschaft,* he preferred it to restorationist politics, or for that matter, feudal economic relations.

The intention of Hegel is clear: to unite a fragmented Germany in awareness of need for action. By logical extension, other aspects of Hegel's worldview become equally evident: that the touchstone for measuring human emancipation is history, and that social function, therefore, cannot be considered apart from historical design. Because of this double aspect, Lefebvre noted that the relationship between personal liberty and social necessity is central to the thought of our times, and nowhere is this better stated than in Hegel.[24]

He offers a "positive" concept of freedom in relation to law
and social order that stands apart from and yet embraces a
pronounced conservation. The *Philosophy of Right* is an attempt to evaluate critically all past estimates of the nature
of the free society and the free conscience. And in distinguishing between family society (community) and civil society (society writ large) Hegel had a tremendous impact on
sociology, especially the tradition of work that Ferdinand
Tönnies exemplified.[25]

The most challenging social question taken up in the
Philosophy of Right is the relation of egoism to sociality. Hegel
rejects the utilitarian theory that decisions are best resolved
by the pleasure-pain principle. The challenge is made in
terms of the French Revolution. Before he had formulated
the polarity of egoism and altruism, Hegel was convinced
that the Revolution was a vision of an age of true justice.
However, it was no less than a desire for freedom that moved
men everywhere to become critics of existing establishments.
For Hegel, the French Revolution, like the Protestant Reformation, was a world revolution, and not simply a national
upheaval. Its specific content ended in death and despair,
while its radical aims nurtured a generation of rebellion.
But the ultimate betrayal of the purposes of the Revolution,
by one class after another, one political faction after another,
caused him to evaluate the liabilities in those Enlightenment
tenets that were converted into slogans of the Revolution.[26]

Starting from the premise that the individual makes his
future only in ways calculated to expand personal happiness,
utilitarianism is a negation of freedom because it can envi-
sion no purpose to life beyond individual pleasure. As a doctrine about society, the principle of utility reduces itself to
the assertion that rulers should act with Olympian detachment to offset the follies of selfish ambition. To Hegel, this
confusion between the "ought to be" and the "is" of politics
was made because the Revolution, following Rousseau, saw
in the state a General Will and a popular consensus, not the

actual historical unfolding of Rational Will. This resulted in an irrational insistence that the state reflects a system of stratification—for example, Montesquieu's system of checks and balances. The utilitarian notion that laissez faire should be the leading political principle because it is economically viable represented the first step in the demise of the Revolution. For Hegel, it demonstrated that French social theory could not distinguish politics from economy.[27]

In its utilitarian usage, freedom is only the egoistic right of the person over and against the collective will of humanity. Real freedom, freedom as rational, negates egoism because its point of departure is the spirit of the rulers (the holders of state power) and not the general spirit of the people (the society). The vogue of hedonism represents, to Hegel's way of thinking, not the achievement of freedom, but the alienation of man from freedom. This is a necessary outcome of a perspective that regards the products of history as both subjective and capricious, responsible more to an irrational general will than to law. Here we have the first indication that Hegel is dissatisfied with a pure theory of society, and that instead he will seek to create a "synthetic" political sociology.

The French Revolution, and particularly its intellectual forerunner, Rousseau, are primary targets of Hegel's efforts to frame a political sociology, precisely because the Revolution and Rousseau announced the birth of reason in society. The opposition to Rousseau is expressed first in his condemnation of rule by men rather than rules of law, second in his criticisms of the principle of social equality, and third, in his opposition to establishing the popular will as a basis for political life. Beneath Hegel's disenchantment with the course of the French Revolution was his larger theoretical concern over the relationship of social contract to natural right.

In Rousseau, Hegel saw the essential forerunner of his own view of freedom and its relation to political authority. In the betrayal of the revolutionary impulse, he saw a need to reassert reason in the state in order to replace reason in society. Hegel's extended polemic is worth quoting at length to appreciate the character and extent of his revolution against the idea of the social contract as a civil affair. "If the state is confused with civil society, and if its specific end is laid down as the security and protection of property and personal freedom, then the interest of the individuals as such becomes the ultimate end of their association, and it follows that membership of the state is something optional. But the state's relation to the individual is quite different from this. Since the state is mind objectified, it is only as one of its members that the individual himself has objectivity, genuine individuality, and an ethical life. Unfortunately, however, as Fichte did later, Rousseau takes the will only in a determinate form as the individual will, and he regards the universal will not as the absolutely rational element in the will, but only as a "general" will which proceeds out of this individual will as out of a conscious will. The result is that he reduces the union of individuals in the state to a contract and therefore to something based on their arbitrary wills, their opinion, and their capriciously given consent."[28] In this, Hegel defends the civil society that Rousseau was so concerned to demolish as divisive and alienating.

What Hegel meant by sociality is not easy to discern. First, it involves integration with other individuals in family, clan and group relations, and second, the processes of civil society. Third, at a more developed state of universal history, sociality entails the rationalization of ideals through the state. In terms of problems of the state, Hegel becomes most demanding. We cannot will our connection to the state any more than we can will our alienation from it in periods of decay. Rousseau's advice to simulate the moral qualities of primitive man, if not the social conditions of antiquity (prehistory) is to Hegel tantamount to the illusion that man can escape his historical commitments. Hegel's organicism rejected the possibility of a complete dissolution of ties and relations between men and nations. When this takes place, you are no longer dealing with social forces as such, but with random persons. The freedom of the social contract is, therefore, an illusion of those who cannot rise above civil society. To Hegel, the social contract is vicarious freedom ending "in the maximum of frightfulness and terror."[29]

Alienation of the *honnête homme* from decaying feudal society made of Rousseau a critic. But his voluntarism gave to his thinking a nostalgic glow and an irrational substance, which cast doubt on the possibilities of ever reaching the good society. Hegel, starting from a strictly formalistic desire to place man in a total system of historical infallibility, frowning upon the waste and horror of revolution, nonetheless (if inadvertently) became a crucial link in modern theories of social revolution. He paid strict attention to the real sources of historical generation—the economically sanctioned civil society and the politically sanctioned state. Once the Hegelian social system was complete, with its hierarchical chain moving and grinding its way from the individual to the state, it was but a step away to frame a historical hypothesis moving from nationalism to internationalism, and from the middle-class state to the classless society, or carried to the extreme, the anti-state. And this bold step Marx took. The trouble was that "history" and "logic" parted company. It turned out that national interests were everywhere to prevail, while international concerns were more likely to find expression in war than in global forums of good will. In this, Hegel rather than Marx was prophetic.

The connection of law to freedom is dual for Hegel. In one capacity, law has as its actual content the processes that form the evolution of society independent of human will. In this way, freedom is related to necessity in that the former presupposes an elemental conformity with objective, historical ideals. But the relation of laws to freedom in civil society seemingly has for its chief content the customs, rules and traditions through which freedom becomes linked to coer-

cion rather than to nature's way. If the spirit of law embodies the spirit of freedom, and if freedom cannot exist without duties and obligations in the juridical sense, we are once
more left with the polarization of individual autonomy and
political responsibility.

In one sense, the existing law of the state becomes the
archetype for the conduct of individual wills. The theory of
freedom thus becomes an elaborate scheme for maintaining the status quo, of keeping political power in the possession of those in a position to maintain and interpret the
meaning of law. Reason becomes nothing but the reality
embodied in the state structure, freedom, and the knowledge that the state is the foundation of consciousness and
self-consciousness (*bewusstein und Selbst-bewusstein*). These
were indeed the conclusions of the *Philosophy of Right* emphasized by neo-Hegelians like Treitschke in the quest to
prove the ideal origins of the political state.[30]

A different meaning emerges from a more balanced appraisal of Hegel's analysis of freedom and the legal superstructure. If there is, *in fact*, a correspondence between a
social system and a moral-legal order, then to move contrary to the spirit or content of law is to move against freedom itself, for it would destroy that unity of the people under the state upon which law is based.[31] This statist element
in Hegel's thought has drawn the support of Straussian in-
terpreters, who like Steven B. Smith in *Hegel's Critique of
Liberalism*, have been drawn to Hegel's social philosophy
narrowly conceived as an assault on modern, that is, Hobbesian liberalism.

There is strong evidence that Hegel himself preferred to
place a constitutionalist construction on legal matters, as in
the case of his analysis of civil rights for religious groups.[32]
Hegel assumes a condition of society under law that would
overcome the alienation that stems from a world without
justice, a universe of collective authority. Under the impulse
of creating an ethical social order, men can achieve a form

of freedom having greater durability than the spurious demand for the direct abolition of social order. It is this aspect
of Hegel's theory of law that accounts for post-Hegelian efforts to locate more precisely the connection of law and social emancipation. Hegelianism was sundered at just this
point: if the emphasis was put on law and social institutions,
a conservative result was guaranteed; if the emphasis was
placed on the changing contents of law and society and the
steady need for human emancipation, then a radical result
was assured.

Ethics, in the same way as law, is for Hegel the essential
content of freedom. In this he is perhaps closer to the Judaic than to the Greek tradition, since there is no functional
difference in his thought between law and morality. Implicit
in Hegel's position is the proposition that the good is defined by the free conscience, whether such a conscience
resides in the self, the state or the universe. Since the ethical world of concrete social life is the idea of freedom, morality no less than logic has for its objective content the doctrine of necessity. If we accept the premise that moral
obligation is the human response to objective necessity, the
absence of responsibility (even in the juridical sense) implies the absence of moral choice. The presence of necessity in human events limits our options to what is possible,
but it does not destroy options as such. If every act is a free
act, there can be no question of sorting right from wrong.
The right becomes amoral, something settled by arbitrary
coercive power. Hegel was thus led to reject Hobbes's power
thesis because it rested on the same sort of psychological
hedonism that disregards the norms and values of society
and the state. The right to make decisions is the characteristic of an ethical man—that is, a free man. This right, operating within a vortex of historical necessity, is considered by
Hegel as a hallmark of the free man vis-à-vis the slave.

As in the theory of law, much depends on whether we
define the Hegelian ethical system to mean that freedom

exists because an objective *telos* directs man to goals (almost in the Calvinist sense of predestination), or whether freedom is an expanding category the contents of which change in direct proportion to human evolution. To satisfy the demands of his system, Hegel concludes with an absolutist prescription: freedom is the consciousness of moral-legal obligations. To satisfy his sense of social process, he employs a historical ethos: freedom is the consciousness of rational and real possibilities.

Hegel endowed freedom with a metaphysical content because he desired to carry his historicism to its ultimate conclusion—the identification of the historical evolution of the state with moral purpose. Because of this, freedom, however ingeniously interpreted as a stage of socially based self-consciousness, was unable to get beyond a metaphysical parallelism. Within this system are to be found the root premises of political realism and political idealism. The ethical can have a content only in relation to human action. But action is itself dissolved into spirit, the idea of universal history. Whether man defines his ethical system, or is defined by it, is something Hegel does not resolve, since he would then also have had to declare that history is not the only framework within which to consider the problem of freedom.

In terms of personal morality, freedom remains an insecure abstraction. Freedom requires a "concrete ground," that is, the union of the individual and the universal. Hegel's concrete ground was the state. While law and morality offer freedom within an objective frame of reference, and in this fashion overcome the capricious freedom which is "the will free only in itself," such objectivity remains formalistic and indeterminate.[33] The social locus of human activity is represented by the growth of state, the true representative of the collective will. Hegel grants the reality of personal, inner freedom, Luther's freedom of the soul. But freedom to be organic must be objectified, the impersonal responsibility of a nonsectarian institution. Without such an impersonal force, freedom would be reduced to a psychologically naive peace of soul, or an equally unheroic pecuniary freedom of the economic marketplace. What is needed is a cancellation of such egoism, its transformation into a set of higher truths. Hegel's emphasis on these higher truths of the reasoning mind clearly demarcates him from a shallow romanticism, from efforts to subsume reality with feelings of *Geist*.

The identification Hegel makes between personal will and the will of the state was considered a necessary curative to the flaws in civil society. Civil society represents the superficial world of money relations, the area in which the individual strives for the private accumulation of wealth. Civil society represents the core of degradation, the "spectacle of excess, misery, and physical and social corruption."[34] In civil society, the full horrors of the exchange market are unfolded; the basis of which is the accumulation of private wealth proceeding through the impoverishment of the laboring classes.[35]

Civil society embodies values contrary to those of the state; its own inadequacies generate the Leviathan. Civil society, which is clearly identified with the German bourgeoisie, has as its main human denominator the entrepreneurial personality. The state has for its proper concerns those universal laws and principles guiding all citizens. The latter is therefore freedom. The state replaces either the atomized individual or bourgeois civil society as the chief organizing force of men; polity replaces society as the form for realizing freedom.[36]

To support this position, Hegel presents a damaging empirical characterization of the bourgeoisie as an economic and social force. At the same time, he also offers an idealization of the landed nobility and court aristocracy in charge of the state machinery. In this way, Hegel mirrors the cleavage in German life at the start of the nineteenth century between commercial and inherited aristocratic interests. In his work, one gets a keen sense of how disturbed the Prus-

sian emperor must have felt by the machinations of the bourgeoisie, its pressuring for a greater share of political power
as compensation for its "economic burdens." Hegel partici-
pated in the Prussian celebration by convincing himself that
the political state could somehow stand apart from and above
the socioeconomic cleavages in its historic role as the carrier of freedom. Like equilibrium and consensus doctrines
of the present era, Hegel was more interested in the immediate conditions for maintaining political stability than in
the long-range linkages between the state and the dominant
economic sectors.

Hegel represented the idea of freedom as organically related to the political state, and to the inevitable unfolding
of a *Weltgeschichte* which makes certain the attainment of
absolute truth. In his analysis of civil society, Hegel adopts
the arguments of English classical political economy to ensure for the state a metaphysical position at the expense of
the divisive influences of commercial bourgeois interests.
This was a return to freedom in its abstract form; a retreat
from a scientific concept of social structure to ideological
deliberations on how best to preserve conservative political
values. History became historicism, a tool for proving this
or that emperor to be the bearer of the historical essence.
History ceased to serve as a majestic framework for locating
outstanding problems of man, and served instead to enshrine
the state as the vehicle for realizing equilibrium.

However emphatically Hegel turned the concept of freedom to the sacred interests of the state, there remains the
kernel of "self-consciousness" and "self-creation" which enabled him to consider freedom as residing in the social process. Man in his continuing self-creation, the steady growth
of civilization through consciousness, provides a firm basis
for total emancipation. Only formal freedom reduces everything to the general will. The general will reveals itself as an
assortment of conflicting individual wills, each insisting on
holding itself up as the model for all men. If this process

continues indefinitely, tyranny prevails. Inevitably, a shallow liberalism allows for the will of the one to displace the general will. Such a tyranny would offer the shadow of freedom in place of a substantive freedom: the right of judgment and criticism, but not of rebellion or revolution.[37]

A great deal of attention has been given to the way Hegel subsumed society into universal history, and in so doing, drowned the individual in a cosmic vocation. Hegel realized, nonetheless, that there remains an impulse toward individuality. In his political essays, written two decades before the *Philosophy of Right,* Hegel attempted to retrieve for the area of social personality the "smaller" liberties of dissent, difference and even disaffection from the general commonwealth. Hegel was critical of efforts to curb individual liberties needlessly because this entailed the risk of destroying freedom in general. Reason and knowledge mediate freedom. The rational constitution does not seek to impose the abstract will on every member of society at every level of social intercourse for the obvious reason that such unanimity of opinion is impossible, and for the less obvious reason that personal liberty is the precondition for the formation of general emancipation. It is not that Hegel conceived of personal freedom in contradistinction to necessity, but that true freedom must always allow a measure of freedom *from* authority—that is, liberty.

In Hegel's early view, liberty is denied in two ways. The hedonist negates it, making it a matter of caprice and private will, thereby depriving it of a meaningful historical setting, while the abstract rationalist negates liberty by ruling out the variables in human-forced ideals and standards, and placing a premium on abstract duties and obligations. Hegel offered his theory of negative freedom (liberty) to overcome especially the one-sided conclusions of Kant, Rousseau and Fichte. Positive freedom corresponded to Hegel's theory of history and philosophy as scientific disciplines, while negative freedom corresponded to the practical judgments men must daily make about economics and politics.

The transition from *Selbstbewusstein* to the *Staat* as the perfect embodiment of consciousness in Hegelian terms is the transformation from freedom as contemplative to freedom as active. In the realm of praxis, if a people desire negative freedom alone, freedom from institutional responsibility, they can never achieve moral or political heights. The built-in egoism of the *burgerliche Gesellschaft* would cut the ground out from under freedom, reducing society to freedom *of* rather than *from* market competition. This was the condition of German society at the start of the nineteenth century. As Hegel says: "The obstinacy of the German character has not yielded to the point where the separate parts would sacrifice their particular interests for the whole society, where all would sacrifice their particular interests for the whole society, where all would be united in one general body and where freedom might be achieved in common with free subjection to the supreme political authority."[38] Germany, trapped by the middle-class faith in political particulars (*Kleinstaaterei*) achieved freedom only in the realm of abstraction rather than in history. This charge became a battle cry for the remainder of the century, socialism declaring that this victory in the realm of ideas prevented the growth of democracy, and restorationism declaring that this same condition made Germany effete and lacking in national purpose. Hegel himself saw the problem in stricter terms of universal freedom: Germany should have been the freest of nations. Hegel did not believe that "self-centered activity" makes rational political authority impossible, that society must be at the mercy of brute physical power.

Once positive freedom is anchored to the state, negative freedom, "the self-centered activity," should be allowed to develop unimpeded. The function of liberty is to heighten the prospects of knowledge. The suppression of liberty carries with it the threat of positive freedom, itself being corroded and its historic mission derailed. Hegel insisted upon the free activity of the citizens "in the field of administration and adjudication." Autonomy within a larger national policy is a guarantor of social organization. Hegel was a constitutional monarchist and not just a crude advocate of the discredited divine rights doctrine. And this bias in favor of legality was a constant in his writings. Although he could present no solution other than a conservative solution, he never retreated to the specious comforts of feudalism. We owe to Hegel the complete separation of the conservative conscience from the feudal mind. "Society should leave to the people their maintenance according to law, and each class, city, village, community, etc., the freedom of doing and executing what lies within its sphere.[39]

The young Hegel emerged as an unequivocal inheritor of the *Aufklärung.* "Nothing should be more sacred (to government) than to leave to the free action of the citizens all these matters and to protect it without regard to utility. For this freedom is sacred in itself." Hegel goes on to explain the virtues of individual liberty: "We consider that people are happy to which the State leaves much freedom in the subordinated, general activities, and that political authority infinitely strong which will be supported by the free and untrammeled spirit of its people."[40] Hegel's theory of freedom and liberty amounts to a safety-valve principle of government, since unlimited expression of criticism, far from weakening the state, gives it unlimited strength. Hegel did not show the way in which the negative and positive poles of freedom can be joined without lapsing into the authoritarianism of the God-State. What prevents the leader of state from placing a cap on the valve of criticism when he so pleases? The sectioning off of residual political power into the hands of various elites made it difficult for any "subordinate" activities to be registered. But Hegel did not consider the problem of the dysfunction of reason any more than it was by Rousseau.

With the passage of years, Hegel was unable to resist the blandishments of linking his theory of freedom to the authoritarian state. He indicates that negative freedom is "periled" by its inherent tendency to excess. In this way, Hegel blames the existence of economic inequality and political repression, not on the messianic state, but on the "excesses" of the popular elements. The *vox populi*, expressing itself through dirty monetary advantage and revolutionary unrest, makes necessary a powerful state.[41] His position reflected a political situation in which Germany was divided in fact between a political power wielded by Junkers, the landed nobility of Prussia, and an economic power rooted in urban commerce and industry. In this context, the state did indeed "mediate" the claims of each. But with the subsequent expansion of the business classes, and their amalgamation with the major "old families," the facade of state neutrality was quickly dispelled. History became synonymous with the manifest destiny of the mythic German Empire, and the state became the vehicle through which history would be realized and through which criticism would be distilled.

The leitmotif in Hegel's social thought is the distinction between anarchy and freedom. The movement from society to polity is an obvious effort to get from one to the other. But no such distinction is made between liberty and the state beyond a rather tepid reminder (in the twilight of his career) that "people must participate in legislation and in the most important affairs of state." In the fluid conditions of German life an effective statement would have at least implied, not simply participation, but opposition to the nation-state. This transition from the freedom to participate in the Prussian celebration to opposition to any of its pronouncements was one Hegel could not make once he had staked out the territory of society as the struggle between anarchy and authority. By the close of his career, when he was more concerned with wrapping up his system than in opening up new issues, Hegel fell victim to his own admonition: "When philosophy paints its gray on gray, then has the shape of life grown old."[42] Thus it is that the close of his

Philosophy of Right and Law is neither the summation nor conclusion, but an introduction to the Introduction of the *Philosophy of History*.

Neither political science nor political economy can contain the Hegelian "world mind." History alone is the anchor point and proving grounds of freedom. According to Hegel, social life is a "mundane interest," and the "absolute mind," discontent with the mundane, works out its "transition to its next higher stage."[43] While one is left with the disquieting knowledge that the "absolute mind" is nothing more than Hegel's own mind, there is nonetheless a nobility of spirit motivating his decision to locate the springs of freedom in historical process rather than in philosophical speculation.

Freedom is essentially a changing phenomenon. The more humankind develops spiritually, that is, in the sense of the world mind, the more it becomes aware of its generic self and genetic unfolding—the historical growth of consciousness of freedom. The role of the *philosophy of history* is the "actualization of freedom." World history in Hegel's sense is the progress of freedom because it is the process of the self-realization of the spiritual content of social existence. And conversely, "freedom is itself its own object of attainment and the sole purpose of spirit. It is the ultimate end toward which all world history has continually aimed."[44] At this point, Hegel's kinship with Platonism is most clearly revealed, since just as spirit and freedom are linked, so, too, slavery and dead matter are fused.

Every slackening of spirit involves a retreat to material inertia. Only through the study of history and its lessons are gaps in the fortress of freedom overcome nowhere else. Once freedom becomes manifest in spirit, it becomes practical, something taken up by the *Volksgeist*. Freedom can thus be viewed as the propelling force of hitherto existing societies. When freedom is fully realized through the identification of consciousness and history, society in its profane ceases to exist. What we are left with is a sacral collectivity of human spirit. Before the tide of freedom everything gives way. In his early years, Hegel interpreted this in a radical fashion. Those institutions and constitutions that did not correspond to the *Volksgeist* were doomed because they provided an unreal, irrational bond. "The owl of Minerva spreads its wings only with the falling of the dusk."[45] Here Hegel cautions against a pre-determinist view of social existence. The task of displacing the old involves the ability "to rise above one's little interest." Egoism conflicts with social change. "Too often a reservation is hidden behind the eager concern for the general welfare as long as it coincides with our own interest. Such eagerness to consent to proposed reforms gets discarded as soon as a demand is made upon it."[46]

Contrary to the common view, Hegel did not consider either social or political freedom as abstractly inevitable. Freedom is real, but conditional in its forms. It is thus an active process rather than a passive series of events. In this way, Hegel provided his sociological followers from Marx to Mannheim with a methodological basis for posing the conditions of man's material freedom, just as Hegel himself had traced the evolution of the idea of freedom as spirit.

To the degree he was concerned with human emancipation, Hegel tried to hold with one-rein chariots moving in opposite directions. He hedged on an expansive view of freedom by first identifying freedom with the established political order, and then by assuming that such an order is spiritually sanctioned by the gods of reason. In this system, spontaneous social change becomes "the spirit of negation, i.e., the negation of freedom."[47] It should be noted that Hegel's opposition to civil conflict and political revolution held only when there exists an organic linkage between a conquered people and its prince, or more simply, between the ruler and the ruled. Where no such correlation exists, then rebellion and revolution may be sanctioned. In the case of a rebellion in a conquered province, as distinct from an uprising within a well-ordered state, Hegel notes that in the former situation there may be a social contract, but not an organic tie. In Hegel one sees the heavy emphasis on state-craft, with hardly any corresponding concern for what is now called social justice.

Ever the devoted servant of the concrete, Hegel did intro-duce a more sociological concept of freedom than had pre-viously been known in the history of ideas. He filled the issue of freedom with historical detail, while at the same time showing that the context of freedom is social and hu-man and hence realizable. In so doing, he revolutionized the study of freedom by going beyond the psychological frame of reference (from Hobbes to Rousseau) which had bottled up political theory.

What Hegel sought had nothing in common with political quietism. He felt that the proper end of men, freedom, could be achieved because it is rooted in both the human personal-ity and in the historical *Geist*. If the further growth of man-kind is our self-declared purpose, freedom is not simply what is desirable but what is necessary. Indeed, Hegel's theory of freedom in its panpsychic immensity easily allows for a chiliastic interpretation. He himself forestalled such a view by limiting its practical application to the growth of Germany from absolutism to constitutionalism. But the ends of Hegel's social theories failed to outweigh their pragmatic abuses. It was Hegel who finally separated the issue of political free-dom from personal liberty: the moral absolutists on one side and the social meliorists on the other. But in so doing, Hegel had, no less than John Stuart Mill, set the limits as well as terms of discourse for nineteenth-century struggles between liberal and conservative varieties of sociology.

The return to prominence of neo-Hegelian statist think-ing in the social sciences comes about via the new individu-alism. The political scientists seem attracted to the notion of state autonomy, which in turn becomes the precondition of social welfare and benign neglect alike. It is of no small irony that a Marxian sociology, born out of an initial repudiation of Hegelian idealism and the bourgeois system, currently seeks its regeneration through a return to Hegel. The slogan becomes "bringing the State back in," a vulgar paraphrase of George Homans's urgings of "bringing men back in." As we have seen, the state becomes a Hegelian necessity because his work was deeply rooted in hierarchical perceptions about culture, race, and paradigm of heroism.[48] But Hegel seems to slip away from such self-assured post-modernism into larger visions of the human condition. Every new reinterpretation of Hegel seems normative: constitutional and dictatorial, and anti-liberal and liberal forms of institutional order. Canonical figures are not necessarily consistent. They gain their notoriety through ambiguity as often as they do through clarity. Hegel is most certainly such a case in point.

Hegel leads directly into Marx less because of abstract philosophy than because of concrete political science. Francis Fukuyama has explained as much in his *End of History* volume.[49] While attracted to Hegel for his bourgeois constitutional defense of the state, people such as Fukuyama, and Alexandre Kojeve long before him, well appreciated that something beyond glorifying the state was involved. Hegel's larger vision was rooted in universals, particularly a universal bourgeois state. The current fixation on globalization has thus turned up a rich mine of thought that owes much to Hegel. It was Marx and Engels who first appreciated the potent combination of the national state with the international order as a mechanism to convert philosophy into slogan, and the masses as carriers of emancipation. To those masters of revolution we now turn.

Notes

1. Friedrich Meinecke, *Machiavellism: The Doctrine of Raison d'État and its Place in Modern History.* New Brunswick and London: Transaction Publishers, 1998, p. 350. [Original publication in English, 1957.]
2. Irving Babbitt, *Rousseau and Romanticism.* New Brunswick and Lon-

don: Transaction Publishers, 1991 [original publication, 1919], esp.
pp. 187-219. The new introduction by Claes G. Ryn deserves a careful reading as to how the transition from French to German thought
actually took place.

3. Raymond Aron, *German Sociology*. New York: The Free Press, 1957;
and Auguste Cornu, *The Origins of Marxian Thought*. Springfield,
Ill.: Charles C. Thomas, Publishers, 1957. Both of these works offer
worthwhile introductions to the bridge provided by Hegel from the
rationalist to romantic traditions.

4. J.M. Findlay, *Hegel: A Reexamination*. London: Allen and Unwin, p.
320. This view has clear roots in the views of Karl Popper, *The
Open Society and Its Enemies*. London: Routledge & Kegan Paul,
1945.

5. Leonard Krieger, *The German Idea of Freedom: History of a Political
Tradition*. Boston: Beacon Press, 1951, pp. 125-138.

6. Frederick Engels, *Ludwig Feuerbach and the Outcome of Classical German Philosophy*. New York: International Publishers, 1934 [written
in 1845].

7. Georg Wilhelm Friedrich Hegel, *Lectures on the History of Philosophy*,
trans. E.S. Haldane, vol. 1. London: Routledge & Kegan Paul, 1955.

8. Karl Marx, *The Holy Family; or Critique of Critical Critique* [written in
1845]. In *Marx/Engels Gesamtausgabe*, abt. 1, band 3, Berlin: Bietz
Verlag, 1956. There is a vast and worthy literature on "left" and
"right" Hegelianism in Germany. The work of Sidney Hook, *From
Hegel to Marx: Studies in the Intellectual Development of Karl Marx*.
New York: Reynal & Hitchcock, 1936, Karl Lowith, *Meaning in His-
tory*. Chicago: University of Chicago Press, 1949; and Hans Speier
"From Hegel to Marx: The Left Hegelians, Feuerbach and `True
Socialism'," in Hans Speier, ed., *Social Order and the Risk of War*.
New York: Stewart, 1952 are especially worthwhile.

9. Josiah Royce, *The Philosophy of Loyalty*. New York: Macmillan, 1908,
pp. 213-215.

10. Bernard Bonsanquet, *Social and International Ideals: Being Studies in
Patriotism*. London: Macmillan, 1917, p. 300.

11. Søren Kierkegaard, *Concluding Unscientific Postscript*, translated by
D.F. Swenson and W. Lorie. Princeton: Princeton University Press,
1944, pp. 291-299, 505-512.

12. Georg Wilhelm Friedrich Hegel, *Philosophy of Right and Law*, sec.
270H, 302. For a sound analysis of the philosophic source of Hegel's
theory of state power, see Alexander Kaufman, "Hegel and the
Ontological Critique of Liberalism," *American Political Science Review*, Volume 90, Number 4 (Dec. 1997), pp. 807-817.

13. Georg Wilhelm Friedrich Hegel, *The Science of Logic*, trans. W.H.
Johnston and L.G. Struthers. London: Allen and Unwin, 1929.

14. Edmund Husserl, *La philosophie comme science rigoureuse*, Volume 2,
Section 3, trans. Quentin Lauer, Paris: Presses Universitaires de
France, 1954, pp. 56-57.

15. Georg Wilhelm Friedrich Hegel, *Phenomenology of Mind,* trans. J.B. Baillie. London: Allen and Unwin, New York: Macmillan, 1931.
16. Karl Marx, *Economic and Philosophic Manuscripts of 1844,* trans. Max Milligan. Moscow: Foreign Languages Publishing House, 1959, pp. 45–46.
17. Ludwig Feuerbach, "Gedanken uber Tod und Ensterblichkeit," in *Sammtliche Werke,* volume 3, ed. W. Bolin and F. Jodi. Stuttgart: Bad Cannstatt Fromann Verlag, 1903–1911.
18. Alexandre Kojeve, *Lecons sur la Phénoménologie de l'esprit, professées de 1933 à 1939 à l'Ecole des hautes-études réunies.* Paris: Gallimard, 1957, pp. 412–441.
19. Georg Wilhelm Friedrich Hegel, *Philosophy of Right and Law,* (preface), trans. T.M. Knox. Oxford: Clarendon Press, 1953.
20. Georg Wilhelm Friedrich Hegel, *Philosophy of Right and Law,* para. 142.
21. Georg Wilhelm Friedrich Hegel, *Philosophy of Right and Law,* para. 33.
22. Georg Wilhelm Friedrich Hegel, *Philosophy of Right and Law,* para. 188.
23. Georg Wilhelm Friedrich Hegel, *Philosophy of Right and Law,* para. 297.
24. Henri Lefebvre, "Lois objectives et forces sociales," *La Nouvelle Critique* (May), 1956, pp. 59–73.
25. Ferdinand Tönnies, *Fundamental Concepts of Sociology,* trans. C.P. Loomis. New York: American Book, 1940.
26. Georg Wilhelm Friedrich Hegel, *Hegel's eigenhandige Randemerkingen zu seiner Rechtsphilosophie,* ed. G. Lasson. Leipzig: Felix Meiner Verlag, 1930, para. 273.
27. Georg Wilhelm Friedrich Hegel, Hegel's eigenhandige Randemerkingen zu seiner *Rechtsphilosophie,* ed. G. Lasson. Leipzig: Felix Meiner Verlag, 1930, para. 273.
28. Georg Wilhelm Friedrich Hegel, *Hegel's eigenhandige Randemerkingen zu seiner Rechtsphilosophie,* ed. G. Lasson. Leipzig: Felix Meiner Verlag, 1930, para. 258.
29. Georg Wilhelm Friedrich Hegel, *Hegel's eigenhandige Randemerkingen zu seiner Rechtsphilosophie,* ed. G. Lasson. Leipzig: Felix Meiner Verlag, 1930, para. 258a.
30. For two varieties of a "left" outcome, see Georg Lukacs, *Die Zerstorung der Vernunft.* Berlin: Aufbau-Verlag, 1953; and Herbert Marcuse, *Reason and Revolution: Hegel and the Rise of Social Theory.* New York: Oxford University Press, 1941.
31. Georg Wilhelm Friedrich Hegel, *Philosophy of Right and Law,* para. 153.
32. Georg Wilhelm Friedrich Hegel, *Philosophy of Right and Law,* para. 270a.
33. Georg Wilhelm Friedrich Hegel, *Philosophy of Right and Law,* para. 29, 30.

34. Georg Wilhelm Friedrich Hegel, *Philosophy of Right and Law,* para. 185.
35. Georg Wilhelm Friedrich Hegel, *Philosophy of Right and Law,* para. 243, 244.
36. Georg Wilhelm Friedrich Hegel, *Philosophy of Right and Law,* para. 258, 260.
37. Georg Wilhelm Friedrich Hegel, *Philosophy of History* trans. J. Sibree. New York: Dover Publishers, 1956.
38. Georg Wilhelm Friedrich Hegel, "Die Verfassung Deutschlands," in *Hegel heute; Eine Auswahl aus Hegel's politischer Gedankenwelt.* Leipzig: Meiner, 1934, pp. 11–12.
39. Georg Wilhelm Friedrich Hegel, "Die Verfassung Deutschlands," in *Hegel heute; Eine Auswahl aus Hegel's politischer Gedankenwelt.* Leipzig: Meiner, 1934, pp. 24–25.
40. Georg Wilhelm Friedrich Hegel, "Die Verfassung Deutschlands," in *Hegel heute; Eine Auswahl aus Hegel's politischer Gedankenwelt.* Leipzig: Meiner, 1934, pp. 25.
41. Georg Wilhelm Friedrich Hegel, "Die Verfassung Deutschlands," in *Hegel heute; Eine Auswahl aus Hegel's politischer Gedankenwelt.* Leipzig: Meiner, 1934, pp. 39–40.
42. Georg Wilhelm Friedrich Hegel, *Philosophy of Right and Law,* para. 341–360.
43. Georg Wilhelm Friedrich Hegel, *Philosophy of Right and Law,* para. 344.
44. Georg Wilhelm Friedrich Hegel, *Philosophy of History* trans. J. Sibree. New York: Dover Publishers, 1956.
45. Georg Wilhelm Friedrich Hegel, *Philosophy of Right and Law,* para. introduction.
46. Georg Wilhelm Friedrich Hegel, "Die Verfassung Deutschlands," in *Hegel heute; Eine Auswahl aus Hegel's politischer Gedankenwelt.* Leipzig: Meiner, 1934, pp. 9–10.
47. Georg Wilhelm Friedrich Hegel, *Philosophy of Right and Law,* para. 151.
48. Anna Makolkin, "The European Legacy of Hate: A Semiotic Pathway," *The European Legacy.* Volume 2, Number 2 (part 6), April 1997, pp. 370–375.
49. Francis Fukuyama, *The End of History and the Last Man.* New York: The Free Press, 1993.

4

The Liberal Compromise with State Power: Alexis de Tocqueville

---

"Tocqueville is the first and, throughout the nineteenth century, the major exponent of the view that the modern regime is characterized not by the solidification but by the fragmentation of social class, with the key elements dispersed: power to the masses and to centralized bureaucracy, wealth to an ever-enlarging middle class, and status to the varied and shifting sectors of society which, in the absence of true class, become the theaters of the unending and agonizing competition among individuals for the attainment of the marks of status."

—*Robert A. Nisbet*[1]

One of the great enigmas of political history, never mind political sociology, is how liberalism transformed itself from a stinging critic of state power over society, into the pivotal crusader for state power as a mechanism for instituting social welfare. The process happened so gradually that it took theorists by surprise, and set them to wondering how so ringing an endorsement of local democracy by Tocqueville could so readily be set aside in favor of top-down guarantee-guarantor of equity. In part, the answer is obvious: Tocqueville was in search of the practice and theory of liberty—and liberty resides in the person; whereas, his successors were in search of equity—and equity resides in the society. In that sense, the winds of doctrine that swept the old order away in Europe contain part of the answer to that for which we are searching: how liberalism as an ideology emerges as a compromise between the bureaucratic state and the welfare society.

Despite the obvious aristocratic background of Tocqueville, he was keenly aware of the rising tide of socialism, not so much as a system, but as a pending ideological threat. He perhaps took Marx and the *Communist Manifesto* more seriously than the proletariat for whom its message of the doom of capitalism and the rise of communism was intended. But for all the deep belief in the welfare of the people and the obligation of the state to provide for such welfare, Tocqueville held in deep reserve the political consequences of such socialism. Indeed, even capitalism as a process of increasing administrative controls was troubling to the French giant of ethnography.

But my aim here is not to study this extraordinary figure in general. There is sufficient work on him, not to mention by him. Rather, the purpose of this chapter is to explain why Tocqueville is very much part of the canon of political sociology. He is such both for the brilliance of his writings and for the fact that he declared social welfare to be a condition of the good state. It is less the state writ large rather than policy-making as an everyday activity that defines his major contributions to the formation of a political sociology. For it is in the realm of the human adjudication of events, the tampering with the natural order of things, that he made his biggest contributions. This is not to disparage or dismiss Tocqueville's ethnographic survey of the United States; it is rather to offer in evidence a critical place for this figure in the formation of a discipline that did not as yet have a name.

That Tocqueville has been quite properly enlisted in the cause of a free society, at times from contemporaries with a less than perfect pedigree, is an indicator of how topsy-turvy the world of political ideology—in contrast to political sociology—can and has become. Conservatives have become the standard bearers of Americanism as a supreme value, while liberals have become the critics of an American past that included genocide against Native American Indians and the unconscionable abuses of the slave system. As a result, it is the conservatives who are more apt to consider *Democracy in America* as the appropriate response to *The Communist Manifesto*. At the same time, conservatives have been the standard bearers for a strict interpretation of the Constitution, and all that it implies with respect to the rights of individuals and the limitations imposed on government and its three branches. The liberals, for their part, see trouble when the free conscience runs amuck and denigrates minorities and those less able to defend their own interests. *Democracy in America* is seen more as an anachronism than a shield behind which to rally the troops of a free society. But our purpose will be not to give aid and comfort to any particular ideology so much as to show that Tocqueville represented critical aspects of the canon of political sociology, of the effort to harmonize the interests of the state and the will of the society.

It should be understood that the liberalism of Tocqueville was as much a function of his sentiments as of his thoughts. That is to say, he was an inveterate traveler, what today we might call an ethnographer, or in more sophisticated circles, a cultural anthropologist of advanced societies. While he had a profound sense of theoretical mooring, he did not write big books of theory. His books were elegant in style, but obviously hurried, and more in the nature of extended essays. Tocqueville's musings of a theoretical sort are embedded in the careful examination of American and European civilization—especially the United States, France, and Ireland. Thus, the structure of his work must be teased out of his normal intellectual habitats to be made part of the

canon of political sociology. However, to neglect this protean figure because he worked in a style with which we are
more comfortable in the twentieth century than his associates were in the nineteenth century would be to miss out on
what perhaps was the largest theoretical breakthrough of
the entire epoch in which he lived and worked: establishing
the contours of the liberal state within the bowels of the
egalitarian and democratic society.

Tocqueville well appreciated the difficult intellectual
position in which he stood. Celebrating the unique achievement of America, the sturdiness of its democratic institutions, the uniqueness of its culture and people, the extraordinary degree of voluntary associations as a character of
this society, he could yet be harsh in his judgment of this
same culture for losing touch with the values of tradition
and authority, for the oppressive conformist atmosphere
brought about by the ceaseless quest for equality, and for
the power of an elected majority to make mistakes that are a
product of mindlessness. In attempting to square the circle
of tradition and authority on one side, and innovation and
association on the other, Tocqueville fashioned more than
a picture of America, he offered a blueprint for liberalism
as a way out of the swamp of reaction on one side and revolution on the other. Indeed, Tocqueville's later writings, those
closer to home, made this quite clear.

Writing to his friend, Eugene Stoffels, he half-complained
about and half- celebrated his middle ground: "I please many
persons of opposite opinions, not because they penetrate
my meaning, but because, looking only to one side of my
work, they think they find in it arguments in favor of their
own convictions. But I have faith in the future, and I hope
that the day will come when all will see clearly what only a
few suspect."[2] What then is the "meaning" of Tocqueville's
work? And what is it to "see clearly" into his writings? I would
submit that the driving force is not, as has been suggested
often, ambivalence about democracy. Rather it is a firm

conviction that a liberality of law and custom, one that mediates the claims of "government" (Tocqueville rarely used
the word state) and the desires of "civil life" was the best
way to secure a social order in which "revolutions become
more rare."[3] And that has been the leitmotif of liberalism
for two centuries: to adjudicate differences in such a way as
to maintain order and freedom in some magical equilibrium
that will not spill the blood of innocents. According to
Tocqueville, the key to the good society then is simply that
balance, that equilibrium between general theories and value
systems and "the palpable, direct, and immediate connection with the daily occupations of life."

There were three great events in the lifetime of Tocqueville,
and he covered each of them with enormous skill, a skill it
should be noted that was leavened by his being a practical
politician and diplomat. In some ways, his writings can be
viewed as an expanded version of filing reports on the condition and status of the world for the government of France.
Whether Parisian officials listened is another matter. Indeed,
he couched his commentary in such ambivalent ways that
knowing exactly how or what policies to implement was no
easy task. But Tocqueville's need to report to authorities, instead of assaulting authority in general made him "liberal" in
the quotidian sense of weighing the consequences of specific
actions, no less than in the larger sense of his ideological
proclivities to mediate and moderate rather than to serve the
interests of revolution or reaction. Thus, a political sociology
must be teased out of Tocqueville in ways that are somewhat
more challenging than examining say, the explicit aims of
Marx with respect to the capitalist state.

We should start with Tocqueville's *Old Regime and the French
Revolution*, since this is the source of his writings on the importance of states in forming societies. Contemporary and
classical Marxian complaints about the shortcomings of society often fail to recognize that political culture, in which a
society is embedded, is an independent variable along with

state structure. The special character of Tocqueville's diagnosis of what ails French political culture was to demonstrate the way in which French society—constantly termed politically impotent, debilitated and conflictual—was a function of changes in state structure, that is, political centralization under the Bourbon monarchy. Already visible in the eighteenth century, Tocqueville called attention to a "highly centralized and all powerful" state whose range of activities was prodigious.[4] Tocqueville found "a single central power located at the heart of the kingdom and controlling public administration throughout the country."[5] Tocqueville saw this centralizing tendency of state power as the eclipse of all vitality in the periphery by a metropolitan center.

The problem for society, according to Tocqueville, was the way in which state power absorbed all intermediary organizations and sapped society of its vitality. The capacity of American society to deal with and overcome this French curse became a steady drum beat motif in all of Tocqueville's work. But, in the *Old Regime and the French Revolution,* the warning signs were clear regarding what was to ensue. "In short, the central power had taken to playing the part of an indefatigable mentor and keeping the nation in quasi-paternal tutelage."[6] Correspondingly, while the French people were advancing toward a higher standard of civilization, their political structure was "relapsing into barbarism." Tocqueville went further by noting that "the spirit of local patriotism and strenuous endeavor, and the virile, pioneering virtues it promoted, had passed away. In short, these ancient institutions, while keeping their original forms, had been drained of their substance."[7]

The key factor in draining such participatory energies was not exploitation engendered by the factory system as such, but the tradition of state centralization. "It never occurred to anyone that any large scale enterprise could be put through successfully without the intervention of the State."[8] Tocqueville struck a very modern note in his argument that the tradition of state centralization is the problem to be overcome. The growing force of the state was such as to limit on less than encourage political participation. In a cynical mood, Tocqueville observes that in late eighteenth century France "the only way of getting a Conservative and a Radical to agree was to attack the authority of the central government, not in practice but in principle."[9] Tocqueville constantly strikes a Hobbesian note. It was the inner lack of resolve within the state, rather than any bottom up assault, that was at the core of the revolution to come. "We had so completely forgotten the practice of great human affairs, and we were so ignorant of the role of religion in the government of empires, that unbelief established itself first in the minds of the very people who had the most personal and pressing interest in keeping the state in order and the masses obedient. Not only did they [the leaders] welcome it, but in their blindness they spread it downward; impiety was the pastime of their idle lives." [10] There could hardly be a more severe judgment on the Enlightenment epoch. And even if Tocqueville himself rarely addressed issues of division within the Church as well as the state, one finds in his writings on France a bitter conservatism entirely absent in his writings on the United States. The passion of the French revolutionary project was quickly spent in the absence of a political culture; the compassion behind the American revolutionary project, in contrast, remained durable and successful.

The potential for revolution was subsumed under the problem of restoring society to its rightful place. For Tocqueville, French politics could never be viable until changes took place in the underlying political culture of the nation. The fact that so many different regimes have all proved equal failures demonstrates that it is not any particular set of political institutions, but rather French society itself, which was at fault. State centralization poses a limiting condition on French political life. "So when people say that we have nothing that is safe from revolutions, I tell them that they are wrong, that centralization is one thing. In France there is only one thing that we cannot make: a free government; and only one that we cannot destroy: centralization."[11] This was a theme Tocqueville was to strike repeatedly in his study of political institutions of the West. Alongside this insight that it is political institutions in general, and a tradition of centralization in particular, that have distorted French society, Tocqueville also posits the limits that societal shortcomings pose in implementing new political institutions.

The irony of the French Revolution of 1789 is that it could not overcome the inertia of social traditions. Thus it came to be that the most concerted revolution in human history, one which attempted to remake all of human society and to obliterate everything that came before it, succeeded only in perpetuating and deepening the original tradition of centralization. Far from vanquishing state power, the Revolution only enshrined the state as the ultimate arbiter of behavior. The more Tocqueville looked back beyond the prism of the Revolution and into the forgotten world of the Ancient Regime, the more he came to appreciate the truth that all the bad habits of nineteenth-century France were already inscribed in the institutions and agencies of the eighteenth century. On one hand, Tocqueville's account of political revolution reinforced the original eighteenth-century conceit that revolution is capable of undoing, if not remaking, social relations on a colossal scale. But on the other hand, such long-standing tendencies simultaneously imply the inexorable weight of tradition and the impossibility of wholesale social revolution.

But Tocqueville's innate liberalism, which it should be noted is quite compatible with his enlightened, aristocratic background, compelled him to say that limits posed by custom are not absolute. He opposes a naive fatalism, or for that matter, desperate historicism, in political affairs. "I am tempted to the belief that what are called necessary institutions are only institutions to which one is accustomed, and that in matters of social constitution the field of possibilities is much wider than people living within each society imagine."[12] Yet, unlike Rousseau and Robespierre, Tocqueville well recognized the dangers of trying to remake society anew and too quickly. Ultimately, there is a distinction to be made between politics as a philosophical activity and as a concrete set of problems in governance. Looking at the activities of Rousseau and the *philosophes* in retrospect, it was evident to Tocqueville just how dangerous was the impulse to substitute theory for policy. The tragedy of the French Revolution is that it placed in governance those people with the least amount of practical political knowledge. All the disastrous features of the Revolution flowed from this fact.

Tocqueville is probably the first major figure who observed that revolutions are either caused by or coordinated with rising expectations. "At first sight it may appear surprising that the French Revolution, whose primary aim was to destroy every vestige of the institutions of the Middle Ages, should not have broken out in countries where those institutions had the greatest hold and bore most heavily on the people instead of those in which their yoke was relatively light."[13] At stake is the belief of Tocqueville that the source of revolution is less one of social class or relative economic depravation than political issues. More important than the economic status of the bearer class of revolution, whether it is bourgeois, peasant, or proletarian, is its practical political experience. Tocqueville concurs with Edmund Burke's prophetic estimation that the fateful error of the French Revolution was its systematic exclusion from governance of any of the people who possessed practical political knowledge. It was an error oft repeated in the two hundred plus years since that defining revolution.

The excesses of the French Revolution follow not simply or even primarily from the original and disproportionate influence of the *philosophes*. Rather, they stem primarily from

the fact that a new political class that is incautious or ignorant of the limitations of theoretical knowledge appropri-
ates these ideas. Tocqueville's analysis thus marks a turning
point in political sociology. He rejected the impulse to fault
revolutionary ideas in the abstract for the damages that they
inflict on society. He similarly rejects the socialist ideas, then
quite current, that it is the economic status of the revolutionary class that determines the morality or the immorality
of its actions. Instead, Tocqueville turns his attention to the
manner in which revolutionary or utopian theory can become a dangerous crutch for a new political class that lacks
any concrete idea of governance. In the absence of direct
political experience, revolutionary designs to remake society
are more attractive. Conversely, the utopian mind and the
mind of the statesman are at odds with one another. Char-
acterizing David Hume's disagreement with Denis Diderot
over the value of toleration, Tocqueville concludes, "it was
the Scotsman who was right. Living in a free country, he
had practical experience of freedom; Diderot's was the viewpoint of a man of letters; Hume's that of a statesman."[14]

Tocqueville, considerably before Marx and Mannheim,
proved to be a major diagnostician of the intellectual and
ideological temperament. There is a sociology of knowledge
component implicit in his analysis of the French Revolution. He gave great emphasis to the affinity between the
unconnected intellectual and the revolutionary mindset. It
was not the capacity to reason that failed the intellectual,
but the absence of a stake in the social order. Beyond economic interest, Tocqueville demonstrates how and why revolutionary ideas exercise such a powerful hold on the minds
of ascendant classes. "There are periods in a nation's life
when men differ from each other so profoundly that any
notion of the same law for all seems to them preposterous.
But there are other periods when it is enough to dangle
before their eyes a picture, however indistinct and remote,
of such a law and they promptly grasp its meaning and has-

ten to acclaim it."[15] Such a time is the democratic age—desired by the French but achieved by the Americans.

The problem of revolution and its carrier class is uniquely the problem of revolution writ large in a democratic age. Democratic revolution brings to power a new political class, one which lacks the practical habits of self-governance, and worse, the dedication to restraint required to protect civil society and its voluntary associations. "Since no free institutions and, as a result, no experienced and organized political parties existed any longer in France, and since in the absence of any political groups of this sort exist at present, the guidance of public opinion, when its first stirrings made themselves felt, came entirely into the hands of the philosophers, that is to say, the intellectuals, it was only to be expected that the directives of the Revolution should take the form of abstract principles, highly generalized theories, and that political realities would be largely overlooked."[16] The ideology and culture of the French Revolution was itself fueled by a group that could see the evils of the ancient regime, but were unable to perceive the terror of the new regime.

Tocqueville distinguished between the philosophers and the economists at this level as one might today distinguish between the professors and the policy-makers. While the philosophers confined themselves to general speculation, the economists were able to deal with real problems of government at the practical level. "According to the top economists the function of the State was not merely one of ruling the nation, but also that of recasting it in a given mold, of shaping the mentality of the population in accordance with a predetermined model and instilling the ideas and sentiments they thought desirable into the minds of all. In short, they set no limit to its rights and powers; its duty was not merely to reform but to transform the French nation—a task of which the central power was alone capable."[17] Tocqueville dubbed the goal of social order by means of unchecked state power as "democratic despotism"—a close handmaiden to what Karl Wittfogel[18] was to call in this century "Oriental despotism" and what Walter Laqueur was to refer to as "third world dictatorship."[19]

But at this point, Tocqueville proves himself an adroit theorist. Instead of following in the path of Burke and de Maistre and other opponents to revolutionary movements, he broke with those compatriots with whom he had much in common regarding the limits of theoretical knowledge. Tocqueville believed that the solution to the problem of democracy was, somewhat paradoxically, more democracy. One can readily see how the example of the United States loomed ever larger in the wake of the failures of the French Revolution to achieve its desired reforms. Given the inevitability of democracy thrusting into power a new political class, the problem of the modern age is to educate this class. As a result, Tocqueville favored suffrage reform, public education, and other social legislation that would offer these new popular political classes an opportunity to gain the habits of self-rule.

The metaphysical supposition behind Tocqueville's work, and a posture that spared him from intense despair when looking at the wreckage of the French Revolution, was the recognition that if institutional changes in the distribution of state power had originally worked to change the nature of French society for the worse, then so too might subsequent institutional reforms bring about salutary changes in French society. Not given to a priori thinking, Tocqueville was not bound to doctrines of natural law or natural rights, and even less to presumptions of Augustinian original sin and Rousseauian original goodness. Behind the preference for voluntary association was the creation of agencies and institutions suitable to the practical needs of people. And behind that was a philosophical disposition to indeterminacy, to a society in the process of evolving, rather than one predetermined by history or inheritance.[20]

It might well be that a critical factor in Tocqueville's continuing fame has less to do with what he advocated than it does with his disdain for deterministic visions of revolutionary take-over and management of politics from above. He postulated a plausible, highly pragmatic theory of revolution that accorded with the liberal predisposition then rising throughout Europe and North America. By his emphasis on the political as an autonomous domain of action, Tocqueville was in a position to avoid the pitfalls of revolutionary theory and reactionary anti-theory. He removed the study of political sociology from an area fixated on social classes into the examination of politics as a realm of practice malleable and apart from presumed beliefs in any single source of change.

At the deepest level, Tocqueville's enterprise suggested the futility of any monocausal explanation of political phenomenon. And not until we arrive at Max Weber seventy years later, do we see a similar figure able to move beyond the boundaries of ideology and into a social science writ large. One need only consider the discrete levels of analysis that emerge from Tocqueville's treatment of state and revolution. First, he analyzes the substance of political ideologies; then the conditions of their reception by various political classes; next he moves to the study of the economic and cultural motivations of these actors and their degree and nature of political socialization; and finally, into the study of whole systems, that is, the structural features that constrain or move forward any particular political system or regime.

In such a complex social scientific world, there is no place for the mechanical materialism of a Helvétius or Diderot that would crowd out other explanatory perspectives. Nor was there any need to adopt a blanket Hegelian idealism that would posit transcendental forces of development in opposition to the concrete and the quotidian. It was not hard to detect in so many thick philosophical perspectives a nationalist bias or a racialist bias that crowd out all possi-

bilities of innovation. In so doing, in studying the French
Revolution in so candid a manner, Tocqueville effectively
gave definition to a political sociology that avoided the twin
traps of anarchy and the leviathan. He also provided a set
of problems with which the subsequent Marxist tradition
would relentlessly struggle throughout the nineteenth century, before yielding to the forces of autonomous politics
practiced by the state.

We are now in a far better position to appreciate the special, if intermediary, place of *Democracy in America* in
Tocqueville's world. It occupies the mid-point between two
French poles: the revolutions of 1789 and that of 1848. From
such a perspective, it is little wonder that he held the First
New Nation in high repute. In its Cartesian practicality, in
the openings of its people, in the size of its voluntary association, the United States held out hopes for the Old World.
Indeed, that Tocqueville was able to hold such an extraordinary position as early as the 1830s may say less about his
regard for the American nation than it does about his desperate search for a liberal solution to a Europe in which
fanaticism seemed to triumph from both reactionary and
revolutionary perspectives. Indeed, the opening sentence
of the work states that "nothing struck me more forcibly
than the general equality of conditions among the people."
And while he was no egalitarian in a French context, he
pointed out with a certain grim humor reminiscent of
Voltaire that "in France the kings have always been the most
active and the most constant of levelers." But with some
noteworthy exceptions, the reigns of Louis XI, XIV, and XV
"reduced all ranks beneath the throne to the same degree
of subjection."[21] America was a source of hope and inspiration, but not necessarily a model to be emulated.

The bulk of the first volume, that from chapter three
through seventeen, is essentially an analysis of the political
conditions which permit social egalitarianism to flourish. It
was as if Montesquieu had come to life in the New World,

and his steady progression from the "essential democracy" of the United States based as it on the sovereignty of the whole people, and ensured by a division of powers between municipalities, cities, states and nation, made the entire system operative. Tocqueville well appreciated the role of the judiciary in this structure. Tocqueville realized that it was not the existence of laws and court systems that made the difference, so much as "the American judges have the right of declaring laws to be unconstitutional." Further, it was the unique genius of the system that made them cautious rather than precipitous in the use of this amazing power.[22]

Tocqueville speaks of jurisdiction, not power, tyranny not oppression, constitution not authority. In this, he was well within the legal tradition rather than the economic tradition. It was not so much the sources of things, but their operations, which intrigued him. His fears were expressed in political terms as well. Thus, when speaking in a prophetic mode about "when the American Republics begin to degenerate," his concern was for the "legislative tyranny" inflicted by the majority that held center stage. The broad outlines of *Democracy in America* follow the outlines of the Constitution itself. It was the "base." There was always the comparison of the United States and France in political and juridical terms, rarely in economic terms. In discussing the differences between a president and a king, Tocqueville noted that "in the United States the executive power is as limited and exceptional as the sovereignty in whose name it acts; in France it is as universal as the authority of the state. The Americans have a Federal and the French a national government."[23] The great space given over to this theme in by far the largest chapter of the work is indicative of Tocqueville's acute sense that the question of state power is first and foremost a political consideration.

The liberalism of Tocqueville resides in his uneasy faith in democracy—at least as practiced in America. While granting the imperfections of the system, and allowing that one person can better perform the functions of a political society than a constant din of legislative proposals, he nonetheless provides as sensible a contrast of democracy and despotism as we have in the literature of political sociology. "Democracy does not give the people the most skillful government, but it produces what the ablest governments are frequently unable to create; namely, an all pervading and restless activity, a superabundant force, and an energy which is inseparable from it and which may, however unfavorable circumstances may be, produce wonders. These are the true advantages of democracy."[24] Sentiments such as these have served as intellectual inspiration for a host of social scientists, ranging from Daniel Bell to Seymour Martin Lipset and Daniel Elazar, to draw upon the work of Tocqueville in contemporary studies of American politics. There is a double process at work: there is a long line of theory grounded in the authority of the political process which reached a pinnacle in Tocqueville, just as there is an equally long line of theory grounded in the power of the social and economic process which reached a pinnacle with Marx. The meeting ground of the two parallel traditions remains elusive.

It is critical to note that, for Tocqueville, the problem to be solved is the tyranny of the majority, that is, the functioning democracy itself. It essentially occupies the final portion of the first volume of *Democracy in America*, and the concerns that necessitated a second volume. Tocqueville is in dialogue with himself. First there is the unlimited power of the majority, and then there is the mitigation of such power, and finally the cultural triumph of democracy in one place on earth. For Tocqueville is constantly contrasting America with Europe, nearly always to the benefit of the former. "In the United States politics are the end and aim of education; in Europe its principal object is to fit men for private life. The interference of the citizen in public affairs is too rare an occurrence to be provided for beforehand. Upon casting a glance over society in the two hemi-

sphere, these differences are indicated even by their external aspect."[25]

The questions of slavery and sovereignty, yoked as they
were prior to the Civil War, were deeply disturbing to
Tocqueville. It is clear that he was on the side of freedom
and the North. But such was the nature of Tocqueville that
he could present the Southern argument for "nullification,"
and what we now refer to as secession. Rather than offer a
tendentious argument for the anti-slavery movement, he
points out that the United States was not formed as a "league"
but as a "national government." The will of the majority,
however distasteful it might be at times, remains the binding force sanctioned by the Constitution. And in the contest between Andrew Jackson and John C. Calhoun over the
nature of statehood, Tocqueville leaves little doubt that his
sympathies for the position are with Jackson while his sense
of the powers are with Calhoun. But without predicting the
nature of the conflict, Tocqueville appreciates the fact that
the tendency of the American nation is toward greater democracy and not the rise of an aristocracy in a European
model. "All the aristocracies of the Middle Ages were
founded by military conquest. Inequality was then imposed
by force; and after it had once been introduced into the
manners of the country, it maintained itself and passed naturally into the laws."[26] The entire second volume of *Democracy in America* can be considered a study of how the United
States was destined to be exempt from this process—by culture, manners, tradition and accident of geography. Americans were a "great civilized people" thrust in the midst of
an "uncultivated country." Tocqueville never doubted the
outcome of a war between states that had yet to come, and
whose end could not destroy the unitary character of the
people.

The need for the second volume of *Democracy in America*
emerged as a consequence of trying to understand why the
outcomes of the French and American revolutions were so

different—more concretely, why it was that two nations with similar doctrinal intent met with such a sharp diversity of outcomes. It was Tocqueville's great wisdom as a sociologist that led him to realize that what he derided in others, monocausal explanation, would yield a work lacking in persuasiveness. It was to character, what we now call culture, that he looked for answers. He found one answer in the egalitarian style that pervaded the entire American landscape. Hence, anticipating Veblen, he pointed out that "in the United States the more opulent citizens take great care not to stand aloof from the people; on the contrary, they constantly keep on easy terms with the lower classes: they listen to them, they speak to them every day."[27] Indeed, even the treatment of the slave population stunned Tocqueville by this display of ruling class welfare.

Individualism was combated not just by displays of magnanimity, but by voluntary association. Indeed, if there is a theme picked up by contemporaries it is this steady emphasis on associations large and small, converted into a general theory of communitarianism, as we shall see later in the work. And association works because self-interest "rightly understood" becomes "small acts of self-denial"; such small acts of a cooperate and compassionate nature "disciplines a number of persons in habits of regularity, temperance, moderation, foresight, self-command." The transvaluation of utilitarian theory into a general theory of the common good underlines the associations of the American people, but also insures them from again accepting tyranny as a political style.[28]

Tocqueville was especially intrigued by the distinction between passion and compassion that Hannah Arendt noted much later as the key difference between the French and American revolutions. In Europe, to the victor belonged not only the spoils of war, but also the heads of warriors defeated. But in that act of passion, the seeds of permanent political hostility were clear. In contrast, the American style was to punish lightly. Tocqueville remarks somewhat in astonishment, that "in no country is criminal justice administered with more mildness than in the United States."[29] We are reminded that the European tradition, from the Romans onward, was to slaughter defeated opponents, whereas in the United States, from its very origins, rehabilitation and, if needed, exile were the favored instruments of demonstrating who was in charge. This pattern of compassion carried through not just to the manners, mores, and sensitivities of Americans, but into the conduct of the political process. It helped ensure a careful balance between the majority and the minority, a furtive recognition that balances of force change in society as in nature.

While one might fault Tocqueville with a near idyllic picture of family life, education, the place of women, and the role of child rearing, there is no gainsaying his tough-minded appraisal of how these private virtues play out on the public canvas. But in an especially pithy conclusion to this whole area of private morality he notes a Rousseau-type paradox: "Democracy loosens social ties, but tightens natural ones; it brings kindred more closely together, while it throws citizens more apart."[30] Implicit in this judgment is that the state is curbed in its propensities to intervene in the area of private morals by virtue of the strength of private ties, and what he later refers to as "small private circles." For Tocqueville, the propensity to revolution making is far less in the United States than in Europe because the stake of the people in their land is much higher in America than in Europe; that ideas "which threaten to alter, in whatever manner, the laws of property" are rejected.[31] The equity in rights produces a common denominator in wants. And in such circumstances of consensus revolutions become rare and decreasingly likely. In a rare moment of personal preference, Tocqueville, sounding more like John Stuart Mill than Edmund Burke tells his readers that "personally, far from finding fault with equality because it inspires a spirit of independence, I praise it primarily for that very reason. I admire it because it lodges in the very depths of each man's mind and heart that indefinable feeling, the instinctive inclination for political independence, and thus prepare the remedy for the ill, which it engenders. It is precisely for this reason that I cling to it."[32]

What must continually astonish the contemporary reader of Tocqueville is how succinctly he saw the struggle between state and society, moreover, how he clearly preferred an outcome predicated on the society rather than the state. What makes this critical is a sensibility about political sociology that is only now coming to maturity. In his unique way, Tocqueville established the parameters of social life—egalitarianism, associatiionism, and communitarianism—within which sociology is now struggling. But he did so in the context of a political understanding far greater than that possessed by sociologists. He knew the centrality of politics, of government, administration, legislative, judicial and executive forms of power, and local and national sources of authority. In short, Tocqueville operated within a vortex so much of his times that it only appeared that he was speaking for the ages. Unlike the *philosophes* and the key figures of German romanticism, he started with human interaction in institutional settings, not with general theories of history.

The end of *Democracy in America* reminds us that the search for egalitarianism can "lead to servitude or freedom, to knowledge or barbarism, to prosperity or wretchedness."[33] It led to both as matters turned out. But it took a full one hundred years, until Weber, before such simple truths could be understood. As I indicated in the opening remarks, the canon of political sociology is real, but not as some stepping stone to paradise, not as a railway leading from valleys to mountains; rather, the canon is itself a representation of the struggle—in the realm of ideas as well as politics, in the realm of values as well as ideologies. We turn now to examples of just how the paradox of state and society worked its way out in the tortured world of a Europe moving with equal speed in 1848 to reaction and revolution—frequently confusing the one for the other.

The world of Europe in 1848 was nothing like the America of 1835 about which Tocqueville wrote. Benevolent despotism of the eighteenth century was a mode of government appropriate to a nation of serfs, artisans, and aristocrats, but in an epoch of urban concentration and factory production, such a system became a political millstone, a brake on modernization. As one historian pointed out: "The system of legitimate rule established in Europe after the Congress of Vienna, blind to the transformation of society which the French Revolution had introduced, failed to achieve a lasting stability. And the generation which reached maturity after the Battle of Waterloo lived through a time of bitter conflict, as the world of the past fought to remain alive."[34] The fact of the matter is that the aristocracy did stay alive. However, it did so in a quite new context, one in which the bourgeoisie had carved out a place for itself as dominant in the business sphere, and the working masses had begun to organize trade unions and political parties aimed at the overthrow of the bourgeoisie no less than the aristocracy. Polarization was the basic characteristic of Europe in the period beginning in 1848. And Tocqueville was both part of the old order and a harbinger of the new. Little wonder that a certain ambiguity which had been observed in his attitudes toward the United States surfaced to become a dominant factor in his thinking once he returned to the subject of Europe and its states.

The spirit of the age was one of radicalism and reaction, not liberalism. And the centrist values Tocqueville embodied were remote and increasingly difficult to locate in actual political struggles. He reaffirmed his belief that a republican form of government was ill suited for Europe and France in particular, yet he swore fealty to the Republic and its "ill balanced form of government, promising more freedom and giving less than a constitutional monarchy."[35] Tocqueville cleverly added "there were, so to speak, no Republicans in France." He well appreciated the spirit of fanaticism that had overtaken his land, and the fact that there would be little relief in sight. Indeed, he was correct to note that a radicalism bereft of reason was to dominate for the balance of the century and beyond.

The revolutions of 1848 that swept aside the old order confirmed the role of social class in nineteenth-century definitions of human relations. But far from leading to a consensus, this ineluctable fact widened the basic rift between democratic and authoritarian traditions, between advocates of social reform and those who claimed the need to use state power to overhaul social relations. More exactly, the policy aims of the liberals and conservatives alike were to mute the demands for social justice with much higher concerns for social welfare; whereas, the policy aims of the radicals and socialists were to accentuate the demands of social justice by using the rising working classes as a battering ram for social revolution. Tocqueville made his own position starkly clear: "I hate all those absolute systems that make all the events of history depend on great first causes linked together by the chains of fate and thus succeed, so to speak, in banishing men from the history of the human race. Antecedents, facts, the nature of institutions, turns of mind and the state of mores are the materials from which chance composes those impromptu events that surprise and terrify us."[36]

The battle lines between Tocqueville and Marx were now drawn. For Tocqueville, what doomed the revolutions of 1848, was not so much the weakness of the proletariat or the strength of the bourgeoisie, as it was the rise of political democracy without a corresponding rise of new political leadership. "Universal suffrage had shaken the land from top to bottom without bringing into prominence any new man deserving of attention."[37] In that sense, France, quite unlike the United States, was unable to develop a new political leadership corresponding to new social circumstances. It is a marvelous characteristic of Tocqueville that he confirms such a global judgment by observations such as: "I knew all the men"; "I had seen previously"; "[T]his Assembly was an improvement on anything I had seen before." He went to the Assembly debates, interacted with his friends, and spoke when he was of a mind to do so. Evidence and experience were ever linked in his way of looking at big events.

This linkage raised the sort of issues in the empirical analysis of politics that became fashionable one hundred years later. Indeed, the very inability of political leaders to move beyond the realm of "sermons" and "abstractions" doomed the political process of democratization—at least for a while. "We were unanimously in favor of entrusting executive power to a single man," notes Tocqueville. "But how to elect that man; what prerogatives and what subordinates to give him; and what responsibilities to load on him? Obviously, none of those questions could be dealt with in the abstract; each of them was of necessity linked to all the others and, especially, could be decided only with reference to the particular state of mores and customs in the country. Of course the problems were old, but the novelty of the circumstances made them new."[38] The differences between the empirical and rationalist styles of political sociology could hardly be made plainer.

Beyond the question of style is the matter of substance. Anticipating Weber by seventy years, Tocqueville expressed his concerns about expanding state power couched as a fear of centralization. "So when people say that we have nothing that is safe from revolutions, I tell them that they are wrong, that centralization is one thing." To underscore the point he adds that "in France there is only one thing that we cannot make free: a free government. How could it perish? The government's enemies love it, and the rulers cherish it." Concluding in an unusually bitter mood, Tocqueville noted that while "it is true that rulers notice that it occasionally exposes them to sudden, irremediable disasters, that does not make them disgusted with it. The pleasure of meddling with everything and holding everybody in the palm of their hands makes up for the danger."[39] The deep sense of contrast with legislative behavior in the United States was never far from his mind. Just how the American Revolution could use the French intellectual tradition as a model and yet far exceed his own country in the execution of democratic norms is a problem with which Tocqueville wrestled but never quite resolved. He had a sneaking suspicion that this had to do somehow with character, values and norms. But to have moved in that direction would have placed him back in the camp of the rationalists, especially German idealism—a place he hardly wanted to enter.

The aftershock of the 1848 revolutions impacted more than the French nation. Tocqueville had widely traveled in Germany and was profoundly aware that the force of "German organization" represented a dangerous confirmation of revolutionary fears. The failure of legislative power to topple German absolutism meant that neither the people nor the princes of Germany would submit to decrees and arguments. The political rubble "left room for the violent revolutionaries, who had always maintained that Germany could be led to unity only by the complete destruction of all its former governments and the abolition of the old social order." And if the starting point of Tocqueville and Marx differed, the concluding point was quite similar. "On all sides riots took the place of parliamentary debates. Political rivalries turned into class warfare, the natural hatreds and jealousies of the poor against the rich became socialist theories in many places, especially in the small states of Germany and in the great Rhine valley."[40] The monarchies transformed themselves into miniature garrison states, and the Prussian suppression of Saxony heralded a higher form of centralization. The King of Prussia, "a man of parts but with little common sense, had been wavering between fear of the revolution and eagerness to profit from it."[41] Tocqueville brilliantly explained how the King of Prussia became, at one and the same time, the champion of the welfare state and the leader of a military power with which to be reckoned. In this way, centralization entered a new level and a new realm— one to be explored by Weber at a much later date, but with the same fierce concerns over the damaging role of centralization and autocracy.

The line that runs from Montesquieu to Tocqueville is clearly not the same as that which moves from Rousseau to Marx. But in the very dialogue between civic association and state collective inheres the essential thread that defines the full range of options open to political sociology as nineteenth-century practice. But having said that, it must be understood that Tocqueville was the first to frame the issues in such a way as to make plain the policy choices for the West. That Tocqueville did so by a steady reference to real people residing in real nations only strengthened the unique nature of his contribution. His work enhanced the scientific study of comparative politics, but far more importantly, it revealed the social bases of political liberty and tyranny alike.

Notes

1. Robert A. Nisbet, *The Sociological Tradition*. New Brunswick and London: Transaction Books, 1994 (original edition, 1960), p 183.
2. James T. Kloppenberg, "Everybody's Tocqueville," *The Tocqueville Review* Vol. XVII, No. 2, 1996 (reprinted in *Newsletter of the Committee on Intellectual Correspondence*, Whole Number 2, Spring-Summer, 1998, pp.36–37).
3. Alexis de Tocqueville, *Democracy in America* (in two volumes). All references to this work are to the Henry Reeve Text of 1835–1840, as retranslated by Francis Bowen in 1862, and as further corrected and edited by Phillips Bradley in 1945. New York: Alfred A. Knopf, 1945, (vol. 2), pp.265–278.
4. Alexis de Tocqueville, *Old Regime and the French Revolution*. All references to this work are to the translation by Stuart Gilbert. New York: Doubleday/Anchor Books, 1983, p. ix.

5. Alexis de Tocqueville, *Old Regime and the French Revolution*. p. 57.

6. Alexis de Tocqueville, *Old Regime and the French Revolution*. p. 41.

7. Alexis de Tocqueville, *Old Regime and the French Revolution*. pp.16–17.

8. Alexis de Tocqueville, *Old Regime and the French Revolution*. pp. 68–69.

9. Alexis de Tocqueville, *Old Regime and the French Revolution*. p. 170.

10. Alexis de Tocqueville, *The Old Regime and the Revolution*, edited by Francois Furet and Francoise Melonio. Chicago and London: The University of Chicago Press, 1998, p.207. Alas, the chapter on Tocqueville was completed just before the appearance of a brilliant new edition of his masterpiece on the French revolutionary century. The translation by Alan S. Kahan is seamless—perhaps the best thing that can be said of a translation—and the opening essay by Francois Furet is written with such intimacy and depth that it is best to permit its reading without summary or paraphrase. Happily, I feel that my overall assessment requires no retooling in the light of Furet's effort, but for a sense of the inner life of pre-Revolutionary France it is now a standard by which all other assessments, including my own, will need to be judged.

11. Alexis de Tocqueville, *Recollections: The French Revolution of 1848*. All references to this work are to the edited version of J. P. Mayer and A.P. Kerr, in the translation by George Lawrence. New Brunswick and Oxford: Transaction Publishers, 1987, p.170.

12. Alexis de Tocqueville, *Recollections: The French Revolution of 1848*, p. 76.

13. Alexis de Tocqueville, *Old Regime and the French Revolution*, p. 22.

14. Alexis de Tocqueville, *Old Regime and the French Revolution*, p. 153.

15. Alexis de Tocqueville, *Old Regime and the French Revolution*, p. 13.

16. Alexis de Tocqueville, *Old Regime and the French Revolution*, p. 205.

17. Alexis de Tocqueville, *Old Regime and the French Revolution*, pp. 158, 163.

18. Karl Wittfogel, *Oriental Despotism*. Ann Arbor: Books on Demand-UMI, 1990 [reprint].

19. Walter Laqueur, *The Political Psychology of Appeasement*. New Brunswick and London: Transaction Publishers, 1980.

20. Contrary to academic mythology, Tocqueville was not the first to write a strong defense of the United States, or a sharp comparison with the foibles of the French Revolution. That honor belongs to Friedrich Gentz, whose book on *The French and American Revolutions Compared*, preceded *Democracy in America* by several decades. The work was translated by John Quincy Adams, and most recently published by Henry Regnery Publishers (Gateway Editions) in Chicago in 1955, with an introduction by Russell Kirk.

21. Alexis de Tocqueville, *Democracy in America*, pp. 3–5.

22. Alexis de Tocqueville, *Democracy in America*, pp. 102–109.

23. Alexis de Tocqueville, *Democracy in America*, pp. 128–129.

24. Alexis de Tocqueville, *Democracy in America*, pp. 261–262.
25. Alexis de Tocqueville, *Democracy in America*, p. 330.
26. Alexis de Tocqueville, *Democracy in America*, pp. 438–439.
27. Alexis de Tocqueville, *Democracy in America (volume two)*, pp. 111–112.
28. Alexis de Tocqueville, *Democracy in America (volume two)*, pp. 130–131.
29. Alexis de Tocqueville, *Democracy in America (volume two)*, pp. 176–77.
30. Alexis de Tocqueville, *Democracy in America (volume two)*, pp. 210–214, 226–227.
31. Alexis de Tocqueville, *Democracy in America (volume two)*, pp. 265–273.
32. Alexis de Tocqueville, *Democracy in America (volume two)*, pp. 304–305.
33. Alexis de Tocqueville, *Democracy in America (volume two)*, pp. 349–352.
34. Theodore S. Hamerow, *Restoration, Revolution, Reaction: Economics and Politics in Germany, 1815–1871*. Princeton: Princeton University Press, 1958, pp. 56–74.
35. Alexis de Tocqueville, *Recollections: The French Revolution of 1848*, pp. 200–201.
36. Alexis de Tocqueville, *Recollections: The French Revolution of 1848*, p. 62.
37. Alexis de Tocqueville, *Recollections: The French Revolution of 1848*, p. 104.
38. Alexis de Tocqueville, *Recollections: The French Revolution of 1848*, p. 176.
39. Alexis de Tocqueville, *Recollections: The French Revolution of 1848*, p. 170.
40. Alexis de Tocqueville, *Recollections: The French Revolution of 1848*, pp. 235–236.
41. Alexis de Tocqueville, *Recollections: The French Revolution of 1848*, pp. 244–245.

5

Utopianism as Scientific Sociology: Marx

"Ideology defeats and consumes itself even as it is in the process of being fulfilled; ideology exterminates its true believers. Marxism is the ideology that first spread the world over, the first ideology that gave the world a significant push to unite. Perhaps this is precisely why Marxism is condemned to vanish and to deny its own mission."

—*Milovan Djilas*[1]

The utopian spirit derives its appeal from being inherently optimistic and forward looking. This spirit is nowhere better exemplified than in the thoughts of Marx and Engels. The sense of eternal progress was the bequest of the Enlightenment that was most characteristic of their thought. Such a faith in the future was rapidly absorbed into the literature of nineteenth-century sociology. All human nature was seen as malleable; all moral goals were framed in the course of history; all history was a progressive march toward egalitarianism. But once the theory sought to get beyond the slogans, the tightly woven garment called Marxism began to show some threadbare spots; none were more apparent than the gap between the founders of scientific socialism themselves.

Engels defined the dialectic as "the science of the general laws of motion and development of nature, human society and thought." On this definition practically the entire range of knowledge falls within the scope of dialectics. Engels's elaboration and extension of Marx's essentially economic analysis of social change led him to suggest that the materialist conception of history was based on a set of immutable laws which could be applied to the physical universe, the biological realm, and the social world. (Georg Lukács's earlier view was that Engels misunderstood Marx when he extended the dialectical analysis outside the realm of history and society. But it was this extension that permitted later generations to characterize Marxism as sociology.) Engels completely failed to consider "the *dialectical relation between subject and object in the historical process*, let alone give it the prominence it deserves."[2] George Lichtheim also comments that the application of the dialectic to nature results in a choice between two unattractive alternatives: it is "to read an element of purposive striving into the structure of reality: in other words, to revert to romanticism," and second, it reduces the concept of dialectical change to a tautological proposition, in which any happening whatever is equal to a qualitative change from one state to another.[3]

Marxism, for generations of people, came to mean what Engels rather than Marx said it meant. *Anti-Dühring* in particular was the most influential text for two generations of socialists. It contributed to the development of scientism and positivism in both German Social Democracy and later in Soviet polemics on partisanship and objectivity in social research. For his part, Marx did not set forth his views on social science in any systematic fashion, nor did he ever speak of a dialectics of nature. Marx "permitted" Engels to have the exclusive say in this area.[4] According to Jordan, it was Engels who, unwittingly perhaps, "established the tradition which ascribed to Marx a coherent monistic system of materialist metaphysics in the accepted sense of this term, comprising a philosophy of nature, and a theory of society, each derived from a common set of first principles and logically supporting each other."[5] As a result, when one speaks of Marxian sociology, one is also referring to a schism within this tradition between socialism as a doctrine of society and dialectics as a doctrine of nature. This was a schism not simply between two colleagues, but between two worldviews inhabiting the same ideological frame of reference.

Marx was empirical in analysis, if not always in temper. Throughout, he condemned "a priori construction" and "drunken speculation." His analysis of social change arising from the interacting processes of nature, society and human consciousness, nevertheless, cannot be transmuted into an all-encompassing explanatory device. Engels, for his part, undertook his study of mathematics and natural science to convince himself that precisely such a holism could be achieved. He came to believe that "in nature, amid the welter of innumerable changes, the same dialectical laws of motion force their way through as those which in history govern the apparent fortuitousness of events; the same laws as those which similarly form the thread running through the history of the development of human thought and gradually rise to consciousness in the mind of man; the laws which Hegel first developed in all-embracing but mystic form, and which we made it one of our aims to strip of this mystic form and to bring clearly before the mind in their complete simplicity and universality."[6]

Engels dampened the distinction between the unique character of social development and development in nature by minimizing the role of human volition and maximizing the deterministic aspects of society. His historical materialism can never adequately comprehend this; consequently, his correspondence theory of knowledge is unable to explain that consciousness is social before it is individual, that is, that the process by which knowledge is attained and always set in concrete interactionist context.

It is ironic that Marx directed much of his attention in his early works towards a critique of classical materialism for its failure to take account of the role of human consciousness. The origins of Marx's epistemology are to be found both in German idealist philosophy and in his critique of mechanical materialism, summarized in the *Theses on Feuerbach* and elaborated in other works. Bottomore and Rubel have argued that Marx was not concerned with either ontological or epistemological problems.[7] This does not, however, render the attempt to find the nature of his epistemology a meaningless exercise. The task is made more difficult by the lack of any systematic exposition in his writings on this subject.

Much has been written about Marxism and the concept of "false consciousness," but little about the process of attaining "true knowledge" in Marxian terms. It is possible to discern three stages in Marx's thought on this subject. In the first period Marx maintained that true consciousness could only be attained through the creative activity of man, that is, through overcoming alienation in the social process connected with labor. This naturalization of Hegel had an essential drawback. It failed to determine the exact causes of social change. In the second period, Marx revealed a preoccupation with the class character of knowing, with the social sources and economic interests that define and delimit knowledge. In the final phase, he came to believe that the attainment of true knowledge would only be possible with the revolutionary overthrow of class society, that is, the politicization of the working class and its vanguard through the seizure of state power. It is this latest stage which Avineri is referring to when he states that "Marx's epistemology thus conceals an internal tension. It tries to solve the traditional epistemological problems, but it tacitly holds that human consciousness could operate according to the new epistemology only if the obstacles in its way in present society were eliminated. Hence Marx's epistemology is sometimes divided against itself: it is both a description of consciousness and a vision of the future."[8]

It is impossible to understand Marxian sociology outside the context of Hegel's philosophical idealism, since the foundations of his epistemology and material conception of history arise from his connection to German historiography in general and Hegel's philosophy of history in particular. Marx shared with Hegel a series of basic assumptions about history. Worth noting are their shared belief that history falls into distinctive epochs; these epochs represent a shift in development from East to West. In addition, they believed that history is progressive, revealing improvements in cultural as well as material conditions. This of course is what both shared with the Enlightenment tradition. And while Hegel located the high point in history in German Protestantism, Marx postponed his high point to a Universal Communism yet to come into existence. The importance of this high point is that, for Hegel, the agency of history is the *Geist* or Spirit; whereas for Marx it is the social class uniquely gifted to see the contours of the future and seize state power to bring about that future.

According to Hegel, what appears as an external object is a projection of consciousness. Mind as self-consciousness knows the nonexistence of the distinction between the object and itself, because it knows the object as its self-alienation. The actual character of the object constitutes estrangement from self-consciousness. Since the object exists only as an alienation from self-consciousness, to take it back into the subject would mean the end of objective reality and thus of any reality at all. For Hegel, the highest stage of absolute spirit is attained with the abolition of alienation and the return of consciousness to itself. According to Marx, this is nothing but the self-objectification of the philosophic mind; Hegel's philosophy suffers from the illusion that the object of philosophy is philosophy itself—an illusion that Feuerbach addressed by demanding a materialist interpretation of theology.

History exists so that truth can be revealed. It thus be-comes a metaphysical subject of which human individuals are the mere representatives. "Hegel's view of history pre-supposes an abstract or *Absolute Spirit* which develops in such a way that mankind is only a Mass, a conscious or uncon-scious vehicle for Spirit. Hence Hegel provides for the de-velopment of a speculative, esoteric history within empiri-cal, or exoteric history. The history of mankind becomes the history of the *abstract spirit* of mankind, thus a spirit *beyond* man."[9] This point was also made in the *Economic and Philosophic Manuscripts*,[10] where Marx states that Hegel, in the *Phenomenology* reduces the material world and the prod-ucts of man's activity to mere thought entities and products of abstract mind.[11] Thought takes its own action for sensu-ous, real action.

Despite the severity of his intellectual assault, Marx ac-knowledged the seminal influence of Hegel on his thoughts.[12] Indeed, although he was closer in point of view to the materialist Feuerbach, he recognized the essential brilliance of Hegel in contrast to the pedestrian qualities in Feuerbach. In 1844, in the manuscript entitled "Critique of the Hegelian Dialectic and Philosophy as a Whole," he praised Hegel's conception of the origins and development of man, that is, for his understanding that man creates him-self in a historical process, of which the driving force is hu-man labor. "The outstanding achievement of Hegel's *Phe-nomenology* is thus first that Hegel conceives the self-creation of man as a process, conceives objectification as loss of the object, as both alienation and the transcendence of this alienation; that he thus grasps the essence of *labor* and com-prehends the objective man...as the outcome of man's *own labor*."[13]

Hegel's "error" inheres in the fact that he sees only the positive, and not the negative side of labor. "The only labor which Hegel knows and recognizes is *abstractly mental la-bor*."[14] It is only the abstraction of man—self-consciousness, not active man—who is made the subject; man's objective essence, therefore, according to Hegel, is his alienated self-consciousness. Alienation is a purely spiritual phenomenon, the overcoming of which leaves unchanged existing social and political institutions. The "negation of the negation," that is, the superseding of alienation—mind recognizing that objects which appear to exist outside it are merely a phenomenal expression of consciousness—is a confirmation of a pseudo-essence. Self-conscious man, who denies the reality and independent existence of the material world, confirms his abstract self as his true self. In summary, Marx says, "within the sphere of abstraction, Hegel conceives labor as man's act of self-genesis." This act of self-genesis appears "first of all as a merely formal, because abstract act, because the human essence itself is taken to be only an abstract, thinking essence, conceived merely as self-consciousness.... Real man and real nature become mere predicates—symbols of this esoteric, unreal man and his unreal nature."[15]

Marx identifies human consciousness with the process of man's shaping reality. Man shapes nature: reality is always social reality, what Feuerbach earlier described as anthropological philosophy. "The production of ideas, of conceptions, of consciousness is directly interwoven with the material activity and the material relationships of men; it is the language of actual life. Conceiving, thinking, and the intellectual relationships of men appear here as the direct result of their material behavior. Consciousness can never be anything else except conscious existence, and the existence of men is their actual life-process."[16]

The basic premise of the argument in *The German Ideology* is that historiography must proceed from the existence of social individuals, who are distinguished from animals not by the fact that they think, but by the fact that they have a culture, that is, produce their means of subsistence. What people are coincides with what they produce and how they produce it. When this fact is realized, history ceases to be a

collection of dead facts, or an imaginary activity of imagined subjects, as it is with the idealists.[17] History has been
speculatively distorted by Hegelian idealism; historical
change is not an abstract act of "self-consciousness" but a
completely material, empirically verifiable act. The materialist conception of history, proceeding quite inexorably from
the Feuerbachian legacy, "arrives at the conclusion that all
forms and products of consciousness cannot be dissolved
by mental criticism, by resolution into "Self-consciousness"
or transformation into "apparitions," "specters," "fancies"
etc., but only by the practical overthrow of the actual social
relations which gave rise to this idealistic trickery."[18]

The social world exists as a necessary condition for the
process of social and personal awareness. It is only natural
that man, as a living, sensuous being, equipped with material powers, should have real natural objects as part of his
world. "A being which has no objects outside itself is not an
objective being. Objects in the world must become the objectification of man, assisting him in realizing and confirming his individuality. Man as a human natural being has to
confirm and manifest himself as such both in his being and
in his knowing."[19] It follows, therefore, that "knowing" cannot be limited merely to mental activity.

On this ground Marx attacked those who styled themselves
as "Young Hegelians." He did so by employing Feuerbach's
materialism *sans* mechanism. Marx praised Feuerbach for
making the social relationship of man to man the basis of
his theory, while, for Engels, his work represented the convergence of humanism and materialism in the theoretical
sphere.[20] Feuerbach's most serious limitation, according to
Marx, was that he saw man only as a sensuous object, not
man as sensuous activity. This was reflected in a materialist
critique of religion and theology rather than society and
economy. Feuerbach's view revealed a double limitation: first,
he failed to see that the world is more than an abstract
"given," but the product of the activity of a succession of

generations, continually in a process of change. Second, he did not recognize that the ultimate task of philosophy is not merely to supply an adequate cognition of the world, but a framework for changing the world in anticipated directions.

The Young Hegelians were subjected to an even more severe attack for their claims to have revolutionized philosophy when in fact they attacked not the actual existing world but merely the phrases of this world, that is, German idealism. They adopted Feuerbach's critique of the Hegelian dialectic as their own, and reduced the whole process of history to the relation between the rest of the world and their own philosophy. Bauer, for example, far from moving beyond Hegel's *Phenomenology*, had simply learnt "the art of transforming real, *objective* chains existing outside *me* into *merely ideal*, merely *subjective* chains existing *in me* and hence the art of transforming all external, sensuous struggles into mere struggles of thought."[21]

Stirner also assumed that ideas dominated past history and that real conditions were modeled on man and his ideal conditions, that is, on the nature of man, thus making the "history of the consciousness men have of themselves the basis of their real history." The "Critical Critics" were further rebuked for believing that they had arrived at the beginning of the knowledge of historical reality, while excluding from the historical process the theoretical and practical relations of man to nature, that is, natural science and industry. For Marx, reality, viewed by classical materialism as a passive object of perception, is shaped by men and reacts on men. This point is made in the First Thesis on Feuerbach: "The chief defect of all previous materialism (including Feuerbach's) is that the object, actuality, sensuousness is conceived only in the form of the *object or perception,* but not as *sensuous human activity, practice (Praxis),* not subjectively. Hence in opposition to materialism the active side was developed by idealism—but only abstractly since idealism naturally does not know actual, sensuous activity as such.

Feuerbach wants sensuous objects actually different from thought objects: but he does not comprehend human activity itself as *objective*. Consequently, he does not comprehend the significance of 'revolutionary,' of 'practical-critical' activity."[22]

The second stage in Marxian thought was far less sanguine about the realization of knowledge through labor and the overcoming alienation through self-understanding. By the late 1850s, or what might be called the *Grundrisse* period, Marx had grown weary of the possibility of individual self-realization—or for that matter, the philosophical character of the process of knowing. He had also grown weary of labor as a sheer learning experience. Rather, he saw the problem of knowledge in terms of the problem of social systems.

Knowledge under capitalism is purely instrumental. It is a source of alienation because of its one-sided demystification of experience. Capitalism gives a scientific character to production, but does not give a scientific character to the relationships of human beings within the production process. The process of labor, which in the earlier phase was to be the source of knowledge and liberation, is thereby reduced within capitalism to an element of technology and little else. "The development of the means of labor into machinery is not fortuitous for capital; it is the historical transformation of the traditional means into means adequate for capitalism. The accumulation of knowledge and skill, of the general productive power of society's intelligence, is thus absorbed into capital in opposition to labor and appears as the property of capital or more exactly of fixed capital, to the extent that it enters into the production process as an actual means of production. The tendency of capital is thus to give a scientific character to production, reducing direct labor to a simple element in this process."[23]

When Marx turns to the question of knowledge under communism in the middle period or economic stage, leisure and labor become factors. In a mood almost reminiscent of

Aristotle, he sees the need and the possibility of "leisure time" for the "higher activities." In the realm of communist freedom both leisure and labor define and determine the character of what we know. And in this world of communism, practice becomes equated with experimental science on one hand and historical science on the other, the latter being the accumulated wisdom of society as a whole: "Free time, which includes leisure time as well as time for higher activities, naturally transforms anyone who enjoys it into a different person, and it is this different person who then enters the direct process of production. The man who is being formed finds discipline in this process, while for the man who is already formed, it is practice, experimental science, materially creative and self-objectifying knowledge, and he contains within his own head the accumulated wisdom of society."[24]

In this second stage of the Marxian vision of knowledge there is a liberating power of the economy per se. The way in which economic transformations permit exact knowledge is no longer a matter of individual effort, no longer a matter of knowledge searching for its true opposite; but rather the way in which economic evolution, first one-sidedly through the capitalist expansion of natural science, and then multidimensional through the socialized concept of the human sciences, permits a knowledge without distortion. False consciousness dissolves in social practice rather than in introspective or even experiential reflections.[25]

At this time Marx came to believe that social practice had its roots and origins in work. His criticism of Adam Smith's negative attitude towards work in the *Grundrisse*[26] indicates a basic infusion of sociologism into the earlier materialism of the 1840s. Marx spoke of labor as an entity existing for others, or labor establishing itself objectively as its own non-being. Labor exists as a mere potentiality of creating values: "the entire real wealth, the world of real value and likewise the real conditions of its own realization are placed in opposition to it as entities with an independent existence."[27] The injustice of capitalism is precisely due to the deprivation of wealth from those who produce wealth—the laborers.[28]

The *Grundrisse* reveals that Marx retained his belief in the possibility of human emancipation expressed in the early writings. But his work in the interim "economic" period gave him a heightened awareness of the strength of the economic and ideological forces operating against labor. He became less optimistic about the possibilities of attaining knowledge through labor since the increasing mechanization of industry dehumanizes the worker and divorces him from the intellectual potentialities of the labor process. His writing at this time indicates a more economic view of the source of knowledge and a skeptical attitude towards the possibility of overcoming alienation through self-understanding. Knowledge and practice are still intimately related, but the emphasis is now placed on the class struggle and the movement of larger social forces. Marx came to see the question of knowledge in terms of the overall problem of social change—hence the emphasis placed on the class character of knowledge and the revolutionary practice of the proletariat. Revolutionary practice came to be regarded as both the foundation of the knowledge and the criterion of truth.[29]

In the third stage, which is by 1875, Marx was arguing that the existence of inequality in capitalist society rendered the attainment of true knowledge impossible. In the *Critique of the Gotha Program*, he maintained that equal rights for labor meant simply bourgeois rights: the rights of the workers are proportional to the labor they supply, and labor is used as a standard measurement of worth. "This equal *right* is an unequal right for unequal labor. It recognizes no class differences, because everyone is only a worker like everyone else. *It is therefore a right of inequality in its content, like every right*."[30]

Marx consigned to the "realm of necessity" the sphere of productive human activity, the sphere that in the 1840s he had believed to be the arena where man would attain true consciousness of himself and his world. The realm of freedom began only beyond it, with the attainment of state power by the proletariat. We find therefore a concern with the attainment of state power, and, on the theoretical level, a move from political economy to political sociology. "The early Marx was anticipating the imminent rise of revolutionary 'consciousness' in response to a developing capitalism; the later Marx was investigating the lack of such 'consciousness' despite a developed capitalism."[31]

The crucial role of practice is retained throughout, although the modes of practice change in the three stages. Man acts upon the world, from which he derives his knowledge of it: first, in the social laboring process, second in the character of the class struggle, and third in the struggle for control of state power. Action not directed towards the theory and practice of social change will lead, not to knowledge, but to the furthering of an illusory ideology. Marx's theory of knowledge is therefore closely connected to his view of history and the process of man's advancement—not economic history alone, but the relationship between political change and economic exploitation.

Marx took from Hegel the idea that reality is not mere objective datum, but is shaped by man through consciousness, and combined it with a materialist epistemology derived from both the anthropological materialism of Feuerbach and the earlier naturalism of Diderot, Holbach and Helvétius, which took full cognizance of man's role in shaping his social world. Marx could never agree that consciousness is nothing but a reflection of the material conditions of man's existence, the position later adopted by Engels and Lenin, for this view is antithetical to his belief in the possibility of human emancipation through social practice. This emphasis on the social rather than the psychological clearly endeared Marx to a later generation of sociologists. But it was to create troubling problems in understanding how a social system is both inevitable and yet the product of human wills.

Knowledge is intended to serve the partisan interests of the proletariat, which are both the most exploited class and the embodiment of the true interests of society, so that human emancipation will follow the emancipation of the proletariat. The working class can, by its own efforts, liberate humanity, for only this class is in a position to understand the laws of social development and to perceive history as the working out of these laws. "When a class attains consciousness of what it is doing, of the role it plays in production, it discovers the secret of the whole society of which it is a part."[32] This explains Marx's insistence on workers' associations as representative of a constructive effort to prepare the way for self-emancipation. Productive forces and social individuals appear to capital only as means, but they must provide the material conditions for effecting social change on the part of the proletariat.

The basis of Marx's theory of social change is his analysis of man as a social animal. Men perform labor, i.e., they create and reproduce their existence in daily practice, by working in nature and eventually consciously changing it. Society and nature are part of a single system, so that social evolution is observable in the growing emancipation of man from nature and in his growing control over nature. Marx maintained that ultimately the natural sciences would lose their abstract material or idealistic tendency and become the basis of social science, as they were already the basis of the technological order in an estranged form. Natural science, through the medium of industry and technology, had already prepared the way for emancipation in economy and society. "Human history itself is a *real* part of *natural history*—of nature developing into man. Natural science will in time incorporate into itself the science of man, just as science of man will incorporate into itself natural science: there will be *one* science."[33]

This statement led Marxists to argue that "dialectical analysis is valid for any content. By incorporating the experimental sciences...and using them to verify itself, it can therefore discover, even in Nature, the complex but still analyzable Becoming."[34] This view comes upon the hard fact that in terms of Marx there are no basic assumptions that the acceptance of dialectical materialism is a pre-condition for gaining scientific truth. Marx believed in the independent existence of the external world and denied the independent existence of mind without matter, but these were not the premises from which a holistic view of dialectical materialism was inferred.

The only evidence we have that Marx embraced the historical materialism of Engels, or his copy theory about sensations being images of objects in the external world, comes from Engels himself (plus the fact that Marx approved the publication of *Anti-Dühring*). The fact that Marx and Engels collaborated over a period of fifty years does not mean that work by biographical fiat constitutes a spiritual union. This impression of intellectual commonality gained currency as a result of Engels's effort to disseminate Marx's views over the thirteen-year period separating his death in 1895 from that of Marx in 1882. It is less a matter of intellectual fusion than strategic dissemination.

Engels made several contradictory statements about the unity of science, which have implications for later disputes over the question of whether Marxism is the ultimate philosophy or the end of all philosophy. He appeared to exempt dialectics from the predicted positivistic dissolution of all philosophy,[35] and adopted a didactic approach to scientists who believed they could escape its laws: "Natural scientists may adopt whatever attitude they please, they will still be under the domination of philosophy. It is only a question whether they want to be dominated by a bad, fashionable philosophy or by a form of theoretical thought that rests on acquaintance with the history of thought and its achievements. Natural scientists allow philosophy to prolong a pseudo-existence by making shift with the dregs of the old metaphysics. Only when natural and historical science have adopted dialectics will all the philosophic rubbish, outside the pure theory of thought, be superfluous, disappearing in positive science."[36]

Engels's adversary in the unfinished manuscripts, published under the title *Dialectics of Nature,* was "narrow-minded empiricism," which he contrasted with his own "moderate materialism." In this work, and in *Anti-Dühring,* he distinguished three fields for the application of dialectics: nature, history and human thought. The realm of knowledge was divided into three components: the exact sciences, biological sciences and historical sciences, with different degrees of truth obtainable in each.[37] The first group includes all sciences dealing with inanimate matter. The sciences are generally susceptible to mathematical treatment, and certain results obtained in them are final and ultimate truths. The ultimate truths found in the second group is platitudes of the type: "all female mammals have lacteal glands." But eternal truths are in an even worse plight in the historical sciences, which can offer ultimate truths of the sorriest kind, such as "Napoleon died May 5, 1821."[38] Engels's argument for the relativity of knowledge was distorted by Lenin in favor of the Hegelian notion of the concreteness of truth.[39]

Lenin argued that no particular thing could be comprehended unless it is examined in a universal context that reflects the structure of reality as a whole. Thus the determination of particular things presupposes knowledge of universal concrete principles, which are found in the laws of dialectics. On the basis of these laws, knowledge of absolutely true empirical propositions is obtainable, since if the premises are true; the conclusions must be true. His view led to latter-day claims that dialectical materialism is in possession of immutable and incontrovertible truths. The fallacious reasoning of this theory has been adequately discussed elsewhere.[40] It is sufficient for these purposes to establish a distinction between the modest claims of Marx on behalf of dialectical materialism, and the grandiose claims of his followers on behalf of historical materialism.

The copy theory of perception, which maintained that sensations and concepts were "copies, photographs, images, mirror-reflections of things," was based on Engels' approach to the problem of knowledge. Engels had argued that matter not only preceded spirit, but that it was also the cause and source of the evolution of consciousness. The justification for this claim was supposed to be provided by the laws of the materialistic dialectic.[41] Engels adopted a common sense, naively realistic approach to the problem of knowledge. He was not particularly concerned with the epistemological question concerning the relation of thought to reality, and believed that any problems that might arise could be simply disposed of. For Engels, "There was no doubt that we know things as they actually are and not as they appear to us, for whatever we experience—feelings, thoughts, impulses, volitions—is the effect of the external world acting on the human brain."[42] The "dialectics of the brain" were only the reflection of the forms of motion in the real world: these basic laws of motion were always the same irrespective of whether they referred to the motion of physical bodies, human society or thought. Experiment and practice, he believed, would be sufficient to overcome any objections to this theory. "Thought and consciousness...are products of the human brain and man himself is a product of nature, which has, developed in and along with its environment; hence it is self-evident that the products of the human brain and man himself is a product of nature, which has, developed in and along with its environment; hence it is self-evident that the products of the human brain, being in the last analysis products of nature, do not contradict the rest of nature's interconnections but are in correspondence with them."[43]

Lenin claimed that his theory of knowledge proved that there could be no limit to social knowledge: the only difference could be between what is known and what is not yet known. He assumed that a corresponding relation existed between sensations and external reality, mediated by class interests to be sure, by virtue of which the world is knowable. Nature, which for Engels and Lenin exists independently of human beings and yet is completely knowable, was for Marx a nullity, a nothing. The humanized world is knowable because it is world shaped by man according to his needs. In 1844 Marx wrote: "It is clear...that thinghood is therefore utterly without any *independence,* and *essentiality vis-à-vis* self-consciousness; that on the contrary it is a mere creature—something *posited* by self-consciousness."[44] In this inheres the fundamental naturalism and anti-dogmatism of Marx's theory of knowledge.

Any theory of knowledge that propounds that sensations are literal copies of objects and that of themselves they give knowledge leads towards fatalism and mechanism. It was against such mechanism that Marx had proclaimed that human beings make their own history, albeit not in ways always imagined. His theory of knowledge was based on the assumption that the world around us was not a "thing" given directly from all eternity, but was constantly molded by man's theoretical and practical activity. In that sense, he presaged the essential impulse of modern relativity.[45]

Marx rejected the Hegelian principle that the idea and reality are identical, and argued that philosophical thought alone could never overcome the discrepancy between them. This goal could only be achieved through revolutionary practice, leading to the abolition of private property and the establishment of socialist society. The revolutionary practice which changes the world and the knowing process were, for Marx, inseparable. The knowing subject, in his view, should be conceived as a socially active person, the representative of a particular social class—not as a passive recipient of sensations, which are wrought in the senses by out-side causes. The destruction of Marx's original conception is most apparent in the *partinost* view of philosophy, where it is maintained that the philosophy of dialectical material-ism is the foundation of scientific socialism, providing it with a coherent world view, a criterion of truth, and a uni-tary method over and above the particular sciences.[46] Through such reasoning, Marxism at one and the same time was converted into a series of dogmatic platitudes, and made inoperative in helping to explain any specific science or social science by virtue of the re-entry of Marxism as an abstraction.

The universalistic tendencies in Marxism resulted in con-verting Marxism into a ritual ordering of events rather than a descriptive science. The great advantage in seeing and judg-ing Marxism as part of the tradition of sociology rather than economy is that in the crucible of testing its general proposi-tions in the light of new findings, Marxism is preserved from ossification and obfuscation. Those who wanted Marxism as a secular new theology have given up the most vital aspect of Marxism: its ability to help explain and predict movements in the social world. But this outcome was made inevitable by the nature of scientific materialism as such, a view with con-flict as the necessary means and communism as the neces-sary end. As a result, science itself became falsified.

Marx accepted as his primary responsibility the analysis of social and economic systems, particularly how these sys-tems become transformed over time, and how contending classes are the instruments for bringing about such changes. Although he made occasional bows in the direction of a universal worldview, such as in the Preface to *Das Kapital,* he never explicated a *Weltanschauung* that would be appli-cable to both the physical and the social sciences. His aims were ambitious, but not grotesque: to explain the processes of social development as a dialectical movement in which human volition and conscious behavior play a vital role. He may have been a determinist, but he was not a pre-determinist. He accepted the idea of laws and law-like behavior in human events, but not as something apart from and over against the will of ordinary people. The fundamental relations contending social forces and classes enter into; change these forces and relationships, and the inexorable features of the laws of society, likewise, are subject to alteration make what is "inexorable."

What made Marx limit his effort to the social order is the presumption, increasingly subject to challenge, that man, unique among biological species, and certainly far beyond the capacity of inanimate objects, is both the subject and the object of history. At any time, he is confronted with limited or at least finite options, but he is not limited to the pursuit of any one of these options. In some curious way, Marx wrestled with policy options to an inconclusive point: meliorating changes were possible, but only if historical inevitabilities were not sacrificed. But as long as this dualism was in force, socialism as a movement became constantly roiled in debates about class capitulation and collaboration. Every effort at melioration was subject to attack by the determinists, while every determinist slogan was subject to critique by the meliorists. Marxism in practice could no more resolve the case for human potential in theory than any other political or social doctrine of the nineteenth century.

The possibility of error came from both sides, from the meliorists and determinists alike. The so-called scientific interpretation of Marxism reduces to a predeterminism, to a physicalism that eliminates the need for struggle and, hence, puts an end to the essential dramaturgy of Marxian socialism: a system that is ubiquitous, incomplete, and essentially far less open to empirical scrutiny than, say, the errors and terrors of capitalism. Thus, the volitional aspects in Marx permit precisely what the predeterminism in Engels tends to dampen: revolutionary action by exploited actors. The socialist legacy is ambiguous; in addition, the problem of knowledge is ubiquitous. The implausible task of Marxism was to transcend ambiguity and dissolve ubiquity. What is set forth by Marx in *stages* is presented by latter-day socialism as *options*—or at the least, different ways of viewing the relationship of socialism to the accumulation and uses of knowledge.

What emerged over time in Marx represents three clearly defined options for a socialist vision of scientific knowledge and the process of human liberation. It is no accident that "mechanistic" versus "dialectical" visions of exact knowledge competed for preeminence in the formative period of Soviet socialism. Metaphysical versus positivist interpretations of knowledge has continually vied for attention in Western socialism. As a result, a huge struggle between "early," "middle," and "late" varieties of Marxian analysis have found representatives at one time or another in different movements of the struggle on behalf of socialism.

Socialism had such a towering figure in Marx that the impulse to justify any given course of action by doctrinal references becomes overpowering. Unlike the philosophical preeminence of Thomas Aquinas within the Roman Catholic Church, which was established centuries later by papal edict, the preeminence of Karl Marx emerged out of the special circumstances of nineteenth-century Europe. The struggle for socialism at that time inevitably required legitimization and justification in Marx.

Since then, while there can be no satisfactory answer concerning "periodicity" in Marx, or even which aspect of Marxism is specifically suited to what form of socialist vision, we can at least show how each of the major expressions within contemporary socialism (social democracy, Old-Left Bolshevism, New-Left Revisionism) reflects the peculiar historical antecedents that are to be found in Marx's thought. The socialist vision of knowledge concerns less the matter of knowledge and more that of democratic horizons. The socialist movement has cleaved not nearly as much over the doctrinal contents of Marxism as over the right to access to certain forms of knowledge. This right is either guaranteed or blocked by how one evaluates the relationships of Marxism itself as a body of knowledge to the general accumulated knowledge of the sciences and social sciences.

Marx's attitude toward the problem of knowledge exhibits three basic stages—corresponding to his philosophic, economic and political concerns. In Marx these three stages correspond to three strategic responses by socialism as a system to the problem of knowledge. The first "philosophic" stage covers Marx's attitudes between 1840 and 1848 highlighted by his writings in the *Economic and Philosophic Manuscripts of 1844–1845*. The second "economic" stage, comes after the production of *The Communist Manifesto,* and is largely contained in the *Foundations for a Critique of Political Economy*. The final "political" stage corresponds to Marx's growing movement away from an economic determinism to a political variable of state power and cannot simply be spoken of in "long-run" terms, but as the essential pivot in the immediate practical struggle, just as the economic arena is the essential area of class contradictions. For Marx, the *class contradictions* manifested in the economic realm resolve themselves in the *class struggles* that take place in the political realm. How Marx viewed knowledge profoundly affected how socialism generally reacted to the question of the positive fruits of science and technology.

Althusser's four-fold classification represents an improvement over earlier formulations of the "young Marx" and the "mature Marx." He gives us the following period table: "1840–44: the Early Works; 1845: The Works of the Break; 1845–1857: the Transitional Works; 1857–83: the Mature Works."[47] But he too has considerable trouble with these formal categories. Phrases like "the works of the break" and "the transitional works" express a sentiment more than a temporal reality. I will concentrate on three distinct and distinctive views of the relationship of knowledge to society and of science to socialism.

Hyppolite sees in Hegel's philosophy "a remarkably creative attempt to give a philosophical account of spiritual
relations and to describe the human situation, in the course
of which we believe we have found the source of Hegel's
dialectical thought. To Hegel what is fundamental in experience is the experience of spiritual relations and their development: the relation between man and man, between the
individual and society, God and man, between master and
slave." [48] That is an apt description of the tasks laid out by
Hegel in *The Phenomenology of Mind*. And while a certain
formal continuity does exist between Hegel and Marx, it is
hard to confront the evidence and deny that Marx was mo-
tivated by a total reversal of philosophical priorities: the
materialization of the spirit which he derived from
Feuerbach; the relationship between man and man as an
uneven contest of superordinate and subordinate classes
which he derived from classical economics from Smith to
Ricardo; and the study of how to break and not simply comprehend relationships between master and slave, derived
pragmatically from the French Revolution and theoretically
from the European Enlightenment. The rupture between
Hegel and Marx is real enough, whatever the methodological linkages through dialectic. What must be established is
how Marx viewed the process of exact knowledge as a function of socioeconomic conditioning and political liberation.

In his synthetic study of Marxism, Rudolf Schlesinger
concludes with a clear economic interpretation of Marxist
doctrine, as if it were consistent from start to finish.[49] His
interpretation corresponds with the second phase in Marx,
and the second type of socialist vision. Marxism is considered a theory of social dynamics, and nothing else. It is impossible to prove its basic tenets except by the way in which
the freeing of one class from the clutches of another proves
to be the key independent variable. This transition from a
political economy to a political sociology is precisely the
characteristic of Marxism in its later stages—one that is far

less addressed than the earlier transition from a philosophic to an economic perspective in Marxian socialism.

For Marx and for the socialist tradition generally, there could be no theory of knowledge without a theory of society. The sources of knowledge are connected to the act. The nature of that act may change over time, located first in the minds of laboring individuals, then in the character of economic class struggles, and finally in the competition for domination and control of state authority. But whatever the modality, true knowledge is derived from exact practice, not as an arbitrary slogan, but as an article of faith within the Marxist-socialist tradition.

Marx was taking on the history of philosophical theory, especially the Platonic-Aristotelian world, in which a series of great dualisms were not only sanctioned but encouraged: the gap between mind and matter; man and nature; and theory and practice. For Marx, this series of dualism is the substance of alienation in history. What appears as a series of fundamental distinctions in the history of philosophy, represented to Marx nothing more than the inabilities of all class society to resolve the differences between true knowledge and false consciousness. Avineri understood this point in noting the distance between theory and practice in the world of Aristotle, and in viewing Marx as an effort to bridge that gap.[50] Theory and practice became aspects of social existence.

Aristotle located both theoretical and practical expressions of knowledge within a naturalistic and not a transcendental realm of theoretical knowledge. Marx himself appreciated the naturalistic character of Aristotle's thought and expressed this in his rejection of the "vulgar" materialism of Lange and Buchner.[51] The larger position Avineri takes is sound. The classical conservative view does hinge on an unresolved dualism between theory and practice—with the former elevated to new heights.

Our concern is with the way in which a periodic tabulation with Marx led to a differential view of the role of knowledge in the life of man and society. At first, Marx saw knowledge as related to history rather than action: "history is a true natural history of man;"[52] and at the same time that history is located in societal consciousness, it is brought down from its Hegelian pedestal. Marx did this by naturalizing the world of knower and known. During this first period, he favors naturalism rather than materialism: "Consistent naturalism or humanism distinguishes itself from both idealism and materialism, constituting at the same time the unifying truth of both. We see also how only naturalism is capable of comprehending the act of world history."[53] The problem of knowledge becomes a relational problem, an experientially determined and defined event: "The way in which consciousness is, and in which something is for it, is *knowing*. Knowing is its sole act. Something therefore comes to be for consciousness in so far as the latter knows this *something*. Knowing is its sole objective relation."[54]

Marx often referred to the one-sidedness and limitations in Hegel—usually with reference to the *Phenomenology*. During this period the problems that Marx dealt with in terms of knowledge derived precisely from what Hegel referred to as absolute knowledge, or the way in which the individual transcends his alienation through the act of knowing an external environment. Exact knowledge becomes the basic modality for liberation. What Marx does deal with and Hegel was unable to get at, is the role of labor and work in the process of learning. Marx accepted the Hegelian framework, but through the labor process understood the role of the learning process: "The only labor, which Hegel knows and recognizes, is abstractly mental labor. Therefore, that which constitutes the essence of philosophy—the alienation of man in his knowing of himself, or alienated science thinking itself—Hegel grasps as its essence; and he is therefore able to gather together the separate elements and phases of previous philosophy, and to present his philosophy as the philosophy. Hegel knows what the other philosophers did—that

they grasped separate phases of nature and of human life as
phases of self-consciousness—from the *doings* of philosophy.
Hence his science is absolute."[55]

What we have in this first stage is what might be called
the educative path to human liberation: knowledge as a liberating device, and work as the basic learning instrument
for the realization of such liberation. Hegel gave Marx his
first deep commitment to the idea of communism as the
society of total labor dedication. This is not just a naive stage
in Marxist development, but the Enlightenment ideal in its
Germanic form, in its specifically naturalized version of the
Hegelian vision of coming to truth, coming to grips with
the problem of knowledge. Socialism (or communism in this
sense) is not much different from Hegel's vision of absolute
knowledge—a society in which every person is realized in
the free pursuit of self-understanding through social labor.

By the time of *The Communist Manifesto*, Marx had broken away from the German philosophic tradition and the
German juridical tradition that Hegel inadvertently had
spawned. In one of the most biting paragraphs in the *Manifesto*, Marx and Engels announced their liberation from the
idealist vision of knowledge as well as the capitalist vision
of society. "The robe of speculative cobwebs, embroidered
with flowers of rhetoric, steeped in the dew of sickly sentiment, this transcendental robe in which the German socialists wrapped their sorry 'eternal truths,' all skin and bone,
served to wonderfully increase the sale of their goods among
such a public. And on its part, German socialism recognized
more and more its own calling as the bombastic representative of the petty-bourgeois Philistine."[56] Marx took as his
next task moving beyond his criticism of Philistinism, Chauvinism and the meanness of this model man, into a more
economic view of the source of both knowledge and its
distortion.

The second stage in Marxian thought was far less sanguine about the realization of knowledge through labor and

the overcoming of alienation through self-understanding. By the late 1850s, or what might be called the *Grundrisse* period, Marx had grown weary of the possibility of individual self-realization—or, for that matter, the philosophical character of the process of knowing. He had also grown weary of labor as a sheer learning experience; rather he saw the problem of knowledge in terms of the problem of social systems. Knowledge under capitalism is purely instrumental. It is a source of alienation because of its one-sided demystification of experience. Capitalism gives a scientific character to production, but does not give a scientific character to the relationships of human beings within the production process: "The process of labor, which in the earlier phase was to be the source of knowledge and liberation, is thereby reduced within capitalism to an element of technology and little else has absorbed into capital in opposition to labor and appears as the property of capital, or more exactly of fixed capital, to the extent that it enters into the production process as an actual means of production. The tendency of capital is thus to give a scientific character to production, reducing direct labor to a simple element in this process."[57]

When Marx turns to the question of knowledge under communism in this middle period or economic stage, leisure and labor become factors. In a mood almost reminiscent of Aristotle, he sees the need and the possibility of "leisure time" for the "higher activities." In the realm of communist freedom both leisure and labor define and determine the character of what we know. And in this world of communism, practice becomes equated with experimental science on the one hand and historical science on the other. The latter being the accumulated wisdom of society as a whole: "Free time—which includes leisure time as well as time for higher activities—naturally transforms anyone who enjoys it into a different person, and it is this different person who then enters the direct process of production.

The man who is being formed finds discipline in this process, while for the man who is already formed, it is practice, experimental science, materially creative and self-objectifying knowledge, and he contains within his own head the accumulated wisdom of society; both of them find exercise in it, to the extent that labor requires practical manipulation and free movement, as in agriculture."[58]

In this second stage of the Marxian vision of knowledge there is a liberating power of society per se. The way in which economic transformations permit exact human knowledge is no longer a matter of individual effort, no longer a matter of knowledge searching its true opposite; but rather the way in which economic evolution, first one-sidedly through the capitalist expansion of natural science, and then multidimensionally through the socialist concept of the human sciences, permits a knowledge without distortion. False consciousness dissolves in practice rather than in introspective or even experiential reflections.

Engels, in particular, sought intellectual confirmation of socialism through the natural sciences. Basically Marx and most other socialists—pre- and post-utopian—considered the natural sciences as a common social property, rather than the special property of those in possession of dialectical reasoning. Since the physical sciences are in the "interests" of all contending social classes, such sciences are said to be in the general domain, largely undistorted by ideological considerations. It is the social sciences, specifically the science of political economy, which represents the specifically socialist contribution to the march of science. For it is in the transformation of "classical" or "bourgeois" political economy as a study in the propertied sources of inequality, into a socialist political economy that starts with the class struggle itself (rather than with property) and concludes with the elimination of such struggles through the termination of antagonistic classes, that one locates the knowledge input of socialist doctrine into the general scientific corpus.

At this second stage in the evolution of Marxian socialism, there was an assumption to automaticity, or spontaneity as the Russian Marxists were to call the economic vision of the transformation of capitalism into socialism. It remained a task for the third and final stage in the evolution of Marxist thought to develop a framework for showing how these inexorable economic properties were, in fact, or in future values, linked to the political mission of an industrial working class. As Marxism became more linked to "free will" and less to "determinism," so too did the tasks for bringing about socialism move increasingly to the political realm and decreasingly to the production realm. Much, if not all, of Marx's late writings were taken up with the analysis of civil warfare in the United States, revolutionary conditions in Spain, national liberation in Poland and Russia, and so on. The more remote were the prospects for a European socialism, the more Marx focused on the processes by which classes came to power, rather than the process of class competition in the economic marketplace.

As a result, the concept of knowledge became saturated with that of history—no longer economic history alone, but the relationships between political change and economic exploitation. Engels summed up this classical position in his essay on "Socialism: Utopian and Scientific": "The materialist conception of history starts from the proposition that the production of the means to support human life—and, next to production, the exchange of things produced—is the basis of all social structure; that in every society that has appeared in history, the manner in which wealth is distributed and society divided into classes or orders is dependent upon what is produced, how it is produced, and how the products are exchanged. They are to be sought not in the *philosophy*, but in the *economics* of each particular epoch."[59]

Engels's point of view still represented a somewhat earlier vision, and it was Marx who uniquely took the question of knowledge one step further in his biting and cynical re-

sponse to the Gotha Program. It was here that Marx confronted not only the trade unionization of socialism, but
also his own earlier Baconian vision of the emancipating
properties of knowledge. Inequality, in its very existence,
makes a society based on true knowledge impossible: "This
equal right is an unequal right for unequal labor. It recognizes no class differences, because everyone is only a worker
like everyone else; but it tacitly recognizes unequal individual
endowment and thus productive capacity as natural privileges. *It is therefore a right of inequality in its content, like every
right.* Right by its very nature can only consist in the application of an equal standard; but unequal individuals (and they
would not be different individuals if they were not unequal)
are only measurable by an equal standard in so far as they
are brought under an equal point of view, are taken from
one *definite* side only, e.g., in the present case are regarded
only as workers, and nothing more seen in them, everything
else being ignored."[60]

One can easily understand how delighted Lenin and the
latter-day revolutionaries were with Marx's *Critique of the
Gotha Program* because it was a confrontation of socialism
with liberalism. Liberalism, which had made the most over
its concern with the free exercise of knowledge and had
been most forthright in championing equal rights and the
rights of the free spirit, became a fundamental protagonist
in the communist vision of knowledge. The ultimate cut
was the equation of a Prussian constitution and the
Bismarckian emphasis on the freedom of science with the
liberal emphasis on freedom of conscience: "*Freedom of conscience'?* If one desires at this time of the *Kulturkampf* to remind liberalism of its old catchwords, then it surely could
have been done in the following form: Everyone should be
able to attend to his religious as well as his bodily needs
without the police sticking their noses in. But the Workers'
Party out at any rate in this connection to have expressed its
consciousness of the fact that bourgeois 'freedom of con-

science' is nothing but the toleration of all possible kinds of *religious freedom of conscience* and that for its part it endeavors rather to liberate the conscience from the specter of religion. But there is a desire not to transgress the 'bourgeois' level."[61]

There is a slow, but by no means uncertain evolution in Marx's thinking from individualistic and philosophic reasons for why we can accumulate exact knowledge, to a final stage in his thinking of why, as a result of political, social and economic conditioning, we cannot achieve such knowledge, short of a political revolution. Knowledge that leads away from the making of a revolution, from the theory and practice of social change, is no longer knowledge—but only false consciousness.

At this point a major ambiguity in the socialist legacy rears itself. One view of the Marxian approach to knowledge is that of a continuum: from magic, rites, rituals at the primitive end, to theology at the most sophisticated end. For Engels, there was no doubt that ideology, the most troublesome of forms to express something more than mysticism and something less than pure science, comes into existence to express class interests and not personality defects.[62] History distinguishes between ideological systems and conscious deceptions. There is furthermore a clear correlation of types of social systems and forms of ideological expression. And while ideologies are conditioned by the stages reached in scientific development no less than national peculiarities, they exist and persist primarily to defend class interests. Hence, the root condition for the elimination of ideology is the end of class exploitation.[63]

Increasingly the activist camp displaced this sociological view of ideology, particularly theorists of the communist revolution. Lenin considers ideology as a simple quantitative distinction in ideas.[64] Ideology is said to contain a range of ideas from false notions of the ruling class to the true notions of the revolutionary class. On Lenin's premises, ideology is reduced to a heuristic principle for regulating theory. He thus finds no difficulty in employing terms like "scientific ideology" and "religious ideology." With Lenin, ideology no longer was a special relation of ideas to material institutions as it was in Marx. Political alliance replaces class affiliation as the touchstone for estimating ideologies.

Admittedly, Lenin was dealing with a political context requiring immediate ideological choices. He was confronted with a situation demanding a wholesale commitment to certain policies on the part of an elite and its following. In this context, Lenin contributed to a wide realization that oppressed and oppressor cannot automatically transcend ideological boundaries; that ideology is indeed a barrier to be passed. Thus a revolutionary conflict, insofar as it engages the mental energies of the combatants, is no intellectual idyll, but rather a hard-fought struggle between ideologies. What Lenin did not understand, and what was already apparent to the psychological school of Michels, Sorel and Pareto, is that ideology first and foremost functions symbolically to galvanize men into action. Ideology contains an irrational element without which it could serve no moral or political end, and this end exists quite apart from the intrinsic needs of a scientific sociology.

With this double legacy of perceiving ideology both as something less than science (i.e., a secularized theology) and, contrarily, as something more than science (i.e., the source of revolutionary energy), the sociological vision of sociology as a liberating force becomes considerably muddied—not to say muddled. It is scarcely any wonder, therefore, that under socialism, or at least for most of the Soviet system, social science came to be considered as everything from a manifestation of bourgeois false consciousness to the embodiment of the highest principles of precise knowledge. In this sense, the very sophistication of the socialist theoretical tradition to that ubiquitous concept of ideology has been a source of profound sociological discontent—permitting and even encouraging a struggle not only over ideas but whether it is fitting and proper to even express certain ideas. In this way, the nature of the socialist approach to knowledge is intimately bound up with the basic political questions of freedom of expression and the rights of criticism and self-criticism without the necessity of punishment for being declared wrong or in error.

Quite apart from the personal evolution in Marx's thinking, and apart too from the fact that each of these three types of approaches have developed adherents within the socialist camp, is the question of whether socialism is a sociological system. This constitutes the next stage beyond bourgeois consciousness in a social science of liberation, or is in fact simply the next stage in the evolution of those social sciences. This becomes an extremely touchy and fundamental point throughout the twentieth century. What we constantly confront is not simply the Marxian or socialist vision of society, but just as definitely the sociological vision of the Marxist theories or socialist theories for the promulgation of change and consciousness.

Whether Marxism is part of social science knowledge, or is itself the generalized expression of social science in a "post-bourgeois" context, divided many socialist scholars, who on other grounds might line up on the same side. Even within one collection of papers, in tribute to Lukács's *History and Class Consciousness*, one finds sharp disagreement on the primacy of socialism over sociology, or vice versa. The British sociologist, Tom Bottomore, writing on class structure and social consciousness, notes: "The intellectual uncertainties of the present time, to which Lukács alludes, are revealed in the disarray which prevails within some established ideologies (notably Marxism itself), and in the emergence of a confusing variety of new doctrines, or new styles of thought (for example, in the student movements) which seem to be only loosely connected with social classes or indeed with any identifiable social group which could be seen as a potentially effective agent of social change. We have long since passed out of the era in which the real consciousness of social groups, expressed in their beliefs and actions, could be discussed as mere 'psychological false' consciousness, and be contrasted with 'rational consciousness' enshrined in the ideology of a Communist party."[65]

It is evident that even for Bottomore, the Party does not embody Marxism as a body of authentic knowledge, while in turn (and perhaps the more serious admission) Marxism by no means embodies the entire range of scientific truths. In contrast, Istvan Meszaros, a most able interpreter of twentieth-century socialism, has no doubt whatsoever that contemporary events confirm rather than refute the general propositions of Marxism. Beyond that, in quite orthodox fashion, he entertains the view that whatever analytic problems arise, do so within a Marxian context: "Marx's general analysis remains as valid as ever, since it does not concern the 'developed' countries, nor the 'underdeveloped' ones, taken separately, but the capitalist world system as *whole*, with all its inherent structural contradictions, whatever particular forms of 'exception' they may—indeed must—assume at different times and in different socioeconomic settings characterized by varying degrees of industrialization. In an object dialectical framework of reference, working 'exceptions' constitute the general 'rules' which, in an unending interchange, are made into new 'exceptions' and new 'rules,' thus both modifying (concretizing) and confirming the general conception itself."[66]

What we have in Meszaros is a variation on a standard theme that history may be imperfect, but doctrine remains always perfect. This is the source of utopian as well as ideological thinking in Marxian sociology. The difficulty in this position is the inability to identify counterfactuals, the inability to ever show at what point another can legitimately replace one doctrine, or knowledge in its abstract form can be overthrown by another system or another paradigm. At what point does modification of an old system yield to its overthrow? One can, for example, still manufacture an Aristotelian epicyclical theory of planetary revolution, but it is far simpler to change the system and make the sun the center and the earth a rotating periphery. The incorporation of social science into the Marxian corpus led to relativity of systems and multiplicity in analysis. But beyond that, social science led to the yielding of Marxism itself as a predictor of systems, to a larger set of truths about the nature of society, and no less, the nature of socialism.

Early utopias envisioning a perfect order were superseded by small-scale versions in utopian communities. "Scientific socialism" then held that utopian socialism was doomed to failure in a hostile capitalistic world. As the Soviet experience elicited anti-utopias, utopianism has been unable to resolve its own contradictions in an imperfect world. This tragic outcome is an opportunity for sociology in its study of human interactions to analyze both the possibilities and the inherent limitations of proposed social systems. By monitoring the rich variety of social experience, it may help to restrain some of the fanaticism that now surrounds us.

Apart from the coinage of the word by Sir Thomas More, utopia is as old as the idea of perfection itself. In the Platonic world of the "idea of ideas" there was the perfect number, the perfect circle, and the perfect society. Indeed, *The Republic* itself is a study of the good as implanted in the social and political order, although modern critics often speak of these dialogues as if Plato were in search of an empirical description of alternative social orders. Indeed, it was Aristotle who began the first systematic study of the varieties of rule and how they measured up to ideal notions of the good.

During most of the history of Christendom, the idea of utopia was writ large: Augustine, Campanella, More, Rousseau. Whether man was held to be innately good or evil, the need for a more perfect order, at least as an ideal to which all humanity would strive, was enshrined in literature and in life throughout the course of Western civilization until the arrival of the Enlightenment.

But as the arrival date of utopia was postponed by its advocates, and social life became more complex, more oppressive, more subject to divisions of labor and distinctions of race, religion, and ethnicity, the drive was on for utopia writ small, some piecemeal down payment to prove that the future was now. Weitling, Owen, Fourier, and countless others developed intimate concepts of perfection—places in the world that could also function as places for the heart to find haven, secular retreats that suspiciously shared many of the properties of monasteries and religious orders. As a number of historians like Leo Gershoy observed, the utopias that emerged from the Enlightenment inverted the relationship of people to polity and of the stratification order itself.[67] Utopias came to be linked with populist causes rather than to elitist prescriptions. Priests and commoners, bishops and princes, changed positions. Nonetheless, and best intentions notwithstanding, the existence of superordinate and subordinate roles continued well intact with utopian communities.

It was this sense of utopia writ small that came under sharp attack in the early nineteenth century, or post-Enlightenment epoch, first by the socialists and then by the anti-socialists, or counter-utopians. But our present concern essentially involves the basis of the socialist attack on utopianism, the resulting juxtaposition of so-called scientific socialism with utopian socialism, of the analysis of whole systems with the practical art of living in minute and partial systems.

If I may be permitted a bibliographical digression—this entire process of utopian constructions has been brilliantly and variously described by Western social and intellectual historians. We have Frank E. Manuel, who wrote *Utopian Thought in the Western World*;[68] a few years earlier Melvin J. Lasky's extraordinary compilation, *Utopia and Revolution: On the Origin of a Metaphor*,[69] gave the first systematic study of the specific conditions of twentieth-century efforts to institutionalize perfection; and now we have Yaacov Oved's outstanding study, *Two Hundred Years of American Communes*, which updates the earlier potpourri turn-of-the-century studies of the first 100 years of utopianism in American context.[70]

The critical tradition of Karl Mannheim, in particular the empirical analysis of the social filtering of knowledge in the utopian experience, has had very few legitimate successors.[71] Instead, such sociological work as has been performed in contemporary America tended to be in cameo. The work of Bennett Berger,[72] Rosabeth Moss Kanter,[73] and Benjamin Zablocki[74] provided careful studies of communes, albeit with different emphases and even quite different conclusions. This research is based less on classical utopianism than on the pragmatic prerequisites of communal living, of utopia as the practice of small groups. But our concern here is for utopianism as a big issue, as questions of economic systems again writ large.

My specific charge is with the socialist response to utopianism. And here we must return to the sacred text of Frederick Engels, the pamphlet entitled *Socialism: Utopian and Scientific*.[75] Essentially, Engels's position, which it should be noted has gone unchallenged within socialist circles, albeit with increasing discomfort, is that utopian socialism was the last cry of religious socialism of medieval times, an effort to plant the seeds of the perfect hereafter in secular order on earth. Engels praised the radicalization of this process, by the St. Simonians and Owenites, as proof positive that the longing for socialism was deeply embedded in the common man. Engels essentially believed that the German Christian and socialist utopians alike were doomed to failure because the larger social and economic order of capitalism was hostile to any egalitarianism, however experimental or limited in context it might have been. The utopians were utopian in a double sense: in trying to establish a per-

fect subculture in an imperfect larger world and in an ob-
tuseness to the forces allied to confound and destroy such
attempts. These clever observations were, however, not followed up with a satisfactory resolution.

What Engels offered in place of utopianism, as a community process was socialism as a scientific system. This was
predicated essentially on an analysis of capitalism and ultimately on the overthrow of an exploitative larger society in
accord with the laws of production and the interests of a
proletarian class. But much depended on the word *ultimate.*
How distant was the ultimate? When would fundamental
changes happen? What was the measure of scientific socialism: the community, the nation, or the whole world in con-
flagration? These issues, which were to engage the energies
of Bolshevik successors to the founders of scientific socialism, would not go lightly into the night. These issues also
became the stuff of post-Marxian European sociology. Impatient with the course of the revolution and disbelieving
what did finally take place in the name of socialist revolution, the socialists were driven in two directions: toward
politics and away from sociology; or toward sociology and
away from politics. Thus ended the ultimate effort to t engi-
neer social change—a predictor in theory of practical failures to come.

As the outlines of socialism in one country, the Soviet
Union became clear; counter-utopian formations took center stage. There was Yevgeny Zamyatin's savage *We,*[76] followed by George Orwell's *Nineteen Eighty-Four,*[77] among others. The very phrase "scientific socialism" began to take on
ironies of unexpected dimensions, until the cataclysmic and
fantastic revelations in Solzhenitsyn's masterpiece trilogy,
The Gulag Archipelago.[78] Science, far from saving socialism
or giving it a new dimension, only resulted in the fulfillment of the Sorelian prophesy: a disintegrated, even de-
mented, form of bureaucratic rule that led to anything but
egalitarian outcomes. Rather, it substituted political tyranny

for economic exploitation as the core agent of rule. Indeed, two "scientific" forms of socialism emerged from the Soviet experience: Stalinism and Trotskyism. But neither captured the popular imagination; both struggled for the small leavings from the intellectual table. It could hardly be otherwise, since both varieties of Bolshevism derive from Vladimir Lenin, who abstractly spoke of the "withering away of the State", but concretely advocated a fierce control "over the parasites, the sons of privilege, the swindlers and suchlike guardians of capitalist traditions". Utopianism came to a crashing halt with the tasks of actual administration, with "swift and severe punishment" since, as Lenin noted, "the armed workers are practical people and not sentimental intellectuals".[79] Indeed, neither Lenin nor his heirs could be accused of undue sentiment.

The atrophied character of communist ideology in its Soviet Stalinist phase gave impulse to a renewed, if somewhat tailored, thrust of utopianism elsewhere in the world during this same contemporary period. Sometimes the commune movement was based on a religious-social ideology like the Hutterian Society of Brothers in the United States, while at other times, as in the Kibbutz movement of Israel, it rested upon a largely, although not exclusively, secular view that communal living would make everything from sexual affairs to child rearing to work patterns simpler and nobler. In more recent formations, utopian colonies were set up to satisfy a non-ideological yet wide array of mixtures and motives. Socialism remained an abstract if positive ideal, but its force in everyday communal affairs receded, even emptied, of content, as the magnitude of totalitarian systems became apparent to radicals no less than to conservatives in the West.

The issue of socialism and utopianism, far from being resolved over time, remains a contradiction. In part, this is a psychological problem—or better, motivational. If, as George V. Plekhanov realized, the transformation of capitalism into socialism was axiomatic or determined by events operating behind the backs of men,[79] as Marx declared it to be in his less sophisticated moments, the need for participation in revolutionary struggle seemed terribly diminished. Plekhanov's tortured and brilliant efforts to salvage the "role of the individual of history" became dubious. Furthermore, actual science may be a fine rallying cry for academics and intellectuals, physicists and economists, but it is scarcely the sort of general myth that can serve as an organizing concept or a catapulting agent.

In such a cul-de-sac, it is little wonder that the idea of socialism itself came apart at its sociological seams. While those still in a position to make free decisions tended to choose a "socialism with a human face," another more disciplined portion of socialists turned to communism for the quick fixes: to the dictatorship of the proletariat, to the organized activities of the talented few—the NKVD pulse feelers of the nation, the operators of the metaphysical railroad of history—in short, the advanced leadership of the Communist party of each nation. In such an environment, utopianism as social practice was doomed—but so too was any notion of science as socially benevolent.

It is little wonder then that socialism sprouts utopian wings whenever and wherever it is free to do so. It restores the balance of community, limits the force of order, and reduces the notion of equity to life-size manageable proportions. But, of course, the life cycle of utopianism is precisely that of the life cycle of socialism—a demand for equity followed by a reshuffling of the social order, which in turn leads to a separation of leaders and followers, strong and weak, dissidents and loyalists. The life cycle of The People's Temple in Jonestown, Guyana, so brilliantly document by John R. Hall in his book, *Gone From the Promised Land*, explores the degree to which a Jim Jones can emerge in a cloistered communal context no less than a Joseph Stalin can emerge in a sprawling national context.[80] Utopianism too has proven inept to resolve its contradictions: those posed by scientific socialism to be sure, but also its own set of assumptions that small is beautiful or at least organizationally manageable.

Where does this excursion into the ideology of utopian and scientific variations on the socialist theme leave us? In all this but a metaphor? If so, a metaphor for what? The foibles of humankind? The unquenchable faith in social justice? The socialist part of utopianism seems ever dimmer: in part moving into reform movements in the West, and even capitalist modes of economic relationships in places like China and Eastern Europe. The utopian faith in the "new man," so touchingly expressed by Ernesto "Che" Guevara at the dawn of the Cuban Revolution, seems less like a revolution betrayed than a utopian myth gone plain sour.

This tragic outcome for socialism and utopianism alike also served as an opportunity of moment for sociology. The irreducible context of social systems remains the individual—the person is the bedrock of all systems. Utopianism, writ large or small, involving masses or cults, comes upon the person—what Arendt,[81] following Kant, termed the judging, willing and thinking being. Not institutions but individuals are and always have been the exclusive repositories of rationality. The inventors of utopianisms are also its destroyers. The awesome responsibility lodged in systems, leaders, and movements can be shattered by the far more potent force of individuals who will not participate in all this, will resist through silence if not outright defiance. Only individuals can construct the utopianism, the perfect system, in our personal worlds or even our own minds. The Hegelian world mind after all turns out to be an invention of real minds.

If there is a lesson in this long history of the romance of utopianism and socialism, this on-again, off-again romance of false options, it is that individuals break all known barriers, resist all known confines, shatter all rules and regulations that make no sense. The "normative" structure may exist, but it is a bargain between the rational faculties of the

individual and the confrontation of the world and its interests. Norms are also a commitment to shared purposes and
common goals that define the human condition. Owen's
harmonic society[82] and Becker's heavenly city[83] merge, and
what passes for socialism, or any other system of economic
rule, becomes a pale reflection of the highest aspirations of
the rational mind.

Socialists, scientific and utopian, took cold comfort in
sociology, in the study of human interactions filled with
imperfections and doomed to cycles of optimism and pessimism, successes and failures, small advances matched by
sometimes larger retreats. In a century marked by amazing
developments in applied technology, used for equally and
extraordinarily devastating purposes, the sociological imagination must confront pretensions to the perfect: not as in
the pre-social scientific world of the anti-utopian opposing
the utopian, but rather as citizens and surveyors meeting in
the nooks and crannies of giant societies and individual
minds alike. And with the work of such younger scholars as
Paul Hollander,[84] Vladimir Tismaneanu,[85] and Nicholas
Eberstadt,[86] the analysis of the false options of perfect systems continues.

For those who still insist that, at the end of the long trek
for truth, socialism offer the answer, let it be a socialism
that offers justice and freedom, not pseudo-science and utopian vision. The great Polish philosopher, Leszek
Kolakowski,[87] put the case for socialism both modestly and
well when he said to the Solidarity leader Adam Michnik,
"We need a socialist tradition conscious of its own limitations, because the dream of final redemption is despair in
the cloak of hope, the greed for power in the gown of justice." But having admitted to the prospects for such an outcome, it is also fit and proper to point out that previous
social history argues more persuasively against such an opti-
mum fusion of collective organization and personal aims.
In any event, the tasks of social research in a highly volatile

age are to monitor the rich variety of human relations rather than beat the drums darkly for any single millennial vision. To do so might limit our apocalyptic beliefs of what will occur in the future, but it clearly restrains the great fanaticism that surround us in the present.

The problem is that this cry of the heart by those who want a socialism without terror have a difficult time pointing to a Marxian system that delivers on such a pledge. The State, far from dissolving, becomes stronger and more unshakable as the final resting-place of the Marxian vision. It could not end in any other way. Once conflict became the dominant mode of human conduct, and economic relationships that which people fought over, any regulatory mechanism was bound to insist upon a statist structure that could bridle, if not harmonize such a reductionist universe of psychological competition and economic egotism. Marxism as a routinized response to human diversity became itself a critical pivot in statism, and in the very evils of the state used to rally the vast public to the cause of social justice. It would be sad enough to report this as a noble cause gone sour. But the ultimate tragedy is in the human lives extracted in the name of grand theorizing, in the countless victims, from Ukrainian peasants in the 1930s to Khmer Rouge soldiers in the 1980s. Genocide is never random. It is always a function of a theory run amuck—rooted in the primeval animosities of simple individuals expanded to take on the postmodern credos of complex intellectuals. In such circumstances, states trump societies.

Notes

1. Milovan Djilas, *Fall of the New Class: A History of Communism's Self-Destruction.* New York: Alfred A. Knopf Publishers, 1998, pp. 294, 300.
2. Georg Lukacs, *History and Class Consciousness* (New Edition: 1967) London: Merlin Press, 1971, p. 3. For an excellent recent symposium on the relations between Hegel and Marx, see "Reconsidering the Hegelian Legacy," particularly the commentaries by Sven-Eric

Liedman, Sean Sayers, and Howard Williams. *The European Legacy: Toward New Paradigms,* Vol. 2, No. 3 (May) 1997, pp. 538–573.

3. For a broad, useful analysis of change in Marxism, see, George Lichtheim, *Marxism.* London: Routledge and Kegan Paul, 1961, pp. 253–54.

4. David Joravsky, *Soviet Marxism and Natural Science.* New York: Colombia University Press, 1961, p. 6; and George L. Kline, "Recent Soviet Philosophy," *Annals of the American Academy of Political and Social Science.* January 1956, pp. 126–138.

5. Z.A. Jordan, *The Evolution of Dialectical Materialism.* London: Macmillan, 1967, pp. 11–12.

6. Friedrich Engels, *Anti-Duhring.* Moscow: Foreign Language Publishing House, 1959, p. 17 (first published in 1885).

7. Tom B. Bottomore and Maximilian Rubel, "Introduction" to *Karl Marx: Selected Writings in Sociology and Social Philosophy.* London: Penguin, 1970, p. 36.

8. Shlomo Avineri, *The Social and Political Thought of Karl Marx.* Cambridge: Cambridge University Press, 1970, p. 69.

9. Karl Marx and Friedrich Engels *The German Ideology Writings of the Young Marx on Philosophy and Society,* edited by Lloyd D. Easton and Kurt H. Guddat. New York: Anchor Books, 1967, p. 382 (first published in 1846).

10. Karl Marx, *Economic and Philosophic Manuscripts,* edited by Dirk J. Struik. New York: International Publishers, 1937, p. 176 (first published in 1844).

11. Ibid.

12. Karl Marx, *Capital.* London: George Allen & Unwin, 1957, p. xxx (first published in 1873).

13. Karl Marx, *Economic and Philosophic Manuscripts,* edited by Dirk J. Struik. New York: International Publishers, 1937, p. 177.

14. Karl Marx, *Economic and Philosophic Manuscripts,* edited by Dirk J. Struik. New York: International Publishers, 1937, p. 177.

15. Karl Marx, *Economic and Philosophic Manuscripts.* edited by Dirk J. Struik. New York: International Publishers, 1937, p. 188.

16. Karl Marx and Friedrich Engels *The German Ideology Writings of the Young Marx on Philosophy and Society,* edited by Lloyd D. Easton and Kurt H. Guddat. New York: Anchor Books, 1967, p. 414.

17. Karl Marx and Friedrich Engels *The German Ideology Writings of the Young Marx on Philosophy and Society,* edited by Lloyd D. Easton and Kurt H. Guddat. New York: Anchor Books, 1967, p. 415.

18. Karl Marx and Friedrich Engels *The German Ideology Writings of the Young Marx on Philosophy and Society,* edited by Lloyd D. Easton and Kurt H. Guddat. New York: Anchor Books, 1967, p. 431.

19. Karl Marx, *Economic and Philosophic Manuscripts,* edited by Dirk J. Struik. New York: International Publishers, p. 181.

20. Karl Marx and Friedrich Engels, "The German Ideology," *Writings of the Young Marx on Philosophy and Society,* edited by Lloyd D. Easton and Kurt H. Guddat. New York: Anchor Books, 1967, p. 388.

21. Karl Marx and Friedrich Engels, "The German Ideology," *Writings of the Young Marx on Philosophy and Society,* edited by Lloyd D. Easton and Kurt H. Guddat. New York: Anchor Books, 1967, p. 379.

22. Karl Marx, *The Holy Family. Writings of the Young Marx on Philosophy and Society,* edited by Lloyd D. Easton and Kurt Guddat. New York: Anchor Books, 1967, pp. 400-401.

23. Karl Marx, *Grundrisse der Kritik der politischen Okonomie,* (1857). Edited and translated by David McLellan. London: Macmillan and Co. Ltd., 1971, pp. 134-35.

24. Karl Marx, *Grundrisse der Kritik der politischen Okonomie,* (1857). Edited and translated by David McLellan. London: Macmillan and Co. Ltd., 1971, pp. 148-49.

25. Irving Louis Horowitz, "Socialism and the Problem of Knowledge," *Essays on the Future of Socialism.* Edited by B.P. Parekh. London: Croom & Helm Ltd. 1974.

26. Sidney Hook (1936) *From Hegel to Marx.* New Brunswick and London: Transaction Publishers, 1992.

27. Karl Marx, *Grundrisse der Kritik der politischen Okonomie,* (1857). Edited and translated by David McLellan. London: Macmillan and Co. Ltd., 1971, pp. 100-101.

28. Allen W. Wood, "The Marxian Critique of Justice," *Philosophy and Public Affairs, Vol. 1,* No. 3 Spring 1972, pp. 242-282.

29. Marx, Karl (1845) *Theses on Feuerbach. Writings of the Young Marx on Philosophy and Society,* edited by Lloyd D. Easton and Kurt H. Guddat. New York: Anchor Books, 1967, p. 401.

30. Karl Marx, (1875) *Critique of the Gotha Programme.* New York: International Publishers, 1938, p. 9.

31. Leonard Krieger, "Marx and Engels as Historians," *Journal of the History of Ideas, Vol. 14,* 1953, pp. 397-98.

32. Sidney Hook, *Towards the Understanding of Karl Marx.* New York: John Day, 1933, pp. 159-160.

33. Karl Marx, (1844) *Economic and Philosophic Manuscripts,* edited by Dirk J. Struik. New York: International Publishers, 1938, p. 143.

34. Henri Lefebvre, *Dialectical Materialism.* London: Jonathan Cape, 1969, p. 107.

35. Friedrich Engels, (1885) *Anti-Dühring.* Moscow: Foreign Language Publishing House, 1957, p. 40.

36. Friedrich Engels, (1872) *Dialectics of Nature.* London: Lawrence & Wishart, 1941, pp. 243-244.

37. Friedrich Engels, (1885) *Anti-Dühring.* Moscow: Foreign Language Publishing House, 1957, pp. 122-129.

38. Friedrich Engels, (1885) *Anti-Dühring.* Moscow: Foreign Language Publishing House, 1957, p. 125.

39. Vladimir I. Lenin, (1908) *Materialism and Empiro-Criticism. Collected Works,* Vol. 13. London: Lawrence & Wishart, 1938, pp. 114-130.

40. Z.A. Jordan, *Philosophy and Ideology.* Dordrecht: D. Reidel Publishing Co., 1963. pp. 377-384.

41. Gustav Wetter, *Dialectical Materialism*. New York: Frederick A. Praeger, 1960, p. 490.
42. Z.A. Jordan, *Philosophy and Ideology*. Dordrecht: D. Reidel Publishing Co., 1963, p. 324.
43. Friedrich Engels, (1885) *Anti-Dühring*. Moscow: Foreign Language Publishing House, 1957, p. 55.
44. Karl Marx, (1844) *Economic and Philosophic Manuscripts*, edited by Dirk J. Struik. New York: International Publishers, 1938, p. 180.
45. T.B. Bottomore, "Karl Marx: Sociologist or Marxist?" *Marxism*, edited by Michael Curtis. New York: Atherton, 1970.
46. Gustav Wetter, *Soviet Ideology Today*. London: Heinemann, 1966.
47. Louis Althusser, *For Marx*. New York: Pantheon Books Random House, 1969, pp. 35–39.
48. Jean Hyppolite, *Studies on Marx and Hegel*, edited and translated by John O'Neill. New York and London: Basic Books, 1969, p. 17.
49. Rudolf Schlesinger, *Marx: His Time and Ours*. London: Routledge & Kegan Paul Ltd. 1950, p. 429.
50. Shlomo Avineri, *The Social and Political Thought of Karl Marx*. Cambridge: Cambridge University Press, 1970, p. 131.
51. Karl Marx, (1875) *Critique of the Gotha Programme*. New York: International Publishers, 1938, p. 80.
52. Karl Marx, (1844) "Critique of the Hegelian Dialectic and Philosophy as a Whole," *Economic and Philosophic Manuscripts of 1844*. New York: International Publishers, 1964, p. 182.
53. Karl Marx, (1844) "Critique of the Hegelian Dialectic and Philosophy as a Whole," *Economic and Philosophic Manuscripts of 1844*. New York: International Publishers, 1964, p. 181.
54. Karl Marx, (1844) "Critique of the Hegelian Dialectic and Philosophy as a Whole," *Economic and Philosophic Manuscripts of 1844*. New York: International Publishers, 1964, p. 183.
55. Karl Marx, (1844) "Critique of the Hegelian Dialectic and Philosophy as a Whole," *Economic and Philosophic Manuscripts of 1844*. New York: International Publishers, 1964, p. 131–132.
56. Karl Marx and Friedrich Engels, (1848) "Manifesto of the Communist Party," *Basic Writings on Politics and Philosophy*, edited by Lewis S. Feuer. Garden City, New York: Doubleday & Co., 1959, p. 35.
57. Karl Marx, (1857) *Grundrisse der Kritik der politischen Okonomie*, edited and translated by David McLellan. London: Macmillan & Co., Ltd., 1971, pp. 134–35.
58. Karl Marx, (1857) *Grundrisse der Kritik der politischen Okonomie*, edited and translated by David McLellan. London: Macmillan & Co., Ltd., 1971, pp. 148–49.
59. Friedrich Engels, (1880) "Socialism: Utopian and Scientific." *In Basic Writings on Politics and Philosophy–Karl Marx and Friedrich Engels*, edited by Lewis S. Feuer. Garden City, New York: Doubleday & Co., 1959, p. 90.

60. Karl Marx, (1875) *Critique of the Gotha Programme.* New York: International Publishers, 1938, p. 9.
61. Karl Marx, (1875) *Critique of the Gotha Programme.* New York: International Publishers, 1938, p. 21.
62. Friedrich Engels, (1845) *Herr Eugen Duhring's Revolution in Science (Anti-Duhring).* New York: International Publishers, 1939.
63. Friedrich Engels, (1846) *Ludwig Feuerbach and the Outcome of Classical German Philosophy.* New York: International Publishers, 1941.
64. Vladimir Lenin, (1908) *Materialism and Empirico-Criticism: Critical Comments on a Reactionary Philosophy.* Moscow Foreign Languages Publishing House, 1947.
65. Tom Bottomore, "Class Structure and Social Consciousness," *Aspects of History and Class Consciousness,* edited by Istvan Meszaros. London: Routledge & Kegan Paul, 1971, pp. 61–62.
66. Tom Bottomore, "Class Structure and Social Consciousness," *Aspects of History and Class Consciousness,* edited by Istvan Meszaros. London: Routledge & Kegan Paul, 1971, p. 62.
67. Leo Gershoy, *From Despotism to Revolution.* New York: Harper & Brothers, 1944.
68. Frank E. Manuel with Fritzie P. Manuel, (1979) *Utopian Thought in the Western World.* Cambridge: Harvard University Press.
69. Melvin J. Lasky, *Utopia and Revolution: On the Origin of a Metaphor.* Chicago: University of Chicago Press, 1976.
70. Yaacov Oved, *Two Hundred Years of American Communes.* New Brunswick: Transaction Publishers, 1988.
71. Karl Mannheim, *Ideology and Utopia: An Introduction to the Sociology of Knowledge.* New York: Harcourt, Brace & World, 1959.
72. Bennett M. Berger, *The Survival of a Counterculture: Ideological Work and Everyday Life Among Rural Communards.* Berkeley: University of California Press, 1981.
73. Rosabeth Moss Kanter, *Commitment and Community: Communes and Utopias in Sociological Perspective.* Cambridge, MA: Harvard University Press, 1972.
74. Benjamin Zablocki, *The Joyful Community: An Account of the Bruderhof: A Communal Movement Now in its Third Generation.* Chicago: University Press, 1980.
75. Friedrich Engels, *Socialism: Utopian and Scientific.* Chicago: Charles H. Kerr & Co, 1908.
76. Yevgeny Zamyatin, *We.* New York: The Viking Press, 1973.
77. George Orwell, *Nineteen Eighty-Four.* New York: Harcourt, Brace & Co, 1949.
78. Aleksandr Solzhenitsyn, *The Gulag Archipelago, 1918–1956: An Experiment in Literary Investigation.* New York: Harper & Row, 1973.
79. Vladimir I. Lenin, *The State and Revolution.* (1917) Peking: Foreign Langauge Press, 1976. 123–124.
79. George V. Plekhanov, *Utopian Socialism of the Nineteenth Century.* Moscow: Foreign Languages Publishing House, 1959.

80. John R. Hall, *Gone From the Promised Land: Jonestown in American Cultural History*. New Brunswick: Transaction Publishers, 1987.
81. Hannah Arendt, *The Life of the Mind*, 2 vols. New York: Harcourt Brace Jovanovich, 1977.
82. John Fletcher Clews Harrison, *Quest for the New Moral World: Robert Owen and the Owenites in Britain and America*. New York: Scribner's, 1969.
83. Carl Becker, *The Heavenly City of the Eighteenth-Century Philosopher*. New Haven: Yale University Press, 1932.
84. Paul Hollander, *The Many Faces of Socialism: Comparative Sociology and Politics*. New Brunswick: Transaction Publishers, 1983.
85. Vladimir Tismaneanu, *The Poverty of Utopia: The Crisis of Marxist Ideology in Eastern Europe*. London: Routledge & Kegan Paul, 1988.
86. Nicholas Eberstadt, *The Poverty of Communism*. New Brunswick: Transaction Publishers, 1988.
87. Leszek Kolakowski, *Metaphysical Horror*. Oxford: Basic Blackwell, 1988.

sociologism that often converted to remoteness from the political process as such.

Durkheim's *anti-politique* concerns with the state were orchestrated around a series of propositions about the education of the young, the role of family in institutionalizing moral behavior, and the place of law in orchestrating the collective conscience. He paid scant attention to such liberal concerns of political sociology as the interconnection of social class and organized political power. Rather, Durkheim preferred to "link the corporations to economic sociology, because of the close relations they maintain with industrial and commercial life."[3] As the converse of Marx, Durkheim prefigured both the rise and demise of sociology as an integrated paradigm—but one based on consensus rather than conflict.

Durkheim's emphasis on socialization at the expense of politicization helps to explain the frequent critiques of his ambiguous legacy. Such interests as Durkheim manifested in order, community, and solidarity derived from his powerful belief in moral education, which translated into the professional rhetoric of our age, and served to approximate the goals of political socialization. Durkheim's pursuits help to explain why students of the history of European ideas have not resolved arguments about his political ideology. Durkheim himself formulated a description of the European state in entirely functional terms; hence, ideological factors became a function of primary social groups, not of political allegiances.

Several normative themes are evident in Durkheim's work; each associated with the problem of rights versus obligations. Conservatism, or collectivism in the form of solidarity, clusters along with obligations in one corner, while liberalism, or individualism in the form of human rights, occupies an opposite side. Durkheim treats the state as a dialectical package—an entity which includes castes, classes, or communes which may or may not be designated as politi-

6

Social Order without State Power: Durkheim

"Equality is not enough to ensure that the force of the state must be recognized as a liberation. Heavy doses of civic education and manipulation by a great legislator and by censors are needed to keep the civic self alive."

—Judith N. Shklar[1]

A curious and intellectually disconcerting fact is that founder of modern sociology—and certainly the father c sociologism—Émile Durkheim, was instrumental in givin birth to political socialization, a field of investigation assc ciated with political science. Durkheim played a far lesse role in the development of political sociology, an area c study that remains largely in the eminent domain of soc ologists. Indeed, it is Raymond Aron's contention tha Durkheim's aim was the overthrow of the political by th social.[2] Every thing in him argued for such a position: hi deep interest in consensual rather than conflictual mode of leadership; his appreciation of the role of education an law rather than force and violence in the affairs of mer and an intellectual heritage that rested squarely on th Montesquieu to Tocqueville line of analysis. His was cal, but one which is nonetheless entirely a product of society. The state is an organ of social thought, ultimately responsible for translating social activities into moral purpose. This faith in moral development is at the heart of political socialization and is essential to Durkheim's approach to political theory.

The conservative interpretation of Durkheim focuses on his rejection of the Enlightenment conception of man as an intrinsically moral being, capable of perfection and of mastering himself and his world. It favors a conception of the individual as a product of society, in whom must be inculcated moral discipline to restrain the passions and recall the individual's obligations to society, a collective force which is infinitely greater than any of its individual members. Those who argue with Durkheim's conservatism claim that because he was preoccupied with the problem of order, he failed to place in proper perspective the political sources of social conflict. Critics argue that Durkheim studied society as a whole but failed to deal adequately with specific groups, that he subordinated the claims of individuals to those of society, and that he neglected the issue of power and violence in the body politic.

Robert Nisbet asserts that the intellectual parameters of Durkheim's sociology are derived from the conservative reaction to the Enlightenment, with its stress on the primacy of society and the need for authority in all aspects of social relationships. Nisbet links Durkheim with Freud in this regard, claiming that each contributed to a shift in ideas away from rationalistic categories of volition, will, and individual consciousness "to those aspects of behavior which are in a strict sense non-volitional and non-rational."[4] Nisbet goes on to claim with substantial justification that Durkheim is more radical than Freud, in that he locates the sources of human conduct and values in social conditions external to the individual; whereas, for Freud, non-rational influences on behavior have their origins within the individual psyche.

"It is this supreme emphasis upon society and all its mechanisms of constraint that makes Durkheim's reaction against
individualist rationalism more basic than Freud's, and it is
this emphasis in all its ramifications that places Durkheim
securely in the conservative tradition."[5]

From a markedly different perspective, Lewis A. Coser
has argued that Durkheim, in his general sociology, placed
such great emphasis on the antinomy between society and
the individual that he was unable to perceive the importance of contending subgroups within the social system.
Although his sociology developed in the context of *fin de
siècle* France, Durkheim perceived social conflict as a departure from equilibrium, or as evidence of social pathology.
His conservative tendency to think in terms of the whole,
ignoring struggles between the parts, was nowhere more
evident than in his failure to deal with class conflict. He
simply assumed economic competition would be gradually
eliminated (along with social inequality) as societies moved
from mechanical to organic solidarity. Coser asserts that
Durkheim's intense devotion to "society," or the modern
nation-state, and his desire to implant a secular morality to
buttress the foundations of the Third Republic seriously
obscured his vision and contributed to his failure to take
"theoretical cognizance of the role of governmental force
and violence or of political power and coercion."[6]

Others have argued the case for Durkheim's liberalism
differently. Anthony Giddens disputes Coser's point, noting that Durkheim did not ignore the question of political
power or conflicts among subgroups within society.[7] In *The
Division of Labor,* Durkheim treated political power as directly dependent on the degree to which a division of labor
had developed, positing an inverse correlation between the
two. Although the range of state activities becomes more
extensive, autocratic forms of political domination progressively diminish, and there is a corresponding expansion of
moral individualism. Durkheim later modified this position

to allow for the fact that the centralization of political power may vary independently of the complexity of society—hence the important role assigned to occupational associations as a counterweight to the powers of state in Durkheim's political theory.

Giddens maintains that Durkheim's liberalism in politics is not a momentary aberration from a generally conservative approach to the study of society, and that "orthodox" interpretations ignore basic aspects of his writings while misconstruing others.[8] Talcott Parsons, for example, minimizes the significance of *The Division of Labor* as a general framework for the remainder of Durkheim's writings. Consequently, he presents Durkheim's work as an ahistorical, near model-building attempt to deal with the problem of order. In *The Division of Labor,* Durkheim recognized that the abolition of a forced division of labor in the transition from mechanical to organic solidarity required major institutional changes, principally in the relationship between the state and the revived occupational associations.

Giddens further argues that change was the central issue informing Durkheim's writings. He felt the need to explain the transition from traditional to modern society, and he recognized a need for structural and institutional changes in French society to realize the ideals of the 1789 Revolution. Giddens acknowledges that, for Durkheim, change was to take place progressively, by slow accretion, not through revolution. Conflict was considered pathological when it threatened to disrupt the existing fabric of society. For this reason, Durkheim believed that class conflict could not be the vehicle for attaining social reorganization. In fact, class conflict inhibited the chances of its occurrence because it polarized competing interests and had as its goal the aims of merely a segment of society.

Durkheim failed to consider the possibility that a forced division of labor might be linked to oppressive political institutions, and that it might persist as long as the political structure remained intact. The idea of the state as an instrument of class domination plays no part in his analysis. The role Durkheim assigned to the state as the protector of individual rights places him within the mainstream of individual rights, and thus of liberal political theory. Yet these rights, whether they are derived from sociological or natural law premises can be of little practical significance while basic social and economic inequalities remain. Precisely these considerations formed the basis of libertarian analyses of the limitations on individual freedom and growth within class society. Durkheim's solution to the problem of social inequality, the takeover by the occupational associations of the traditional role of the family as inheritors of wealth, may be seen as an attempt to solve the problems posed by socialist premises, beginning from the assumption that socioeconomic classes fulfill coordinate functions rather than provide a source of conflicting interests. Durkheim reached conclusions and suggested remedies for the problems of his time that were quite distinctive.

Durkheim's approach to political socialization is best understood within the framework of his views on morals and authority, and specifically his concept of individualism. Nisbet is undoubtedly correct that the theme of authority "runs like a leitmotif through all of Durkheim's works. Second only to community, it is the dominant theme of his sociology and philosophy."[9] Durkheim perceived the social question as a moral question, involving the relationship of individuals to existing society. The society problem for him, therefore, centered on the need to devise appropriate moral rules of an authority whose superiority they acknowledge:

It is not a matter of putting a completely new society in the place of the existing one, but of adapting the latter to the new social conditions. At least, it no longer stirs questions of classes; it no longer opposes rich to poor, employers to workers—as if the only possible solution consisted of diminishing the portion of one in order to augment that of the other. But it declares, in the interest of both, the necessity of a curb from above which checks appetites and so sets a limit in the state of disarrangement, excitement, frenzied agitation, which do not spring from social activity and which even make it suffer. Put differently, the social question, posed this way, is not a question of money or force; it is a question of moral agents. What dominate human relations is not the state of our economy but, much more, the state of our morality.[10]

These rather typical passages have given rise to a wide variety of interpretations. In one of the most authoritative statements on Durkheim's approach to individualism and morality, Raymond Aron points out that "Durkheim wants to stabilize a society whose highest principle is respect for the human person and fulfillment of individual autonomy, a conservative or a rationalist-liberal interpretation of his thought is suggested."[11] Giddens sees this fusion of individualistic rationalism and collective norms as an ideal rather than a limit: "In Durkheim's writings obligation or constraint are not to be identified simply with restriction or denial, that is are not to be interpreted as simply placing limits on a range of potential individual actions in a given situation."[12]

The evolution of moral individualism associated with the division of labor and the changing content of collective consciousness as societies move toward solidarity make possible a widening range of individual thought and activity. Authority and obligation not only restrain behavior, they contribute toward shaping and developing it. Steven Lukes has adopted a similar position, arguing that the interpretation of Durkheim as fundamentally anti-liberal and anti-individualist, perhaps even as a forerunner of twentieth-century nationalism and totalitarianism, is based on "a selective misreading of certain of his writings and, in some cases, a mistaken importation into his centralized guild socialism of the connotations of Fascist corporatism."[13]

Aron, Giddens, and Lukes each maintain that Durkheim's

attempt to eliminate the false antithesis between the individual and society, and between authority and freedom,
places him within the tradition of Montesquieu and de
Tocqueville; for their common goal was a revitalized and
strengthened liberalism. The substance of these conflicting
claims can be found in Durkheim's writings on moral individualism, authority, and the state.

Durkheim's views on morality shed light on his doctrine
of political socialization in several ways: they reveal his sense
of the importance of the group as the source and object of
moral life, the place of the individual in relation to the group
and society as a whole, and his dualistic conception of human
nature, in which private passions are seen as requiring moral
discipline and submission to authority. Durkheim clearly
viewed the moral disarray of his time as a problem in social
order rather than in personal disorders (which he recognized with great discomfort). His proposed solution was an
authoritarian moral discipline designed to avoid anarchy
both in society and within the private lives of individuals.

Durkheim felt that a science of ethics could serve as a
rational, secular basis for the judgments required by moral
facts, while at the same time not destroying the *sui generis*
religious character "which is inherent in them and which
distinguishes them from all other human phenomena."[14] In
the preface to the first edition of *The Division of Labor* (1893),
he argued that his attempt "to treat the facts of the moral
life according to the method of positive sciences" did not
mean extracting ethics from science—rather it meant treating moral facts as phenomena like others by observing them,
describing them, classifying them, and seeking laws to explain them.[15] The task of a science of ethics was to distinguish ideals and moral beliefs which were most appropriate
to changes in the conditions of collective existence but which
were still largely hidden from the public consciousness. This
purpose could be achieved only by observing reality and
separating it from the ideal. In practice this meant studying

moral rules scientifically, as they manifested themselves in social behavior.

The essay "The Determination of Moral Facts" provides the clearest formulation of Durkheim's moral sociology. He argued that moral rules, whatever their specific content, imply a notion of obligation, which is the first characteristic of moral life; goodness is the second. Moral rules are obligatory because they come from society, which constitutes a moral authority and is therefore able to impose on moral rules an obligatory character. These two aspects of morality cannot be isolated empirically; they are combined in different proportions in different actions and in different societies. The notion of moral goodness can apply only to actions that are social in nature: that is, a moral rule cannot have an individual for its object. The method for determining the necessary conditions for calling a moral is to "examine the communal conscience."[16] This method reveals that: "(i) The qualification 'moral' has never been given to an act which has individual interests, or the perfection of the individual from a purely egotistic point of view, as its object; (ii) If I as an individual do not constitute *in myself* a moral end, this is also true of the other individuals who are more or less like me; (iii) From which we conclude that, if a morality exists, it can only have as object the group formed by the associated individuals—that is to say, society, *with the condition that society be always considered as being qualitatively different from the individual beings that compose it.*"[17]

The task of a science of ethics is to rationally determine the one set of moral judgments possible for a society at any given time. Durkheim's position was not wholly determinist. He did make vague allowances for circumstances in which new values emerge from the existing moral order. A science of ethics then "allows us to take up a position between these two divergent moralities, the one now existing and the one in the process of becoming."[18] Durkheim had great faith that in principle there could be scientifically ascertainable answers to ethical concerns. Once the needs of society were determined, no further justification for adopting scientific requirements was necessary. The diversity of individual moral conscience and the general mediocrity of the average man precluded making individual judgments binding. "In the sphere of morality, as in other spheres of nature, individual reason has no particular prestige as such. The only reason for which one can claim the right of intervention, and of rising above historical moral reality in order to reform it, is not my reason nor yours; it is the impersonal human reason, only truly realized in science...the science of moral facts puts us in a position to order and direct the course of moral life. The intervention of science has as its end, not the substitution of an equally collective ideal which expresses not a particular personality but the collective itself more clearly understood."[19]

As the creator and guardian of civilization, society both transcends the individual and contributes all that is of value in his nature. Social rules then are exercised by individuals with moral authority, who in turn impose such authority over the rest of society as obligatory. The fact that society has its own nature and requirements, which sometimes conflict with those of individuals, demands that we "do violence to certain of our strongest inclinations."[20] A system of authority is therefore the basis of moral life, and discipline is the authority in operation. In *Moral Education*, Durkheim argued that "to act morally one must have some authority above him before which he yields." Furthermore, authority has a cohesive function, for it accounts for the efficacy that rules have. "It is the nature of the rules that they are to be obeyed, not because of the behavior they require or the probable consequences of such behavior, but simply because they command."[21]

The acceptance of discipline for its own sake is justified on the grounds that self-control is essential to the integrity of the individual. Without discipline, no society could sustain itself. Morality therefore consists in a state of dependence, and to define it through liberty is inappropriate. "The theories that celebrate the beneficence of unrestricted liberties are apologies for the diseased state. One may even say that, contrary to appearances, the words 'liberty' and 'lawlessness' clash in their coupling since liberty is the fruit of regulation. Through the practice of moral rules we develop the capacity to govern and regulate ourselves, which is the whole reality of liberty."[22]

Attachment to the group is justified on similar grounds: social life is the source of all that is best in human nature. Durkheim's solution to the problem of individual autonomy is that freedom rests on knowledge. In understanding the reasons behind rules of conduct, men will obey them freely and continue to respect their authority.

Durkheim's teleological ethics has been criticized on the grounds that it confuses matters properly belonging to the sociology of morality with questions of pure ethics which are of a metaphysical nature; and further, that Durkheim's method of investigation was not empirical but rationalistic—informed throughout by a Kantian moral imperative.[23] The basic political implications are sufficiently clear: moral acts consist of an obligatory element, supported by repressive sanctions for violations, as well as the positive incentives of ideals. Durkheim's method for determining which acts possessed these characteristics was not to conduct an empirical investigation but to appeal to "common opinion."[24]

The collective conscience tells us that disinterestedness and devotion, prerequisites for moral life, become meaningful only when the object of morality has a higher moral value than individuals. This object or being can only be the collectivity. To act morally is to act in terms of the collective interest. The choice of allegiance lies between God and society. "I myself am quite indifferent to this choice, since I see in the Divinity only society transfigured and symbolically expressed."[25] In appealing to society in general as the object deserving our highest devotion, Durkheim did not distinguish between the real and the ideal or specify which societies embodied ideals that could command allegiance. At the same time that he extolled the virtues of society in general, Durkheim called for a system of moral discipline to remind the individual "what he should do so as not to damage collective interests and so as not to disorganize the society of which he forms a part."[26] There are numerous instances throughout Durkheim's work in which he maintains that society must curb the impulses and appetites of its members, and that the latter must recognize the superiority of society. But the apparently authoritarian implications of his analysis of man's relation to society is muted by his attitude toward political socialization, in which he insists on the need for intermediary groups to counterbalance the authority of the state. And this relationship between groups of citizens and representatives of agencies of power is how Durkheim first comes to a discussion of politics.

Durkheim first traced the origins of the state in *The Division of Labor* within the framework of a progressive movement from mechanical to organic solidarity. This work also sets out a theme elaborated on in his later writings—the conception of moral authority rooted in the collective conscience, which is the basis for every manifestation of social life. Later in his career, Durkheim argued in an almost Rousseauian vein that the state was the "organ of social thought," distinct from the diffuse collective conscience. He came to see the moral superiority of democracy as consisting in a high level of communication between the collective conscience and the individual will.

Durkheim defined the collective conscience in *The Division of Labor* as "the totality of beliefs and sentiments common to the average citizens of the same society" which forms a determinate system with its own life.[27] Although it may be diffuse in every society, it has specific characteristics that make it a distinct reality. "It is, in effect, independent of the particular conditions in which individuals are placed: they pass on and it remains."[28] It is therefore quite distinct from individual consciences, although it can be realized only through them. Further on, he suggests that collective sentiments "have exceptional force because of their collective origin, their universality, their permanence, and their intrinsic intensity."[29] They separate themselves from the rest of our conscience, which is feebler.

The collective conscience was the basis of social cohesion in less advanced societies. Societies characterized by mechanical solidarity are dominated by tradition. "The individual is totally subordinated to the collective conscience which completely envelops one's whole conscience and coincides in all points with it. But at that moment our individuality is nil."[30] The concept of moral individualism emerges as societies move toward organic solidarity. The individual is emancipated from the despotism of the group as a result of the increasing division of labor and the related changes in social customs and law—the shift from penal to restitutive sanctions. In this historical movement, the collective sentiments, which the individual embodies rather than society as an impersonal force becomes dominant. "For this [transition] to be so, the individual personality must have become a much more important element in the life of society, and in order for it to have acquired this importance, it is not enough for the personal conscience of each to have grown in absolute value, but also to have grown more than the common conscience. It must have been emancipated from the yoke of the latter, and consequently, the latter must have fallen from its thrown and lost the determinate power that it originally used to exercise."[31]

In primitive societies, everything social is religious. Indeed, the two words are synonymous.[32] Sanctions are therefore repressive, because a criminal act is one that is committed against society as a whole, and society is possessed of a sacred or religious equality. With the growth of individualism, however, a distinction is drawn between crimes against persons and crimes against the collectivity. The content of collective sentiments had changed.

As social beliefs and practices take on less of a religious character, the individual becomes the object of a kind of religion. "We erect a cult in behalf of personal dignity, which, as every strong cult, already has its superstitions."[33] The common conscience does not disappear, but it comes to consist of more and more indeterminate feelings that leave greater scope for the play of individual differences.

With the decline of social links that comes from likeness, there comes a new form of solidarity. Comte had argued that the division of labor threatened social cohesion by undermining the consensus of moral beliefs. Durkheim maintained to the contrary that "It is the division of labor which, more and more, fills the role that was formerly filled by the common conscience. It is the principal bond of social aggregates of higher types."[34] Social order rests on the complementarity and interdependence of cooperatively functioning individuals and groups. Thus, despite the declining significance of traditional beliefs, modern society for Durkheim is not inevitably tending toward disintegration. The division of labor is the foundation of moral order, for through participation in a subgroup individuals become aware of their dependence on society. Eventually they will come to regard themselves as part of the whole, and altruism will become the fundamental basis of social life. "Thus, it is wrong to oppose a society which comes from a community of beliefs to one which has a cooperative basis, according only to the former's amoral character, and seeing in the latter only an economic grouping. In reality, cooperation also has its intrinsic morality."[35]

Durkheim considers occupational associations, by virtue of their voluntary nature, essential to a democratic order. As a political liberal, Durkheim valued the breadth of individual development possible in modern societies, but as a sociological conservative, he feared the consequences of the unrestricted play of individual impulses, uninhibited by a clearly moral code. In order to avoid the dangers of anomie brought about by the loss of regulative norms of conduct, he proposed the reintegration of individuals into secondary groups, according to the particular social and economic activity to which they dedicate themselves. Occupational organizations were therefore destined to replace territorial and clan or tribal divisions so that ultimately "a day will come when our whole social and political organization will have a base exclusively, or almost exclusively, occupational."[36]

It is evident that Durkheim managed to conflate political representation with social integration. His emphasis on the role of occupations and corporate groups confuses two layers of human organization. He saw anomie as a problem at the margins, hence his concern with *Suicide;* but he also viewed occupational groups as the means of political integration and representation. The difficulty is that the collective consciousness, which acts to integrate individuals socially, does so in a variety of ways that have little if anything to do with occupational role. But unless this notion of consciousness is to avoid the Germanic emphasis on *Geist*, which Durkheim clearly strove to achieve, he must conclude that a concept of society is a priori, something that exists in all human beings. Families, schools, churches, etc. may all be vessels in which human beings originally attain knowledge of the collective conscience. But then Durkheim really is reducing his concept to little more than what is now referred to as political socialization.

Maurice Halbwachs was the only member of the Durkheim circle who seemed to appreciate the cul-de-sac into which the collective conscience ended. I suspect that the Dreyfus Affair fueled Durkheim's animus for things directly political, especially by parties who viewed immediate events too passionately and measured events too intensely. Those individuals were as assuredly the source of societal disintegration as the carriers of the anomic or alienated traditions. In short, Durkheim was the ultimate moderate, the individualist who sought out a sociological middle ground, but as a person desirous of avoiding the risks of societal collapse in the name of political cleansing.

Organic solidarity presupposes a moral person; but such personalism is not to be confused with egoism. It does not promote anomie or the decay of moral authority. Durkheim made this explicit in his comment on the Dreyfus Affair (the 1898 article "Individualism and Intellectuals"), in which he asserted a radical distinction between egoism and rationalist individualism. Durkheim therein distinguished his theory of individualism from the "utilitarian egoism of Spencer and the economists," which he regarded as dying a natural death. He also rejected the individualism of Kant and Rousseau, the set of ideas "which the Declaration of Rights of Man sought more or less successfully, to translate into formulae, that which is currently taught in our schools and which has become the basis of our moral catechism."[37] For the Enlightenment, "the only ways of acting that are moral are those which are fitting for all men equally, that is to say, which are implied in the notion of man in general."[38] This type of individualism has given the human person a sacred quality. It is also "a religion of who man is, at the same time, both believer and God."

What Kant and Rousseau did not understand was that individualist ethics must be derived from society. The individual receives from society even those beliefs that deify him. Individualism is not derived from individuals, and thus not from egoistic sentiments, despite the reliance on a common term. Individualism is thus no less a social institution than collectivism. It is humanity that is sacred and worthy of respect, and the individual deserves respect because he possesses within himself something of humanity. "Individualism thus understood is the glorification not of the self, but of the individual in general. Its motive force is not egoism but sympathy for all that is human, a wider pity for all sufferings, for all human miseries, a more ardent desire to combat and alleviate them, a greater thirst for justice."[39]

The cult of the individual has a religious character. Durkheim assigns it a role formerly played by religion in traditional societies. Once a whole people pursue a goal, it acquires a moral supremacy that raises it far above private goals and thereby gives it a religious character. Durkheim believed that "this religion of humanity [with a] rational expression of the individualistic morality" was the only set of ideals which could hope to perform the cohesive function in an industrial society with a highly differentiated division of labor.[40] The sentiments awakened by this "religion" were the only ones to be found in almost all hearts, the only ones to survive the tides of particular opinions.

An attack on the individualist faith could put national existence in jeopardy, for such an attack constitutes an attack on collective sentiments. "A religion which tolerates acts of sacrilege abdicates any sway over men's minds. Thus the individualist, who defends the rights of the individual, defends at the same time the vital interests of society; for he is preventing the criminal impoverishment of that final reserve of collective ideas and sentiments that constitutes the very soul of the nation."[41] Thus, as Durkheim perceived it, the central issue was less the fate of one unfortunate individual than the need to uphold the moral foundations of the nation.

The division of labor and the development of organic solidarity paralleled the development of contract and the state. The growth of the governmental organ was proportionate to the progress of division of labor, but the state enhanced its functions through public services. Because they administered but did not command, these expanding administrative functions required only restitutive but not repressive sanctions. However, in "Two Laws of Penal Evolution," Durkheim modified this hypothesis, declaring that

the coercive powers of the state could vary independently of
the level of social development. The range of social goods
provided by the state varies with the division of labor.
Durkheim directly confronted the problem of a social distribution of power but failed to pursue the political implications of his analysis of penal evolution.[42]

Durkheim was reluctant to take cognizance of power and
violence, arguing that political society is determined neither by possession of a fixed territorial area nor by density
of population. Instead, it owes its existence to "the coming
together of a rather large number of secondary groups, subject to the same one authority, which is not itself subject to
any other superior authority duly, constituted."[43] The term
"state" refers to the agents of the sovereign authority, and
"political society" to the complex group of which the state
is the highest organ. The state "is a group of officials *sui
generis,* within which representations and acts of volition
involving the collectivity are worked out, although they are
not the product of the collectivity."[44] As such, it does not
embody the collective consciousness, which is a diffuse collection of social sentiments and states of mind. It "is the
center of a particular kind of consciousness, of one that is
limited but higher, clearer and with a more vivid sense of
itself."[45] Nor should it be confused with the secondary organs within the immediate sphere of its control, for these
organs are concerned primarily with administrative and
executive functions.

Reflecting the prevailing organicism of the late nineteenth
century, Durkheim argued that the difference between the
state and its executive agencies is isomorphic to that between the central nervous system and the muscular system.
"Strictly speaking, the state is the very organ of social
thought."[46] This highly abstract definition of the state di-
verts attention away from the facts of state power and toward the moral and symbolic roles of the state. Giddens has
recognized Durkheim's overriding concern with moral ques-

tions: "In Durkheim's conception, the state must play a moral as well as an economic role; and the alleviation of the malaise of the modern world must be sought in measures which are in general moral rather than economic."[47]

In the lectures entitled *Professional Ethics and Civil Morals*, Durkheim's purpose was to analyze the nature of civic morals, or the shared mutual obligations of the state and its citizens. But before one could approach the subject of political obligation, Durkheim thought he should deal with this subject. Durkheim thought it necessary to understand which ends the state normally pursues and should pursue in the social conditions of the day. In answering this question, Durkheim begins by examining and rejecting two traditional theories of the state: the liberal/individualist view, which he associated both with Spencer and the economists on one hand and Kant and Rousseau on the other; and the mystical conception of the state, which he associated with Hegel. The advocates of the first view hold that society consists of an aggregate of individuals. The individual benefits materially, morally, and intellectually from living in society, but the state, of itself, adds nothing. Its role is therefore a minimal one: safeguarding individual rights or administering a wholly negative justice. From the Hegelian standpoint, "it is argued that every society has an aim superior to individual aims and unrelated to them." Nonetheless, "individuals are mere instruments of the state. They should work for its greater glory and rest contented when they receive in return some of the reflected rays of that glory."[48]

Durkheim rejects these views on the grounds that, throughout history, we observe a parallel development of the powers and functions of the state and an increasingly widespread belief in the rights and dignity of the individual. Durkheim argued that the only way of getting over the apparent contradiction was to abandon the postulate that the rights of the individual are inherent and to admit that the granting and protection of these rights is precisely the task of the state. The individual can then be understood to develop without requiring any diminution of the state, "since he would be in some respects the product himself of the state, and since the activity of the state would in its nature be liberating to him.[49]

Against utilitarian individualism, Durkheim argues that man is a product of society: It is society that has raised him above the level of his physical nature. Individuals have a moral existence through the state alone: "Rights and liberties are not things inherent in man as such. If you analyze man's constitution you will find no trace of the sacredness with which he is invested and which confers upon him these rights. This character has been added to him by society. Society has consecrated the individual and made him preeminently worthy of respect. The individual submits to society and this submission is the condition of his liberation. For man freedom consists of deliverance from blind, unthinking physical forces; this he achieves by opposing against them the great and intelligent force, which is society, under whose protection, he shelters. By putting himself under the wing of society, he makes himself also, to a certain extent, dependent upon it. But this is a liberating dependence. There is no paradox here."[50]

Association and group life give rise to a psychic life that is richer and more varied than is possible for the solitary individual. While society enriches individual nature, it also tends to subject that nature to itself, but because the individual "naturally desires what it desires" he will "accept without difficulty the state of subjection to which he finds himself reduced."[51]

History demonstrates to Durkheim that rights are acquired only in and through society, and it is the duty of the state to organize and protect these rights, to bring out all that is best in its citizens by "calling them to a moral way of life."[52] He notes that the concept of individual rights emerges only after the historical demise of collective tyranny: "individualism establishes itself in fact, and...with time, the fact becomes a right."[53] This is only possible, however, if secondary groups are prevented from possessing autonomy and from becoming small societies unto themselves, exerting mastery over their members and molding them at will. The essential function of the state is to liberate individual personalities by offsetting the pressure on them of local, domestic, occupational, and other secondary groups.

On the other hand, to counter any tendency toward despotism or absolutism, the local authority of secondary groups must counterbalance the state's authority. "It is out of this conflict of social forces that individual liberties are born."[54] Durkheim was specifically concerned here with French history rather than general theory. Secondary associations are necessary to remedy both the social and political malaise of *fin de siècle* France: politically, they will protect the individual from the power of the state and, socially, they will provide him with moral rules to regulate his conduct. The latter function is of particular importance in the economic sphere, which is in large part freed from "the moderating action of regulation."[55] In the preface to the second edition of *The Division of Labor,* Durkheim argued that anomie is present in the occupational system to the degree that moral authority is lacking within and among occupational groups. The primary function of associations is therefore moral rather than economic: they have a moral power capable of containing individual egos and maintaining a sense of solidarity among their members.

Durkheim first touched on the problem of the individual's triangular relation to the state and the authority of intermediary groups in the final pages of *Suicide,* where he expressed concern about the growth of the powers of the state after the disappearance of occupational groups at the end of the eighteenth century. The state, confronted by nothing but an unstable flux of individuals, was compelled to assume functions for which it was not suited. Similarly, individuals were no longer subject to any collective control other than the state's, since it was the sole organized collectivity.[56] But since the state was remote from individuals, it could exert only a distant, discontinuous influence over them. Thus Durkheim concludes, "they inevitably lapse into egoism or anarchy."[57]

The remedy for both the danger of unilateral state action and the moral isolation of individuals is for the state to share its authority with occupational groups. "The only decentralization which would make possible the multiplication of the centers of communal life without weakening national unity is what might be called *occupational decentralization*. As each of these centers would be only the focus of a special, limited activity, they would be inseparable from one another and the individual could thus form attachments there without demonstrating less solidarity with the whole."[58]

The institutionalization of individualism through the formation of integrating links between the political and economic orders takes several forms: first, economic relationships are made moral through occupational associations, and second, the state eliminates the forced division of labor to ensure a more just distribution of functions. Organic solidarity presupposes equality of opportunity, and it is the duty of the state to change the laws of contract and property to suit new social conditions. Durkheim argued that contracts between social unequals could not be just, even though they might be socially sanctioned. Consent could be binding only when freely given and, "anything that lessens the liberty of the contracting party, lessens the binding force of the contract."[59] Contracts could be just only when they did not exploit one of the contracting parties. Durkheim identified inheritance as a primary cause of the perpetuation of social injustice and argued that it was incompatible with moral individualism.

Remedying unjust economic relationships requires state intervention and regulation as well as moral reorganization. Durkheim believed, however, that the state was too unwieldy to manage the economy with any degree of competence. The solution was, therefore, to abolish the traditional system of inheritance and to decentralize the management of the economy. Occupational groups, "becoming in a sense, in the economic sphere, the heirs of the family" (but with wider ranging powers) were particularly well suited to fulfilling these tasks.[60]

Durkheim's treatment of the occupational association was closely connected to his analysis of the preconditions for a democratic society. One precondition was the existence of strong secondary groups, and in the modern world these could only be occupational associations. He rejected Montesquieu's equilibrium model, based on the number of people who participate in government, on the grounds that it rested on a confusion between the political state and the social goods: "We must therefore not say that democracy is the political form of a society governing itself, in which the government is spread throughout the *milieu* of the nation. Such a definition is a contradiction in terms. It would be almost as if we said that democracy is a political society without a state. In fact, the state is nothing if it is not an organ distinct from the rest of society."[61]

Government is always in the hands of a minority, chosen either by birth or election. Durkheim's view of democracy contains a peculiar elitist critique of any mandated or representative theory of democracy. In his opinion, excessive politicization reabsorbs the state into the society. The role of the state is not to reflect the unconsidered sentiments of the mass of society, but to give the mass thought a more reflective and rational aspect. In the absence of a strongly defined state consciousness, citizens are not restrained but mimicked in their opinions. The individual critical spirit is allowed full play and everything becomes a matter of controversy. It is not surprising, then, that Durkheim opposed direct representation, because it would almost inevitably lead to representatives applying themselves exclusively to the promotion of their constituents' views—and the electorate would begin to claim this docile attitude on the part of representatives as their obligation to the constituency.

A primary characteristic of democracy is the linkages established between this collective consciousness and the cluster of individual expressions of that consciousness. The moral superiority of democracy lies in its reflective capacity: "To be autonomous means, for the human being, to understand the necessities he has to bow to and accept them with full knowledge of the fact. Nothing that we do can make the laws of things other than they are, but we free ourselves of them in thinking them, that is, in making them ours by thought. This is what gives democracy a moral superiority."[62]

In addition to freeing the individual from the state, secondary groups also give it a capacity for autonomous action. They act as intermediaries in a two-way communication system between the state and its citizens, and they foster the moral aims and sentiments of the collective conscience. They also clarify the distinction between the state and the rest of society, and for this reason it is desirable that they should form the basis of the political structure: "The idea is already gaining ground that the professional association is the true electoral unity, and because the links attaching us to one another derive from our calling rather than from any regional bonds of loyalty, it is natural that the political structure should reflect the way in which we ourselves form into groups of our own accord."[63]

The clearest formulation of state power comes not in any of Durkheim's standard works, but in *L'Année Sociologique*. In his summaries of the literature on political organization, Durkheim was able to show, in a comparative format, how different forms of society cope with problems of authority and order: "In the West, the state has succeeded in superimposing itself on political orders already in existence and divided among themselves by all sorts of conflicts of interest, and it has made it its business and *raison d'être* to merge

them and unify them. In Russia, by way of contrast, it is
unity that is more of a primary factor, and it is the state that
has dispersed the population into distinct political orders,
it is the former which has divided the inhabitants into categories and classes in order to give society a more solid
base."[64] The inversion of state and society represented for
Durkheim the source of autocracy, an order based on coercion rather than consent; and it was of social order based
on consent that Durkheim sought.[65]

Since the Russian State is not a union of classes like the
feudal order, but a union of stratified communes, it was
able to develop a strong policy thrust, despite its autocratic
characteristics.[66] Indeed, Durkheim viewed the Russian State
as the core of Pan-Slavism, and speculated that Pan-German-
ism and Pan-Hellenism drew inspiration from a similar state
structure, although one based on international political interests rather than national or class interests.[67] But the difference between Russian states and Western societies remained a leitmotif in Durkheim's work. His central
preoccupation was how to avoid crisis without resorting to a
total state. In this context his comparison of structures remains fascinating.

Basic to Durkheim's political theory is that democratic
institutions will be strong to the degree that society is pluralist in nature; but pluralism is possible only to the extent
that the state can be bridled. Secondary groups that offset
the power of the state also integrate individuals into the life
of society and provide them with the moral discipline necessary to preserve the democratic order. The strengthening
of intermediary groups and the determination of a new code
of moral rules must avert the disruptive effect of the breakdown of moral consensus, as societies become more complex. Far from lamenting the passing of the all-encompassing *conscience collective* of traditional societies and the passive
conformity that resulted from it, Durkheim believed that in
the process of emerging, the harmonious social order would

allow for greater individual autonomy. His definition of autonomy and freedom was guarded and restrictive, for it was based on social, and not individual, requirements.

Freedom demands moral discipline and the cultivation of a sense of social responsibility through acknowledgment of the authority of social rules. Durkheim recognized the potential infinitude of human wants, and the need for individual submission to the needs of the collectivity when these conflicted with individual needs. "What is needed if social order is to reign is that the mass of men be content with their lot. But what is needed for them to be content is not that they have more or less, but that they be convinced that there be an authority whose superiority they acknowledge and which tells them what is right."[68]

Durkheim's theory of moral authority has led some to charge him with authoritarianism and collectivism. But it has also been argued that his analysis of the occupational associations, the basic units of his theory of moral authority, more closely resembles reformist syndicalism.[69]

The professional associations were suited to the task of economic regulation because economic life was considered too complex to be handled by an awkward and unwieldy state apparatus. Furthermore, despite the apparent authoritarianism of the view expressed above, Durkheim was concerned with injustice rather than exploitation; hence his emphasis on the distorting effects on social relations of inherited wealth and poverty. He felt the division of labor had to be spontaneous: "By spontaneity we must understand not simply the absence of all express violence, but also of everything that can even shackle the free unfolding of the social force that each carries in himself. It supposes, not only that individuals are not relegated to determinate functions by force, but also that no obstacle of whatever nature, prevents them from occupying the place in the social framework which is compatible with their faculties. In short, labor is divided spontaneously only if society is constituted in such a way that social inequalities exactly express natural inequalities."[70]

Durkheim's moral philosophy was basically authoritarian and his political theory overwhelmingly liberal. His abstract definitions of the state as the "organ of social thought" had the effect of leaving his analysis of political power as a residual element in his sociology. With the exception of his observations on Russia, he did not undertake an analysis of the national conditions under which the state is able to separate itself from the rest of society or the circumstances under which the legitimacy of political authority can be questioned. Durkheim gives us little guidance about the possible moral grounds for civil disobedience. He assumes that the activity of a state built on the ethic of moral cooperation would be liberating for the individual. In every case, resistance to prevailing morality is justified only if the suggested substitute is more appropriate to changed social conditions. But the task of determining "the direction in which society is moving" is assigned to a science of ethics, not to individual reason.

Durkheim argued that all moral systems are a function of social organization, and that each society has a morality suited to it. If this position is not qualified to permit some grounds for legitimate resistance to prevailing authority, it ultimately results in a tacit acquiescence to totalitarianism. A theory that does not allow for limiting moral and political obligation is not able to tell us very much when the extreme case becomes normal. For individuals to accept Durkheim's definition that the function of the state is "to think" on their behalf, they must abdicate moral responsibility for social injustice.

Durkheim's exclusion of interpersonal relations from the domain of morals, together with his claim that moral duty consists in acting in terms of the collective interest as defined by an abstract collectivity, effectively eliminates the possibility that a social group or social class may organize

itself and work toward social change. It also leads to a neglect of the problem of distributive justice or economic democracy.[71] Justice is concerned not only with society as a
whole and each of its component members, but also with
the relations of individuals among one another.

This faith in political socialization is self-consciously for-
malist. Direct empirical evidence is adduced only to support his positions. His studies tell us little about the functioning of political parties, the structure of parliaments, the
decision-making process, or the role of the state as executive agency. Durkheim's theory of democracy remains obscure. To argue that the moral superiority of democracy
consists in a high level of interplay between the consciousness of the state and the unreflective sentiments of its citizens is to assume the excellence of a communication network as a criterion of moral goodness. The rejection of a
concept of mass democracy, which is based on the number
of people who participate in government, on the grounds
that "if everyone governs, there is no government," destroys
the conventional meaning of liberalism as such.

Durkheim veered away from liberalism in arguing that a
minority always governs de facto. As a result, he emphasized the importance of the methods or procedures by
which a minority comes to power, and probably paid too
little attention to the legitimacy of such power. This led
Durkheim to conclude that there is only a slight difference
between hereditary monarchy, military dictatorship, and
an elite elected indirectly through occupational associations
for a limited period of time.[72] But how, then, can Durkheim
claim that democracy establishes closer communication
with its citizens than other forms of indirect domination?
And why should this matter? Pareto, arguing from a similar methodological stance, arrived at a far more conservative conclusion.

The most valuable and enduring aspect of Durkheim's
political vision is the idea that secondary (or voluntary)

groups possessing legal authority and status as public institutions are necessary both to offset the power of the state
and to provide individuals with some sense of autonomy
from, and a possibility of participation in, social life.
Durkheim's theory of political socialization is concerned
with conflicts of interest, legal injustice, and the nature of
power. However, his greater preoccupation with moral authority led him to develop an abstract and artificial notion
of the state which failed to account for the rise of bureaucracy and new social formations; worse still, he acknowledged only relative degrees of support for the state, rather
than kinds and degrees of opposition to it. As a result, in
Durkheim's world, one is either socialized into the state or
forced to accept a deviant posture toward its existence—precisely the dilemma which continues to plague advocates of
political socialization as a model for citizen participation in
present-day political science and liberal theory generally.

Durkheim's rage for order produced a vision of how individuals are integrated into, and reconciled to, forms of social authority. But without any corresponding appreciation
of the political and economic sources of disorder, Durkheim
concluded with a view of state power as essentially benign.
As a result, Durkheim provided no consistent framework or
guidelines to his own essentially democratic decisions on
critical features of French and European societies. Having
noted this ambiguous legacy, it would be a profound mistake to dismiss Durkheim on such grounds. His attention to
socializing intermediary organizations can be taken as a distinctive virtue of his thought. Instead of responding to or
following the concerns of Weber, Pareto, Mosca and Sorel,
that is theorists of state institutions narrowly understood,
he is important precisely because of his ambiguity, that is,
the difficulty in separating out the social from the political.
Intermediary or socializing agencies has a deeply political
function that tended to be ignored by the advocates of the
conflict school of political sociology. In short, it was by ig-

noring the state that Durkheim tells us much that is important for political sociology.

In the context of nineteenth century political sociology, the field suffered because of its failure to pay due attention to the inevitably political importance of ostensibly social relationships such as the family, household, status groups, friendship networks, and occupational organizations. These relationships are not simply constitutive of but limited to the domain of *burgerlichtgesellschaft,* as distinct from the state. Rather, it is through these institutions that the majority of society experiences the political; and it is upon these socializing agencies that statist institution rest. From Plato through Rousseau, political education was a coherent concept, and an area of legitimate concern. At some along the line, attention to the relationship between political and pre-political became obscured. Along with Montesquieu and Tocqueville, Durkheim is the lone figure who attended to this relationship in the modern context.

Certain strength resides in Durkheim's admittedly ambiguous relationship to notions of power and state control. While preferring to deal with issues of authority he avoided an excessive reliance upon individualistic extremes of anomie and suicide, or more germane to our own age, to a fractional social science that mirrors divisions at large, with its focus on ethnic, class and occupational divisions. While Durkheim provides a powerful defense of pluralism, his focus on political socialization to a common culture also and more significantly provides a powerful antidote to the contemporary tendencies for pluralism to spill over into factionalism. Given one side of the canon that focuses on themes such as elite machination, legitimization, power, conflict, domination, and state power as ultimate power— and not incidentally, a tradition that is correspondingly tone deaf to issues of consensus and political socialization—the need is great for an appreciation of the other side of the helix, the line of development from Montesquieu to

Tocqueville, to Durkheim. For it is scarcely an accident that it is from this side of the canon in political sociology that we derive the impulse to democratic order rather than revolutionary disorder.

Notes

1. Judith N. Shklar, *Political Thought and Political Thinkers*. Chicago: The University of Chicago Press, 1998, p. 282.
2. See Raymond Aron, *Main Currents in Sociological Thought: Volume Two*. New Brunswick, Transaction Publishers, 1998. It is Aron's contention that Durkheim's search for consensus led him to see beyond the state into society. My own view is rather that this consensual impulse led Durkheim not to take seriously the state at all. But whatever the differences between us on the origins of Durkheim's relative indifference to state power, we share the same belief that it was indeed not a part of his larger sociological perspective.
3. Émile Durkheim, contributions to *L'Année Sociologique: 1893–1913*, in Yash Nandan, ed. New York: The Free Press, 1980, p. 306.
4. Robert A. Nisbet, "Conservation and Sociology," *American Journal of Sociology*, 58, 1952, pp. 167–75.
5. Robert A. Nisbet, "Conservation and Sociology," *American Journal of Sociology*, 58, 1952, p. 174.
6. Lewis A. Coser, "Durkheim's Conservatism and Its Implications for his Sociological Theory," in *Émile Durkheim: 1858–1917*, Kurt H. Wolff, ed. Columbus, Ohio: Ohio State University Press 1960, p. 221.
7. Anthony Giddens, "Introduction" to *Émile Durkheim: Selected Writings*, Cambridge: Cambridge University Press, 1972, p. 48.
8. Anthony Giddens, "Introduction" to *Émile Durkheim: Selected Writings*, Cambridge: Cambridge University Press, 1972, pp. 47–48.
9. Robert A. Nisbet, *The Sociological Tradition*. New York: Basic Books, 1966, p. 150.
10. Émile Durkheim, *Socialism*, Alvin W. Gouldner, ed. New York: The Free Press, 1967, pp. 246–47.
11. Raymond Aron, *Main Currents in Sociological Thought, Volume II*. New York and London: Basic Books/Harper & Row, 1967, pp. 96–97.
12. Anthony Giddens, "Introduction," p. 43.
13. Steven Lukes, "Introduction" to "Individualism and the Intellectuals," *Political Studies*, 18, 1969, p. 18.
14. Émile Durkheim, *Sociology and Philosophy*, 1924. New York and London: The Free Press and Routledge, Kegan Paul Ltd., 1965, p. 62.
15. Émile Durkheim, *The Division of Labor in Society* (1893). New York: The Free Press, 1964, p. 32.
16. Émile Durkheim, *Sociology and Philosophy*, 1924. New York and London: The Free Press and Routledge, Kegan Paul Ltd., 1965, p. 50.

17. Émile Durkheim, *Sociology and Philosophy*, 1924. New York and London: The Free Press and Routledge, Kegan Paul Ltd., 1965, p. 37.
18. Émile Durkheim, *Sociology and Philosophy*, 1924. New York and London: The Free Press and Routledge, Kegan Paul Ltd., 1965, p. 61.
19. Émile Durkheim, *Sociology and Philosophy*, 1924. New York and London: The Free Press and Routledge, Kegan Paul Ltd., 1965, p. 65.
20. Émile Durkheim, "The Dualism of Human Nature and Its Social Conditions" (1914) in *Émile Durkheim: 1858-1917*. Columbus, Ohio: The Ohio State University Press.
21. Émile Durkheim, *Moral Education* (1925). New York: The Free Press, 1961, p. 34.
22. Émile Durkheim, *Moral Education* (1925). New York: The Free Press, 1961, p. 54.
23. Steven Lukes, *Émile Durkheim, His Life and Work*. New York: Harper & Row, 1972, pp. 410-34; and Morris Ginsberg, "Durkheim's Ethical Theory," *On the Diversity of Morals, Vol. I*. Melbourne: Heinemann Ltd., 1956, pp. 41-54.
24. Émile Durkheim, *Sociology and Philosophy*, 1924. New York and London: The Free Press and Routledge, Kegan Paul Ltd., 1965, p. 37.
25. Émile Durkheim, *Sociology and Philosophy*, 1924. New York and London: The Free Press and Routledge, Kegan Paul Ltd., 1965, p. 52.
26. Émile Durkheim, *Professional Ethics and Civic Morals* (1950). Glencoe, Ill.: The Free Press, 1958, p. 14.
27. Émile Durkheim, *The Division of Labor in Society*, (1893). New York: The Free Press, 1964, p. 79.
28. Émile Durkheim, *The Division of Labor in Society*, (1893). New York: The Free Press, 1964, p. 80.
29. Émile Durkheim, *The Division of Labor in Society*, (1893). New York: The Free Press, 1964, p. 100.
30. Émile Durkheim, *The Division of Labor in Society*, (1893). New York: The Free Press, p. 130.
31. Émile Durkheim, *The Division of Labor in Society*, (1893). New York: The Free Press, p. 167.
32. Émile Durkheim, *The Division of Labor in Society*, (1893). New York: The Free Press, p. 169.
33. Émile Durkheim, *The Division of Labor in Society*, (1893). New York: The Free Press, p. 172.
34. Émile Durkheim, *The Division of Labor in Society*, (1893). New York: The Free Press, p. 173.
35. Émile Durkheim, *The Division of Labor in Society*, (1893). New York: The Free Press, p. 228.
36. Émile Durkheim, *The Division of Labor in Society*, (1893). New York: The Free Press, pp. 187-88.
37. Émile Durkheim, "Individualism and the Intellectuals" (1898), *Political Studies* 18, 1969, p. 21.
38. Émile Durkheim, "Individualism and the Intellectuals" (1898), *Political Studies* 18, p. 21.

39. Émile Durkheim, "Individualism and the Intellectuals" (1898), *Political Studies* 18, p. 24.
40. Émile Durkheim, "Individualism and the Intellectuals" (1898), *Political Studies* 18, p. 27.
41. Émile Durkheim, "Individualism and the Intellectuals" (1898), *Political Studies* 18, pp. 27–28.
42. Melvin Richter, "Durkheim's Politics and Political Theory," in *Émile Durkheim: 1858–1917*, pp. 192–93.
43. Émile Durkheim, *Professional Ethics and Civic Morals*, p. 45.
44. Émile Durkheim, *Professional Ethics and Civic Morals* (1950). Glencoe, Ill.: The Free Press, 1958, pp. 49–50.
45. Émile Durkheim, *Professional Ethics and Civic Morals* (1950). Glencoe, Ill.: The Free Press, 1958, p. 50.
46. Émile Durkheim, *Professional Ethics and Civic Morals* (1950). Glencoe, Ill.: The Free Press, 1958, p. 51.
47. Émile Durkheim, *Moral Education, p. 99.*
48. Émile Durkheim, *Professional Ethics and Civil Morals*, p. 54.
49. Émile Durkheim, *Professional Ethics and Civic Morals* (1950). Glencoe, Ill.: The Free Press, 1958, p. 57.
50. Émile Durkheim, *Sociology and Philosophy,* 1924. New York and London: The Free Press and Routledge, Kegan Paul Ltd., 1965, p. 72.
51. Émile Durkheim, *Professional Ethics and Civic Morals* (1950). Glencoe, Ill.: The Free Press, 1958, p. 61.
52. Émile Durkheim, *Professional Ethics and Civic Morals* (1950). Glencoe, Ill.: The Free Press, 1958, p. 69.
53. Émile Durkheim, *Professional Ethics and Civic Morals* (1950). Glencoe, Ill.: The Free Press, 1958, p. 61.
54. Émile Durkheim, *Professional Ethics and Civic Morals* (1950). Glencoe, Ill.: The Free Press, 1958, p. 63.
55. Émile Durkheim, *The Division of Labor in Society,* (1893). New York: The Free Press, 1964, p. 2.
56. Émile Durkheim, *Suicide* (1897), George Simpson, ed. New York: The Free Press, 1966, p. 388.
57. Émile Durkheim, *Suicide* (1897), George Simpson, ed. New York: The Free Press, 1966, p. 389.
58. Émile Durkheim, *Suicide* (1897), George Simpson, ed. New York: The Free Press, 1966, p. 390.
59. Émile Durkheim, *Professional Ethics and Civic Morals* (1950). Glencoe, Ill.: The Free Press, 1958, p. 203.
60. Émile Durkheim, *Professional Ethics and Civic Morals* (1950). Glencoe, Ill.: The Free Press, 1958, p. 218.
61. Émile Durkheim, *Professional Ethics and Civic Morals* (1950). Glencoe, Ill.: The Free Press, 1958, p. 82.
62. Émile Durkheim, *Professional Ethics and Civic Morals* (1950). Glencoe, Ill.: The Free Press, 1958, p. 91.
63. Émile Durkheim, *Professional Ethics and Civic Morals* (1950). Glencoe, Ill.: The Free Press, 1958, p. 103.

64. Émile Durkheim, contributions to *L'Année Sociologique: 1893–1913*, in Yash Nandan, ed. New York: The Free Press, 1980, p. 345.
65. Émile Durkheim, contributions to *L'Année Sociologique: 1893–1913*, in Yash Nandan, ed. New York: The Free Press, 1980, p. 346.
66. Émile Durkheim, contributions to *L'Année Sociologique: 1893–1913*, in Yash Nandan, ed. New York: The Free Press, 1980, p. 348.
67. Émile Durkheim, contributions to *L'Année Sociologique: 1893–1913*, in Yash Nandan, ed. New York: The Free Press, 1980, pp. 353–55.
68. Émile Durkheim, *Socialism*, Alvin W. Gouldner, ed. New York: The Free Press, 1967, p. 242.
69. J.E.S. Hayward, "Solidarist Syndicalism: Durkheim and Duguit," *Sociological Review* 8, 1960, pp. 17–36; 185–202. For a different reading on this point, see Robert A. Nisbet, *Émile Durkheim, with Selected Essays*. Englewood Cliffs, N.J.: Prentice Hall, 1965, pp. 62–63.
70. Émile Durkheim, *The Division of Labor in Society*, (1893). New York: The Free Press, 1964, p. 377.
71. Morris Ginsberg, "Durkheim's Ethical Theory," *On the Diversity of Morals, Vol. I*. Melbourne: Heinemann Ltd., 1956, p. 44.
72. Émile Durkheim, *Professional Ethics and Civic Morals* (1950). Glencoe, Ill.: The Free Press, 1958, p. 78.

7

State Power without Social Order: Sorel

"It is continental democracy with its associated dirigisme that Sorel is attacking. For in linking democracy with ever increasing central government, demagogy, opportunism, and the rule of mass man, he is the representative of a venerable tradition in political thought (going back to Plato) which sees democracy as akin to tyranny."

—John Stanley[1]

One of the classic features of political realism is that the organism known as the state is conceived of as the central nervous system of modern politics. Because this is the case, and because Sorel was, in an exact sense, both a realist and an anti-statist, he sought to anchor his system of political theory to an analysis of the state and its subjects. In the present period it is no longer possible to suppress the significance of the state by maintaining that it serves as the corporeal medium for expressing divine law, or, as is now more fashionably the case, a spiritual medium for expressing natural law. Nor does the classic liberal posture, in which the state is represented as a philanthropic fusion guarding the most sacred rights of the citizens on one hand and the profane rights of property on the other, offer much comfort in a situation in which both political and economic power is concentrated rather than diversified.

It has become a test of political realism to recognize that in no modern, economically advanced social structure does the state perform its functions with Olympian impartiality. Efforts to restate or develop such a perspective are invariably viewed as apologetics, sacred or profane, no matter on what level of abstraction such statements are made. The pernicious idea that the state could have a double standard of being pacific and impartial in relation to its citizens and warlike in its foreign policy only—or therefore, repressive to its citizens and pacific in the conduct of foreign affairs— found no support in Sorel. From Proudhon, Sorel inherited the view of the warlike nature of the state, and the reflection of state coercion in all levels of life.[2] It was Sorel's belief that the external relations of the state, its foreign policy, employment of the art of diplomacy and deceit of the masses in support of "national" causes, were reproduced on an internal level in dealing with issues arising out of the class conflicts.[3]

The importance of Sorel in terms of political theory is that he not only offered a unified theory of the state in space, how it functions locally, nationally and internationally, but also in time, how it functions in different economic systems in history. For Sorel, the state is repressive in the nature of things. Even as it seeks to dispense with goods and services it exacts a price on its citizens and subjects. To speak of this repression as a characteristic dispensable at a higher level of economic existence (like socialism) was for Sorel a contradiction in terms no less than in fact. It is thus illusory to believe that a socialist state would substantially improve or alter the classic relations between leviathan and citizen. Quite the contrary. As he said in a prophetic moment, socialist politicians, if victorious, "would very probably be less able than those of today; they would make more flowery speeches than the capitalists, but there is every evidence that they would be much harder and much more insolent than their predecessors."[4] His evidence was the behavior of socialist politicians within the government and unions. The foundations of a proletarian outlook must therefore begin with a theory of state power that is uniformly valid and universally recognizable as a testable proposition.

Since Sorel owes so much of his appeal in the popular imagination to his qualified defense of violence, it might be wondered how it came to pass that he possessed such an unlimited disdain for the state as the primary instrument of violence. This was, after all, the common coin of the realm in nineteenth-century political theory. The answer is to be found in his sharp distinction between types of coercion. Since this is one of the few occasions in which Sorel takes the trouble to review linguistic distinctions of any kind, there is no question that he placed prime value on the dual form of violence existing in modern society. He first asserts the existence of two types of coercion—acts of authority and acts of revolt. Now the state employs coercion for a very specific end: "to impose a certain social order in which the minority governs."[5] This form of coercion stands in clear contrast to the popular will, to the masses of people. It represents the arbitrary and capricious use of force.[6] In this capacity the state is "in fact, the organizer of the war of conquest, the dispenser of its fruits, and the *raison d'être* of the dominating groups which profit by the enterprises—the cost of which is borne by the general body of society."[7] Precisely this function of the state is disguised behind a veil of popular sovereignty and democracy. One could measure the strength of state power by the currency in official academic circles of theories of divine and natural law.

In many particulars, Sorel's view anticipates the position taken by Lenin, even to the extent of claiming that middle-class democracy is the most perfect chimera behind which the ruling class can perform its distinctive oppressive role.[8] Without belaboring the comparison, and without denying a wide divergence on basic issues, it shall be seen that more than surface resemblance is at stake, this despite Lenin's

summary dismissal of Sorel as muddleheaded.[9] For it should
be noted that Lenin's criticism of Sorel as a muddler was
made with *specific* reference to Sorel's entrance into problems relating to epistemology and the philosophy of natural
science.

The primary illusion of the ruling class, and one which,
when taken up by the avant-garde of the proletariat, becomes
an inverted illusion, a utopian fantasy, is that the goal of
"capitalist society would be a compromise between *conflicting appetites under the auspices of political lawyers* (avocats
politiciens).[10] This illusion functions socially to corrode the
effectiveness of revolutionary elements within society. Reformism becomes the dominant political motif of the proletariat, a reformism expressed in political practice through
the fetish of free elections. "The more readily the electors
believe in the *magical forces of the State,* the more will they be
disposed to vote for the candidate who promises marvels; in
the electoral struggle each candidate tries to outbid the others; in order that the socialist candidates may put the Radicals to rout, the electors must be credulous enough to believe every promise of future bliss; our Socialist politicians
take very good care, therefore, not to combat these comfortable Utopias in any very effective way."[11] A vast literature
has been written to justify the independence of commodity
production from state control in the name of natural law
and the freedom of market exchange. But in this process of
separating functions, the state can more readily assume a
posture secured in legal codes, and accepted by the utopians, of its essential impartiality in relation to the class conflict.[12] It is this bourgeois myth with which utopianism ex-
pects to make a pacific revolution.[13] The doctrine of the
metaphysically secured and juridically applied automatic
harmony of economic interests implies this conception of
the impartial state.[14]

The reality, which the illusion of the popular state beclouds, is that control of the state leads to control of all so-

cial power. The state, for Sorel, is in its very conception an organ of class power, an instrument of one entrenched socioeconomic grouping over all others. The right to rule is bitterly contested precisely for this reason. Every class out of power argues against the state as an institution only so long as it remains out of power. When the elite of a new class assumes control, a transvaluation of socioeconomic values magically occurs. What becomes a focal point of contention is not the legitimacy of the state, but the legitimacy of the old rulers to continue in control of the state apparatus. "When the force of the State was in the hands of their adversaries, they acknowledged, naturally enough, that it was being employed to violate justice, and they then proved that one might with a good conscience 'step out of the region of legality' in order to enter that of justice; when they could not overthrow the government, they tried at least to intimidate it. But when they attacked the people who for the time being controlled the force of the State, they did not at all desire to suppress that force, for they wished to utilize it some day for their own profit; all the revolutionary disturbances of the nineteenth century have ended in reinforcing the power of the State."[15] Sorel argued, not always convincingly, that the proletariat alone can alter this cycle of struggle for state power, for it alone represents social interests rather than selfish interests.

What distinguishes Sorel from Marx in this instance involves the different uses of the term interests. Marx held that the proletarian revolution is the historical completion of the class epoch because it links its particular class ambitions to the general social interest; whereas, for Sorel, the proletarian revolution is the completion of the class epoch because it immediately destroys all specific class interests, leaving behind the altruism of those who make revolution as a general social component. It was this difference which led to a theoretical rupture of socialism and anarchism. What was at stake in this seemingly moral definition of interests

was the major political question: what should the attitude
of the revolutionary be toward the chief instrument of coercion and social domination—the state?

French political theory has been particularly sensitive on
the question of the state. Nowhere else did the bourgeois
revolution take such a pure form, both in its physical cleavage with the *ancien régime*, and, after the downfall of
Mirabeau and Lafayette, in its total annihilation of divine
right theories. Yet nowhere else did the revelation become
so clear that bourgeois aims diverged radically from its universal claims of brotherhood and equality. *Encyclopédistes*
enshrined the bourgeois ideal as the rational, historical ideal,
while the revolution succeeded only in a universal re-divi-
sion of property relations and in enshrining the Middle-class
State as the rational state.[16]

While the lofty aims of overthrowing the sanctity of state
authority was not achieved by the French Revolution, Sorel
nonetheless had hopes, tempered by the ever-present nag-
ging fear of socialist politicians, that the producing classes
would finally succeed where the propertied classes had failed.
In this belief in the sanctity of the masses, in its capacity to
rid society of that cancerous growth, the state, Sorel distinguishes himself from Renan. His primary teacher in historical studies, Renan's infatuation with Germany led him to a
view of an ideal France as a carefully structured hierarchical society, in which a political-military-intellectual aristocracy would control state power and mediate the claims of
the grasping bourgeoisie and grasping proletariat alike.[17]
The state for Sorel, far more than any economic considerations, was the primary element of social decadence. This
belief in the primacy of politics distinguishes Sorel just as
sharply from his economic mentor, Marx, as it does from
his mentor in history, Renan.

Sorel's total rejection of the state as a necessary evil, generated as it was by his pessimistic view of French history, led
to a decisive break in theory and action between syndical-

ism and bolshevism. Whereas Lenin argues for the practical necessity of replacing the bourgeois state with a proletarian state, that is, for a dictatorship of the proletariat, Sorel argues vehemently against either the resurrection or revitalization of the state apparatus. For him, the central task of the producing citizens is not seizure of power but emancipation from state power. "Proletarian violence entirely changes the aspect of all the conflicts in which it intervenes, since it disowns the force organized by the middle class, and claims to suppress the State which serves as its central nucleus."[18] To those who argue that the state, despite its coercive features, is necessary in a modern society because of its enormous role in regulating the economy of the nation, Sorel offers as his rejoinder that while this is the situation based on economies structured on a labor theory of value, it need not be enshrined as the only possible social instrument regulating the economy.[19]

The heart of Sorel's thrust at Marxian political theory is that, although in its theoretical moorings Marxism does not deny the oppressive nature of the State, it places its elimination from the historical scene into a relatively distant future. Marxism assumes an equivocating position in that it places the achievement of certain goals prior to any possibility of eliminating state power. The context of Marxian discussions on future society shifted from the structure of state power to the pre-conditions for an economy of material abundance and cultural achievement, and to the internal political power base that would be required to allow for the harmonious evolution of diverse sections of the economy. It was Sorel's contention that even if these were useful social goals, the need to anchor a theory of state liquidation to such goals, however noble, was for all practical purposes a devious form of support for the continuation and even extension of state power.

Ideologically, such a political sociology supports the state by terming the dictatorship of the proletariat a "higher form" of democracy than the rule of capitalist democracy. Sorel's support for the Bolshevik revolution was on precisely the reverse grounds. The lesson of events in Russia indicated to him that there was "a contradiction between democracy and the mission of the proletariat."[20] He undoubtedly believed that the Soviets would constitute themselves as the Russian phalanx of syndicalism, and in so doing overcome both the bourgeois state and bourgeois democracy.[21]

It was Sorel's belief that orthodox European Marxism of his day, like *Encyclopédism*, placed itself on the side of universal democratic precepts by repeating the time-worn critique of abusive state power, while in fact promoting and promulgating its own version of the bureaucratic state. "In the end the State must disappear—and they [the orthodox socialists] are careful not to dispute what Engels has written on this subject—but this disappearance will take place only in a future so far distant that you must prepare yourself for it by using the State meanwhile as a means of providing politicians with tidbits; and the best means of bringing about the disappearance of the State consists in strengthening meanwhile the Governmental machine." As a final peccadillo Sorel points out that "this method of reasoning resembles that of Gribouille, who threw himself into the water in order to escape getting wet in the rain."[22]

The criterion for reform socialism, therefore, is not simply, or even primarily, the attitude taken on evolutionary or revolutionary means of bringing about a co-operative society of producing classes, but rather whether the preservation of the State is in practice desired or repudiated. Some of Sorel's harshest comments on reform socialism are directed at those who defend with subterfuge and verbal chicanery the need for state machinery. Reform socialism fills bourgeois needs in that it channels the instinct of revolt possessed by the masses into a basis for promulgating the so-called popular state. This popular state is for Sorel the best means possessed by the bourgeoisie of maintaining its stranglehold on the organs of social power, while at the same time allowing it to do verbal shadow-boxing with the wide and varied demands of the producers.[23] Sorel harbored a profound mistrust for those who transform middle class vices into working class virtues. Social reformers like Eduard Bernstein, who at least have the courtesy and honesty to drop the mask of orthodoxy, take great trouble to "explain to the middle class that they do not by any means dream of suppressing the great State machine, but wise socialists desire two things: (1) to take possession of this machine so that they may improve its works, and make it run to further their friends' interests as much as possible and (2) to assure the stability of the Government, which will be very advantageous for all business men."[24]

Revolutionary socialism stands in direct opposition to this line of economic, reform socialism. Since the root and branch of proletarian political action is its organizational purity, that is, the elimination of professional time-servers and professional pundits, the workers will have no need to replenish the state machine or take refuge in false notions of *"L'État populaire."*[25] Their only need will be to destroy it.

Sorel was so taken with the intrinsic corruption of the State-Government apparatus of the French middle class that he tended to equate corruption with impotence and ineffectiveness. This was clearly evident even in his estimate of the Dreyfus Affair. The exposure of the timidity of the government was alone held responsible for the benefits that accrued to labor in consequence of revealed administrative and military corruption in high places.[26] This strengthened Sorel's belief that the state could easily be defeated by the unified power of proletarian uprising. Before the onrushing general strike, the middle class state would quake with fear and capitulate. How to secure power and what to do with power once achieved are passed off by Sorel as minor considerations, tactical matters that are resolvable only at the moment of crisis and revolt.

Like the German Spartacists (who in many ways shared Sorel's attitude toward spontaneity and organization), Sorel was fearful of utopian projections. In consequence, he paid scant attention to the question of political organization. The unfettered action of the masses, the assumption that the myth of socialism would sustain them even in the details of revolutionary change, keynoted the anarchist attitude. The Spartacist uprising of 1919, which can serve as a case study of Sorelian methodology, revealed the disastrous consequences of operating within a pure theory of revolt. All contact with the bureaucratic state and with the bureaucratic socialists was considered alien to the purity of revolution from below. Freedom of action was held in such high repute by anarchism that at critical junctures in contemporary history, when organized direction was imperative for success, none was forthcoming. The myth of anarchism, in both France and Germany, was that it might, by the feather of freedom, overcome the lash of authority.[27]

Several lines of criticism suggest themselves in evaluating Sorel's dire predictions for the future of state authority. In the first place, Sorel was quite incapable of stating just what forms of coercion might be necessary to maintain an advanced technological civilization under proletarian direction. Beyond the generalization that all labor would be evaluated for its social efficacy, he declines to venture an opinion on the contours of socialist society. If we assume, with Sorel, that only problems connected to the labor process would arise in a socialist directed economy, serious questions might be ventured: elementary issues of proper wage norms, hours of employment, gross national income distribution, the role of banking and commercial reserves and the measurement of value itself. Such questions seem to require some specially designated force in society that can both legislate and enforce legislation. The verbal and emotive distinctions between "bourgeois state power" and "proletarian syndicate power" merely disguise the problem of coercion, freedom and the role of the elites. It is on just this point that Michels, Pareto, Mosca and a whole generation of Italian neo-realists took profound issue with Sorel's bland conviction that the future will take care of itself.

The purely regulative, administrative needs of a highly developed industrial civilization suggest that some form of State power is necessary for at least as long as human kind endures. Even presuming a society of extraordinary abundance, decisions regarding how to distribute wealth and assure the continuation of abundance remain. In a more immediate sense, problems of differing cultural and ethnic values, differences in psychological temperament, religion, climate and geography, all have to be dealt with. The disappearance of class antagonisms might indeed make it easier for an administrative force to regulate these problems harmoniously, but that they remain problems to be dealt with is a fact which the history of socialism and social reform since Sorel's time verifies. To put the matter directly, there exists an enormous gap between the elimination of the state whose primary feature is class coercion and the elimination of the state as a law-making and law-enforcing agency. To call only the former, only that condition in which the will of some ruling class is involved, a state, in no way dissolves the state in existential terms. In this identification of the state with class power rather than public authority, Sorel forms a common ground with Lenin in quite total disregard of both of their mentors, Marx and Engels. The consequence of the Lenin-Sorel thesis results not in the liquidation of the state but in a liquidation of the traditional linguistic forms of examining the state in theory and practice.

Because Sorel decries as utopian phrase-mongering all attempts at anticipating problems which might arise in a socialist society, nothing in his work enables one to understand how changes in the rules of conduct can be brought about in a cohesive and coherent form, much less be enforced. In failing to provide a distinction between oppressive class-state functions and civil functions fulfilled by state power from pre-class society to the present, the impact of his critique of the state is severely circumscribed in both time and space to the France of the early twentieth century.

Let us assume that Sorel is correct in saying that history marks the passage from obligations to rights, in itself a difficult assumption since these terms might imply rather than exclude each other. Does this alter the need for some public authority to regulate the harmonious distribution of these rights, or at least ensure that no infractions of these rights occur? What Sorel ignores is that discussion of rights immediately involves questions of obligation, just as in a more general way, discussion of liberty involves discussion of the admissible range of coercion.

Then of course there are empirical problems related to the functioning state in specific contexts at given historical moments. For example, granting that the bourgeois State generates socioeconomic strife by fostering the economic interests of one class over another, does it not have at least the auxiliary function of regulating the civil relations between people and people, and people and things? It was one of the greatest contributions of classic political philosophy, of Hobbes in particular (of whom Sorel knew little, if anything), that this dual functional role of state sovereignty was recognized. As undemocratic and oblivious to the fundamental interests of producing classes as a state may be, it still remains that regulative lever by virtue of which man in an industrial society is guaranteed a certain amount of stability and harmony. Hobbes felt so keenly this relationship of the state to the citizen that he maintained that revolution was acceptable only at that point at which state power failed to provide the people with the security for which it was organized in the first place.

Sorel further failed to indicate that the relationship between the state and the dominant economic forces is not a static relationship. Power is never stationary; power is the measure of disequilibrium. In times of general socioeconomic strife the state may necessarily waver in its allegiances. The shortcomings of the dominant class, any procrastination on basic labor, health and welfare measures, any inability to provide for maximum full employment over a long period of time, any reduction of the economic capacities of the ruling classes, inevitably leads to a situation in which the state may function as an instrument of mass interests over against narrower class interests. Frederick Engels admitted as much when he said: "By way of exception, however, periods occur in which the warring classes balance each other so nearly that the state power, as ostensible mediator, acquires, for the moment, a certain degree of independence of both."[28]

It is in this direction that certain monarchical regimes of seventeenth-century England, eighteenth-century France and nineteenth-century Germany functioned, and it is no less a tendency in the way the state functioned in a Labor Party-governed England, a New Deal America and a government of the "popular front" in France. Such distinctions are not reducible to logic chopping, for they cut through the essentially one-sided Machiavellian view of the state held by Sorel.

How in point of fact a state apparatus functions at a particular moment is far less a matter of general theoretical or historical principles than a concern for sociological investigation. There is a significant distinction between *the primary purposes* of the state and the *total functioning* of the state. In like manner there is a clear logical disjunction between how the state conducts itself *sometimes* and how it conducts itself *always*. These types of distinctions, which would either validate or invalidate Sorelian theory, were brushed aside. In consequence, capricious interpretations were put upon his view with impunity. Even the most perfect examples of state power operating to protect the interests of industrialists and militarists (Nazi Germany and Fascist Italy) sought and received sanctuary in Sorel's political philosophy.

A third and ancillary criticism of the Sorelian theory of statecraft is his naive faith in the conviction that the state is *always* intimidated by proletarian violence. If we assume with Sorel that the state is an arm of the dominant economic forces of society, then the question of how difficult or complex it is to replace one state power with another can be seen for what it is—a problem of concrete history. When state power is viewed through the perspective of the myth of the general strike, which, it might be added, involves a myth Sorel does not discuss—the total disunity of the ruling classes and the total unity of the ruled classes—analysis of the state vanishes into personal wish-fulfillment. To assume, as Sorel does, that a vigorous and prospering middle class state would succumb to a vigorous and prospering proletariat, or that this economic condition is best for revolutionary activity, is naive. Classes most often succumb when they have decayed, not when they are healthy.

A state apparatus tends to remain intact long after the class which gave it its original nourishment ceases to perform decisive economic functions. The final break-up of feudalism in France occurred no later than 1715; yet the actual transference of political power, i.e., of state power, did not take place until 1789—this in a social situation in which the *ancien régime* was neither particularly vigorous nor numerically powerful. This historical example is merely indicative of the many elements that must be present before state machinery can be replaced. It is historically more accurate to say that the unification of social aims which grips large masses at points of revolution is in itself a reflection of weakness and disorganization on the part of the dominant ruling classes. It is not, as Sorel maintained, something which automatically comes about through the establishment of the myth of the general strike.

In sum, Sorel suffered from an inability to distinguish between government and state, between the machinery of administration and the machinery of exploitation. It is widely realized, for example, that the frequent South American revolutions, however fratricidal, do not touch the economic foundations of state sovereignty. The same can be said for counter-revolutionary movements in Italy and Germany during this century. What is at stake in this distinction is of major consequence. When the structure of government is considered to be an administrative apparatus, there is no need, either on radical or conservative grounds, to assume the "withering away" of government with the destruction of the coercive features of state power. The failure to bear this distinction in mind subjected Sorel to a position in which the only legitimate alternative to state power is a power vacuum. From Sorel's standpoint, government is merely a subsidiary appendage to the state apparatus and no possibility of developing a rational approach to the politics of socialism is possible. This lack of elementary distinctions, which is characteristic of Sorel's writings, led him to hasten his abandonment of objective political analysis in favor of the greener pastures of a voluntary philosophy of history and an atavistic psychology.

Sorel's theory of the state, while on the surface a vigorous defense of revolutionary possibilities in mass action, is at its core more closely related to fantasy than to science. It offers no guarantee that the syndicate, the fundamental unit of proletarian organization that is to become the center of polity under socialism, will not reproduce every miscarriage of human rights committed by the State in class society. As Michels brilliantly noted: "The more syndicalism endeavors to displace the axis of working class policy towards syndicalist action, the greater is the danger it runs of itself degenerating into an oligarchy. Even in the revolutionary syndicalist groups the leaders have frequent opportunities of deceiving the rank and file. The treasurer of a strike, the secretary of a trade union, even the participator in a conspiracy or the leader upon a barricade, can betray those from whom they have received their instructions far more easily and with much more serious consequences than can a socialist member of parliament or a municipal councilor. French syndicalists," continues Michels, "arbitrarily restrict their one-sided theory to the political party alone, as if it were not inevitable that like causes should produce like effects when their action is displayed upon the field of the syndicalist movement. They reason as if they were immunized against the action of sociological laws of universal validity."[29]

Its exemption from social laws is the personal embodiment of utopian reasoning in Sorel's syndicalism. The mythological basis of his doctrine of the State, far from being an asset to a revolutionary theory of society, proved to be Sorel's greatest liability, for he reproduces a portion of the pragmatic acquiescence: an acceptance of the spontaneous and apocalyptic view of social change. The very view of history and change that Sorel ridicules in Enlightenment philosophy, becomes his supreme ideological burden. And since he eschewed the possibility of a scientific sociology, he was left with a dogmatic emotivism emulating in ferocity anything produced by internecine tendencies of medieval society.

The question of the relationship between democracy and coercion has come to play an increasingly important part in contemporary studies of political thought and behavior. As recent major discussions have made rather clear, whatever the philosophic pose, the problem of democracy cannot be resolved outside analysis of the coercive features that the state steadily employs.[30] The distinctions between democratic and authoritarian modes of rule are not so much questions of the economic supports of government as they are quantitative differences between the use of coercion and consensus.

Democracy is more easily identifiable with the ends to which coercion is put and the limits with which coercion may be employed to secure these ends than it is with purely formal or semantic appraisals of universal qualities of democracy. On the sociological side, it is likewise more important to identify the level of democracy with types of class structure than with a simple numerical majority or plurality covering many classes. It was the virtue of Aristotle's view of democracy that he identified it in just such economic and class terms. It is likewise a decided asset in Sorel that he saw the problem of democracy in this two-fold way: as related institutionally to the problem of coercion, and as related sociologically to the problem of economic classes. This is a starting point for any mature political sociology.

The first stage in Sorel's argument was to distinguish between violence and force. Basically an act of force is said to represent an act of officialdom—of established authority. Force is that which is employed by the state to defeat its only potent adversaries—those able to employ counterforce.[31] Now counterforce, the force not of established authority but of producers in capitalist society (and by inference, the middle class in feudal society, the industrialists in mercantile society, etc.), is given the designation of violence. "A terminology which would give rise to no ambiguity" would be one in which "the term violence should be employed only for acts of revolt," while "the object of force is to impose a certain social order in which the minority governs."[32]

Sorel did not think himself arbitrary in advocating the use of violence to counter the force of the state. To be sure it was his primary theme that "whether we approve or condemn what is called the *revolutionary* and *direct method,* it is evident that it is not on the point of disappearing."[33] The establishment of a correlation between subjective ambitions and the objective use of force led Sorel to an empirical and not merely a normative guide for the advocacy of violence. *It is not that force simply ought to be employed, but that it is employed.* Advocacy is not to be confused with description.

The problems involved in jumping from description to prescription in political theory are clearly evident in Sorel. For the fact that violence is used as counterforce is not logically an argument for its continued use—only a statement of

fact. That Sorel makes this jump hurriedly is indicative of
the loose empirical evidence supporting his contentions. It
was after all in "warlike France" that Sorel saw the most
insidious inroads of the "pacific spirit" in both domestic
and foreign affairs and in both the proletariat and the middle
class. The statement that violence is the main fact of the
growth of civilization has far-reaching consequences for
Sorel's *Weltanschauung,* since another anchor point of his
theory of force and violence is that civilization, through its
continued stress on utilitarian modes of behavior, does indeed negate the warlike spirit. The gravity of Sorel's paradoxical position might be summed up by pointing out that
if violence is an objective fact of socioeconomic existence,
why the need to urge producers to adopt violent tactics as
the only road to emancipation? On the other hand if violence
is progressively being replaced by other methods of reconciling social antagonisms, where is the objective basis for
the prolongation of the method of violence? On this theoretical polarity Sorel floundered badly. The political about
face that Sorel periodically underwent is indicative of an
essential confusion between arguments based on moral sentiments and arguments based on empirical measurements.

Sorel's view of coercion is fundamentally conditioned by
an acceptance of the Marxian view of the supremacy of the
class struggle over all other forms of human association and
rivalry: "The class struggle is the alpha and omega of socialism."[34] The struggle between plebeians and patricians, poor
and rich, has roots as far back as Hellenic civilization. The
unequivocal and categorical presentation of this struggle is
the underlying source of socialism's strengths.[35] As long as
economic roots are clearly divided between owner and
owned, employer and employed, there is no question in
Sorel's mind that power remains the sole basis for resolving
differences. What he resents most in modern society are
those social forces which tend to obfuscate primal economic
relations, i.e., the lower middle classes and the aristocratic

echelons in the labor movement. This vast middle economic sector operates to vitiate and neutralize class warfare, and beyond that, to assume power by mediating the claims of wealth and privilege against those of labor and poverty.

The political reflection of this middle portion of the economy is liberalism and democracy. This sector corrupts the purity of both the *haute bourgeoisie* and the proletariat by proclaiming a series of reformist platitudes that dulls the edge of violence. "The whole future of democracy might easily depend on this *lower middle class (basse bourgeoisie)*, which hopes to make use of the strength of the really proletarian organizations for its own great personal advantage. The politicians believe that this class will always have peaceful tendencies, that it may be organized and disciplined, and that since the leaders of such sane syndicates understand equally with the politicians the action of the State, this class will form an excellent body of followers."[36] Democracy is therefore not a form of political rule sanctioned by the ruling classes, but an economic tactic of the weak. Those *basse bourgeois,* alienated from the cleansing force of social production, offer it up to the masses. Its major function is to secure State control with the minimum political strife.[37]

The divergence of Sorel's view from traditional Marxian political theory, which asserts that democracy is the most efficient political shell for the *development* of capitalism, is important from a theoretical point of view. In this divergence is revealed the gulf between Sorelian syndicalism and Marxian socialism. Spontaneity and mass action became the highest ideals, replacing political organization and parliamentary action. Socialism is emptied of all democratic content. The liberating violence of the revolutionary situation becomes an end in itself. Whatever justification for revolution inhered in Marx's socialism, the effort to establish a broader and more pervasive form of democracy is dissipated by the anarchist repudiation of any specific program for social change. This Sorel did through a rejection of the worth of social consensus and also through an assertion of the negative character of democracy.[38] Of equal interest is the agreement *in principle* between fascism and syndicalism on the decadence of the middle classes. The facts are something else again. Fascism relied heavily for its support on the lower middle classes. It was when this stratum of the population became discontented with its share of the national produce, disenchanted with the goals of proletarian socialism and disaffiliated from bourgeois democracy, that fascism and Nazism were in a position to come to power. As one authority points out: "The Nazis recruited their millions from the middle class parties as well as from the non-voters."[39]

Just as the producers are the bulwarks of modern social revolutionary movements, so, too, the lower middle strata of the economy have come to perform a similar function in social counter-revolution. Far from playing the role Sorel attributed to them, the lower middle class, "the protagonists of repressed nature, the victims of instrumentalized reason," has in modern history not infrequently exhibited profoundly warlike and anti-democratic attitudes.[40] In contrast to this is the propensity of labor in developed capitalist societies exhibiting rapid social mobility to eschew the method of violence where possible. Labor unions tend to hold their power of organization as an ultimate weapon—to be used only where all other means of gaining their ends fail. The method of violence tends to be employed by the proletariat when other methods are not available. This point needs to be made in view of Sorel's belief in the instinctual proclivity to violence on the part of the producing classes.

It was Sorel's contention that "no historical experience justifies the hope that a democracy can be made to work in a capitalist country, without the criminal abuses experienced everywhere nowadays." Instead of granting the possibility that socialism may develop a form of democracy which cancels out political-criminal associations, he enshrines this

relation between democracy and criminality into an instinctual, permanent verity: "we ought to learn from experience
that there is no way of bringing about their disappearance."[41]
This is clearly reduced to the view that democracy is at best
a disguise for coercive activities. Since this is the case, democracy cannot be utilized by the producers as a method of
greater worth than that of force, since the two terms describe antagonistic social interests. Thus, the social changes
required are capable of being brought about by violence that
the proletariat brings to bear on the force of middle class
democracy.

Democracy in itself cannot be an instrument of progress
or even an indication that greater progress has occurred. It
can only be an instrument cleverly disguising the defense of
the status quo. Sorel further makes the interesting observation that the social cohesion which democratic rule tends to
promote is not in fact a consequence of the ability of education, persuasion and knowledge to render the method of
violence obsolete in settling conflicts, but is in reality a social product of force itself. "Social unity presses upon us
from all sides, so to speak, in the ordinary course of life;
because we feel, almost always, the operation of the effects
of hierarchical authority which imposes uniform rules on
citizens of the same country."[42] It is coercion, legal and extra-legal, which underlies the unity of the nation far more
effectively than supposed common economic and social interests. This being the case, the maintenance of social unity
was for Sorel no more an argument for the promotion of
pacific means as against violent means, than were social divisions for the promotion of a democratic polity.

Cutting across Sorel's argument and cushioning it from
criticism is the idea that parliamentary activities and all
political products of the modern democratic state are fig
leaves in the great struggle *between* force and violence, between owner and producer.[43] Sorel has a disquieting reproach
for reform socialists who are under the impression that so-

cial revolution is a consequence of fine rhetoric made in the councils of the politically powerful. "From the moment one has anything to do with elections, it is necessary to submit to certain general conditions which impose themselves unavoidably on all parties in every country and at all times. If one is convinced that the future of the world depends on the electoral program, on compromises between influential men and on the sale of privileges, it is not possible to pay much attention to the moral constraints which prevent a man going in the direction of his most obvious interests. Experience shows that in all countries where democracy can develop its nature freely, the most scandalous corruption is displayed without anyone thinking it even necessary to conceal his rascality."[44]

He goes on to compare the activities of parliamentarians to financiers who place worthless stock on the commercial exchange. Both offer commodities that are intrinsically worthless.[45] For in this transformation of democracy into parliamentary demagogy, the actual socioeconomic needs of the masses are continually violated. Instead of being the sensitive instrument through which such needs are registered, democracy becomes the enemy of the producers, functioning as the shell through which politician and professor, socialist and capitalist alike, thwart the ambitions of laboring classes.[46] Democracy *promises* the good life for these masses; it *secures* this good life only for the economically prosperous.[47] In addition, democracy is, by definition, a form of political rule, not a method of direct popular rule. This dichotomy becomes particularly clear when a parliamentary system is developed to act as the legislative arm of state power. Through the machinery of these state-dominated parliaments, and the educational system it brings into existence, democracy carries on the task of coercing the masses with an effectiveness and mendacity unknown to the ancients.[48]

The appeal of Sorel's position is evident to all who have been disconcerted by the division between liberal democratic pledges and practices. He made it clear that power is the basis of political change. The force of democracy can be essentially conservative, particularly when it obstructs the desire for change behind a veil of electoral procedures.

What is lacking in Sorel's appraisal, however, is an appreciation of the possibility that power can be consciously represented by democratic procedures. If one source of power confronts another source of power directly, in the field of combat, this does not mean necessarily that in every instance this is the logically superior method of resolving political or economic differences. The fact that force is the purest way of resolution does not constitute logical proof that it is the only or the most desirable way. For, as one critic of Sorel indicates: "It may be, on occasion, necessary to fight, and cowardice not to; but fighting is always at best a necessary evil, and there is nothing ennobling about it. Quite the contrary. It is perfectly possible to admire initiative, *élan* and determination without falling into the evil position of admiring combativeness in its own right."[49] This prescriptive attitude towards violence, rather than its necessity, separates Sorel from liberal socialism more profoundly than any specifically doctrinal differences.

Surely the growth of civilization and the worth of democracy itself rests not so much on how it obfuscates conflict, but on how it points to a resolution of conflict within commonly accepted rules. Too often, critics of democracy call any non-violent resolution of differences obfuscation; this is because they start with a definition of society as lawless. But democracy, in providing rules of procedure, offers a method of channeling and directing behavior, despite the contentions of critics. Democracy can clarify the relative strength of contending forces in a conscious way. Democracy therefore is perhaps the most reasonable expression through which the issues dividing men can be resolved. The fact that power remains basic political capital in existing societies is no serious critique against the employment of democratic procedures. Quite the contrary. The abuse of democracy is perhaps the soundest argument for broadening the scope of human involvement in political processes. This involvement would perhaps better reflect the actual balance of power sources than is the case at present. It thus may be argued that what is needed at this juncture in history is not the overthrow of democratic procedures, nor the substitution of Sorel's method of direct violence, but a stipulation of the contents of democracy in functional rather than normative terms: that is, into terms which have utility and relevance for the masses of men in a scientific and technological civilization—namely, a general theory of social organization.

Still another potential shortcoming in Sorel's theory of proletarian violence is the fact that raw power may often resolve antagonisms to the detriment of the great mass of people. If the numerically few possess overwhelming power, in the form of the state for example, then the popular will might be thwarted time and again. It is the ideal of democracy, and a genuinely functioning ideal in many of the lower layers of human intercourse, that it registers the wants, complaints and ambitions of the group or class out of power. A democracy is a real entity only in so far as its employment of coercion is so circumscribed as to allow those out of power, and perhaps without hope of achieving power, to share in the general material and cultural advances of society. It might be argued that the potentials of democracy are never fulfilled in a society rendered antagonistic by diverse economic interests. But such an argument is an empirical one, and does not necessitate an either-or posture with regard to the value of the democratic process itself. Democracy has, in the context of class society, a double function, corresponding to a negative and positive role of social authority. In the first instance it is a technique for reducing violence, and in the second place it is a technique for reaching rational consensus. What Sorel lost sight of was that the concept of rendering decisions in a non-violent way did not necessarily carries with it an assumption of philistinism. The radical critique of society does not imply therefore a radical *technique*, i.e., the method of absolute violence, but only the application of the historically evolved tools for the best possible social decisions. Sorel substituted a formal radicalism of content, a formal denunciation of the state, for the elimination of the problems connected with its genesis and evolution.

Judicial review, constitutional amendment, parliamentary statute, executive veto and the like, are elements (even in capitalist democracy) which mitigate and abate, no less than disguise the basis of political domination. That these activities of democracy are taken as a consequence of the potential power of various revolutionary currents in society is, it would seem, just as strong an argument for increasing the sensitivity of democracy to revolutionary approaches as it is for attempting a return to primordial modes of settling social and economic antagonisms. Contrary to Sorel's insistence, a reasonable defense of democracy would not rest upon subterfuge and reformism, but would show the essential sufficiency of political democracy for even the most radical far-reaching transformations in the economic institutions of human society. The degree of democratic safeguards possible in a given revolutionary context is an empirical question, which in no way cancels the values of democracy in modern society as such. In present society the methodological base of democracy is criticism. It is the social force of popular power—potential and actual.

Democracy functions for Sorel as a protective mask for carrying on the coercive acts of the state with impunity and without criticism. It will occasion little surprise therefore that, for Sorel, democracy plays a like role in the relationship between the bureaucracy and the masses. That is, democracy, instead of being an instrument of popular control, is essentially a protective covering for the machinations of the bureaucracy. In Sorel's opinion, "the greatest danger which threatens syndicalism would be an attempt to imitate democracy." Since democracy is seen exclusively in terms of its being "a political form of the middle class," the aims of laborers cannot be resolved within the framework of democratic procedure.[50]

This appeared as the decisive feature of Sorel's political thought when appropriated by fascist ideology. It too condemned democracy as an exclusively middle class phenomenon that corrupts and distorts the heroic instincts and appetites of *il popolo*.[51] The demagogic potential of Sorel's view of democracy is socially realized in a context in which the standpoint of an "out-group" (not necessarily from a lower economic strata) sees itself frustrated by the effete virtues of the going institutional concern. The heroic passions revealed in direct action can only be suppressed in the immorality of democracy. In this way anti-democracy becomes a moral credo.

It should be noted, however, that Sorel's views do not coincide with Vilfredo Pareto's argument that bureaucracy is built into all contemporary social structures since they rationalize power relations in advanced societies. Sorel condemns the bureaucratic tendencies in modern civilization for talking on behalf of the producing classes while acting to frustrate their most elementary ambitions. The bureaucracy is for Sorel a powerful sub-class, with a will to survival that cannot easily be stifled, even by the conquest of socialism. Its tendency, to the contrary, is to become a special class, with a firm managerial mandate. The bureaucracy is recruited in the main from professional elements—engineers, lawyers, clerks and economists. There "natural tendency is to become a little aristocracy; for these people, State socialism would be advantageous, because they would go up one in the social hierarchy."[52] The producing classes, even if successful in the social revolution, even if they seized control of the economic foundations, would be faced with the immense and drawn-out task of uprooting the bureaucratic aristocracy. Sorel's solution to this problem, the formation of an independent and strictly proletarian seat of power, tends to obscure the differences between the legitimate demands made by highly advanced technological societies for trained personnel at managerial and administrative levels, and the excessive waste created by an indolent group of bureaucratic time-servers.

Sorel assumed that every social need would be fulfilled within the framework of purely proletarian economic activity. These social needs would in short order create, from the working class itself if necessary, managerial and administrative elements which would separate themselves out from actual productive processes. Lawyers, engineers and clerks would no more perish in a society of producers than they would in any other advanced industrial structure. Sorel's failure to discuss such eventualities, on the basis of their being essentially non-demonstrable and utopian, confirms the suspicion that he frequently confused political ideals and sociological realities.

In political life generally, Sorel sees the outlook of European social democracy as an essentially compromising force. Just as social democracy mediates the claims of workers and employers in economics, the bureaucracy mediates these opposing claims in political life. There is a functional kinship between social democracy and bureaucracy. It is this entire economic stratum between the polarity of producer and owner that Sorel views with the greatest suspicion and mistrust. The pious rascality of the legal profession in medieval life, for example, has in no form been curbed in capitalism. It has merely been transplanted to a new and fertile ground. Whether industrial barons or church fathers are the great beneficiaries of the machinations of the lawyers is secondary. They form the higher echelon of the bureaucracy precisely because of their ability to deprive the producers of their fruits within the framework of the law.[53] Dominant classes utilize other segments of the bureaucracy in much the same way. The capabilities of the bureaucracy are turned to specific class needs. Its services are always offered to those in political control. Older revolutions did not disturb the bureaucracy because its essential task of confounding proletarian needs remained built into new systems of oppression.

The state represents the interests of the owners as against the led. Sorel insists that the needs of the masses can only be fulfilled in direct conflict with the politicians from outside the structure of politics. This high caste of state organization is described by Sorel as being "people whose wits are singularly sharpened by their voracious appetites, and in whom the hunt for fat jobs develops the cunning of Apaches (*ruses d'apaches*).[54] Proletarian strength is tested not only, or even primarily, against the bourgeoisie as such—but more especially against the bureaucracy developed by the bourgeoisie in the course of its evolution. The distinction is important, for it points up that the type of class warfare Sorel had in mind centered primarily in the political sphere, in the sphere of state power. To beseech the wealthy for economic advantages, as socialist politicians and labor aristocrats do, is reformism. To abolish the *political* rule of capital, the governmental machinery it has erected, is the central goal of revolutionary socialism.

Sorel took seriously the question of the overthrow of the old capitalist political order. We know that he remained interested in the *Mafia* and *Camorra,* secret and extra-legal terrorist organizations in Italy, during his entire life. They served as examples to him of how it is possible to maintain a semi-militarist organization operating outside the official State machinery, a force that shared the tenacious fanaticism of the manipulators of the State and yet escapes corruption by class society.[55]

Sorel's steadfast opposition to social legislation and social reconstruction through educational advances grew from this regard for the direct method. He worked within an association of terms: the direct method of violence is the revolutionary approach, the indirect method of legislation and education is the reformist approach.[56] By adopting this equation Sorel felt himself to be a thoroughly consistent socialist, since any amelioration of the economic antagonisms of class society only provides the ruling, exploiting class with a longer, stronger lease on life. For if "all social legislation is nothing but an element of proletarian decadence," it becomes obvious that the path to change is not gradual but apocalyptic, involving a confrontation of the chief rivals for power in any given age.[57]

Sorel cast his spontaneous socialism in the form of the psychology of slave and master. True to his belief in the primacy of the political, he generally preferred to picture the class conflict in vivid images, rather than in economic terms. "The masses who are led have a very vague and extremely simple idea of the means by which their lot can be improved; demagogues easily get them to believe that the best way is to utilize the power of the State to pester the rich. We pass thus from jealousy to vengeance, and it is well known that vengeance is a sentiment of extraordinary power, especially with the weak."[58] The mass of producers is thereby induced to subdue their discontent in quiet and pious ways, never really achieving the power they possess as producers. The only escape Sorel allows is revolutionary practice, the method of direct violence. Unlike the bulk of socialist intellectuals and politicians, he disallows the co-existence of immediate reform policies coupled with long-range revolutionary policies.

In adopting this socialism without tactics, Sorel reveals how thoroughly his commitment to and feeling for the problem of achieving socialism rested on psychological rather than economic grounds. "The only means by which this pernicious influence of the demagogues may be wiped out are those employed by Socialism in propagating the notion of the proletarian general strike; it awakens in the depths of the soul a sentiment of the sublime proportionate to the conditions of a gigantic struggle; it brings to the fore the pride of free men; it forces the desire to satisfy jealousy by malice into the background; and thus protects the worker from the quackery of ambitious leaders, hungering for the flesh pots."[59] Clearly, the core of politics for Sorel is not the outcome of the class war, but the mode in which the battle is waged. Cole put the matter rightly: "What attracted him was the struggle, not the prospect of victory, except when he was thinking of the latter, not as victory, but as the defeat of the other side."[60]

The enormous bureaucracy, subsidized and underwritten as it is by the bourgeoisie, expands to where it can lead a flourishing existence in quite different and varied economic soil. Bureaucracy becomes an independent political variable even in socialist politics. In this way Sorel perceived a relative independence of political life from its economic sources. He also perceived the potential of bureaucratic management to one day congeal as an economic entity rivaling older productive classes. The class allegiance of bureaucratic-minded politicians is continually being purchased. "The reinforcement (of power)[61] of the State is at the basis of all their conceptions." Indeed, the more perceptive politicians are "already preparing the framework of a strong, centralized and disciplined authority, which will not be hampered by the criticism of an opposition, which will be able to enforce silence, and which will give currency to its lies."[62]

To Sorel the huge and vital growth of productive techniques in the twentieth century makes possible an ultimate and final break with the bureaucratic state. "Modern production requires mutual action of the workers, a voluntary co-ordination of the systematic productive relations, that transforms an accidental agglomeration into an army shown to possess a common enterprise."[63] Thus, the answer to state power is economic power. The answer to the bourgeois state founded on terror is the proletarian syndicate based on voluntary association. The unusual aspect of this alternative to the state is that Sorel derived it in large measure from reform socialism. Like Eduard Bernstein and German revisionism generally, Sorel was mistrustful of the implications inherent in the concept of the dictatorship of the proletariat. He feared what totalitarianism held in store for the producing classes. For, as Bernstein noted, the consequence of the strengthening of state power would be a further separation of the proletariat from the actual implements of political rule and control.[64] This tendency of politics to separate itself from economics represented for Sorel a corresponding extension of the division of society into masters and slaves.[65] This is not for Sorel allegorical theorizing. What is involved is a further development of the conflict between the masses and the bureaucratic machinery. This political conflict has an historical evolution of its own that is not resolved automatically in the course of economic transformations.

The bureaucracy quite clearly cannot maintain itself without masking its relations to the proletariat. The disguise takes the form of concessions to the laborers in the course of the *political* strike. This phenomenon is, properly speaking, not a strike at all, but only a series of party maneuvers. It was, for Sorel, the logical labor tactic of reform socialism, particularly in Germany.[66] "Enfeebled classes habitually put their trust in people who promise them the protection of the State, without ever trying to understand how this protection could possibly harmonize their discordant interests; they readily enter into every coalition formed for the purpose of forcing concessions from the Government."[67]

The political strike is the precise opposite of the proletarian strike in that it at least implicitly accepts the notion that several classes can co-operate towards the same specific economic goal. Broadly speaking, the political strike was an effort made by German socialism and its leaders, Bernstein and Kautsky, to satisfy the ultimate demands of the working class for emancipation by gradually resolving the problem

of its vast political disenfranchisement. The banner of reformism might well have read: from political power to economic supremacy. This for Sorel was anathema, since it involves an ultimate commitment both to co-operating with
the class enemy, and what is worse, absorbing in producer
organizations the worst features of the bureaucratic state.[68]
"The political general strike presupposes that very diverse
social groups shall possess the same faith in the magical
force of the State; this faith is never lacking in social groups
which are on the downgrade."[69] This quest for alternatives
to revolution, in Sorel's view, separated Marx from the bulk
of the Marxists.

The issue of reform or revolution pressed as hard in France
at the turn of the century as it did in Germany. The general
failure of the condition of the producers to deteriorate in
either an absolute or relative sense, the fantastic growth of
industrial output in Western Europe at the time, and the
development of the trade union movement on a mass, industrial scale, contributed to the growing feeling that socialism might be realized by strictly legal, evolutionary methods. Sorel improperly saw in Jean Jaurès the French
counterpart to German revisionism. He drew this false image from a single fact: Jaurès's position on the function of
the strike ran counter to Sorel's in every major detail. First,
Jaurès held that the proletariat must be deeply convinced of
the goals sought through the general strike, and not just be
exclusively concerned with the mechanics of the strike. Second, a large section of public opinion and not merely a proletarian elite must be willing to support the legitimacy of
the general strike. The third point is best stated in Jaurès's
words: "The general strike must not seem like a disguise for
violence, but simply the exercise of the legal right to strike.
More systematic in method and vaster in scope than usual,
it is true, and with a more clearly marked class character."[70]

The ideological conflict between reform and revolution,
of which the debates concerning political strikes versus the

general strike is but a fragment, forms a continuing pattern in French political thought.[71] Indeed, among the advanced European countries, only in France can one speak of a steady questioning of reformism, rather than its unconscious acceptance as the only road for people to take in order to adequately adjust to his social milieu. Radicalism in France has therefore tended to consider reform policies not so much as a way of life, as a challenge to the traditional life of those people impacted.[72]

Ultimately, reformism is a futile road for the producing masses because, in Sorel's view, an instinctual, psychological propensity for violence possesses the proletariat. In witness of this, we should note that Sorel at no point in his writings found it necessary to criticize the character of productive relations in capitalist society. Andreu has indicated that not a single line against capitalism as a regime of production will be found in Sorel's writings.[73] This is an astonishing fact in view of the extent to which socialist literature in the nineteenth century made use of Marx's argument against the efficiency and effects of capitalist production on labor. This being the case, why the producers should be desirous of taking up arms against the bourgeoisie in deadly combat is held to be less a matter of economic tensions than the psychological compulsion to assert its class muscularity and purity. The political union of diverse economic elements is criticized with such a viewpoint in mind. "The political general strike does not presuppose a class war concentrated on a field of battle in which the proletariat attacks the middle class; the division of society into two antagonistic armies disappears, for this class of revolt is possible with any kind of social structure."[74]

Lurking beneath the psychological dimension of proletarian purity was a view common to many revolutionary thinkers in Europe after the death of Marx: substantial alteration would be required in theory to account for disturbing peculiarities in proletarian practice. As long as the social consciousness of the working class found appropriate expression in trade union activity, an implicit threat to a revolutionary standpoint was ever present. This is so since trade unionism, when left at the level of economic wants, involved an acceptance of the existing economic order and its ways of promoting men up the social ladder. Thus, Sorel was led to the conclusion that "the proletarian general strike and the political general strike are diametrically opposed to one another."[75] The latter receives its sustenance from parliamentary democracy and the state bureaucracy, the former from consistent opposition to these pernicious blandishments of capitalist existence, which frequently manifest themselves in the economic ambitions of the proletariat. The true face of bureaucracy can only be uncovered through the steady opposition to encroachments on proletarian heroism and purity. As long as the state and its bureaucratic apparatus is seen as a neutral element of capitalist society, or even as a force sometimes receptive to working class interests, the possibility of developing a revolutionary situation tends to be undermined. For, as Sorel would have it, the bureaucracy will then be in a position both to manipulate and to corrupt producers of the wealth of society.

The idea of ideological purity as necessitating a total separation of labor from the bureaucracy extended even to the need of keeping separate proletarians and professors, the intellectual bureaucracy. Just as the syndicate is to grow outside and independent of the juridical and legislative devices of the state, so, too, it is to maintain careful watch over the intelligentsia, even that portion of it which professes sympathy for proletarian aims. Because practice resides in the proletariat, it alone can be the instrument of real change. The intelligentsia can at best perform auxiliary functions in the social revolution. Sorel was convinced that any relation other than dependence upon the producers would be equivalent to injecting impure ideological modes of thought that could only lead to an equivocating and procrastinating working class. Indeed, sociological methods that would take cognizance of alternative modes of action in a specific context would serve to undermine the mythological basis of mass action. In this way the intelligentsia, like the bureaucracy, comes to preach the gospel of reformism.[76]

Sorel is aware that his position on bureaucracy is extreme and raises more questions than it answers. He therefore sought to distinguish the political bureaucracy from the future proletarian elite. This he was able to do by relating the former to advocacy of the political strike and the latter to the proletarian, revolutionary strike. There will be no bureaucracy, in the historic meaning of the term, under socialism. Administration is to replace bureaucracy.[77] But as is often the case with Sorel, after indicating the general features of future society, he does not indicate the precise mechanism by which proletarian administrators will be able to avoid differentiating themselves from the laborers to form, once again, a distinctive social and political elite. What we are thus ultimately left with is Sorel's insight into the multilevel sources of political friction, without a corresponding ability to show the possibilities for non-antagonistic forms of social organization. Sorel pushed the central problems of socialist political theory into the utopian future. In so doing he abandoned the whole range of problems with which political sociology must grapple.

It is easy enough to summarize the crudities in Sorel's view of the relation of the masses to the bureaucracy: his one-sided concentration on the political forms of rule, the consequent absence of serious analysis of the economic sources of bureaucratic strength, his imprecision as to the actual mode of operation of bureaucratic apparatus and types of people involved in this apparatus, his linguistic vagueness on questions of control and levels of control of the state, his failure to clearly distinguish between the legitimate managerial functions of a highly developed industrial society and illegitimate power function exercised by an ex-

ploiting class. These are serious deficits indeed. They stem
in part from Sorel's blind adherence to a partisan notion of
truth and in part from the pragmatic values implicit in his
approach to revolutionary action.

The ray of light penetrating shady vagueness and inaccu-
racies is Sorel's perceptiveness, particularly his insistence on
seeing the state and its bureaucratic apparatus as a self-per-
petuating phenomenon. It is an apparatus that might change
hands with succeeding revolutions, but an organism that nonetheless has remarkable qualities of endurance, much like institutional religions. That the bureaucracy may concentrate
further and evolve to a point where, independent of older
established classes, it might constitute itself as a political and
economic force is a possibility Sorel raises that cannot be dismissed lightly. The bureaucracy, which can come to power
only with the support of one or another contending economic
classes, has shown signs of constituting itself as an entity over
and apart from these classes, and in effect forms a distinctive
social entity. Whether the bureaucracy can ever be a class in
the classic sense of economic ownership of productive processes is still a future contingency. What can no longer be
doubted is the bureaucracy's capacity for economic management and also social demands of a kind not normally associated with either the bourgeoisie or the proletariat.[78]

To justify elitist distinctions and to defend them in the
name of State authority is to Sorel tantamount to surrender-
ing freedom to the false god of security. Those who make
the guarantees, the mass bureaucratic network, attempt to
make good by controlling economic and political upheavals
through manipulation of the legal machinery of government.
In so doing, the bureaucracy insidiously constitutes itself as
a class independent of either industrialists or producers.
This Sorel sees as the binding element between State capitalism and State socialism. The reconciliation of social needs
and economic ambitions is not solved, in Sorel's system, by
viewing material abundance as the automatic regulator of

human strivings and passions. Such a hierarchical approach is too often a disguise for putting off into the future serious consideration of root problems of political sociology: the precise relation of authority to freedom, social control to individual fulfillment.[79]

It was Sorel's prime merit as a political theorist that his ambiguous hopes for the future were not allowed to conceal concrete issues of the present. His focus by now has become common political science currency, as it sheds light on the general features of the state. The bureaucratic components of the state, the effects of violence on the masses, the adopted stance of bureaucracy within various economic systems—on such vital issues as these, his work and insight assure him a significant place among efforts to construct a synthetic theory of politics. In doing so he drew a line in the sand with conventional theories of democracy and the idea of progress. And, perhaps inadvertently, he also distinguished the realities of the "hard state" with the pieties of the "soft society."[80]

Notes

1. John Stanley, *The Sociology of Virtue: The Political and Social Theories of Georges Sorel*. Berkeley and Los Angeles, University of California Press, 1981.
2. Pierre Joseph Proudhon, *La guerre et la paix; recherches sur le principe et la constitution du droit des gens* (Paris, 1861), Vol. II, chap. xi.
3. Georges Sorel, *Matériaux d'une théorie du prolétariat* (Paris, 1919), pp. 29–30.
4. Georges Sorel, *Réflexions sur la violence*, p. 265 (199–200); and 256–257 (194).
5. Ibid., p. 257 (194).
6. Ibid., pp. 153–154 (127–8).
7. Ibid., p. 249 (189).
8. Of particular interest in any comparison of the two men are the following writings of Lenin: *The State and Revolution* (Selected Works, Vol. 7) (New York, n.d.); *The State* (Selected Works, Vol. 11) (New York, 1943); *Collapse of the Second International* (Selected Works, Vol. 5) (New York 1943).
9. Lenin, *Materialism and Empiriocriticism* (Moscow, 1947), p. 301. While

this statement is widely cited, the context of Lenin's remark has not been indicated. Thus, even Georg Lukács, in *Die Zerstorung der Vernunft* (Berlin, 1954), p. 27, has drawn a general characterization of Sorel from Lenin's few words on Sorel's philosophy of physics.

10. *Réflexions sur la violence*, p. 311 (229).
11. *Réflexions sur la violence*, p. 184 (146).
12. Georges Sorel, *La décomposition du marxisme* (Paris 1908, 1910), pp. 13–14.
13. *Matériaux d'une théorie du prolétariat*, p. 36.
14. On several occasions Sorel recommended Vilfredo Pareto's *Les systèmes socialistes* as a significant critique of the doctrine of the harmony of economic interests in a class-divided society. The underlying political power thesis held by Pareto, its *realpolitik* extension of Marx's efforts, accounted in large measure for Sorel's endorsement of it.
15. *Réflexions sur la violence*, pp. 28–29 (46).
16. For a penetrating account of this divergence between aims and achievements in the French Revolution, see Harold J. Laski, *The State in Theory and Practice* (New York, (1935), pp. 241–249; and his study, *The Rise of European Liberalism: An Essay in Interpretation* (London, 1936), pp. 227–236.
17. For Renan's views, see "Questions contemporaines" and "La réforme intellectuelle et morale," in *Oeuvres complàtes d'Ernest Renan* (Paris, 1947), Vol. I. p. 23, 513–514.
18. *Réflexions sur la violence*, p. 29 (46).
19. Ibid., pp. 170–171 (138).
20. *Matériaux d'une théorie du prolétariat*, p. 53.
21. *Réflexions sur la violence*, pp. 437–54 (303–11).
22. Ibid, pp. 170–1 (138).
23. *La décomposition du marxisme*, pp. 26–29
24. *Réflexions sur la violence*, pp. 238–239 (182).
25. *La décomposition du marxisme*, pp. 26–27.
26. *Matériaux d'une théorie du prolétariat*, pp. 283–284.
27. The idea of paralleling syndical socialism with Spartacism was first offered to me by Aviva L. Futorian. For information on the extent to which Rosa Luxemburg's theory of spontaneity coincided with Sorel's doctrine of the political apocalypse, see her essay, *The Russian Revolution* (New York, 1940), pp. 46–47; also her program on the demands of the Spartacus League, adopted by the German Communist Party on December 31, 1918, published in *Illustrierte Geschichte der Deutschen Revolution* (Berlin, 1929), pp. 259–263. A very useful estimate of the Spartacists' anarchist tendencies is in Carl E. Schorske, *German Social Democracy: 1905–1917* (Cambridge, 1955), pp. 318–321.
28. Frederick Engels, *The Origin of the Family, Private Property and the State*, in *Marx/Engels Selected Works* (London, 1950), Vol. II, p. 290. The exact wording in this version differs in emphasis from the ear-

lier Kerr edition of the same work (p. 209). Nonetheless, the impact of Engels's statement is to introduce the fact of the existence of the state in pre-class history, a state which is not primarily a tool of a class. His statement further enables us to distinguish the point in human history when the state is transformed from an instrument of public authority into one of class authority. For a concise exposition of this point, see Stanley W. Moore, *The Critique of Capitalist Democracy: An Introduction to the Theory of the State in Marx, Engels, and Lenin* (New York, 1957), pp. 17–57.

29. Roberto Michels, *Political Parties: A Sociological Study of the Oligarchical Tendencies of Modern Democracy*, p. 347.
30. *Democracy in a World of Tensions*, edited by Richard McKeon (Chicago, 1951). See also on this Arne Naess, *Democracy, Ideology and Objectivity: Studies in the Semantics and Cognitive Analysis of Ideological Controversy* (Oslo and Oxford, 1956).
31. *Saggi di crittica del Marxismo* (Palermo, 1903), pp. 38–40.
32. *Réflexions sur la violence*, pp. 256–257 (194).
33. Ibid., p. 95 (90).
34. *Matériaux d'une théorie du prolétariat*, p. 67.
35. *La décomposition du marxisme*, pp. 22–24.
36. *Réflexions sur la violence*, p. 265 (199).
37. *La décomposition du marxisme*, p. 25
38. *Matériaux d'une théorie du prolétariat*, pp. 384–389.
39. Cf. Peter Gay, *The Dilemma of Democratic Socialism: Eduard Bernstein's Challenge To Marx* (New York, 1952), pp. 207–212.
40. Max Horkheimer, *Eclipse of Reason* (New York, 1947). pp. 121–122.
41. *Réflexions sur la violence*, p. 298 (220–1).
42. *Réflexions sur la violence*, p. 392 (279).
43. For a brief, pointed examination of anti-parliamentarianism in Sorel, Pareto and Lenin, and psychological co-efficients of authoritarianism see Jules Monnerot, *Sociology and Psychology of Communism* (Boston, 1953), pp. 31–33, 146–147.
44. *Réflexions sur la violence*, p. 341 (247).
45. Ibid., p. 342 (248).
46. *Insegnamenti sociali della economia contemporanea*, pp. 397–398.
47. *Les illusions du progrès* (4th edition), pp. 276–277.
48. *Matériaux d'une théorie du prolétariat*, pp. 72–73.
49. G.D.H. Cole, *A History of Socialist Thought*, Vol. III, Part I, p. 386.
50. *Réflexions sur la violence*, p. 268 (201).
51. Cf. Curzio Suckert Malaparte, "Fascism as a Counter-Reformation and Anti-Risorgimento," in Herbert W. Schneider, *Making The Fascist State* (New York, 1928), Appendix 30, pp. 352–356.
52. *Réflexions sur la violence*, pp. 190–191 (150–1).
53. *Réflexions sur la violence*, pp. 313–314 (230–1).
54. Ibid., p. 221 (171).
55. Michael Freund, *Georges Sorel: Der revolutionäre Konservativismus* (Frankfurt-am-Main, 1932), pp. 63–64.

56. *Matériaux d'une théorie du prolétariat*, pp. 73-74.
57. *Insegnamenti sociali della economia contemporanea* (Palermo, 1906), p. 278.
58. *Réflexions sur la violence*, p. 244 (186).
59. *Réflexions sur la violence*, p. 246 (187).
60. G.D.H. Cole, *A History of Socialist Thought*, Vol. III, Part I, p. 383.
61. Sorel's original statement does not contain the translator s phrase, "of power." It simply reads: "Le renforcement de l'État est à la base de toutes leurs conceptions."
62. *Réflexions sur la violence*, p. 250 (190).
63. *Matériaux d'une théorie du prolétariat*, p. 162.
64. Eduard Bernstein, *Socialism théorique et social-democratique pratique* (Paris, 1900), pp. 226-228.
65. *Réflexions sur la violence*, p. 253 (191).
66. Eduard Bernstein, "Der Streik als politisches Kampfmittel," in *Neue Zeit*, XII, No. 1, 1894, pp. 689-695. This article contains a defense of the political strike, and of revisionist labor tactics in general, as opposed to the purely proletarian strike. See also *Der Streik, sein wesen und sein wirken* (Frankfurt-am-Main, 1906), pp. 109-117.
67. *Réflexions sur la violence*, p. 236 (180-1).
68. *La décomposition du marxisme*, pp. 10-11.
69. *Réflexions sur la violence*, pp. 236-237 (181).
70. Jean Jaurès, *Studies in Socialism*, "The General Strike and Revolution," (London, 1906), pp. 106-129.
71. It is important to distinguish the three types of strikes with which Sorel deals. First, there is the *proletarian* general strike, which is a protracted workers' strike at the bastions of government as such. It has as its chief aim the overthrow of capitalist society. Sorel restricted the content of socialism to this type of general strike. The *political* general strike is connected to the proximate goals of socialists in parliament and government generally. The political strike is a symbolic strike, revealing the extent of mass support for socialist political claims. The third type of strike is the more familiar *economic* strike, having as its aim the improvement in the status of the laborers. Political ends either do not enter, or enter only elliptically. Sorel was relatively indifferent to the economic strike. Like most social revolutionaries, although he supported the right of workers to improve their conditions of life, he was fearful of the reform ideology that ordinarily accompanies the purely economic strike.
72. Political and philosophical thought in France after the conclusion of the Second World War bears witness to the extent to which it was still caught up in the historic debates of reform versus revolution. Raymond Aron has inherited the constitutional reform tradition from men like Millerand. In his justly famous essay, *The Opium of the Intellectuals* (London, 1957), he attempted to puncture the "myth of the proletariat" and the idea of the inevitability of revolution in general. Albert Camus has offered a different phase of this debate

in his *L'homme révolte* (Paris, 1951). Here, State terror is counterposed to rational terrorism, with a firm plea being made for the rebel over and against the revolutionist. The two contemporary views which show the most in common with Sorel are those of Emmanuel Mounier and, to an even larger extent, Maurice Merleau-Ponty. Mounier, the direct inheritor of the mantle of Peguy, offered, up to his death, the most consistent defense of revolutionary socialism from the viewpoint of the Catholic apocalypse. In particular, see his collection of essays in two volumes, *Feu la chrétienté* (Paris, 1950), and *L'espoir des désespérés* (Paris, 1953). Like Sorel, Merleau-Ponty is insistent on the special role of the proletariat in shaping the future of history. The proletariat is said to have a unique revolutionary destiny because it is the only class which embodies real universality and consciousness of historical direction. See in particular his *Humanisme et Terreur* (Paris, 1947 and *Les aventures de la dialectique* (Paris, 1955). Here we see just how much of the Sorelian legacy has been retained by present existential *philosophes* and *literati*.

73. Pierre Andreu, *Fédération* (Paris, 1947), cited in James H. Meisel, "Sorel Revisited," *University of Toronto Quarterly*, Vol. XIX (1949), p. 54. For Sorel's praise of capitalist production, see *De l'utilité du pragmatisme*, pp. 350–351.

74. *Réflexions sur la violence*, p. 233 (179).

75. Ibid., p. 228 (175).

76. *Matériaux d'une théorie du prolétariat*, pp. 73–74, 132–133.

77. *Introduction a l'économie moderne* (Paris, 1922), p. 247.

78. The following works have emphasized that common to different economic systems is a unique inversion of the political state and the national economy—an inversion accompanied by a much larger role for the state bureaucracy. See Franz Neumann, *Behemoth: The Structure and Practice of National Socialism* (New York, 1944); C. Wright Mills, *The Power Elite* (New York, 1956); Milovan Djilas, *The New Class: An Analysis of the Communist System* (New York, 1957); Joseph A. Schumpeter, *Capitalism, Socialism, and Democracy* (New York. 1947).

79. It should be mentioned that Sorel arrived at his position on the pivotal role of bureaucracy in modern society independent of, and prior to, Max Weber. The fact of their remarkable perspectival similarities has thus far not received the attention it merits from comparative sociologists. Talcott Parsons's justly famous *The Structure of Social Action* (New York and London, 1937), which deals extensively with the work of both Weber and Pareto, ignores Sorel's germinal efforts completely. Reinhard Bendix's *Max Weber: An Intellectual Portrait* (New York, 1960) likewise makes no mention of Sorel. The excellent essay by J. P. Mayer, *Max Weber and German Politics: A Study in Political Sociology* (London, 1944), while noting Weber's "European Outlook" does not indicate that Sorel shared with Weber the founding of the sociology of bureaucracy. What makes this so amazing is that Roberto Michels and Vilfredo Pareto had many years earlier

already documented Sorel's role. While the literature of Weber in English is extensive, the best single source for his views on bureaucracy is contained in *From Max Weber: Essays in Sociology,* translated and edited by H. H. Gerth and C. Wright Mills (New York, 1946), esp. pp. 196–244.

80. Two first-rate general studies of the moral foundations of Sorel's critique of the state and society—especially as it existed in France— are John L. Stanley, *The Sociology of Virtue: The Political and Social Theories of Georges Sorel.* Berkeley and Los Angeles: University of California Press, 1981; and Arthur L. Greil, *Georges Sorel and the Sociology of Virtue.* Washington, D.C.: University Press of America, 1981.

8

Legitimizing the Bureaucratic State:
Weber I

"Durkheim explained why all men were rational, and Weber, why some were more rational than others."

—Ernest Gellner[1]

In the study of legitimacy, all political sociologists are the children of Max Weber; just as in the study of revolution we are the offspring of Karl Marx. This is as might be expected since Marx paid scant attention to what happens after revolutions succeed, as if such questions were unworthy of speculation in advance of revolution. It was left to Weber—more a democratic Kantian than a bourgeois Marxian—to explain how social systems come to sustain themselves over time through a combination or permutation of charismatic, traditional, and rational-bureaucratic modes of domination. Weber himself appreciated the complexities of the problem of legitimacy. And this is indicated by his allusion to the special circumstances surrounding the Papacy. He saw such church forms of legitimacy as a function of the "charisma of office"—the so-called magical leadership potency is less derived from the personal qualities of any given pope than it is from the institutional properties of a world historic

church. Weber was more concerned with the secular context of religious agencies than with the religious beliefs of
social actors. So then, what is one to make of these various
distinctions? The answer Weber gives is rooted in the notion of ideal types. Social systems are not pure, but represent an amalgam of diverse forms of domination.

Weber's preeminence derives in no small part from the
failure of Marx to acknowledge State domination as theoretically distinct from class repression. It was religion, and
in particular the evolution of religious patterns of accumulation in rural economies, and not development or bureaucracy, that originally provoked his break with neoclassical
political economy and Marxism in particular. Thus, as the
welfare state evolved in Germany, Russia and the United
States as an independent institution, Marxism as a theory
seemed inept, if not entirely blind, to this evolution of political forces in various institutional guises apart from economic relationships. Weber as a social theorist understood
well the Marxist myopia, the congenital incapacity to see
the working class as anything but an enemy of the state and
the bourgeoisie as anything other than the engine driving
the state. In such a theoretical vacuum, the need of the time
became obvious: to give substance to the evolution of politics as an autonomous process. Thus, Weber displaced revolution and class with development and bureaucracy, and in
so doing gave political sociology a lasting life apart from
political economy.

These new sets of distinctions carried Weber to a new
sense of super- and subordination, of domination, or politics as the main activity of the state. As someone who took
legal definitions seriously, Weber understood the Hegelian
essence: the central concern of the state was the protection
and expansion of the nation. Indeed, Weber derived from
Marx an appreciation that the state as legitimated through
appointment or election, nonetheless retained a capacity
for coercion. But coercion no more than beneficence ex-

hausted the meaning of state power. Far from being a benign condition, the state is based on a monopoly of physical coercion, a controlled situation legitimated by laws and
customs of leaders and masses. The rule of law is not some
abstract credo for Weber, but the instrument by means of
which the exercise of power is not only possible but found
acceptable by wide masses of people through its legal response to equity of the citizenship. Legitimacy became distinct from liberty. Weber thus retained his European biases,
despite an awareness of the American experience and its
uniqueness. Indeed, one might argue that the greatest triumph of Weberian analysis is neither to be found in America
nor in Europe, but rather in China. In its most recent evolution the political leadership has sensed the need to open
the economy to the free market system, while at the same
time continuing, even strengthening its control over the
machinery of State administrative functions. In this stunning development, a presumably Marxist society has turned
"theory" on its head—with the state becoming the "base,"
while the economy becomes the "superstructure."

We have then in Weber the "father" of social systems and
bureaucratic politics alike. It is little wonder that those who
claim to wear the crown of Weber are certain that their man
speaks for a view of political sociology that offers an acceptable formula for describing the relationship of class, status
and power. The core of Weber's views on the state were not
so much a belief in the efficacy of power, a long-standing
predicate of political philosophy from Plato through Hobbes,
but a belief in the efficacy of the legal system to compel all
branches of the population to accept its grand design, its
sovereign rule, its sense of the national will.

If there is a specifically Germanic property to sociology,
it derives from the search that stretched from Hegel to Weber for understanding the sources of authority, or more
specifically, order. While much is made of Weber's approaches to the sources of capitalist development in the so-

called Protestant ethic, and a corresponding interest exists
in his efforts to understand the sources of political change
in the notion of "charisma," the essence of the Weberian
synthesis was in the notion of authority. Indeed, even his
notions of individual leadership as lodged in charisma indicated as much. It was not just leadership as an attribute of a
person, but authority as broadly accepted by those out of
power that gripped Weber's attention.

Weber held that there were essentially three types of authority: traditional forms based on dynastic inheritance;
rational-legal varieties based on an broad acceptance of rules
and norms; and charismatic authority predicated on faith
in a person of exceptional qualities of either a secular or
clerical sort. But this essentially historical evolution of forms
of authority does not in itself delimit the content of politics.
The admixture of the three types of authority instead serves
to disguise the potential for democracy or autocracy. A process defines Weber's world more than a structure. The tension between civil society and state power is a shifting activity. Varieties of authority are thus the playing field on which
the struggle over the distribution of power takes place.

One can best appreciate this process element in Weber's
political sociology by contrasting his efforts with that of the
Franco-Italian school of sociology. From Michels to Sorel
and Mosca, it was the exercise of power—sometimes naked,
more often disguised, in the modern industrial epoch—that
fascinated these figures far less concerned with legal norms
than political actions. In Weberian terms, on the contrary,
power was virtually identified as illegitimacy. In this, Pareto
was aligned with the so-called German School of political
theory. Its uses and abuses were wrapped in each other and
in the transgression of legal statutes or authority as such.
And while we shall emphasize the Weberian context, it should
be clear that the incapacity of sociology to treat power and
authority within the same paradigm was a contributing element to the ultimate dissolution of classical European soci-

ology. For it surrendered to political science, or at least political theory, the study of power. Which to break that authority reduced sociology to a one-sided search for either the sources of legitimate authority or the mechanisms.

At a later stage and in an American context, Talcott Parsons understood as much; in *The Structure of Social Action* he attempted to include Weber and Pareto as part of the same study of social dynamics. But that attempted synthesis between authority and power, normative values and pecuniary interests, failed precisely because this great American sociologist attempted to convert the problem of authority to one of the interplay of state and economy, and in so doing seriously weakened the study of politics as an autonomous art form. It suffices at this point to appreciate the extent to which sociology showed early in its development the sort of truncated form of development that led to an arbitrary, and ultimately tragic, separation of the analysis of authority and power, law and force, and ultimately, legitimacy and illegitimacy. In other words, the outcome of Parsonian thought was the very reverse of his inputs. It was a system that terminated in a dualism, in a schism, from which the social sciences are only now trying to recover.

Weber escaped this later dualism by separating his thought from that of Michels and the power school. He saw authority as an entity distinctly apart from power. And here, Weber wedded Kant to Hegel. The internalization of respect for law, for values, gave authority a source of connection to the state, apart from crude reliance on force. This internalization was axiomatic—much like the way in which human beings come to understand the logical structure of mathematical reasoning. In this, Weber separated himself from the Machiavellian and Hobbesian traditions alike, apart from the idea that power was an ultimate value. Just as Plato rejected the argument of Thrasymachus in *The Republic,* so too did Weber reject the notion of the Franco-Italian school of sociology that power is a club, and that elites are determined exclusively by their hold on segments of population, over whom they rule. The German State, with its unique linkage of welfarism, militarism and state power, may have frightened and disheartened Weber, but it also gave him an awareness of just how complex the issue of state and society actually is. The effort to make Weber part of a continuum with Pareto, undertaken by Parsons, led to intellectual confusion, and ultimately to chaos. Even Parsons in his later years was led to mute his idea of power and authority as a simple continuum.

Before going further then, it is best to unpack the discrete points of entrance into political sociology, or at least Weber's political sociology. In a strong bow to the French tradition of Montesquieu, Tocqueville and Durkheim, he understood that the issue that was to preoccupy the twentieth century would be the political capacities of the rulers and not the economic conditions of the ruled. One might say that in his analysis of German "political immaturity," he cut to the core of this volitional rather than determinist source of the anti-democratic tradition. "The reason for such immaturity is to be found in its apolitical past, in the fact that it was not possible to catch up on a century of missed political education in a single decade, and in the fact that rule by a great man is not always a means of educating the people politically." He goes on to sat that "the danger does not lie with the masses, as is believed by people who stare as if hypnotized down into the depths of society. The deepest core of the sociopolitical problem is not the question of the economic situation of the ruled, but of the political qualifications of the ruling and rising classes."[2]

Weber followed up this view of the importance of political culture with a blistering critique of determinism and historicism. The distinction between politics and science depends on avoiding the import of human goals in empirical examinations. Indeed, beyond leadership, is its capacity to lead by containing conflict within constitutional norms. "It is utterly ridiculous to suppose that it is an 'inevitable' feature of our economic development under present-day advanced capitalism, as it has now been imported into Russia and as it exists in America, that it should have an elective affinity with 'democracy' or indeed with 'freedom' (in any sense of the word), when the only question to be asked is: how are all these things, in general and the long term, possible where it prevails."[3]

Lurking beneath Weber's concerns is the problem of democracy in environments where such a liberal order is either unknown, untried, or untested. Bureaucratic centralism, a trait of Nazism and Communism alike, surfaces in his study of the situation of constitutional democracy in Russia—or better, its absence. Liberal democracy can only be brought about by "organs of self-government, and for this very reason it seems vitally important for liberalism to understand that its vocation still lies with the struggle against both bureaucratic and Jacobin centralism, and in working to spread the old, fundamental, individualist notion of 'inalienable human rights' amongst the masses, rights which have come to seem as 'trivial' to us in Western Europe as black bread is to a man who has enough to eat."[4]

Even allowing for Weber's huge contributions to the study of leadership and political education, the problem of containing conflict within constitutional forms—and the nature of liberal democracy as an option to the bureaucratic pathos, the issues of legitimacy and regime survival—was not entirely resolved. Weber had to introduce the notion of charisma, or personality, in a public setting, as a fourth distinct area of political sociology in order to account for real world combinations and recombinations of state power. Even in such instances of pseudo-democratic forms, such as one now finds in Egypt, India, and Mexico, it is clear that the major binding single-party units could survive intact after the demise of an originating leadership only with great difficulty, or better yet, only insofar as the state machinery remained

intact. It is a tribute to the work of Weber that he anticipated the great difficulty with which political systems would
manage problems of succession and leadership without an
appropriate sense of the normative legal basis of democratic
politics. Systems of rule can be mandated by constitutions,
but democracy can come about only over time and in special circumstances.

It soon became apparent that the notion of charismatic
authority was a special condition of a transitional stage, rather
than a general law of political development.[5] Where institutions were durable and powerful in their own right, such a
concept has great operational worth—whether in describing
the leadership of the Roman Catholic Church or a representative socialist or Third World country. However, in other
nations, especially in nations in which a democratic ethos is
remote, the party apparatus itself was subject to extreme pressures, and with the fall of charismatic figures, multi-party dissolution rapidly occurred. However, the state as such did not
dissolve. This happened to a lesser degree in societies capable
of shifting the basis of power from the individual to the societal. But this in itself served to confirm Weber's concerns
about new political formations. It is no longer possible to
subsume all or most developing societies or developing powers under the rubric of charismatic authority. They move either toward the social bases of democracy or the statist bases
of dictatorship. The character of economic structures only
beclouds such tendencies in the political sphere.

This need to reach out for a more embracing political
concept of development, one that took into account the
phenomena of party, class, and state under praetorian conditions, led Weber to the study of illegitimacy no less than
legitimacy. For it became evident to Weber that in the twentieth century military might had become pre-eminent in
determining the structure of state power and social welfare
alike. The Wilhelmine-Prussian System made room for both.
Furthermore, Weber knew that the management of the

political system was not based on anything remotely resembling a Rousseauian social contract, but was simply a rearrangement of elites lacking in either electoral or popular support. These new structural configurations that emerged in Europe and elsewhere remained of such a profound nature that it was no longer feasible to speak of a crisis in legitimacy. Rather, it became necessary to explore what the new configurations of power were and how they contributed to the formation of the new normative framework, quite unlike what characterized democratic societies. To these states that combined modernization and state power one can affix the term norm of illegitimacy.

The original utilization of the norm of illegitimacy concept was to explain what appeared to be the crisis of democratic formations throughout Europe after World War One. It was clear then, and even more so now, that the model employed by Weber has a range of applicability to many parts of the developing world. For the so-called crisis of legitimacy has become common parlance with respect to the socialist as well as capitalist economies of the post-World War Two epoch. We have an expanding literature of the growing significance in the breakdown of legitimacy in the West,[6] and a similar sort of literature covering the contemporary evolution of post-communism.[7]

Weber's concern is not so much with the breakdown of legitimacy as with the normative standing of militarized politics equal to, if not greater than, the older capitalist and socialist orders alike. What Weber holds is that we are witnessing not simply a crisis of legitimacy but at the same time new forms of institutionalizing power, that is, of making the state central to society. Seen in this way, problems of legitimating do not necessarily evaporate, but they do take on a more specialized meaning—since we can now examine the problem of legitimacy as long standing rather than the conventional mode of crisis-thinking on ways of maintaining legitimate authority.[8]

The crisis factor in the legitimization process has common roots, yet different forms of expression, given the structural differentiation of political systems in the "three worlds." In Western capitalism and democracy, those societies most characterized by parliamentary representation, the problem has been that within a mass society there has been a stretching out effect of representational government. When a constituency is small, the relationships between the representative and those who are represented are direct and organic. But as the size of parliamentary governments is held constant, and citizen size continues to grow, the ratios of representation change. As a result, those who represent constituencies are themselves nearly as anonymous, remote, and removed from popular consensus as executive officers or even appointed officials. This stretching out effect generates a problem of non-choice, a feeling of helplessness before world historic events presumably beyond ordinary control. This, in turn, leads to at least a short-term fall-off of interest more conventionally labeled by political scientists as a problem of political alienation in a democracy.[9] But whatever labels are attached, widespread agreement exists that the sense of distance between those who rule and those who are ruled is in large part the source of the legitimacy crisis in the West.

When we turn to the panoply of socialist and social democratic economies, the problem of legitimacy shifts, but only quantitatively. In nations with a broad culture of liberty and individualism, even the rise of heavy intervention to ensure the social well being of the whole society (as in Scandinavian nations) did not topple regimes. But in nations lacking such normative capacities and traditions (as in Eastern Europe and Russia for the most part), communist movements were unable to survive the initial seizure of power. In those societies where the basis of legitimacy was presumably based on the doctrine of direct popular participation, alternatively called the dictatorship of the proletariat, socialism of the whole people, the rights of the masses, and so on, it became apparent that illegitimacy continued to be the leitmotif of politics itself.[10] Characteristic of the socialist situation, with its single party pre-eminence and parliamentary government reduced to rubber-stamping executive authority, different political structures yielded the same sort of disastrous outcomes. Communist systems revealed the problem of non-choice and a problem of a fall-off of popular interest, or a decline in political mobilization and participation. Weber understood that only when rational-legal authority is secure could the state overcome the problem of apathy, alienation, and ultimately, a crisis in legitimate authority. In the absence of voluntary associations, or even the rights of individuals not to participate, legitimacy dissolved as the social system itself shriveled.

Weber is careful not to confuse political legitimacy with national hegemony. Neither the classic models of the American nor Soviet revolutions could boast hegemonic rule by the *de jure* procedures of claiming legitimacy for a revolutionary elite or party. In the case of the American Revolution claims of legitimacy for what Seymour Martin Lipset aptly termed the "first new nation" divided the colonists and resulted in the emergence of United Empire Loyalists who, for the most part, settled in Canada. One authority, Leslie F.S. Upton, put the matter thus: "The American Revolution was a civil war between British subjects and particularly between British Americans. The Loyalists were the losers. They were the first 'un-American' Americans, interrogated by committees, condemned without judge or jury, smeared in the press, expelled from their jobs, and deprived of their possessions. The American mind can tolerate any crime but that of failure: the grand sweep of American history dispersed the Loyalists in oblivion."[11] In doing so, the normative basis of American society was secured.

The Soviet Revolution was unable to resolve its cleavages in a similar normative fashion. As a result, Russian society

was compelled into a permanent condition of warfare between contending forces—or between Bolshevik hegemonists
and social democratic pluralists. As David Lane notes, the
immediate consequence of the Soviet state was civil war:
"From 1918 to 1921, the country was enveloped in the chaos
of civil war and foreign intervention: it was a period known
as 'War Communism.' For much of the time the Bolsheviks
ruled only one-seventh of Russian territory, mainly the Great
Russian areas of the country, the remainder being occupied
by the other government."[12] It is this cleavage that made the
Soviet State vulnerable, not so much to external threat, but
to Hobbesian schisms. Without legitimacy the State becomes
an instrument of terror. But terror is not a constant. It becomes subject to diverse forces operating within the State
bureaucracy. Thus, even at points of maximum revolutionary
fervor, in Weberian terms, legitimacy is never quite secure.

The success of a revolution is itself a phase of legitimizing a regime. This may be followed by institutionalization,
which operationally refers to the emergence of hegemonic
rule, or at least a broad-based consensus between the holders of power. Creating an institutional framework is often
as difficult and exacting a task as leading a successful revolution. Indeed, it has become an iron law of socialist revolutionary politics that the cadre formed in making a revolution is inevitably displaced by one formed to carry through
its stated tasks. In that post-revolutionary process very few
of the original "old revolutionists" survive the bureaucratic
processing. But quite beyond legitimating and institutionalizing phases is what might be termed the "highest stage" of
revolution making—solving the riddle of succession. And
here is where Weber is most helpful—and hopeful.

The crucial point in the revolution comes when there is a
need to transfer power from one person or group to another
person or group, and to do so without the destruction of the
governing and bureaucratic networks as a whole. The serious
problems that arose in the transference of power after the

death of Lenin in the Soviet Union and of Mao in the People's Republic of China is a clear indicator of just how serious a matter succession can be in totalitarian regimes. Far even beyond Dahl's question: "after the death of original leader, then what?" This is clearly not the place for a full-blown discussion of problems of leadership and succession. It is sufficient to note the three phases of revolutionary evolution: legitimization, succession, and institutionalization.

When viewed against such a historical background, urging older forms of legitimating upon new states is a far less attractive moral imperative than would at first seem apparent. It might well be argued that the function and structure of military politics in developing regions has increasingly come to provide a solution to the crisis of legitimacy by turning the political structure upside down: by institutionalizing forms of illegitimate authority that are admittedly derived neither from the electoral process, nor the direct will of the people, but simply by a presumed national need best understood by those who lead, and best implemented by those who are led. Thus, the Third World, faced with monumental problems of modernization at the economic level, mobilization at the political level, and militarization at the organizational level, has moved toward a style of governance that deserves to be understood on its own terms.

The presumption that such Third World forms only provide a benchmark on an evolutionary scale which is still considerably behind either Western or socialist forms of government, does not appreciate the ironic situation that has ensued: legitimacy, like illegitimacy, is a process and not a substance tied to any one type of economy. To understand Weber is to appreciate the degree to which the issue of political legitimacy is tied to that of political instability or to illegitimacy as such. For what we want to know is not just what it takes for a society to survive but what are the mechanisms of collapse and of breakdown. And here Weber proves to be an excellent guide.

The norm of illegitimacy arises in a context where structural requisites for legitimate authority are absent. When authority can be institutionalized neither through the mechanism of class/mass, nor through law/authority, then illegitimacy exists in fact. The norm of illegitimacy is serviceable both to the internal needs of the political/military order which gives direction to national policy and to an international/multinational order which delimits the directions of any one nation in the world economy. Illegitimacy, like legitimacy, is intended to produce mass political mobilization and, at the same time, reduce unauthorized violence or acts of terror. Illegitimacy becomes an instrument to prevent rather than to stimulate untrammeled social change.

The norm of illegitimacy is guaranteed and underwritten by a combination of internal and international elites that view a circulation of government power as beneficial to larger global interests. Hence, it is usually carried forth by military or quasi-military forces, sometimes overturning civilian regimes, and other times overturning military regimes, but always circulating elites while minimizing the risk of civilian authority in the Third World. Such military sponsored change often serves as a political distributive mechanism without being an economically distributive mechanism. Since no government undergoing a constant set of political rotations at the top can legitimate itself, either in electoral terms, or through direct participation, political illegitimacy becomes institutionalized.

Revolutionary cadres serve to prevent any undue entrenchment of special, sectarian interests. Hence, it serves to overcome structural deformities in the older political system. But it does so by risking further social revolution and systemic overhaul. As such the norm of illegitimacy is a mechanism for problem management rather than problem solving. Its purpose is to institutionalize elite authority without the conventional calcifying effects of older interest group formations that are attached to race, class, or religious interests instead of the profession of state power directly. But what then occurs is the internalization of such interest groups. They become attached to the State machinery, instead of to popular demands and discourse.

The norm of illegitimacy presupposes a conflict model, just as theories of legitimization for the most part presuppose consensus models. In propositional forms: when a consensus apparatus becomes inoperative, political-military regimes turn to a norm of illegitimacy rather than risk formlessness and widespread upheaval as a whole. The "new order" thus permits the institutionalization of crisis as a normative political pattern, rather than presume norms of legitimacy which are largely absent in most new nations.

A considerable amount of work on illegitimacy took place outside the framework of political sociology and served to extend the work of Weber. The more recent studies have served to provide a deeper understanding of the subjective side of the process, which accompany the breakdown of legitimacy and, parenthetically, make possible the emergence of dictatorial regimes in a virtually permanent state of crisis. Clifford Geertz pointed out that for virtually every person in every society some attachment flow more from a sense of natural, even spiritual, affinity than from social or political interaction.[13] He went on to note that in modern societies the shifting of such ties to the level of political supremacy has increasingly come to be considered as pathological. An increasing percentage of national unity is maintained not by calls to blood and land, but by a vague, intermittent and routine allegiance to a civil or military state supplemented to a greater or lesser extent by government use of police powers and ideological exhortation. In modernizing societies where the tradition of civil authority is weak, and where technical requirements for effective welfare are poorly understood, primordial attachments serve to demarcate autonomous political units. What finally emerges, according to Geertz, is a theory that authority comes only from the inherent coercive nature of such primordial attachments, or what in fact in my own terms I have come to call the norm of illegitimacy.

Georges Balandier enriches this Weberian notion of the primordial or spiritual source of permanent strife by speaking of the desacralization of power. This process of desacralization of traditional leadership of kings and chiefs was inevitable since the power of those sovereigns and chiefs was legitimated by references to colonial governments rather than native groupings. Such authority rarely rested on any intrinsic merit of such systems of rule. Hence, the transition from the patrimonial to the bureaucratic type of authority does not take place in the Third World the way it earlier did in either the First or Second worlds. Because these colonial political systems were so varied, different reactions to the experiences of post-colonial transformation were inevitable. Bureaucratic desacralization did not bring about the terrible effects feared by former rulers, but it did result in types of rule that attempted to combine hierarchical and egalitarian forms rather than displace the latter by the former. Balandier notes that the process of modernization was set in motion by the colonial adventure.[14] But that very adventure created political distortions that led political parties, social ideologies, and military regimes to seek out forms of institutionalization quite different from the older European and American societies. All human societies produce politics, and none are resistant to historical processes. On the other hand, this universal proposition comes upon the particular: namely, that Third World politics produces national, ethnic, racial, and religious demands that lead to a different set of norms than in either the First or Second worlds. The issue is not necessarily one of democracy, but of stability. And it is here, with the reintroduction of genocidal systems in places as remote as Rwanda and Cambodia, the militarization of tribal power, in places as far apart as Nigeria and Yugoslavia, that the breakdown or the lack of legitimacy becomes a source of breakdown and collapse.[15]

An area in need of far greater emphasis than it received at the hands of Weber is the relationship between electoral politics and state legitimacy. Specifically, why should it be that elections, that monument to constitutional legitimacy, should fail to prevent military dominion, authoritarian take-overs, and the constant rotation of self-appointed leaders? In many states, where democratic norms are weak, a regime is more likely to be overthrown the smaller its margin of victory.[16] This can be broadened into a generalization by noting that the narrowness of an electoral victory seems to impair a government's legitimacy, thus making a military coup against it more likely. Yet, in North America and Western European political democracies, where the system itself and not the party process provides legitimization, similarly close elections, while engendering bitterness and charges of vote tampering, ironically serve to unite the nation and prevent militarist outcomes. While a tradition of competitive elections may itself reduce differentials of winning from losing, it also stimulates a norm of illegitimacy based on charges, often launched by military technocrats, that the electoral process is wasteful, divisive, and fruitless. And if one examines the sad roster of Latin American nations which once had vigorous presidential elections, and far from routine campaigns, few of them have endured. It is the quasi-democracies, the basically single-party states (Mexico, Cuba, and to a lesser extent Venezuela and Costa Rica) that have shown greater resistance to illegitimate authority than the former democracies of the area. But then, one might well argue that single-party states are themselves a special case of illegitimate authority. Admittedly, these concerns move a considerable distance from Weber, in geographical no less than theoretical terms.

Nonetheless, it is the relationship of military technocracy, with its singular incapacity to generate a new form of legiti-

macy that serves to confirm the wisdom of Weber. Although
the norm of illegitimacy invariably requires high military
participation, many military systems were and remain transitional—such as in Greece, Spain, and Portugal. It is con-
ceivable that military rule can become institutionalized and
hence develop a sense of quasi-legitimacy without the constant rotation of power. This is certainly what took place in
Chile under Pinochet. The military regimes essentially institutionalize their power, regularize the political processes
in order to solve the problem of succession, and in this way
create political forms that stabilize rather than rotate elites
in power. Military directives are intended to prevent civilian
opposition from reaching power in the foreseeable future,
but they also serve to move away from the highly personal
military dictatorships of previous years, and incorporate
themselves as the only institution capable of leading the
nation into economic and social transformation. Since time
is a crucial element in legitimization, the ability of a military to maintain itself in power far longer than either they
or their opponents originally thought possible, represents a
move away from democratic norms into a new type of authoritarian legitimacy, one in which the armed forces serve
as a ruling class. The problem is the notorious incapacity of
military leaders to serve as civil servants. Hence, the absence of legitimacy breeds a cycle of permanent revolution
or at least steady discontent.

The crucial test for the new states is the same as for all
societies: can such essentially non-democratic agencies of
authority achieve high levels of productivity without inflation or labor unrest? Can it achieve political stability without mass apathy and alienation? Can it create a stable pattern of succession without recourse either to the democratic
distemper or without resorting to authoritarian repression?
But to pose the issue in this essentially Weberian manner is
already to appreciate the degree to which the economy is an
engineered artifact, something that is controlled by human

forces in their guise as political directors of the levers of power. Far from the nineteenth-century idea of the economy as a force operating behind the backs of men, is the late twentieth-century idea that the economy is very much in the front of men—an instrument of society to be managed, manipulated and controlled in order to achieve the ends of power, or if one is more benign, the ends of stability. The Keynesian Revolution itself is part of the new tendency to view the economy as an element very much within human control. Monetarist policy has as its metaphysical presupposition that the control of the flow of capital, and decisions about disbursement of wages, can offset so-called natural tendencies toward exploitation and domination.

The same problems exist now, as did a century ago, only without the baggage of theory that claimed inevitable and infallible outcomes. States old and new have tended to accept pragmatic criteria in place of historical ones. Three things remain as elusive as ever: whether or not short-run tendencies can produce long-range economic benefits to large numbers; whether the costs of maintaining a norm of illegitimacy (high military and policy power) dry up economic distributions rather than expand services; and finally whether the very success at the economic level may engender new classes and social formations and hence new demands for legitimacy and the institutionalization of authority based on democratic or populist premises. For the present, the drive toward legitimization of authority has had contradictory results: seriously weakening civilian authoritarian forms of rule, serving to institutionalize military authority and police power, and stabilizing the world economy as a free market zone, with yet a heavy dose of social welfare considerations. Those who like their political systems simple are faced with troubling times. Those prepared to follow in Weberian tracks will at least have a keen sense of the evolution of the twentieth century.

Seymour Martin Lipset has well articulated the relationship of conflict and consensus in the process of legitimating state power. What he indicates about the American origins of democracy merit deep appreciation. "Democratic norms and rules developed largely through the struggles of various groups—religious, ideological, sectional, economic, professional, and so on—against one another, but particularly against the group which controls the polity. In many cases, the opposition forces that struggled for rights for themselves were not themselves committed to democratic ideology, but in the context of conflict they helped institutionalize democratic rights and form democratic norms."[17] This is as good a statement of Weberian thought, as we have to describe a contemporary world in which social welfare and state power both hold forth in the name of democracy.

It needs to be understood that Weber spoke of "legitimate domination" and not just legitimacy as such. The word domination is strong and intentional. It underscores a flinty, near-Hobbesian element, to Weber's thinking. The political universe is not simply a world of static equilibrium, or for that matter, a bland world of liberal pathos. Domination may be legitimate or illegitimate, but it serves as a bracing reminder that the state is not just a friend to mankind, but an arena in which dominance is more than a game, it is a reality. The Weberian problem imperceptibly shifts from the study of legitimacy to the dual problem of opposition to centralized state power and the political incapacity of the new ruling classes thrust into governance in the former Soviet Union, China, and other parts of the developing world identified as "Third"—neither capitalist nor socialist in their economies. Having understood this, Weber is then able to move onto a discussion of law and order in modern societies: opposition to an overweening bureaucratic state in the First World, the problem of democratic inexperience in the Second World, and the lack of stable social classes in the Third World. Again, I admit to an extrapolation from Weber's texts, but the evidence from those texts seem to confirm the direction in which his thought has taken throughout a variety of social systems and political orders.

Notes

1. Ernest Gellner. *Plough, Sword and Book: The Structure of Human History.* London: Collins Harvill, 1988. p. 128.
2. Max Weber "The Nation State and Economic Policy," *Political Writings.* Lassman and Speirs, editors. Cambridge: Cambridge University Press, 1994, pp.25–26.
3. Max Weber, *Selections in Translation* W.G. Runciman, editor. Cambridge: Cambridge University Press, 1978. p. 282
4. Max Weber, "On the Situation of Constitutional Democracy in Russia," *Political Writings,* Lassman and Speirs, editors. Cambridge: Cambridge University Press, 1994. pp. 67–68.
5. I have made three previous passes at trying to understand Weber and the issue of legitimacy. They are in Irving Louis Horowitz "Party Charisma: Practices and Principles, Ideological and Institutional Bases of Party Charisma," and "Intra-Country Variations in Party Charisma," in *Three Worlds of Development: The Theory and Practice of International Stratification.* New York and London: Oxford University Press, 1965. "Political Legitimacy and the Institutionalization of Crisis," *Comparative Political Studies,* 1 (1): 45–69, 1968; and "The Norm of Illegitimacy: The Political Sociology of Latin America," in Irving Louis Horowitz, Josue de Castro, and John Gerassi (eds.), *Latin American Radicalism: A Documentary Report on Left and Nationalist Movements.* New York: Random House: London: Jonathan Cape, 1969. pp. 3–29. Perhaps this time I have succeeded, or at least come closer to an understanding.
6. Alan Wolfe. *The Limits of Legitimacy: Political Contradictions of Contemporary Capitalism.* New York: The Free Press/Macmillan Publishing Company, 1977.
7. Julius Jacobson. *Soviet Communism and the Soviet Vision.* New Brunswick: Transaction Books/E.P. Dutton, 1972.
8. Max Weber, "The Types of Legitimate Domination" *Economy and Society* (volume 1). New York: Bedminister Press, 1968, pp. 212–245.
9. D.C. Schwartz, J. Aberbach, A.W. Finifter, et al. "Political Alienation in America." A special supplement to *Transaction/Society,* 13 (5) (July/August), 1977. pp. 18–53.
10. Bogdan D. Denitch. *The Legitimization of a Revolution: The Yugoslav Case.* New Haven and London: Yale University Press, 1976.
11. Leslie F.S. Upton, ed. *The United Empire Loyalists: Men and Myths.* Toronto: Copp Clark Publishing Company, 1967. pp. 1–7
12. David Lane. *Politics and Society in the USSR.* New York: Random House, 1971.
13. Clifford Geertz, ed. *Old Societies and New States: The Quest for Moder-*

nity in Asia and Africa. New York: The Free Press/Macmillan, 1963. pp. 105–57.
14. Georges Balandier. *Political Anthropology.* New York: Pantheon Books, 1970.
15. Alfred Stepan. *The Military in Politics: Changing Patterns in Brazil.* Princeton, New Jersey: Princeton University Press, 1971. pp. 79–84.
16. Martin C. Needler. "The Closeness of Elections in Latin America," *Latin American Research Review,* XII (1), 1977. pp. 115–21.
17. Seymour Martin Lipset, "Three Lectures on Democracy," *Extensions* (spring) 1998. pp. 3–12.

9

Defining the Boundaries of Law and Order: Weber II

"It was perhaps never before in history made so easy for any nation to become a great civilized power as for the American people. Yet, according to human celebration, it is also the last time, as long as the history of mankind shall last, that such conditions for a free and great development will be given. The areas of free soil are now vanishing everywhere in the world."

—*Max Weber*[1]

All major elements and tendencies in modern sociology take Max Weber seriously—even if he seems more cited than read. Certainly, for the first half of the century, he was the touchstone that measured all varieties of serious macroscopic analysis of large social systems. Marxists appreciate his keen sense of historical specificity. Functionalists celebrate his capacity to stay close to explanatory variables. Traditionalists respect his sense of the place of religion and convention in social life. And liberals date Weber as the main source of their own commitment to a scientific standpoint over ideological persuasions. It is almost as if Weber provided not just a theory of status legitimization, but in his person was a special form of legitimization to the American sociologist.

Parsonians identify with Weber's notions of bureaucracy and
social stratification; Mertonians identify with Weber's concepts of career patterns of scientists and theologians and
their stimulus to social change; and Millsians identify with
Weber's concepts of authority and the dysfunctionality of
raw power no less than with the belief that at its source
every problem is a moral paradox. Explaining just how this
canonical condition emerged on American soil is the essential task of this chapter.

We know from Hans Gerth that whatever linguistic limitations Mills had in German, he nonetheless "loved to pore
over the Weber materials" which Gerth had translated. If
Mills never did quite make up his mind about Weber, it was
less a response to Weber's writings directly than it was a
mixed set of feelings toward those, like Gerth, who mediated his reading of the great German. Perhaps Marianne
Weber, in her biography of Max Weber (a work which, by
the way, Mills helped to support), best captured his essential spirit of dedication to freedom over tyranny, principle
over expediency, and conscience over dogmatism:

> Weber always judged political events on the basis of one thing to
> which he clung all his life: Intellectual freedom was to him the great-
> est good, and under no circumstances was he prepared to consider
> even interests of political power as more important and attainable for
> the individual. Not for reasons of expediency, but only in the name
> of conscience does a man have the right to oppose the conscientiously
> held different beliefs of others.[2]

Here then is the essence of the Kantian as social theorist,
the political sociologist who separated the "is" from the
"ought." Weber was a European par excellence; but, like
Tocqueville, he traveled widely. He viewed events in grand
world historic terms. Even when he came to the United States
and observed "the Greek shining the Yankee's shoes for five
cents, the German acting as his waiter, the Irishman manag-
ing his politics, and the Italian digging his dirty ditches. His
real interests were focused not on the persons performing

such roles but on the 'Yankee' for whom the work was being performed."[3] True enough, this was circumscribed by his general belief in the waste created by capitalism. However, unlike the muckraking tradition that wafted out of the stench of the Chicago stockyards, unlike the studies of ethnic minorities, racial groups, and psychologically dislocated and sociologically deformed types, Weber's works uttered no cry for social change, for just laws, or for extending human rights. Such ideological posturing was simply foreign to Weber's legalistic style. Like the abstract "generalized other" of the symbolic interactionists, he saw only the "hopelessness of social legislation in a system of state particularism." Thus, Weber's globalism clashed with the reform instincts of Chicago-style sociology, with its personalist emphasis on welfare and life cycles.

It is therefore ironic, if understandable, that the larger world of American ideas paid scant attention to Weber. There was the whiff of patronizing in his writings on the United States. Quite unlike Tocqueville, Weber never dug into that which made the United States a unique culture. It remained some sort of strange aberration. It threw off the yoke of European oppression, but Weber never understood that it also threw overboard the stifling load of an Old World culture. Thus, it was not until the European migration as a result of Nazism, fascism and communism that Weber was discovered in America. And those native sons like Mills were attracted to Weber precisely because of their own alienation from an American nativist tradition.

Weber was concerned with power and authority, euphemisms in his hands for state and society: how they became legitimated, how status depends on authority. The world of the Chicago School, even its conservative anthropological echelons, never could accept such global formulations, which seemingly denigrated status in deference to power and authority. It is small wonder that while Weber himself viewed his work as on a scale with that of Marx, the provincial soci-

ology of the Midwest saw him as one more footnote to the
power-and-authority school that could claim such an unlikely
blend as Plato, Machiavelli, Marx, and Rousseau. From the
American perspective it was indeed the case that what Weber conceived of as "world historic" trends were simply the
decayed reflection of crumbling European intellectual edifices musing over their own past while taking a breather
from war. Certainly that was the judgment from the American heartland: the one sector of sociology that was less than
worshipful of Weber—and, not incidentally, the source of so
many of Mills's early approaches.

Weber has little to say of the demimonde, of the under-
world in which life is not "rationalized and bureaucratically
structured" but basically unstructured, deviant, and marginal.
He directly relates even the notion of charisma to political
authority, rather than leadership styles in general. This reflects Weber's general neglect of the dysfunctional and personal elements in his system of social stratification—a theme
that has been developed by many of Weber's American commentators. In sharp contrast, Mills's shorter essays are concerned with sailors in search of sex, prostitutes in search of
respectability, and issues in deviance generally.

Weber was "discovered" by a special kind of American—
the worldly eastern sociologist trained in Europe, or at least
learned in the languages and customs of central and northern Europe. Learning about Weber was sifted through a fil-
ter called *The Structure of Social Action.*[4] The mood of the
Chicago School in the thirties was analytic rather than synthetic, symbolic rather than historic. How was the Chicago
School to know of Weber's interests in such things as the
ecology of the city, property rights, the personal situation,
and plebeians and patricians when the Parsonian filtering
process tended to minimize Weber's *Wirtschaft und
Gesellschaft* precisely at those admittedly rare points where
he ceased being systematic and grand, world historic and
theoretic?[5] This was only to come at a later, postwar stage

with the translations by Don Martindale, which revealed that an entire layer of Weber's works lay undiscovered, unexamined in the Parsonian synthesis.

It was the economists and political theorists who gave some depth to the early discovery of Weber. Frank Knight and Edward Shils were drawn to Weber, less for any formulation of state and society, than because of a sense that here was a thinker who combined in his person the solidity of social science as an empirical discipline with such investigations as a liberal enterprise. Curiously, the sociologists, their disclaimers notwithstanding, fit into a similar mold. Parsons, Merton and Mills may have feuded amongst themselves on a host of professional issues, but on the unity of sociology and the liberal imagination, they stood as one—at least until Mills broke ranks with liberalism at the end of his brief career. But one might note that he also broke with the idea of sociology as a discipline that stands above and beyond ideology in general and Marxism in particular.

The American response to the European Weber is thus considerably more differentiated than pre-World War Two sociology allowed for—and for reasons not entirely trivial by any means. The East Coast developed styles of sociological research that increasingly became gentlemanly and remote in form and bureaucratic in substance. It was obviously easier to place Weber in this kind of professional context. In the postwar period, West Coast analysts rekindled an interest in Weber by shifting the emphasis from Weber as a theorist of social stratification to Weber as the political sociologist par excellence. There was also a clear shift in how West Coast thinkers like Reinhard Bendix and Seymour Martin Lipset operated with the data—even though many of these men were originally products of the East Coast or even Europe. There was an increasing emphasis on qualitative over quantitative findings. The basic valuation posture remained unchanged. Sociology on the East and West coasts retained an insistence on detachment over involvement, and pure research over applied research. In such matters, the newer Western style was a perfect complement to the Columbia-Harvard-Yale approach to Weber. Generally, when the European Weberians examined the relationship of rich and poor, elites and masses, their personal sympathies were largely with the poor and the masses, but their professional interests were clearly focused upon examining the rich and the elites.

The role of Talcott Parsons in disseminating the spirit of Max Weber as a European orthodoxy can scarcely be overestimated. The design of *The Structure of Social Action* gives a critical anchor to a select cluster of Weber's writings. As translator of *The Protestant Ethic and the Spirit of Capitalism,* and later, with A.M. Henderson, of *The Theory of Social and Economic Organization,* Parsons set the tone for what was considered the essential Weber for a long while. The very idiosyncrasies of the Parsonian lexicon found their way into the corpus of these translated works. If in the 1930s Parsons's definition of *Weberstudien* was rooted in the essay on the relationships of Protestantism to capitalism, by the fifties, when there were a much heavier number of translations available, the emphasis was shifting from Weber as illustrative of a "voluntaristic theory of action" to Weber as "illustrative of universalistic and functional specificity." It was also Weber as the analyst of the "Western World" and of the "Anglo-Saxon" world to whom Parsons responded and resonated. He saw or created Weber in his own image: someone who understood both "the uniqueness of our social system" and "its precarious state of instability."[6] Weber *contra* authoritarianism was the political motif, and Weber *contra* traditionalism was the sociological motif.

The ways in which science can service the needs of totalitarianism and of modern bureaucratic structure tended to be profoundly minimized by Parsons. This is partially a consequence, hypothetically at least, of the Weberian tendency to minimize, although not ignore, the dysfunctionality of bureaucracy. The rise of fascism did temporarily shake Parsons's insular belief in conservative solutions and led him to emphasize, between 1945 and 1949 at least, checks upon authority rather than the rationality of authority.

It was not only what Weber stood for on specific issues that attracted Parsons, but also the sense that Weber (unlike Durkheim, Marshall, Pareto, or even Freud) made possible considerations of the social system within the framework of a general sociological theory. Inadvertently, to be sure, Weber allowed for the evolution of a kind of sociological imperialism in which everything from family and personality to politics and economics could be viewed as a subsystem of sociology.[7] In introducing his first volume of selected papers, Parsons notes the existence of two big problems for social science: the development of a unified language, which is converted into a need for a conceptual scheme; and a theory of the relation of institutional structures and human behavior. On the latter score, Parsons identifies his view of function with that of Weber, since, says Parsons, only when human motivation is linked to the operations of a social system are generalizations about people "sociologically relevant."[8] Supplying a conceptual scheme and a general theory, Weber offered Parsons a way of transforming sociology from a parochial discipline, confined to local, small, and middle-sized issues, to a universal discipline dealing with large-scale issues, in which total systems proceed in Panglossian fashion always and everywhere toward increased rationality.[9]

To be a Parsonian became, in the middle of the twentieth century, the only way professionals within American sociology could tolerably deal with big issues without being dismissed to the revolutionary margins. Indeed, developing an optional social systems approach became the only way that American economics and political science—often in the guise of people like David Easton—could move beyond the impasse created by Marxism as a political doctrine rather than an intellectual outlook. Parsons's own awareness of this undoubtedly accounts for his profound early animus toward Marxism and socialism. He adopted a cold, analytic stance with respect to any sociology that came within sniffing distance of a positive appraisal of "dialectics" or any other aspect of Marxism as a worldview. This militancy differed markedly from his Olympian disregard of critics in general.[10]

Robert K. Merton, insofar as he represented a response to Weber, was not so much interested in systematizing as in secularizing the great European scholar. Weber became one of the classic father figures to whom the good sociologist turns for inspiration—specifically, for new ideas about old themes. The great theme of bureaucratization in modern society, for example, was for Merton not an illustration of universalistic-instrumentalist action, but rather a challenge for further social science research into problems of professionalization. With some concern, Merton felt this approach provided an opportunity to "build a Solomon's House for sociologists"—with what telling effect remains to be demonstrated.

Bureaucracy as a theme enabled Merton to critically treat what Weber had failed to deal with substantively: the dysfunction of certain bureaucratic structures; the administrative consequences of exaggerated conformity and maximum rule-boundedness; and above all, the possibility that Weber's pessimism, if not uncalled for, may have been slightly premature—since, as a matter of fact, "bureaucracy is a secondary group structure" oriented toward depersonalized achievement of "certain activities" only when primary group relations fail to solve problems and "run counter to these formalized norms."[11] The trend toward increasing bureaucratization in industrial societies raised for Merton a set of critical problems, which he outlined; many of his students in subsequent years filled in the intellectual crevices. But the overwhelming impression given by Merton's sociology is of problems to be solved rather than structures to be either applauded or overthrown.

Merton's use of Weber's sociology of religion is also dramatically different from that of Parsons. Instead of offering a propaedeutic review of Weber's position, Merton tried his hand at a slightly adjacent, related, but markedly distinctive problem: the differential tendency for German Protestants to pursue scientific career patterns more frequently than Catholics. The results of Merton's investigation were not particularly astonishing, nor were they intended to be. In a bibliographical postscript to his classic essays on social theory and social structure, Merton says that the results arrived at, at the empirical level, were "conceived as an effort to follow: and extend the mandate that Weber had opened up."[12] But the role of the "religious factor," even in a world of scientific discovery, is one by which Merton placed great store.

To underscore Merton's non-polemical attitude toward the work of Weber, it should be noted that one of his most important papers, employing roughly the same analysis with respect to Protestantism and the rise of scientific societies in England, was published in *Science and Society,* which at the time was (and has remained) an avowedly Marxian journal. The problem of capitalism and its relation to the Protestant Reformation, particularly how it ramifies outward, is seen by Merton as a scientific problem bequeathed to modern sociology by Marx and Weber, stripped of its inherited ideological squabbling over whether economy or religion is the originating causal base of social development. The scientific problem in turn is seen as a social problem—an issue in the status of democracy.[13]

Merton responded to Weber as the sort of scholar who, above all, represented global considerations rather than some form of localism. Merton is no "Easterner," but like Parsons, in this sense, a cosmopolitan figure entirely in touch with the world of European learning. Just how important Merton views this European context to be is reflected by his criticism of provincialism, rejected twice in the same sen-

tence of his Acknowledgments to his omnibus collection
Social Theory and Social Structure. It might also be noted that
the Europeans stood in awe of Merton as the paradigm of
American sociology as a science. In a new volume paying
tribute to him in terms that barely escape being labeled the
cult of personality, while put in the form of a query, the
answer is not left too much in doubt. "Is Merton the first of
the great American sociologists to expose himself to doubt,
the realm of probability, the recognition of the constitutive
limits of knowledge of the social world, or is he rather the
last and most astute exponent of an intellectual tradition
which is fundamentally illuminant and scientistic in its basic
convictions, a man whose intellectual finesse has permitted
him to elaborate tools far ahead of his time which can tackle
the cognitive difficulties that the present generation of sociologists has increasingly become aware of?" [14] One is left
with a choice, a plethora of Weberian virtues.

Pitirim Sorokin is acknowledged as having helped him
escape from the provincialism of thinking that effective studies of society were confined within American borders and
from the slum-encouraged provincialism of thinking that
"the primary subject-matter of sociology was centered in such
peripheral problems of social life as divorce and juvenile
delinquency." But since Sorokin had already gone off to
"become absorbed in the study of historical movements on
the grand scale," the search in Europe focused very heavily
upon Marx, Durkheim, and Weber; and the problems selected for study by Weber—bureaucracy and the social structure, and the role of religion in social change—were upper-
most for Merton over a long span of years.

Even in Merton's more recent papers, such as "Social Conflict over Styles of Sociological Work," the impact of Weber
upon Merton's liberal-heterodox view of the sociological
field is noticeable. He argues for a Weberian middle position,
against value free and partisanship alike, and for Weber's
concept of a sociology which is *Wertbeziehung*—value relevant.

To the charge that value relevance is a fuzzy halfway house, Merton responds much the way Weber did: its very ambiguities allow for open debate and differing evaluations.

To be described as a figure by which others have been influenced is not necessarily a form of flattery. Weber was, for Mills, as he was for Parsons and for Merton, a part of the classic tradition in sociology. But unlike either Parsons of Merton, Mills derived his consciousness of Weber second-hand, from German émigré sources. Mills learned about Weber from Hans H. Gerth, himself a German sociologist. But because of his Midwest intellectual links, Mills found his interest in Weber tempered by a range of considerations raised by American classic figures, such as Thorstein Veblen in economics, George Herbert Mead in social psychology, and John Dewey in philosophy. From the outset, Mills was uncomfortable with the role of interpreting Weber. What he did, in effect, was to convert Weber into a proper pragmatist, as he was later to do with Marx. This is most obvious in the 1946 introduction that he and Gerth wrote for the translations of Weber's essays. Like Dewey and James, Mills saw Weber as "one of the last political professors who made detached contributions to science, and, as the intellectual vanguard of the middle classes, were also leading figures."[15] In the hands of Mills, Weber became the teacher and exemplar of intellectual courage, a moral rather than intellectual leader. It was not the refined pedagogic aspects of higher education that attracted Mills, but the moral infusion of politics that struck a responsive chord.

Aside from the introductory essay to *From Max Weber*, Mills wrote little about Weber that did not carry at least an implicitly critical tone. In part this derived from ambivalence in his early association with Gerth at Wisconsin. This critical tendency was pushed even further and harder by Mills the further removed he was from Wisconsin. For it was Gerth who was responsible for the monumental project of translating Weber's religion—sociology, and it was Mills who placed decreasing emphasis on the Weber legacy. After Mills's collaboration with Gerth terminated, it would appear that his fascination with Weber diminished sharply. Early in his career, Mills appreciated the fact that Weber was something less than a radical savior of sociology. He understood that Weber's kind of identification of charisma with irrationality was linked with totalitarianism, something of which Weber did not approve but against which he had no intellectual defense. Similarly, Weber's belief that bureaucracy would remain fairly stable throughout revolutionary shifts in power was a generalization that Mills felt did not obtain for twentieth-century bureaucracy.[16] It astonished Mills, even toward the close of his career, that this highly questionable formulation of the bureaucratic continuity should remain unchecked and uncriticized for so long among his professional peers.[17] It is rather curious that Mills mistook Weber's pessimistic acknowledgment of the role of administrative bureaucracy in the modern state with an approval for such a tendency. Georg Lukacs, writing in his Stalinist phase on the "decline of reason" in the West made the same malicious error later.

There was one aspect of Weber's thought that Mills picked out as potentially revolutionary in its consequences—the difference between Marx and Weber on the social organization of modern capitalism. Marx's idea that capitalism represents anarchy of production was subject to Mills's sneering criticism. He saw this as one of Marx's basic generic errors. He stood with Weber in understanding that what makes capitalism viable, or at least durable, is that in its statist form capitalism is rational and planned in the extreme.[18] Mills also learned from Weber that what made the development of a true revolutionary experience so difficult in modern capitalist society was that rationality had shifted from the individual and become lodged in the total institution. Because of this, the increased education of modern man had no revolutionary consequences; it only went to feed the needs

of the all-encompassing institution for happy and well-edu-
cated robots.

Mills's positive linkage to Weber was based on several
extrapolations: the role of capitalist political economy in
the formation of the modern state, and the sacrifice of the
intellect involved in outfitting the scientific soul for policy
needs of the bureaucratic state. Weber's supposed ambiguity on how to handle these relationships was translated by
Merton as the need for intellectual heterodoxy, but as translated by Mills it became the need for intellectual commitment in combating state authority.

Mills saw in Weber the need to connect intellect with power
and not to shy away from the challenging dangers of possible
corruption through power. The choice had to be squarely
faced between which value element should rule: intellect or
passion. Both Mills and Weber were contemptuous of fears as
to whether intellect could be saved by avoiding problems of
power and authority; neither quite brought themselves to
appreciate the compromising nor bargaining aspects of power.
At the very root, one would have to say that this fierce devotion to intelligence is what Mills learned from Weber. Methodologically, Mills learned from Weber to deal with society
as Parsons had done, as a complete social system—but he went
a step beyond that, dealing with evolving social structures in
a comparative context. It was Mills's hope to transform, via
Weber, systematic sociology into historical sociology, without
losing touch with empirical reality.[19]

The history of European sociology, and the selective absorption of that history by Mills and the radical tradition
generally, represents an intense, albeit symbolic, struggle
between the northern European, and Germanic, vision of
the field and the Franco-Italian, or southern-tiered, vision.
Without making too much of geographical distinctions (after all, Marx the internationalist was of German background),
it can be said that each of these two broad-ranging macro-
sociological schools of thought had a distinct emphasis.

For Mills, as for Weber, authority was the linchpin of the social system. Every phenomenon stemmed from authority: legitimacy of a political regime, charismatic and bureaucratic forms of organization, the process of legalization of the social system, and the insinuation of cultural hegemony into a society. Authority resulted from internalization and absorption by the mass of superordinate and subordinate relationships. Over time such political as well as economic inequalities became enshrined as norms. Ultimately, such relationships became values of the system. But Mills was much less comfortable with a valuational approach than was Weber. He saw Weber as vaguely accepting and not just examining bureaucracy and power—a point others have made before and since. In this context, the alternative power model of Michels, in particular, served to rescue power analysis from normative theory. The tendency of organizations and their leaders to accept an oligarchical model was termed an "iron law". But Michels never surrendered his socialism to cynicism.

The chief architects of the Franco-Italian school—Michels, Sorel, Pareto, and Mosca—were less analytically profound, but more to Mills's liking than were their middle of the road Germanic counterparts. For them, as for Mills, the key to political dominance was power. The imposition of power by one group over another made for authority, law, and the dominant culture. Michels, Sorel, and Mosca presented the world as an arena of struggle. Yet the power of one person or system over another in some ironic way could never be legitimated, could never be internalized as Weber envisioned in his concept of authority. Underwriting the Franco-Italian school was the notion of mass behavior as a volatile source of change not readily harnessed to an elite ordering of events. Only Pareto, anticipating the fascist sense of order, argued the case for caution against any casual linkage between mass behavior and social control. Ranging from anarchism to socialism, the expression of the indomitable individual will could be suppressed, but acceptance of such suppression never could be internalized or legitimated as long as inequality remained a social fact. For all the weakness in Mills's theory of power, the fact remains that he uniquely understood the need to connect that much abused term with the functions of authority. In so doing, Mills made the effort to unite Weber and Michels—an enterprise also undertaken in less ambitious but perhaps more satisfactory ways by Seymour Martin Lipset. But in the end, such fusion's created the ground for ambiguity rather than clarity. The state neither dissolved, nor did the society become truly benign. As a consequence, the struggle in American political sociology between liberal and radical perspectives sharpened over the gravesite of Weber, with little relief in sight as long as European categories were superimposed onto American reality.

The difference between authority and power, between Weber and Michels in particular, gave birth to other differences, which, when transplanted to an American context, led to sharp cleavages in the major schools of sociological thought. For the Weberians, the emphasis became consensus among the polity, bureaucratization in government, and legal norms. For the Paretians, the process was reversed: power determined the course of American destiny. The system somehow could never be legitimated given the existence of class differences and deep political antagonisms. As a result, the conflict model became dominant among the followers of this latter school. To do serious work in sociological theory meant coming to terms with this bifurcated inheritance.

Mills's own intellectual uncertainties with respect to authority and power, consensus and conflict were shrewdly disguised rather than resolved. The notion of a "classic tradition" included Weber. By addressing himself to "big problems" and the "big picture," Mills obscured the core of these inherited sociological disputes but did not necessarily resolve them. Once the rhetoric behind the big picture was examined, differences of the most acute sort began to become manifest. It was simply no longer possible to hold the European tradition intact. Later conflict theories, like those of Lewis A. Coser, Ralf Dahrendorf, and Jürgen Habermas, made this clear. Mills himself, more out of intuition (or perhaps irritation) than sociological logic also knew this to be the case. He was shrewd enough to know those theoretical disputations over the status of authority and power, or consensus of conflict, could yield either conservative or radical outcomes, depending on concrete circumstances. Hence, Mills was driven back to the results of analysis rather than any search for, or commitment to, general theory.

There is an air of ease and familiarity in Mills's writings about Weber; he incorporates him into his own corpus, rather than making distinct pronouncements about him. Mills does not show this same sense of ease in writing about Marx, and so it is hard to say whether Weber was more or less important in Mills's development than were Mannheim or Marx. Given Mills's sociological eclecticism, it is best not to attempt weighting these great figures, but simply to examine what aspects of Weber helped to fill Mills's intellectual shopping basket. For, if one cannot rightfully be a "Millsian" outside a wide tradition, this in part derives from Mills's own sense of employing theory for concrete research ends, rather than determining what these research tasks should be on the basis of completing or adding to a theoretical scaffold.

Typical of Mills's theoretical eclecticism is the remark in *The Sociological Imagination* on the theoretical foundations of *The Power Elite*: "I had to take into account the work of such men as Mosca, Schumpeter, Veblen, Marx, Lasswell, Michels, Weber, and Pareto."[20] In that most Weberian of works, *Character and Social Structure,* Gerth and Mills nonetheless make much of the significance of the two traditions of Freud and Marx. But they will be perfectly content if, for these two names, their readers prefer substituting Mead and Weber.[21] Mills later amplifies the methodological function of a shopping-basket view of theory—a view not at all out of character with Weber's open-ended approach to "theory construction": "Sometimes I can arrange the available theories systematically as a range of choices, and so allow their range to organize the problem itself. But sometimes I allow such theories to come up in my own arrangement, in quite various contexts. At any rate, in the book of the elite I had to take into account the works of such men as Mosca, Schumpeter, Veblen, Marx, Lasswell, Michels, Weber, and Pareto."[22]

This helps to illustrate the arbitrariness of singling out the influence of any one sociologist upon Mills's intellectual development. Yet, insofar as doing so helps us frame Mills in an appropriate intellectual setting, the task remains marginally worthwhile.

This is not to suggest that Weber's work had little or no influence on the young Mills. It most certainly did, especially in the area of social psychology. Mills saw Weber as providing the necessary social-structure cement in an American world of individualistic psychology where minds were discussed without regard to bodies, where people were discussed without regard to publics, and in which interactions were granted without analysis of collectivities. Weber provided the intellectual sourcebook for collective psychology by giving strength and backbone to individual motivation. To quote again from *Character and Social Structure*: "No matter how we approach the field of social psychology, we cannot escape the idea that all current work that comes to much, fits into one or the other of two basic traditions: *Freud,* on the side of character structure, and *Marx,* including the early Marx of the 1840s, on the side of social structure. We have no objection, if the reader prefers, to use the names of George H. Mead and Max Weber, although of course they differ from Freud and Marx in many important ways."[23]

Yet, in the very next sentence, the "two basic traditions" become Freud and Mead, rather than Freud and Marx. "The

reason we are drawn, again and again, to Sigmund Freud
and George Mead is that they try, more effectively than the
others to show us man as a whole actor instead of man as a
set of traits, as a bundle of reflexes."[24] By the time of *Images
of Man*, Mills had even fewer specifics, preferring the rhetoric
of the "master trends" rather than the "master works." This
constant shift in intellectual peerage reflects both intellectual
confusion and a calculated eclecticism. In any event, Mills's
casting about makes "influence tracing" just about impossible as an exercise in pure theory or doctrinal impact.

The fusion of sociology and psychology in a historical
context was certainly Weber's lasting contribution to Mills's
thinking. This contribution was made more important by
virtue of the absence of a distinctive psychological orientation in the work of Marx. Certainly, the mature Marx took
pride in the absence of psychological interpretations. His
American followers, especially those politically active in the
1940s and 1950s, saw little problem with this. With the exception of Vernon Venable, Erich Fromm, and Herbert
Marcuse, the psychologizing of Marx hardly had begun when
Mills came to maturity. Hence, Weber loomed larger in
Mills's thoughts than perhaps he might have in a later period
of the 1960s and 1970s, when the early Marx of alienation
had been rediscovered with a vengeance by psychologists
and sociologists alike.

Mills grew increasingly disquieted by the impact of Weber upon American sociology. Weber's preemptive role with
respect to structural functionalism certainly did not go unnoticed. If macro-sociological tradition was described solely
by the difference between Merton and Parsons, that in itself
provided Mills with a *prima facie* reason to look beyond Weber
for answers. Mills became uncomfortable with the legalistic
and conservative bureaucratic tendencies manifested in
American writings on Weber. Thus, without any overt manifestation of a rupture with Weberian theory, which would
have meant a formal break with his mentor Gerth as well,

Mills simply never returned to Weber once his relationship with Gerth was intellectually completed. *Character and Social Structure,* which was begun during the Second World War but which appeared in print far later in Mills's career than he really wished, must thus be seen not as a work written "in between" *White Collar* and *The Power Elite* but as a long-delayed publication of the Wisconsin era. Indeed, Mills underscored this by virtually repudiating his work on social psychology with Gerth. Whether for personal or professional reasons, the outcome was the same: a denial of the place of personality in the formation of systems of power. As a result, Mills, like the Marx he adopts, was bereft of a political psychology with which to explain anomalies in public conduct of political personages.

Whatever else transpired on the intellectual journey of Weber's thought from Europe to America, it is an ineluctable fact that its cutting edge was lost in the process. In part this is because Weber's consistent enemies at home were right-wing nationalists. The struggle for scientific objectivity, value-relevance without ideological determinism, was undertaken in a context of intellectual jingoism, Prussian manifest destiny, and the alarming bureaucratization of state power. Prewar (and wartime) America, the period from 1936 to 1946, from Parsons's early celebration to the Gerth-Mills collection, presented a somewhat different picture. Weber became an American "answer" to Marxism. It was the remnants of an old left that were contested by the neo-Weberians. The roots of Weber at Columbia and Harvard, and later at the University of California (which in an odd way synthesized the conservative tendencies in neo-Weberian thought during the McCarthy period), offered an analytical framework of authentic power that did not overly depend upon the Marxist tradition. Again, this became especially so in the postwar period, which was mired in Leninist and Stalinist orthodoxy. It was at the unique moment when new tendencies in Marxism had yet to emerge and old tendencies in

Weber had crystallized and dissolved that Mills came upon
Weber. The philosophy of pragmatism and the sociology of
knowledge were behind Mills by the end of the Second World
War. The sense that this was to be an American century had
just taken root. Under the circumstances, all Mills could
rightly do was extract those elements in Weberian thought
that were serviceable to radical aims or were at least capable
of dampening the chauvinistic implications of the American celebration of triumph. This was Mills's approach until
the time came when Weber, too, could be treated as an element in rather than the essence of contemporary America
social thought.

Mills made it clear that there were several important aspects of his relationship to Weber's legacy. First, *Character
and Social Structure* was his least favorite book. He confessed
to coming close to a public repudiation of this fine work. In
part, he completed it as a repayment to Gerth for many past
kindness', in particular, the co-editorship of *From Max Weber*. By the time *Character and Social Structure* appeared, Mills's
formal association with Gerth had long since ended. Weber
came to be employed as a bridge to other theories of social
philosophy: "Max Weber defines motives as a complex of
meaning, which appears to the actor himself or to the observer to be an adequate ground for his conduct. The aspect of motive, which this conception intrinsically grasps, is
its social character. Motives are accepted justifications for
present, future or past programs or acts."[25]

But it was the way in which "social character" issued into
"social structure" that proved most appealing to Mills:
"Weber's use of the notion of structure enabled him to transcend the individual's own awareness of himself and his
milieu."[26] It was Weber as the primary representative of the
European macroscopic tradition, in contrast to the molecular tendencies in American sociology, which proved most
attractive to Mills. "Weber's analytic and historic essay on
bureaucracy has not been repeated or checked in the same

way (as the molecular), however much of it has been criticized and used. Macroscopic work has not experienced the sort of cumulative development that molecular work during the current generation of sociologists has."[27]

This sense of scope brought about the highest praise Mills was to tender to Weber: "The ethos of Max Weber was the climax of the classic German tradition."[28] However, even this praise carried with it an explicit criticism. Just as Ludwig Feuerbach was for Friedrich Engels not only the highest expression of classical German philosophy, but also its end, so, too, did Mills see Weber as the highest expression of classical German sociology, but also its end.

Ultimately, Mills's animosity toward liberalism, or better perception of liberalism as the enemy of radicalism, especially its sociological manifestations, led to a break in intellectual affinities with this highest expression of German thought. It was sociology itself that needed the closest critical scrutiny. But it should not be thought that Mills was alone in his recreation of Weber. The left-wing critical theorists have found in Weber an amenable critic of modern rationality, so that, with Jürgen Habermas, this radical grouping made of Weber the supreme critic of the state, of institutional rationality, of the iron cage.

Mills had two specific problems with Weber's notion of rationality: first, its general linkage to the process of bureaucratization; second, its specific linkage to the structure of modern capitalism. There was simply no way Mills could square this circle. Even as early as 1946, he was critical of Weber's nostalgic liberalism, which empathizes with cultural freedom but remains relatively blind to economic exploitation:

> Weber identifies bureaucracy with rationality and the process of rationalization with mechanism, depersonalization, and oppressive routine. Rationality in this context is seen as adverse to personal freedom. Accordingly, Weber is a nostalgic liberal feeling himself on the defensive. He deplores the type of man that the mechanization and the routine of bureaucracy selects and forms. The narrowed professional, publicly certified and examined, and ready for tenure and ca-

reer. His craving for security is balanced by his moderate ambitions and he is rewarded by the honor of official status. This type of man Weber deplored as a petty routine creature, lacking in heroism, human spontaneity, and inventiveness: "The Puritan was the prototype of vocational man that we have become."[29]

Since Weber identifies capitalism as the embodiment of rational impersonality, the quest for freedom that informs Mills and his other intellectual mentors is reduced to irrational sentiment and privatization. As a consequence, Weber's objectivity becomes defensive. "Weber represents humanist and cultural liberalism rather than economic liberalism "Weber's own work is a realization of his self-image as a cultivated man concerned with.all things human. And the decline of the humanist and the ascendancy of the expert is another documentation for Weber of the diminished chances for freedom."[30]

Mills's later defense of "plain Marxism," and his increasingly strident attack on "liberalism as a dead end," must each be seen as an ultimate rejection of Weber; a final settling on Weber as the anti-Marx, rather than as the sophisticated "bourgeois-Marx" with which he had started his intellectual examination. By the time Mills produced *The Marxists,* his animosity toward liberalism and his rejection of this "creed" for Marxism was so complete that any further serious consideration of Weber was out of the question. It is clear that Mills came to consider the same cluster of figures he formerly admired—Weber, Mosca, Michels, Mannheim, etc.—as representative of "the firm ideology of one class inside one epoch; specifically the urban and entrepreneurial middle class." As a result of Mills's final settlement of accounts with the "classic tradition," essentially by his turn toward Marxism, the last vestige of support for Weber vanished.[31] Mills never resolved what this polarization did to his earlier statements on the continuities between Marx and Weber and on German sociological profundity. Rather, sociology itself somehow became the enemy of progress; the source of the confusion was thus neatly externalized.

Mills had a peculiar relationship not simply to Weber but to European sociological doctrine in general. While Mills celebrated the virtue of large-scale macroscopic thinking and breathtaking analysis on epochal subjects, there was scarcely that fine attention to detail that characterized the more empirical and earlier aspects of his work. In this sense, Mills and Parsons were diametrically opposed. For Mills, the "classical European tradition" represented an unfurling of the banners of social research, a flag of legitimacy providing ideological fuel in times of intellectual turmoil. For Parsons, however, one has the distinct impression that the empirical world was served up to the theoretical construct of Weber's worldview. The actual contents rather than the style of sociology became its "classical tradition" within Parsonian thought. As a consequence, the tone, not to mention the content, of Parsons's *General Theory* was diametrically in contrast to Mills's *Image of Man*. Parsons took the ideas of German sociology seriously. Mills took seriously only the sentiments—the underlying thrust, which took sociology into large-scale areas of historical and social analysis. Perhaps that is why, despite the severity of their differences, a peculiar sort of respect is manifest between Parsons and Mills.

The sense of discontent that Mills expressed about Weber in his later work stemmed in part not so much from any single proposition as from the amorphous theory of value neutrality. For Mills, such formal academic demands for not politicizing the classroom and lecture hall in practice represented bureaucratic support by Weber for Imperial Germany, or more gently, a denial of the overall policy considerations created by social research. Mills thought of Weber as a sociological Brahms, an old-fashioned medieval craftsman rather than a precursor of German Nazism. The absence of a cutting edge, the feeling that Weber was somehow removed from the social struggle, was ultimately more weighty to Mills than any single theoretical proposition. Whatever else Weber represented, he was the architect of academic freedom as academic responsibility. And Mills, whatever else he was, represented academic freedom as freedom from constraint. This philosophical gap between freedom as discipline and freedom as liberty could not be bridged—at least not by Mills. The disjunction between Weber and Mills on the public role of sociology is so wide and deep that, in retrospect, it is a tribute to Mills's personal loyalties to Gerth that he could restrain himself from overt criticism of Weber's work.

The identification of the neo-Weberians, such as Edward A. Shils, Seymour Martin Lipset, and Reinhard Bendix, with an increasingly conservative political posture also alienated Mills's affections from Weberian thought. The neo-Weberians from Chicago and California led the charge against Mills at that very point in time, circa 1956–1962, when older functionalist canons were breaking down in social science. This is scarcely the first time that followers of a major contributor to social thought have gone their separate ways. However, so uniform was the hostility to Mills among the inner circle of Weber's biographers, commentators, and translators that Mills can be forgiven if he somehow, albeit less than forthrightly, came to identify Weber himself as at least partially the intellectual source of his own professional miseries.

Nor were Mills's miseries merely intellectual; personal resentments flared. Hans Gerth made it quite clear to all who would listen that he felt himself to be the senior author of the essays in *From Max Weber*; that, in point of fact, Mills insinuated himself into the project only because he, Gerth, needed an American citizen to be listed as co-editor for the book as a passport to publication. It must be remembered that this collection had its origins during the Second World War and that Gerth as a German national did in fact suffer a certain alienation from mainstream publishing and professionalism. In truth Mills was, even in 1945, a supreme stylist, while Gerth, to put it mildly, was not a graceful writer or translator. The primary role of Mills was in editing the editor's work on Weber. In addition, Mills helped to place the extensive introductory essay on Weber within a meaningful American as well as English-speaking context. If the strictly biographical portions of the introduction are clearly written by Gerth, the political analyses and implications are just as clearly the mark of Mills.

These sorts of negative experiences with colleagues, with translations, and finally with Weber's corpus eventually led Mills to a personal review of where he wanted to go. It clearly was away from the history of sociology, and into sociology as a key to history. Yet, even at the end, when Mills's affections for sociology were at low ebb, he could not bring himself to disavow a filial connection with Weber. Along with Marx, Weber was held supreme.[32] "Marx and Weber are greater than, for example, Mosca or Durkheim" since "every line they write is soaked in knowledge of history."[33] Weber offered clarity and profundity—and whatever "personal troubles" he occasioned, he was central to the public presentations of American sociology across the political and intellectual spectrum—a decent judgment that Weber himself might well have appreciated.

But the fate of Weber did not entirely come to rest with the sociologists. In the second half of the twentieth century, Weber was demonized by normative theorists such as Leo Strauss, who saw in Weber the apostle of nihilism and relativism—a world of views without judgments. Alasdair MacIntyre, for his part, continued in this critical vein, considering Weber as a principal source for modern bureaucratic technique and an amoral positivism—a position MacIntyre borrowed lock, stock, and barrel from Georg Lukács's critique of Weber in *The Decline of Reason*. The charges against Weber fall flat once it is understood that Weber attempted to describe the totalitarian future of unbridled state power—not to sanction such uses.

Nevertheless, the sociologists, in their sublime ignorance of any tradition other than their own, seemed oblivious to problems posed in Weber's line of *political* analysis. As a result, the best and the brightest identified him with a liberalism unsullied by weakness. What happens to Weber in a world in which liberalism, or the vital center, fails to hold? In such a world, it remained for people like Arthur Schlesinger to bail out of the causes of liberalism, while Weber was improperly made part of the arsenal of the bureaucratic state—even as he himself loathed that state. The enormous crimes of the Nazi system, the quiescence of many post-Weberians in the face of gigantic wrongs, would not disappear in the gentle breezes of an affluent post-war America.[34] Individualism increasingly became an instrument of conservatism. Collectivism likewise became the monopoly of revolutionists. And in the process, Weber's centrist impact on intellectual life in America was badly spent. It became one more sociological vision in search of a mass base. In sociology at least, the center did not hold and, with its erosion, the sources of Weberian thought evaporated.

Notes

1. Max Weber. *The Agrarian Sociology of Ancient Civilizations.* London: Routledge/Chapman & Hall, 1988, p. 348.
2. Marianne Weber. *Max Weber: A Biography*, translated by Harry Zohn. New York: John Wiley Sons, 1975, p. 120.
3. Hans H. Gerth and C. Wright Mills, eds. *From Max Weber: Essays in Sociology.* New York: Oxford University Press, 1946, p. 15.
4. It is not that the work of Weber went unnoticed or was unknown prior to the efforts of Parsons. But Parsons "internalized" or "operationalized" Weber. The working sociologist learned from Parsons how to use (Duncan might say abuse) Weber's work. See Talcott Parsons, *The Structure of Social Action: A Study in Social Theory with Special Reference to a Group of Recent European Writers* (New York: McGraw-Hill, 1937).
5. In this respect, Don Martindale's work rounds out our vision of Weber considerably. See the translation he and Gertrude Neuwirth made of *The City* (Glencoe, Ill.: Free Press, 1958), and, in particular, his "Prefatory Remarks: The Theory of the City." See also Don

Martindale, *The Nature and Types of Sociological Theory* (Boston: Houghton Mifflin, 1960, pp. 377–90). For a sound and impartial appraisal of the Chicago School, see John Madge, *The Origins of Scientific Sociology* (New York: The Free Press of Glencoe, 1962, pp. 88–125).

6. Talcott Parsons, "Introduction to Max Weber." In *The Theory of Social and Economic Organization*, translated by A.M. Henderson and Talcott Parsons, edited with an Introduction by Talcott Parsons. New York: Oxford University Press, 1947, pp. 82, 84.

7. Irving Louis Horowitz, "Introduction to the New Sociology." In *The New Sociology*. New York: Oxford University Press, 1964, pp. 14–15.

8. Talcott Parsons. Essays in *Sociological Theory Pure and Applied*. Glencoe, Ill.: Free Press, 1949, p. x.

9. On this point see Robin M. Williams, Jr., "The Sociological Theory of Talcott Parsons," in *The Social Theories of Talcott Parsons*, edited by Max Black. Englewood Cliff, N.J.: Prentice-Hall, pp. 161, 1969.

10. See Parsons's unusual polemical reaction to Llewellyn Z. Gross's "Preface to a Metaphysical Framework for Sociology." *The American Journal of Sociology* 67 (September 1961): 125–36. Parsons's comment was carried in the same issue, pp. 136–40.

11. Robert K. Merton. "Bureaucratic Structure and Personality." In *Social Theory and Social Structure*, revised and enlarged edition. Glencoe, Ill.: Free Press, 1957, pp. 204–5.

12. Robert K. Merton, "Puritanism, Pietism, and Science." In *Social Theory and Social Structure*, p. 595.

13. Robert K. Merton, "Science and Democratic Social Structure." In *Social Theory and Social Structure*, pp. 560–61.

14. Carlo Mongardini and Simonetta Tabboni, *Robert K. Merton and Contemporary Sociology*. New Brunswick and London: Transaction Publishers, 1998, p. 10. See also Robert K. Merton, "Social Conflict over Styles of Sociological Work." *Transactions of the Fourth World Congress of Sociology* 3 (1959). Reprint No. 286, Bureau of Social Research publication, pp. 34–35.

15. C. Wright Mills with Hans Gerth, "A Marx for the Managers." In *Power, Politics, and People: The Collected Essays of C. Wright Mills*, edited by Irving Louis Horowitz. New York and London: Oxford University Press, 1963, pp. 54, 68–69.

16. H.H. Gerth and C. Wright Mills, Introduction to *From Max Weber*. New York: Oxford University Press, 1946, p. 25. C. Wright Mills, "Two Styles of Social Science Research." In *Power, Politics, and People*, pp. 557–558.

17. C. Wright Mills, "Two Styles of Social Science Research." In *Power, Politics, and People*, pp. 557–558.

18. C. Wright Mills, "The Nazi Behemoth." In *Power, Politics, and People*, p. 171.

19. C. Wright Mills, *The Sociological Imagination*. New York: Oxford University Press, 1959, pp. 25–49.

20. Ibid., p. 202.
21. C. Wright Mills and H.H. Gerth, *Character and Social Structure: The Psychology of Social Institution.* New York: Harcourt, Brace & Co., 1953, p. xiv.
22. Mills, *The Sociological Imagination*, pp. 202–203.
23. Mills and Gerth. *Character and Social Structure, p. xiv.*
24. Ibid.
25. Mills, *Power, Politics, and People*, pp. 442–443.
26. Mills, *The Sociological Imagination*, p. 162.
27. Mills, *Power, Politics, and People*, p. 557–558.
28. Mills, *The Sociological Imagination*, p. 48.
29. Gerth and Mills, *From Max Weber*, p. 50.
30. Ibid., p. 73.
31. C. Wright Mills, *The Marxists.* New York: Dell Publishing Co., 1962, pp. 27–39.
32. C. Wright Mills, ed. *Images of Man: The Classic Tradition in Sociological Thinking.* New York: George Braziller, 1960, p. 12.
33. *Ibid*, p. 13.
34. Guenther Roth, "Marianne Weber and Her Circle," Introduction to *Max Weber: A Biography* by Marianne Weber. New Brunswick and London: Transaction Publishers, 1988, p. lii.

10

The Unhappy Alliance of Democracy and Dictatorship: Horkheimer, Benjamin, and Neumann

---

"The Nazis showed us the depths of which human beings are capable; the Communists have shown us the same depths while manipulating a social vision. The faith in science, the belief in progress, the ideals of liberty, equality and fraternity, have all been paraded before us in a murderers' masquerade."

—*Charles Frankel*[1]

I wish to examine two aspects of German immigration to the Western democracies, especially the United States and Great Britain. The first is the sheer transformation brought about by the process of migration and changing cultures, and the second, the changes brought about in the areas of political sociology and political philosophy by the special people who left Europe for the New World. I do not necessarily seek to offer a full explanation of this complex historical and ideological issue, but rather an analysis that attempts to avoid the maze of sociological generalizing that has grown up around the politically inspired migration of scholars.

I seek to understand the common denominators, or better, the root elements that led René Koenig to locate the source of the German sociological exodus in the virulent nationalism of the 1920s, and to argue that the fusion of conservative and radical elements in post-1933 National Socialism was a culmination rather than a cause of social scientific breakdown in Germany.[2] As Otto Neurath interpreted this plight: "We are like sailors who must rebuild their ships on the open sea without benefit of a dock, or an opportunity to select the best replacement parts."[3]

The first aspect I shall examine is who left and who stayed. The evidence indicates that the German intellectual migration was overwhelmingly a German-Jewish and an Austrian-Jewish migration. Whether the sense of Jewishness in a particular scholar was weak or strong, whether the families involved were assimilationists or Zionists mattered little in the final decision. Likewise, Jewish marginality or centrality was an ephemeral concern for those who converted the dreams of German nationalism into the nightmares of German-sponsored crematoria. Those who would deny or trivialize the Jewish factor as central to intellectual migration from Germany are foredoomed to give tortured, pained, and ultimately impoverished explanations to a central tragedy of twentieth-century German history.[4] For what is central is not the migration from one country to another of networks of intellectuals, but ultimately, the destruction of a people and, with it, the decimation of social science in select national contexts as a relatively recent part of the Western democratic tradition.

The second aspect, no less important, which also receives remarkably short shrift in the literature, if it is not glossed over entirely, is that those who escaped tragedy nearly uniformly rejected the possibility of migrating to the Soviet Union in favor of migration to the Western democracies. Even those whose Judaism may well have been suspect, but certainly whose commitment to socialism was widely heralded, chose for their collective home away from home the "decadent" capitalist West over the "advanced" communist East.

Right-wing intellectuals, those caught in the entrails of traditional nationalism and the dictatorship of the bureaucracy had every right to reject Soviet appeals to class solidarity across national boundaries. The precedent for doing so had already been set by competing claims of race and class after World War One.[5] But the left-wing intellectuals had no such simplified fallback position. They had to reject Soviet communism after empirical observation and theoretical study.[6] I shall leave for others the disquieting result: an emigration pattern which sent German-speaking radicals seeking safety to the capitalist West without ever coming to terms frankly with what this meant for their ideological commitments to the left.[7]

It was clear by the late 1920s that something dramatic had gone wrong with the Soviet communist "experiment." To the great credit of social science scholarship in Germany, both those of Jewish and Christian origins—and in the latter category one must point to the towering achievements of Karl August Wittfogel,[8] and Joseph Schumpeter[9]—many problems in Soviet society were dealt with frankly and critically. This critique of Soviet life, first a trickle and then a torrent, helped to determine the character, the time, and the place of the migration when it finally had to occur. That there was no corresponding critical analysis at the theoretical level of socialism as a long-term value commitment must be reckoned a consequence of the utopian strain in social science ideology. But by 1933 it was no longer a "dialectical tension" that could readily encompass a Soviet solution to the Nazi system. Communists, socialists, and social democrats for the most part fled west.[10]

These two factors are essential to any larger reconstruction of exile patterns. Jewish survival has uniformly depended upon a relatively democratic society, in which individuals, not types, races, or classes of people are judged. Social science survival likewise depends upon a democratic society, in which analysis is distinct from ideology, and in which mistakes are punishable by scholarly rebuke rather than soldierly bullets. I would like to explore this twin phenomenon of Jewish marginality and social science marginality as part of the history and legacy of German migration during 1933–1945.

John Lukacs noted that "when in Germany something becomes respectable, it is chewed over, swallowed, ruminated, again and again."[11] He specifically had in mind the intense nostalgia for the Weimar period that became a myth of exile after World War Two. Yet this topic of German intellectual migration might properly be considered a by-product of the larger theme of decadence and democracy in the pre-Hitlerite period. What adds credence to this assessment is that not a few of the younger Weimar figures, just coming into prominence in the 1930s, gave special attention to problems of power, interest, and freedom in their mature work: Herbert Marcuse,[12] Henry Pachter,[13] and Hans Morgenthau[14] to name a few.[15] Hopefully, in the analysis of the German-Jewish migration of intellectuals to America and England, the excesses of pathos and bathos can be avoided and some sense of the past as it informs the present can be gained.

The commitment of German-Jewish social scientists to classical German culture has long been taken for granted–, as indeed it should be even on the basis of such fragmentary autobiographic evidence as exists.[16] Not simply autobiography, but the great themes of German culture occupied Weimar and Viennese Jewry alike. The dorsal spine of German sociology had in common with Austrian economics an interest in the large issues of class, stratification, and race, coupled with philosophical concern regarding how freedom and order are absorbed in volatile societies. It is a tradition which to its lasting credit has been empirical, but more than that, it has been clinical. Nor can its contents be reduced to some abstract caricature like *Verstehenstheorie der Verstehenden Soziologie*.[17] The richness of analysis, its unparalleled outburst of achievement, stems from this symbiotic merger of social stratification and social psychology—of which the work of Hans Gerth and C. Wright Mills on social psychology is perhaps one example,[18] and Reinhard Bendix's volume on work and authority in industrial society provides an equally representative outcome.[19]

I make no claim that these works exemplify specifically Jewish themes. Such a claim would be easily refutable and absurd on the face of things. But it is certainly no mistake or exaggeration to claim that such themes are easily absorbed within Old Testament concerns and have found parallels among the great German-Jewish theological teachers Franz Rosenzweig,[20] Martin Buber,[21] and earlier, Hans Kohn.[22] Rosenzweig in particular wrote on a set of themes that ran parallel to the sociological interests of Weimar Germany.

What I would claim is that the Jews gravitated to big themes, and hence often to the social sciences, because their fates were caught up and determined by a Weberian perspective. They could neither intellectually accept nor emotionally act upon the crude notions of national interest common to a Gustav Schmoller on the right or a Vladimir Lenin on the left. Even Jewish social-activist scholars in Germany, such as Karl Liebknecht and Rosa Luxemburg, had a hard time accepting Leninist doctrines of political partisanship and party discipline. Nor should we forget that many of the classical texts of social research written in German, from Georg Simmel to Paul Lazarsfeld, were in fact products of a Jewish tradition which saw in German a universal language to express its social scientific ideas. This is not to deny the impact of more prosaic factors: Jews were essentially locked out of the administrative-bureaucratic apparatus. Hence, the structure of occupational opportunities moved large numbers of Jews into academic pursuits and political participation in radical groups at one end, and others, toward taking up business and shop keeping activities. Before the Nazi consolidation of power, German society, oriented as it was toward the supremacy of the state, paid relatively scant attention to this phenomenon—at least in terms of ethnic and religious membership.[23]

The overwhelming proportion of Jews amongst leading *Weltbühne* writers, as members of the *Institut für Sozialforschung,* and in leadership roles in the Social Democratic Party, make it plain that German-Jewish participation in select activities can scarcely be reduced to the structure of employment of opportunities, especially since such opportunities were precisely to be found in largely bourgeois enterprises, and not in radical sectors of society.

Recent documentation tends to confirm German Jews as a general cultural phenomenon common to Germany, Austria, Hungary, and parts of Switzerland. This is not to say that the constituent elements of this culture are completely different from other cultures, it is to say rather that their Judaic background served as an organizing set of values distinguishing German-Jewish culture from others. The German Jews offer a particularly interesting case of a group which, despite considerable pressure in Germany from the emancipation onwards to assimilate in the sense of becoming wholly absorbed into German society, resisted. Instead, they developed a specific German-Jewish identity that survived against great odds. Indeed, the pressures from within as well as from without the group to denounce and reject that identity were at times enormous. More recently, this pressure has been exerted not so much because of its link with Judaism as because of its past association with German culture.[24]

This German-Jewish formation, as it was expressed by the members of the social science communities, and epitomized by its so-called "critical theory" wing, was caught between the Charybdis of capitalism—which they despised as a system of exploitation (whose fruits they nonetheless enjoyed), and the Scylla of communism, which they despised as a system of worse exploitation (whose bitter fruits they often escaped, unlike their Russian-Jewish counterparts). When the chips were down, and they certainly were down between 1933 and 1945, members of this influential, if small, network made decisions not on the basis of competing ideological claims or even economic conquests pure and simple, but rather on the basis of political and juridical considerations of which societies afforded the greatest opportunity for personal survival and further intellectual growth.

A parallel theme is that, while some moved as a coherent group, such as the Frankfurt School in sociology and the Vienna Circle in philosophy, German Jews shared an animus for dictatorship rather than any unified theory of society and/or religion. This too is common to a Jewish life, which from the Talmudic to the Midrashic traditions shared a common hatred of tyranny rather than a unified vision of Jewish culture.

Once this framework is appropriately considered, the overwhelming preponderance of German-Jewish cultural participation not only in the life of society but in the first massive critiques of totalitarianism becomes understandable. Acceptance of the German nationalism or the fascist totalitarianism of the 1920s was out of the question. Only those Jews who found comfort in ideological sadomasochism could accept fascism as more than an aberration. Their critique of communism, and not incidentally communism as it related to the Jewish question, determined their patterns of exile.

Scholars have not so much tended to deny categorically but rather to minimize, even trivialize the above position. An all too typical case in point is Tom Bottomore's work on the Frankfurt School. In that work he miraculously dismisses the centrality of Jewishness in German-Jewish thought and at the same time entirely skips over the main point: why this socialist-learning group, committed to socialist reason and the end of irrational capitalism, came to the United States and England. "What is most striking of all," Bottomore writes, "in the analysis of fascism (more particularly, National Socialism in Germany) by Horkheimer and Adorno is that they virtually identified it with anti-Semitism, or at least came to view it almost exclusively from this narrow perspective." But it turns out that this "narrow perspective" asserted nothing less—in the work of Horkheimer and Pollock at least—than the "primacy of politics over the economy, and domination exercised through 'technological rationality' and through the exploitation of irrational sentiments and attitudes among the mass of the population (e.g., anti-Semitism)."[25]

The monumental break with Marxist orthodoxy that such a view portended a break that made possible the exact analysis of totalitarianism on the right and left, is something that Bottomore cannot admit much less celebrate. Otherwise, he would have to draw the further conclusion that this sense of the primacy, or at least autonomy of politics, also encouraged a migration to the capitalist West rather than to the communist East, and in addition, that such a line of analysis was powerful and broad-ranging precisely because it focused on the Jewish condition.

This is not intended to single out one individual; indeed, the tradition of neglect has its own lineage.[26] Nonetheless, the intermingling of the Jewish question and the political question provided a fertile soil for the critique that unambiguously determined the movement of German-speaking intellectuals during the exile period. Even those who did not share any powerful sense of Jewish centrality in their political or sociological analysis seemed quite willing to study anti-Semitism once transplanted to the free soil of the West.[27]

The powerful anti-capitalist sentiments of the German-Jewish social science community hardly needs further application. Indeed, even among figures in philosophy and psychoanalysis, where the impulse to anti-capitalist sentiments might be expected to have been muted, the consensus at this level is high. What does require further study is the disquieting if tacit support for the statist element coexisted with an unqualified anti-capitalist posture. Here is where the consensus not so much unravels as goes off in different directions.[28] For the need to come to grips, if not altogether to terms, with the totalitarian system in the Soviet Union challenged the anti-capitalism no less than it served to reinforce the pro-socialism beliefs of this German-Jewish intellectual community.

I should briefly like to discuss how these contrasting themes were played out in the actual critical work in which various groups and individuals were engaged. In the remaining portion of the chapter, I wish to focus on some representative critiques of communist performance, critiques that became absorbed in the American ethos and were further nourished by a wide range of American scholars, from conservative to radical. Given the prototypical nature of this German and largely (but hardly exclusive) Jewish analysis, its exact contents are of more than antiquarian interest even fifty years later.

Those who, like Leo Lowenthal, were examining the sociological roots of totalitarian culture, were hard put to accept simplistic varieties of partisan Marxist "explanations" of fascism as a species of capitalism in its dying stage and of communism as a new blossoming of humanism.[29] Indeed, Lowenthal identified the psychological seeds of anti-Semitism with the projection of Jews as victims of paranoid projections and as the embodiment of those projections. While specific forms of fascist and communist totalitarian mentality differed, they shared a generalized commitment to making moral judgments based on abstract types: class, race, or religion. The use of background variables to develop notions of good and evil proved uncomfortable to the inheritors of Weimar, for whom such morally centered literature was not the beginning of a "new moon" but the end of a humane tradition. Thus, while socialist-oriented scholars like Lowenthal were eager to believe in differences between National Socialist and communist cultural forms, ultimately it was their sameness that contributed to both scholarly critique and personal decisions to migrate to a democratic West.[30]

Radical members of the German and Austrian intelligentsia were quite knowledgeable of fervent changes in the Soviet landscape after the death of Lenin. And these key figures reported back their profound misgivings. Thus, as early as 1927, six years prior to the assumption of power by Hitler in Germany, Walter Benjamin could report from his visit to Moscow the following: "Moscow, as it appears at the present, reveals a full range of possibilities in schematic form: above all, the possibility that the Revolution might fail or succeed. In either case, something unforeseeable will result and its picture will be far different from any programmatic sketch one might draw of the future. The outlines of this are at present brutally and distinctly visible among the people and their environment."[31]

This letter to Martin Buber is but a mild illustration of the disillusionment felt by Benjamin. One can only imagine that his personal discussions upon returning to Berlin were far more candid and less guarded about the disastrous turns of the Bolshevik Revolution. But the Frankfurt School, having cut itself off from liberal capitalism and Zionist Judaism, had no choice but to support the myths of communism in theory when it sought the benefits of capitalism in practice.

It would be largely inaccurate to make any claim that German-Jewish scholars went west rather than East because of specific anti-Semitic policies of the Soviet State. But even those who made sharp distinctions between Nazism and communism, such as Franz Neumann, migrated to the West.[32] In other words, while a great preponderance of scholars who fled from fascism were Jewish, their reasons for going to the United States were only rarely linked to a frank disbelief in Soviet applications of the national question. Indeed, the late 1920s and early 1930s were the period of the great Soviet illusion on the Jewish question. Birobidjan was targeted as a Jewish homeland in which the Yiddish language would have official status. In the early stages, Jews were involved, albeit *sotto voce*, in the highest ranks of the communist parties of both Russia and Germany, and Jews were especially prominent in the development of Marxism-Leninism in a wide variety of fields ranging from philosophy and literature to the social sciences.

There were some disquieting rumbles and even early purges in professional life. But as Aleksandr Solzhenitsyn was later to remark, these were discounted as purification rituals against peasants and workers.[33] It was only with the turning of the screw in the late 1930s against intellectuals, the rationalists of the regime, that serious questions were raised about the Soviet system in elitist circles.[34] In a sense, this makes the exile of German-Jewish scholars to the Western democracies all the more remarkable since it was a decision taken singly rather than collectively, against the general features of totalitarianism—left and right—rather than as an emotional response to particularistic policy features of the Soviet Union against its own Jewish people, or as part of Soviet policy in general.

If I place strong emphasis on German-Jewish critical responses to Soviet Communism, it is not to distort the nearly uniform opposition of German-Jewish social scientists to fascists and Nazi doctrines, and certainly not to deny their sense from whence derived the main threats to their autonomy and academic livelihood. It is clear that German Jews, across the ideological board, opposed fascist ideology and practice. To emphasize this, however, is to repeat the obvious and belabor the well known.

Thus, I take the position that the critique of Soviet communism, made as it was by scholars often holding socialist and radical beliefs no less than liberal and conservative persuasions, was trans-ideological: that is to say, German-Jewish intellectual behavior tapped religious and ethnic roots that led to similar types of analysis by diverse types of scholarship. This helps to explain the near-uniformity of exile patterns to the democratic West.

I have chosen as representative critiques made by the Vienna School of socialist economists and the Frankfurt School of neo-Marxian sociologists. While one can readily draw upon individuals of all persuasions with similar and shared visions of Soviet Marxism, and one should add by non-Jew and Jew alike, it is clear that by emphasizing these two clusters, one can effectively establish the motif and leitmotif of this chapter.

It should be evident to all but the most obtuse and jaundiced that the migration of German-Jewish scholars was not the cause but the consequence of the breakdown of social science in Germany as an autonomous civilized activity. Even the best of those who remained yielded on questions of the autonomous nature and humane purposes of social science. Carl Schmitt saw the decisive question of moment as the relationship of state to politics, with scarcely a place for autonomous society.[35] Werner Sombart[36] slowly eased his thesis about the Jews and modern capitalism into a general theory of a state that stood outside the class system and over all forms of religious pluralism.[37] Hans Freyer had little trouble converting sociology as a simple historical phenomenon originating out of bourgeois society's feeling for the situation into a specific fascist feeling for sociology.[38]

The last gasp of nineteenth-century romanticism turned into a conservative twentieth-century anti-romantic historicism. Aims and goals were commingled with desires and dreams of conquest. The Weberian idea of a social science as something apart from a social ideology rapidly disintegrated. The great masters of German social thought—Weber, Töennies, and Simmel—passed away. Their legacy was carried into exile by Lazarsfeld, Lowenthal, Cahnman, Bendix, and countless others. But those who remained were no less lacking in talent. They were rather lacking in nerve. They became part of the generalized malaise of Nazism, and worse, contributed to the malaise by a collapse of verve. The young went to war, whilst the old either paraded forth doctrines which rationalized the spirit of *revanchism* and racism in clever ways, or more often lapsed into silence.

The Austro-Marxists are chosen as a prototype for a number of reasons. They represented an organic group dedicated to coming to terms with problems in Marxian economic theory, and did so in an uncompromising fashion. They represented a group somewhere between social democracy and bolshevism as a unified political style. They shared in common Jewish ancestries if not Zionist persuasions. The pattern of exile was different because the Austrian School, which by common consent started in 1904 and ended with Dolfuss's semi-dictatorship in 1934, included many people who had passed away or retired prior to the worst infections of Nazism. Some members of this group sought a freer atmosphere in Europe during the Weimar period, while others did in fact migrate to the West. But the purpose of treating this group seriously is less the phenomenon of exile than the intellectual groundwork of criticism that they provided of totalitarianism in general, no less fascism on the right and bolshevism on the left.

This is not to say that the Austrian Marxists passed their final years in Vienna cafes. Friedrich Adler died in Zurich, a bastion of democracy compared to either Germany or Austria after 1937. Otto Bauer fled to Prague, Czechoslovakia; and when the Nazi Wehrmacht menaced that forsaken country, he took refuge in Paris. Indeed, on the day of his death in 1938, the London *News Chronicle* published his appeal to world conscience to save the 300,000 Jews of Austria. Rudolph Hilferding, perhaps the most central figure in this group, also fled to Zurich, where he resided between 1933 and 1938. He then went into exile in Paris. In 1941 the Vichy police handed him over to the Nazis. There is some doubt about how he died: some accounts claim he took his own life in prison; others claim that the Nazis murdered him.

Again, we see a group of dedicated German-speaking scholars, Jewish and socialist, fleeing from tyranny to the capitalist democracies—such as they existed before the catastrophic
destruction of prewar-Europe.[39]

I want again to emphasize that my remarks are intended
as a specific response of a German-Jewish group of sociologists and social scientists to the totalitarian environment as
it emerged in Central Europe during a critical juncture between 1924 and 1934, and not as a full-bodied evaluation of
the Austrian-Marxist School of thought. Indeed, with the
publication of Bottomore's work on the subject, the need
for such an elaborate introduction is fortunately obviated.[40]
While it may be questionable, as Bottomore claims, that
Austro-Marxism and the Frankfurt School represent "two
extreme and contradictory forms of Marxist thought" (the
former sociological and the latter philosophical), it is the
shared ethnic and religious backgrounds of its members,
not to mention overlapping networks and cohorts, that must
herein be of interest. For it is the unity of prewar European
German-Jewish life which led to a strangely similar rendition and rejection of Soviet society early on by these two
"extreme and contradictory forms of Marxism."

Let us start our brief excursion with a cursory look at the
Austrian Marxists of the 1920s and 1930s. Why did the
Austro-Marxism of Otto Bauer, Max Adler, Rudolf
Hilferding, and Karl Renner remain overshadowed by other
intellectual currents and exert such little long-range impact?
The answer must be sought, not in the development of capitalism as a historical phenomenon, but in the development
of communism as an ideological aberration. It was the very
emphasis of Austro-Marxism on political practice that made
its members cognizant, early on, of Soviet political practice.
In 1936, Otto Bauer put the matter bluntly and properly:

> The dictatorship of the proletariat has become something entirely
> different from what was originally conceived by those who established
> it. It is not the dictatorship of freely elected Soviets. It is not the 'supe-

rior form of democracy' that Lenin imagined, 'without a bureaucracy' or policy, or a standing army. It is not the free self-determination of the working masses exercising their rule over the exploiting classes. It has become the dictatorship of an all-powerful party bureaucracy which stifles all freedom of speech and action even in the party itself, and it dominates the people by means of the powerful apparatus of the state and economic bureaucracy, the police, and the army. This development was inevitable. Only this bureaucratic dictatorship was able to accomplish the social revolution, but at a certain stage of development which Soviet society is rapidly approaching, this bureaucratic dictatorship will become an obstacle to further development. The evolution of the dictatorship has established the bureaucracy of the party, the state and the economy as the master of the Soviet people.[41]

The Austrian School of Marxism, far more than the German School, saw this bureaucratization of Soviet politics clearly and decisively. They were not heeded, less because of their *closeness* to the marrow of reality, than because of their *distance*. In a climate of being reviled by the Soviets as ideological forerunners of revisionism and ignored by the Anglo-American economists as being individuals more concerned with economic fossils than with real world model-building, the Austrian School of Marxism, however prescient, tended to be either denigrated by the East as anti-Leninist or downgraded by the West as anti-Keynesian. There was indeed truth in both critiques: but it only served to remind this group of its marginality, indeed of its Jewish cosmopolitanism. The enemies of socialists emphasized the Jewish character of its ideological leadership, to which the Austro-Marxists could only respond by reciting the shibboleths of its "class analysis," its deep-seated belief that the Jewish question would be readily resolved within the framework of the national question. The evolution of Soviet communism soon put an end to that option. Dispersal through migration was a practicality, a sad but intellectually fortuitous resolution.

The specific contributions of the Austrian school were many: they noted the mechanisms of the transformation of industrial capital into banking capital, which thus created finance capital; they were the first to indicate the fusion of capitalism and the bourgeoisie with the military in Germany, thus making possible National Socialism as an operative system along with the emergence of political economy as state capitalism; they showed how the working class rather than the capitalist system is burst asunder under conditions of modern statism; and they put an end to the deterministic myth of proletarian triumph as a function of universal history. But ultimately it was the failure of nerve in the Austrian School that limited its outreach, not to mention its study of capitalism as a historical phenomenon.

Max Adler epitomized this theological bent in the Austro-Marxian School, a refuge in neo-Thomistic formulas, by distinguishing the collapse of communism as a movement from the preservation of communism as a theory.[42] There was no letting go of illusions—new reality was broken on the shoals of old theory. The impact of the Austrian School—the most brilliant group of socialists rivaling if not surpassing the Frankfurt School—provided the seeds of doubt even more than a confirmation that the transition process in politics would not run smoothly or in keeping with vague predictions about an egalitarian future.

Unlike the German Marxists, the Austro-Marxists did not maintain a distinct identity in the exile period. In part, they left for different places as *political* exiles rather than as a unitary *intellectual* cadre. Their roles in the Social Democratic parties of Germany and Austria, including acting as conduits between general political issues and specific efforts at Jewish defense and self-organization, came to a crashing halt with the triumph of the Nazi party.[43] In part too, the Austrian School's personnel was dismembered early on in the Nazi epoch. Not only was Rudolph Hilferding either a suicide or a victim of murder in Paris, but such figures as Robert Danneberg died in the concentration camp at Auschwitz. Ultimately, the hopes of this group, their sure sense of optimism about a socialist Austria, proved less serviceable than the pessimism of the Frankfurt School, with its limited faith in nation building and nation-builders. It is to them that we now turn.

While many members of the Frankfurt School were Jewish, they shared a sense of Judaism that was defined more by Karl Marx[44] and Heinrich von Treitschke[45] than by Buber or Rosenzweig. That is to say they identified Judaism with the process of bourgeoisification (read contamination) in Weimar German society. Even the most sensitive of the Frankfurt group, Max Horkheimer, lapsed into a vicious, banal argument by analogy. As late as 1941, writing from an idyllic exile in Morningside Heights, he was moved to discuss the moral equivalencies of Judaism and Nazism—not their fundamental opposition. The following passage is not atypical, in which the apostle of socialist rationality noted: "the language of market mentality, Jewish slang, the vernacular of salesmen and traders who have long been humiliated, survive on the lips of their suppressers." Horkheimer continues in this vein of Jewish self-hatred:

It is the language of winks, sly hints, and complicity in deceit. The Nazis call failure *Pleite,* he who does not watch his step in time is *meshugge,* and an anti-Semitic song says that the Americans have no ideas *was sich tub.* The instigators justify their program by saying that once again all was not quite kosher with the Jews. Getting through by hook or crook is the secret deal, and even the SA troopers' envy the Jewish brains that they cudgel. They imagine that the Jewish shrewdness they strive to imitate reflects the truth that they have to deny to themselves and to destroy. If this truth has once and for all been discarded and men have decided for integral adjustment, if reason has been purged of all morality regardless of cost, and has triumphed over all else, no one may remain outside and look on. The existence of one solitary 'unreasonable' man elucidates the shame of the entire nation. His existence testifies to the relativity of the system of radical self-preservation that has been posted as absolute. If all superstition has been abolished to such a degree that only superstition remains, no stubborn man may wander around and seek happiness anywhere except in unrelenting progress. The hatred of Jews, like the lust to murder the insane, is stimulated by their unintelligible faith in a God who has everywhere deserted them and by the conditional rigidity of the principles they maintain even unwittingly. Suspicion of madness is the unperishable source of persecution. It originates from distrust of one's own pragmatic reason.[46]

Typical of this prevailing attitude are the reflections of Lewis A. Coser. In response to a query about experiencing anti-Semitism, he noted with deep candor that his "identification was surely not with Jewry; it was always with Socialism, Marxism, radical politics." He added, "I remember a few guys who joined the Hitler Youth. One knows that these bastards were anti-Semitic, but our fights were because we were on the left and they were on the right."[47] This was certainly a shared perspective of younger and older German Jews who drifted into both socialism and sociology.

We are talking about an uncomfortable, often reluctant, exodus of select elites, and not a mass exodus of the downtrodden. They had the wherewithal to make decisions. They chose Paris, Zurich, London, and finally, New York, not in order to share a common fate with their religious brethren, but to survive and thrive as socialists, radicals, and sociologists. The categories were believed to be roughly isomorphic by many.

While the primary intention of the Frankfurt School was the critique of fascism, a nearly parallel drive was a critique of communism. Both were believed to be illustrative of the end of reason. From the outset, Herbert Marcuse best exemplified this belief in the dual enemy. Long before his critique of *Soviet Marxism*,[48] he offered, in an abstract, neo-Hegelian manner, the following observations on individualism and collectivism:

> Masses and mass culture are manifestations of scarcity and frustration, and the authoritarian assertion of the common interest is but another form of the rule of particular interests of the whole. The fallacy of collectivism consists in that it equips the whole [society] with the traditional properties of the individual. Collectivism abolishes the free pursuit of competing individual interests but retains the idea of the common interest as a separate entity. Historically, the latter is but the counterpart of the former. Men experience their soci-

ety as the objective embodiment of the collectivity as long as the individual interests are antagonistic to and competing with each other for a share in the social wealth. To such individuals, society appears as an objective entity, consisting of numerous things, institutions and agencies, plants and shops, business, police and law, government, schools and churches, prisons and hospitals, theaters and organizations, etc. Society is almost everything the individual is not, everything that determines his habits, thoughts and behavior patterns, that affects him from the outside. Accordingly, society is noticed chiefly as a power of restraint and control, providing the framework that integrates the goals, faculties and aspirations of men. It is this power which collectivism retains in this picture of society, thus perpetuating the rule of things and men over men.[49]

Scholars of German-Jewish background like Marcuse distanced themselves from both main trends opposed to fascism: capitalist democracy and totalitarian socialism, but with no stated options save utopianism or some ill-defined chiliastic vision—the twin poles of the Judaic longing after a world of perfect justice—but without Jewish practice; that is, without a sense of community and commitment.

Otto Kirchheimer first voiced the notion that fascism and communism were structurally equivalent. The key element binding the two was the conversion of state power into state terror.[50] Terrorism became the mechanism of the state, through police power exercised by specialized military units. In this he broke with Franz Neumann and the other members of the Frankfurt School, who persisted over time in seeing differences between Nazism and communism. World War Two contributed to maintaining this belief in differences, whereas the post-war Cold War rekindled just these analytical concerns.[51]

Several years before his association with the Institute, Kirchheimer investigated the consequences of both the excess of utopianism and the error of party-oriented *realpolitik* for the popular democratic soviets, or councils. A revision, his essay on "Marxism, Dictatorship, and the Organization of the Proletariat" criticized both the "primitive democratic dreams" of Lenin's *State and Revolution* and the authoritar-

ian tendencies of Bolshevik organization. The latter, in particular, according to Kirchheimer, led to an identification
of party with bureaucratic state administration, both intra-
party democracy and the earlier dynamic links to the underlying population.[52] For a centralized and centralizing
party in control of the bureaucratic state, the loss of contact
with their mass base could only mean terror. Here was a
creative (though only implicit) application of the Marxian
analysis of Jacobinism to the Soviet Union, more convincing than Trotsky's uncertain juggling with the slogans of
"Thermidor" and "Bonapartism," or Deutscher's efforts to
preserve such shaky analogies and metaphors.[53]

Given this line of development, the question of where
German-Jewish social scientists of this persuasion could move
and practice their skills become moot. We are dealing with
a problem of marginality, or better multiple varieties of
marginality: Judaism, socialism, and social democracy, sociology itself. All of these required an environment relatively
open, not static in its presumptions, a place where work was
possible, if not easy. Such a notion was the archetype of the
new capitalism embodied by the United States of America,
where countless minorities, revolutionaries, and discontents
had come before, have come since.

The hunt for historical antecedents, for functional equiva-
lents, and analytical parallels is, upon inspection, not only a
reflective process but also a projective one.[54] What is ignored is as important as what is recollected. The cast of
characters, which contributed to empiricism or positivism,
went out of fashion at its point of preeminence. In the broad
sweep, old-fashioned German and Austrian scholarship came
into sharper focus. Younger scholars, also often of Jewish
extraction, saw the German-Jewish exiles as posing the key
issues of the West's struggle with the East, or what I have
elsewhere called the First World and the Second World.

These intellectual antecedents made possible an American theory both beholden to and in rebellion against Ger-

man-Jewish social theory. From right and left the American polarities surface: Nisbet's authority[55] and community,[56] Jaffa's equality vs. liberty,[57] Walter's terror vs. resistance,[58] Strauss's classicism vs. modernism,[59] and Mosse's masses and individuals.[60] But the dramaturgy finally cracked. The dialectical vein began to yield fewer nuggets. Measurement between the poles and not just pronouncements about the poles became central. Why do men rebel? How does one measure authority and community? Under what conditions do equality and liberty appeal to different segments of the same society? One might argue that even here the debt to the exile community is great. After all, it was Paul F. Lazarsfeld who early on emphasized that meaning could be found only essentially through measurement and quantitative research.[61]

In fact, it was not so much the assault from outside as the collapse from within that characterizes the intellectual networks we have been describing. The exile experience could preserve, even enrich the German-Jewish tradition. But, ultimately, it fell victim to its own indecision and indiscretion. It could and then did argue from its special vision the issues of fascism and communism, democracy and dictatorship, order and freedom, but it could not get beyond its own preconceptions. The polarities, the dialects, were as prevalent after the exile experience as before.

Germany remains at the crossroads of the two cultures of West and East. For that reason, German scholarship has itself been broken on the shoals between anti-capitalist and anti-totalitarian traditions. In theory there was a dual inheritance given Western society's intellectuals after two world wars. In practice this same dual inheritance rested upon German society itself. For this reason, the question of the German-Jewish inheritance of America has now become an issue of the American impact on a German intellectual life essentially purged of its Jewish elements. The rise of quantitative analysis has been fueled by this American style. But the place of qualitative research and synthetic analysis has helped transform that style, by making it responsive to larger, contextual issues of American civilization.

Big intellectual transmigration does not just vanish. They are absorbed, regurgitated, and sometimes fertilized. They even lead prodigal children back home. The case of Theodor W. Adorno indicates that a home away from home may not stick intellectually.[62] The desire to return to Germany indicates the considerable pulling power of the fatherland, purged of the twin godfathers of war and destruction. But in the main, the German impact on Western culture, beyond its obviously selective and at times myopic nature represents a testament to the personal security provided by Western democracy.

German-Jewish traditions are an inadvertent testament to the fact that all totalitarian systems are prone to anti-Semitism. Societies built upon irrational premises can be expected to act irrationally when they feel threatened. And this peculiar strain we call German Jewry intuited early on, albeit with fits and starts, what is now reckoned a commonplace of civil discourse; that the physical safety no less than intellectual freedom of endangered minorities can be protected only in an open society. Permit me to recall the 1945 words of the Swiss philosopher and political scientist Hans Barth:

> The disastrous effect of ideological thinking in its radical form is not only to cast doubt on the quality and structure of the mind that constitute man's distinguishing characteristic, but also to undermine the foundation of his social life. Human association is dependent on agreement, and the essence of agreement, be it concerned with common behavior, rational action, or scientific investigation is the idea of truth. If this idea is denounced as ideological, we are left, in Nietzsche's language, with individual quanta of will which, according the measure of their power, arbitrarily determine what truth and justice are to be.[63]

Underneath national, tribal and religious identifications and alienation is the simple fact that the so-called Frankfurt

School proved thoroughly inept in resolving the master dilemmas of political sociology. The entire "school" broke into tiny pieces once issues of a serious nature were confronted: Neumann and Kirschheimer understood the role of law and authority, while Horkheimer and Adorno cared not a whit for the subject. They preferred a world in which stagecraft was a matter of force and power. Some of the group, such as Lowenthal, Benjamin and the ever present Adorno, essentially believed in the power of culture to move the revolution forward in a healthy direction; others, like Marcuse and Horkheimer were far too preoccupied with political psychology directly to pay much heed to cultural struggles. Even the choice of heroes divided the German émigré class. For Fromm, the work of Sigmund Freud was the crowning centerpiece for explaining the present state of human affairs under capitalism; while for Marcuse, Freud was the quintessential reformist, the enemy of revolutionary transformation. What started as synthesis ended as synopsis, of shoehorning the work of towering masters into the dreary analysis of what went wrong in Weimar Germany and why Nazi Germany rather than communist Russia seemed the attractive option of the thirties. So, in theory as in biography, the Frankfurt Group was a pleasant fiction, part of the iconography of the post-Stalinist Marxists more than the canonical evolution of political sociology.

It took the bitter ashes of World War Two to restore meaning and dignity to such simple but easily overlooked words. Even so, questions remain unanswered, such as: what explains the overwhelmingly anti-liberal character of post-World War Two social theory? While scholars like Strauss and Arendt developed a powerful anti-totalitarian consensus, they seemed less certain about the positive values of democratic rule and constitutional order. They could agree on the moral bankruptcy of moral relativism but could not agree on the moral supremacy of liberal societies. The force of the state hovered like a phoenix in émigré thought. Strauss,

Schmitt, Kojeve, and a variety of other post-war figures have been canonized and lionized, but the reasons for the shambles left behind in the wake of the European catastrophe of anti-liberalism went unanswered. Under such conditions, it is little wonder that political sociology shifted not only its intellectual focus but also its geographical center of gravity from Europe to America.

Notes

1. Charles Frankel, *The Case for Modern Man*. New York: Harper & Bros. Publishers, 1955. p 41
2. René Koenig, "Über das vermeintliche Ende der deutschen Soziologie article von der Machtergreifung," in *Kölner Zeitschrift für Soziologie und Sozialpsychologie 36*, 1984, pp. 1–42.
3. Otto Neurath as quoted in Mark E. Blum, *The Austro-Marxists: 1890–1928*. Lexington: The University Press of Kentucky, 1985.
4. Typical of this past tendency to minimize and trivialize the "Jewish Question" is Martin Jay (1973: 136–137). Most recently Jay has taken a far more candid and critical look at "critical theory."
5. E. Kehr, *Economic Interest, Militarism, and Foreign Policy*. Berkeley and London: University of California Press, 1977, pp. 164–173.
6. Walter Benjamin, *Moscow Diary* (orig. 1927). G. Smith (ed.) Cambridge: Harvard University Press, 1986, pp. 132–133.
7. The one noteworthy and singular exception to this political vision of emigration is to be found in Hannah Arendt's classic study, *The Origins of Totalitarianism* (1966).
8. Karl A. Wittfogel, *Das erwachende China: Ein Abriss der Geschichte des gegenwartigen Problem Chinas*. Vienna: Agis Velag, 1926. The culmination of this line of reasoning was in *Oriental Despotism: A Comparative Study of Total Power*. New Haven: Yale University Press, 1957. For a full review of Wittfogel's monumental achievement, see Gary L. Ulmen, *The Science of Society: Toward an Understanding of the Life and Work of Karl August Wittfogel*. The Hague: Mouton Publishers, 1978.
9. Joseph A. Schumpeter, *History of Economic Analysis*. New York: Oxford University Press, 1954, pp. 877–885. Also see *The Theory of Economic Development*. New Brunswick and London: Transaction Books, 1982. The best general statement on Schumpeter that I have come upon is by John E. Elliot "New Introduction to J. A. Schumpeter," in *The Theory of Economic Development*. New Brunswick and London: Transaction Books, 1982.
10. Walter Benjamin, *Reflections*. P. Demetz (ed.) New York and London: Harcourt, Brace & Jovanovich, 1978, pp. 97–130.

11. John Lukacs, "Two-Faced Germany." *The American Spectator* 17 July, 1984, pp. 21–23.

12. Herbert Marcuse, *Reason and Revolution; Hegel and the Rise of Social Theory.* New York: Oxford University Press, 1941. Also see *Soviet Marxism.* New York: Vintage Books/Random House, 1957.

13. Henry Pachter, *The Fall and Rise of Europe: A Political, Social, and Cultural History of the Twentieth Century.* New York: Praeger, 1975.

14. Hans Morgenthau, *Politics Among Nations (first edition).* New York: A.A. Knopf, 1948. Also see *In Defense of the National Interest.* New York: A.A. Knopf, 1951.

15. A recent empirical study has made quite plain not only how central the Austrian School of political economy was to the evolution of Marxism, but just how central in practical terms its leading figures were to the development of prototypical red communes in Vienna. This makes the newer effortless demise of the Austrian School, and its inability to regroup, somewhat easier to understand, since paradoxically, the Austrians were far more rooted in party politics of the Left than were their German counterparts at Frankfurt. See Frei.

16. Hans Morgenthau, "Interview by Bernard Johnson" and "Fragment of an Intellectual Autobiography," in K. Thompson and R.J. Myers (eds.) *Truth and Tragedy.* New Brunswick and London: Transaction Books, 1984, pp. 1–17, 33–386. Louis A. Coser, "Interview with Bernard Rosenberg," in W.W. Powell and R. Robbins (eds.) *Conflict and Consensus.* New York: The Free Press/Macmillan, 1984, pp. 27–52. Reinhard Bendix, *From Berlin to Berkeley: On German-Jewish Identity.* New Brunswick and London: Transaction Books, 1985. Paul F. Lazarsfeld, "An Episode in the History of Social Research: A Memoir" in D. Fleming and B. Bailyn (eds.) *The Intellectual Migration.* Cambridge: Harvard University Press, 1969, pp. 270–337.

17. Theodore Abel, *Systematic Sociology in Germany: A Critical Analysis of Some Attempts to Establish Sociology as an Independent Science,* 1929 edition, reprint. New York: Octagon Books, 1965, pp. 116–159.

18. Hans H. Gerth and C. Wright Mills, *Character and Social Structure: The Psychology of Social Institutions.* New York: Harcourt, Brace & World, 1953.

19. Reinhard Bendix, *Work and Authority in Industry.* New York: John Wiley & Sons, 1956.

20. Franz Rosenzweig, *Hegel und der Staat* (two volumes). München and Berlin, 1920. Also see Nahum Glatzer, *Franz Rosenzweig: Life and Thought.* New York: Schocken Books, 1953.

21. Martin Buber, *On Zion: The History of an Idea.* New York: Schocken Books, 1973. Also see "The Jew in the World," in A. Hertzberg (ed.) *The Zionist Idea: A Historical Analysis.* New York: Antheneum, 1979, pp. 450–453.

22. Hans Kohn, *Reason and Hope.* New York: Schocken Books, 1971. Also see *Religion of Reason.* New York: Schocken Books, 1972.

23. R. J. Brym, *Intellectuals and Politics.* London: George Allen & Unwin, 1980, pp. 64–65.
24. Marion Berghahn, *German-Jewish Refugees in England: The Ambiguities of Assimilation.* New York: St. Martin's Press, 1984, pp. 250–253.
25. Thomas Bottomore, *The Frankfurt School.* Chichester and New York: Ellis Horwood/Tavistock Publication, 1984, pp. 20–21.
26. The level of denial of the Jewish component in the Frankfurt School is astonishing when one considers that writers on this subject are often of a neo-Marxian persuasion, and hence would, if anything, have a tendency to overemphasize rather than deny "background variables" relating to religion and ethnicity no less than those relating to social class and economy. For example, in his exemplary work of more than 400 pages, Martin Jay sees fit to devote only cursory pages to the Jewish backgrounds of the Frankfurt social scientists. Martin Jay, *Dialektisch Phantasie: Die Geschichte der Frankfurter Schule und des Instituts für Sozialforschung, 1923–1950.* Frankfurt am Main: Fischer Taschenbuch Verlag, 1981, pp. 51–54. In all fairness, Jay has made an effort to rectify this shortcoming in subsequent writings. See Martin Jay, "The Jews and the Frankfurt School," *New German Critique,* Winter, 1980, pp. 137–140; and "The Jews and the Frankfurt School," in A. Rabinbach and J. Zipes (eds.) *Germans and Jews Since the Holocaust.* New York and London: Holmes & Meter, 1986, pp. 287–301.
27. Egon Bahr, "The Failure of Critical Theory," in J. Marcus and Z. Tar (eds.) *Foundations of the Frankfurt School of Social Research.* New Brunswick and London: Transaction, 1984, pp. 311–321.
28. A monograph on the general subject of the mutual impact of German and American education has pointed out, rightly, that the scholars who actually penetrated American higher education during the Nazi era were exceptional in their talents but few in numbers. Further, it is by no means the case that "émigré" scholars were as uniformly radical as was the Frankfurt School. Indeed, most scholars involved in American higher education tended to be drawn from the physical sciences, whilst the social scientists actually employed tended to be conservative in their orientations. See David Goldschmidt, "Trans-Atlantic Influences: History of Mutual Interactions between American and German Education," in *Between Elite and Mass Education: Education in the Federal Republic of Germany.* Albany: State University of New York Press, 1983, pp. 1–65.
29. Leo Lowenthal, *Literature and Mass Culture* (Vol. 1: Communication in Sociology). New Brunswick and London: Transaction Books, 1984, pp. 3–18; 291–301.
30. It is not without interest that the one figure who came close to an awareness of Jewish concerns in German Marxism, Lowenthal, shared with his Frankfurt colleagues at home and in exile a myopic inability to address the anomaly of dealing with Nazi anti-Semitism and Stalinist anti-Semitism as made from the same cloth. Even in his brilliant essay on "Judentum und deutscher Geist" we are given an

essay in the classic period—up to Freud and the end of Weimar—but nothing beyond that point. See Leo Lowenthal, *Judaica, Vortage, Briefe.* Frankfurt am Main: Suhrkamp Verlag, 1984, pp. 9–55.

31. Walter Benjamin, *Moscow Diary* (orig. 1927). G. Smith (ed.) Cambridge: Harvard University Press, 1986, pp. 132–133.
32. Franz Neumann, *Behemoth: The Structure and Practice of National Socialism.* New York: Oxford University Press, 1942. See also H. Stuart Hughes, "Franz Neumann: Between Marxism and Liberal Democracy," in *The Intellectual Migration: Europe and America, 1930–1960,* 1961.
33. Aleksandr Solzhenitsyn, *The Gulag Archipelago, 1918–1956: An Experiment in Literary Investigation* (three volumes). New York: Harper & Row, 1975–1978.
34. Aleksandr Solzhenitsyn throughout bitterly calls attention to *la trahison des clercs,* their uniform disregard of Stalinist terror, until it struck the intellectuals as such. See Irving Louis Horowitz "Revolution, Retribution, and Redemption," in *Winners and Losers: Social and Political Polarities in America.* Durham, NC: Duke University Press, 1984, pp. 177–191.
35. Carl Schmitt, *The Concept of the Political (Der Begriff des Politischen).* New Brunswick: Rutgers University Press, 1976, pp. 19–79. See also Leo Strauss' essay *What is Political Philosophy? And Other Studies.* Glencoe, IL: The Free Press, 1959.
36. Werner Sombart, *A New Social Philosophy.* Princeton: Princeton University Press, 1937.
37. One might argue, even persuasively, that *The Jews and Modern Capitalism* is not an anti-Semitic work, but even Sombart's most vigorous defenders do not deny that he became a chief representative of Deutsch Sozialismus, of Hitlerism. See Samuel Z. Klausner's brilliant new "Introduction" to *The Jews and Modern Capitalism.* New Brunswick and London: Transaction Books, 1978, pp. cii–cv.
38. Hans Freyer, *Theorie des objektiven Geistes: Eine Einleitung in die Kulturphilosophie* (3rd edition). Leipzig, 1934. See also *Die politisch Insel: Eine Geschichte der Utopien von Platon bis zur Gegenwart.* Leipzig, 1936. A reasonably good summation of Freyer's work in English is contained in *Modern Sociological Theory,* edited by Howard Becker and Alvin Boskoff, New York: Holt Rinehart & Winston, 1957, pp. 660–665.
39. *Encyclopaedia Judaica.* Jerusalem: Keter Publishing House, 1971, vol. 2, pp. 282–283; vol. 4, pp. 331; vol. 8, p. 479.
40. Thomas Bottomore, (ed.) *Austro-Marxism.* Oxford: Oxford University Press, 1978.
41. Otto Bauer, "Zwischen Zwei Weltkriegen?", in Tom Bottomore (ed.) *Austro-Marxism.* Oxford: Oxford University Press, 1978, pp. 201–203.
42. Max Adler. "Wandlung der Arbeiterklasse?" (orig. 1933), in T. Bottomore (ed.) *Austro-Marxism.* Oxford: Oxford University Press, 1978, pp. 217–252.

43. A.G. Frei, *Rotes Mien: Austromarxismus und Arbeiterkultur, Sozial-demokratische Wohnungs und Kommunalpolitik, 1919–1934*. Berlin: DVK-Verlag, 1984.
44. Karl Marx, "On the Jewish Problem" (orig. 1844), in P.R. Mendes-Flohr and J. Reinharz (eds.) *The Jew in the Modern World*, 1980, pp. 265–268.
45. Heinrich von Treitschke, "A Word about Our Jewry" (orig. 1879), in *The Jew in the Modern World*, 1980, pp. 280–284.
46. Max Horkheimer, "The End of Reason" (orig. 1941). *Studies in Philosophy and Social Sciences Vol. IX*, 1978, p. 5.
47. Lewis A. Coser, "Interview with Bernard Rosenberg," in W.W. Powell and R. Robbins (eds.) *Conflict and Consensus*. New York: The Free Press/Macmillan, 1984, pp. 27–52.
48. Herbert Marcuse, *Soviet Marxism: A Critical Analysis*. New York: Columbia University Press, 1958.
49. Herbert Marcuse, "Some Social Implications of Modern Technology" (orig. 1941), in A. Arato and E. Gebhardt (eds.) *The Essential Frankfurt School Reader*. NY: Urizen Books, 1978, p. 159.
50. Otto Kirchheimer, "Changes in the Structure of Political Compromise," in A. Arato and E. Gebhardt (eds.) *The Essential Frankfurt School Reader*. New York: Urizen Books, 1978, pp. 49–70.
51. The difference between Hirchheimer and Neumann that began before the rise of Hitlerism persisted through the post-war reconstruction period, a period in which both figures were heavily involved in the reintroduction of democratic norms in Adenauer's Germany. It is thus interesting to note a recent paper on this phenomenon and extrapolate from the essay the role of attitudes toward Soviet power in the determination of attitudes toward the composition of German democracy. See Sollner, A. *Emigrantenblocke-Westdeutschland im Urteil von Franz Neumann und Otto Kirchheimer* (mimeographed), 1984.
52. A. Arato, "Introduction," in A. Arato and E. Gebhard (eds.) *The Essential Frankfurt School Reader*. New York: Urizen Books, 1978, pp. 18–19.
53. I first tried to make this point in a critique of Isaac Deutscher's notion of "The Non-Jewish Jew." See I.L. Horowitz, "Liquidation or Liberation: The Jewish Question as Liberal Catharsis," in *Israeli Ecstasies/Jewish Agonies*. New York: Oxford University Press. 1974, pp. 192–204. The same point has recently been made far more succinctly and ably by my Christian friend Paul Johnson in his essay "Marxism vs. the Jews," *Commentary* 77, April 1984, pp. 28–34.
54. Hannah Arendt, *The Origins of Totalitarianism* (new edition). New York: Harcourt, Brace & World, 1966.
55. Robert A. Nisbet, *Twilight of Authority*. New York: Oxford University Press, 1975.
56. Robert A. Nisbet, *Tradition and Revolt*. New York: Random House, 1968.

57. Harry V. Jaffa, *Equality and Liberty*. New York: Oxford University Press, 1965.
58. Eugene V. Walter, *Terror and Resistance: A Study of Political Violence*. New York: Oxford University Press, 1969.
59. Leo Strauss, *What is Political Philosophy? And Other Studies*. Glencoe, IL: The Free Press, 1959.
60. George L. Mosse, *Masses and Man: Nationalist and Fascist Perceptions of Reality*. New York: Howard Fertig Publishers, 1980.
61. Paul F. Lazarsfeld, "Notes on the History of Quantification in Sociology: Trends, Sources and Problems," in H. Woolf (ed.) *Quantification: A History of the Meaning of Measurement in the Natural and Social Sciences*. Indianapolis and New York: Bobbs-Merrill Co., 1961, pp. 147–203.
62. Theodor W. Adorno, "Scientific Experiences of a European Scholar in America," in D. Fleming and B. Bailyn (eds.) *The Intellectual Migration*. Cambridge: Harvard University Press, 1969, pp. 338–370.
63. Hans Barth, *Truth and Ideology* (orig. published as *Wehrheit und Ideologie*, 1945). Berkeley and London: University of California Press, 1976.

11

Modern Capitalism as a Social Phenomenon: Schumpeter

"There is no Schumpeter school, and it seems unlikely there will ever be one.... No one believes passionately in a theorem learned at Schumpeter's knee or gleaned from his writings. He wished to be regarded as just one of those few who nudged economics along a bit. His many admirers do not include followers, nor do the honors bestowed on him include worship."

—*Robert Loring Allen*[1]

The development of capitalism as a historical phenomenon raises difficult issues in social theory generally, no less than in the transmission of ideas from one society to another—in this case, from Austria and Germany in the nineteenth century to the United States in the twentieth century. To summarize a social system in this fashion, as an "ism" rather than a structure, is to take account of a cultural and intellectual superstructure that is still evolving. For some it is a triumph of human organization, for others, it is a tragedy for human equality. And for still others, capitalism is a transitional form—marching on its merry way to one or another form of socialism.

For, as Schumpeter brilliantly understood, capitalism, whatever its empirical successes at the level of production of goods and services, has come to be seen as a system embodying a variety of values: competition, unevenness of reward, reward based on talent not need, trust based on repayment, and repayment based on trust. In some odd way, the United States is the veritable home of exceptionalism as a theory explaining social practice. But to explain this transmission belt in a unique set of circumstances is to show how America drew from German-Austrian theorists the sustenance for its presumed exceptionalism. If America practiced being different from Europe, Germany offered the theoretical underpinnings for sustaining such differences.

The problem of capitalism is not the same as the fact of capitalism. Capitalism as an intellectual superstructure first arises as a consequence of the utopian and Marxian emphasis on capitalism as a systemic link of empirical goods and ethical evils. *The Communist Manifesto* was a dramaturgy as well as historiography. It was a statement about a feudalism that had passed, and a socialism that was sure to follow. Capitalism was seen as the present moment sandwiched in between the past and the future. For most varieties of socialism—scientific and utopian—this historicist's vision provided hope to the hopeless and faith to the faithless.

Whatever kindness Marx bestowed on capitalism: its rationalization of production, its stripping away of theologies of resignation, its transformation impulses in all areas of social life, all were quickly dashed in a moral outburst against the inequities of reward in the capitalist economic system—inequities between capital and labor, rich and poor, men and women, and so on. It is hardly an exaggeration to say that every impulse we share for fairness in human dealings derives from this burning sense that while all people are equal in their biological origins, they are less than equal in their social outcomes. The moral fuel of anti-capitalism was the observable fact that inequities exist.

The intellectual superstructure of capitalism is, therefore, an overriding concern for the potentials of socialism—or better a question of ontological commitment to a fraud, the inevitable transformation of capitalism into communism. The bitter, acrimonious debates in Germany concerning socialism in backward Russia, feudalism in Middle Period China, trade union consciousness in advanced France, etc., were at their root and branch issues of the moral probity of systems and nations. With the emergence of fascism in Italy, Nazism in Germany, and militarism in Japan, the issue of capitalist transformation heated up, it did not die down. For, if National Socialism was the final desperate gasp of a dying system, society had one set of problems. However, if Nazism was simply a series of terrible aberrations that were a consequence of Statist power grabs, then post-totalitarian society had quite another set of issues to confront. Discussions of socialism were either muted or held in abeyance for social research.

Although the scene shifted from Germany due to intellectual migration, the issues did not die away; they were intensified. For, if capitalism was only capable of producing fascism, its own moral worth became exceptionally dubious. And so indeed, a majority of American scholars, under the impact of Horkheimer, Neumann and Marcuse, reacted. But a minority saw fascism as a blood brother of communism, a vulgar biologism well suited to a vulgar historicism. In such a scenario, as devised by Hannah Arendt and Karl Polanyi, it was the democratic content rather than the capitalist form of the West that became central. This split in Weimar ideology forms the intellectual background to the American discussions of capitalism in the post-war environment. It is a schism between nothing less than the anti-capitalist spirit on one side and the anti-totalitarian spirit on the other.

Let us start our brief excursion with a cursory look at the Austrian Marxists of the 1920s and 1930s. Why did the Austrians (and here I presume we are talking about the Austro-Marxism of Otto Bauer, Max Adler, Rudolf Hilferding and Karl Renner) remain overshadowed and with such little impact? The answer, I would claim must be sought, not in the development of capitalism as an historical phenomenon, but in the development of communism as an ideological aberration. Both Otto Bauer, in *Between Two Wars* and Wilhelm Reich in *The Mass Psychology of Fascism* understood that the assault on fascism was incomplete and ultimately incompetent, for it failed to see totalitarianism as the problem.

The Austrian School of Marxism, far more than the German School, saw this bureaucratization clearly and decisively. They were not heeded *because* of their closeness to the marrow of reality. In a climate of being reviled by the Soviets as ideological forerunners of social democratic revisionism, and ignored by the Anglo-American economists as being individualistic, more concerned with economic fossils than real world model-building, the Austrian school, however prescient, tended to be either denigrated in the East or downgraded in the West.

The specific contributions of the Austrian School were to announce the transformation of industrial capital into banking capital, thus creating finance capital; the fusion of capitalism, or a bourgeoisie, with the military in Germany, and hence the emergence of political economy as state capitalism; and the fact that the working class rather than the capitalist system is burst asunder in conditions of modern statism. But ultimately it was the failure of nerve of the Austrian School that limited its outreach, not to mention its study of capitalism as an historical phenomenon. Not a few of its key figures, such as Max Adler, took comfort as well as refuge in theological formulas by distinguishing the collapse of communism as a movement but the preservation of communism as a pure theory embedded in religion.

The dictatorship of the proletariat has become something entirely different from what was originally conceived by those who established it. It is not the dictatorship of freely elected soviets. It has become the dictatorship of an all-powerful party bureaucracy which stifles all freedom of speech and action even in the party itself, and it dominates the people by means of the powerful apparatus of the state and economic bureaucracy, the police, and the army.

There was no letting go of illusions; new reality was broken on the ground of old theory. And here the impact of the Austrian School, the most brilliant group of Marxists perhaps surpassing the Frankfurt School, but certainly their equal in analytical skills, simply crumbled, like the old Austro-Hungarian Empire, and worse, like the Austrian Republic before the Nazi onslaught.

The work of Karl August Wittfogel, a towering scholar, uniquely understood the issues posed by European scholars in the late 1930s: the problem was not "capitalism as a historical phenomenon," but the varieties of social forms and social systems compatible with the evolutionary historical process. It was Wittfogel, through his emphasis on the Asiatic Mode of Production, who opened up a generation of scholarship that accomplished a variety of extraordinary feats within the bowels of Marxism.

First, there was his rejection of unilinear concepts of systemic change. Second, Wittfogel moved beyond a simplistic theory of "capitalist" and "socialist" camps. To the contrary, he properly assumed pluralism in both economic systems, i.e., shading off into each other. Third, he appreciated that Russia was far more than a West European social formation. Quite the contrary, he put forth the notion that Soviet society was led by a ruling class subject to Oriental despotism. In this way the Soviet Empire became both authoritarian and militarized.

Soviet communist scholars, and their acolytes in the West, were haunted by the Asiatic Mode of Production because it made all notions of historical inevitability *prima facie* preposterous. Further, it made clear that, under communism, bureaucracy became the ruling class. But they were also

haunted by Wittfogel's none too subtle insistence that the
Soviet system, with the bulk of landmass east of the Urals
was also "Oriental" in its political system. The new premiers,
like the old czars, did not easily become swayed by the winds
of democracy blowing from the West. The revolutionary
"prototype" might have been the French Revolution, but the
reactionary "archetype" was that of the Mongols who came
west from the great steppes of Asia.

Wittfogel startled the Soviets with the bowels of Marxism
by taking real history and demonstrating the mythic character of its approach to China and Asia during the Stalinist
epoch. Thus, whatever Wittfogel's post-war political blun-
ders—his acquiescence too easily to the witch-hunting mentality—his intellectual contributions are so central to the very
essence of doctrines of inevitability that his place in American political debates is at least as secure as his place in German intellectual history. By showing the centrality of natural resources to the struggle for social control, he linked
issues of economy and environment in an innovative manner. This effort to understand the economy as a natural and
social process was central to European intellectuals who took
Marxism seriously but critically. Schumpeter, in a somewhat
different manner, utilized the language of capitalism as a
process not so much to establish the tenets of class struggle
or the contours of a history yet to appear, but as a conceptual map intended to show capitalism in its modern guise,
not so much as success or failure, but as the operative mode
of all developing societies.

Schumpeter's hero is not the *competitive marketplace* as a
system (as it was with Friedrich von Hayek and Milton Fried-
man) but the economic elite, the *creative entrepreneurs*. Cyclical fluctuations are not a deterrent to economic growth,
nor are they necessarily indicators of capitalist failure. Innovation and technological change are accompanied by
Kondratieff swings. Hence fluctuations, cycles of growth
and stagnation, are part of systemic health. Economic in-

equality exists in a world of dynamic change, and it is not a function of stagnation. Surplus value is defended as a value; while Schumpeter shines the empirical premises shared with Marx, he denies their moral import. This is also true about unemployment: yes, it exists, not an example of capitalist weakness, but as *accredited rewards*. Far from being a moral right, work, or better yet, the quality of work is a key factor in development, since the source of innovation is none other than work as a creative process, and not a natural right of workers or a threat mechanism wielded by unpleasant corporate rulers.

The main thrust of Schumpeter's work was not so much to frustrate Marxian doctrines of systemic transformation by suggesting structural modifications, as with Wittfogel and Hilferding, but rather to totally reverse the moral thrust of the empirical premises by asserting that the creative force in modern society is *entrepreneurship*. If the notion of capitalism is deprived of its worth to its enemies as a term of intense disapproval, then the mobilizing force of socialism is deprived of its chief weapon. By turning the notion of historical evolution on its head, capitalism becomes the source of socialism, not by class struggle, but by the very energies unleashed by the entrepreneurial class. This I take to be Schumpeter's lasting contribution, whether or not he left a "school" of thought like John Maynard Keynes.

The instabilities of capitalism for Schumpeter are nothing to be unduly concerned about, since the miraculous hidden hand of Adam Smith comes back in the form of modern equilibrium theory to save the day. But, alas, it fails to do so because the innovative spirit of capitalism cannot sustain itself within the boundaries mapped out by capitalism as such. And, in a rather bizarre summary by a great social scientist of the twentieth century, Schumpeter concludes a famous essay with one "short and imperfect" sentence: "Capitalism, whilst economically stable, and even gaining in stability, creates, by rationalizing the human, a mentality and a style of life incompatible with its own fundamental conditions, motives and social institutions, and will be changed, although not by economic necessity and probably even at some sacrifice of economic welfare, into an order of things which it will be merely a matter of taste and terminology to call Socialism or not."[2] Like the competitive economy, the modern welfare state is itself as much a product of capitalist evolution as its accompanying consumer culture. Thus capitalism tends to undermine the social values of mutuality, trust, and other elements of the civil society upon which liberal democratic regimes depend. It is the contradiction between economic laisser faire and political liberalism that is at the heart of the capitalist state; it must manage two irreconcilable first principles.

That the weakness of the post-modern welfare state was unknown to Schumpeter at the time is quite understandable, that the strengths of capitalism to create a powerful state to rationalize its interests were likewise unknown to him is less understandable. From Marx through Oppenheimer the belief in the phenomenon of the state rationalizing the interests of capitalism as a system was a commonplace. Yet, one looks in vain for a sense of the state in Schumpeter. He understood the contradictions of the system, and he knew the place of ideology in the modern economy, but not the source of ideology in the modern state.[3]

Schumpeter was no novice in politics, having served as Austrian finance minister during World War One. But his sentiments, as revealed in correspondence, indicate not simply a devotee to conservatism in the abstract, but to a monarchist transition with a power aristocracy at its head. Curiously, these personal predilections reveal clearly Schumpeter's lack of a notion of the modern state. When he does deal with the state it is in terms of the absolute monarchy—of seventeenth- and eighteenth-century notions of the state as a war machine run by monarchists who had less of a public and more of a private agenda. While he may have had leanings in the direction of totalitarianism, especially of the Nazi sort, he never saw the state as a functioning entity to either preserve the economic status quo, or as the instrument for meliorative reform of welfare practices and policies.

Thus, capitalism for Schumpeter was not so much the historic outcome of the democratic system, or for that matter the economic precursor of such a system and an economic order operating in a remote, independent realm. He bequeathed to the post-war generation of the United States a basic problem of the Austrian School: the relation of capitalism as an economic system to democracy as a state system. Whether one presupposed the other, or whether democracy could even exist apart from capitalism, was the sort of problem that disquieted Schumpeter. Indeed, his home grown acceptance of Sombart's idea that the Jews were the emotional as well as logical heirs to capitalism made him congenitally unhappy about prospects of capitalist survival, while his animus for the Jews as an unfairly advantaged group under capitalism made him equally displeased with prospects for democratic growth.

Schumpeter was far more of a sociologist than a political scientist. When he stepped outside of his role as a professional economist he turned toward a mechanism for reducing inequality, not ways to increase repressive order. He understood well the problem of social class. According the Schumpeter, the behavior of people toward one another was perceived as "a very dependable and useful symptom of the presence or absence of class cohesion among them." Further, such relations, the way people behave in social intercourse, were for Schumpeter the "shared social a priori" that made a society possible. In this, Schumpeter was far more the student of Simmel than of Weber. For Schumpeter, the modern welfare system has completed the work of the competitive economy by replacing familial, local and group allegiances with abstract bureaucratic machinery to a remote state. The modern welfare system completed the atomizing work of the marketplace in the area of social welfare and mutuality. Previously, traditional localities handled welfare and were the objects of political allegiance. Along with nationalization and globalization of the competitive economy, the growth of the modern bureaucratic order has effectively eroded all such allegiances.

Schumpeter's choice of patrimonialism as the essential pivot for the rise and fall of social classes betrays this strong identification with sociological rather than political explanations of bureaucracy. As with Weber, patrimonialism, by which he explained changes in class position, was a familial rather than coercive function. Patrimonialism was the means by which vital functions became hereditary and tended to become objects of the law of property. The office-holder or property-holder was a mechanism by which ownership by the nobles became first *de facto* then *de jure* an entity apart from the unified feudal system, a source of income, productive means and an object of tariff. Through this process, the aristocracy became a class, through which the individual emerges from the obligations and attitudes of feudal relationships, becoming in effect a citizen capable of shaping his destiny. Patrimonialism thus substituted in Schumpeter's world for statism. In this view, "state power meant no more than the sum total of the powers of the sovereign."[4]

Schumpeter viewed patrimonialism as achieving its highest level of being in princely domains, but throughout this was a familial affair. Ruling classes were family classes that succeeded. Ruled classes were essentially families and clans that simply never achieved fiscal or territorial ascendancy. It was therefore class function, whether of a military, political or peasant variety, that determined status, and no less, power. Shifts in the power of social class are essentially changes in economic rank. Schumpeter concludes that a class gains or loses position in the same way that it emerges and passes as a class. The problem of class structure is hence a problem in economic hierarchy. As to why such changes in family fortunes occur, Schumpeter, lacking any theory of state power falls back on a theory of individual aptitude, i.e.; those with creative minds and leadership potential survive and thrive. Those lacking such features fall. Dynasties thus rest on aptitudes. "Pure chance," Schumpeter maintains, largely determine specific changes in the fortunes of social classes.

In his more than one thousand page *History of Economic Analysis* one can hardly find a trace of the state. Even his review of historical sociology shows a complete lack of interest in the subject. If the state enters into the picture it is as a regulatory mechanism, a means whereby equilibrium in the economic system can be maintained. His belated bow to the rise of totalitarianism is revealing more for what he does not say than for the analysis. Indeed, the entire discussion of Nazi Germany, Fascist Italy, and Communist Russia takes just six pages of a 1,260-page work! He saw the task of Soviet economists as nothing more than "to hide their fundamental identity with the corresponding 'capitalist' concepts," and his brief remarks on Nazism and Fascism are reduced to unimpressive comments on "methods of teaching economic theory."[5] So, for something more substantial in Schumpeter's views on state and society we must turn to his later thoughts, in particular to his observations on the New Deal era.

Acknowledging this blind spot in the direct study of state power, Schumpeter's work, by extension and extrapolation, offers a coherent account of the growth of the modern welfare state and its relationship with political democracy. The rationalization of modern democratic citizens means that they eschew traditional loyalties, such as patriotism, self-reliance, altruism and mutual assistance. Instead, they must treat the state as economic clients. As rational individuals, new post-feudal citizens, tend to dismiss entrepreneurial efforts, innovation, and risk. Instead, they seek to minimize their tax burden while maximizing their consumption of

social services. This leads both to the growth of bureaucracy and to its crippling deficits that do in fact threaten
the viability of liberal democratic political economy.
Schumpeter, for all his reticence in confronting the state
head on, does appreciate that once the political relationship of citizenship becomes subsumed into the economic
relationship of consumer, modern liberal societies can
scarcely avoid instability. Again, even if Schumpeter himself
was unable or unprepared to pursue his own line of analysis, this insight into the contradiction of politics and economics has been pursued by key figures in the public choice
school, especially by James Buchanan and Gordon Tullock
in the *Calculus of Consent.*

Schumpeter had a pessimistic view of survival prospects
for capitalism equal to that of Marx, but not because of the
threat of totalitarian movements and regimes, rather because
of the inherent destabilizing elements in democracy. "The
reason, the deepest reason, why I think that capitalism won't
survive is the rationalizing effect the system has on our
minds. The effect the system has on doing away with everything traditional."[6] And thus it was the intellectual rejection, the questioning, of traditional loyalties that led to a
breakdown in discipline no less than tradition. He saw in
the American bourgeoisie naivete, an ability to educate its
enemies but not itself on the risks of modernity. "It absorbs
the slogans of current radicalism and seems quite willing to
undergo a process of conversion to a creed historically opposed to its very existence."[7]

While leading his readers right to the gates of the state,
Schumpeter seems to be unable to evolve any sort of theory
of state power as autonomous, as directing through its rationalizing modalities the ability to maintain and extend the
bases of capitalism, by preserving elements of the traditionalism he so believed in, such as entrepreneurialism, competition, and the spirit of innovation. In the absence of a political sociology, he was saddled with a political economy

that saw the state as some sort of sub-head of "social reconstruction." He concluded by seeing the New Deal as anticapitalist, instead of an entity which, in its very autonomy, created a state force capable of maintaining capitalism—not as it was in the eighteenth century, not as the driving force of advanced societies, but as a bridled system driven by new classes, new administrative chieftains, who saw in capitalist relations a tool more than a structure. It is not that Schumpeter was, as has been often claimed, conservative or even reactionary. Rather, it was that, lacking a sense of state power as autonomous and separate from economic conditions, he could only chart the history of modern times as a history of economic theories. And while his analysis was often brilliant, it was even more often wide of the empirical mark.

Schumpeter gave a shining substance to a view of society without the practice of politics. But, in explaining change within family, society and empire, the missing link of State power became an inscrutable dilemma, not just for Schumpeter, but for the entire Austrian School. Rather than treat the issue of power directly, as a group, they had a tendency to simply view the state as an impediment—an obstacle to gaining the good life. But this flew in the face of the constant growth of the State throughout Europe and America, thus making of society a repository of good things, rather than a source of problems unto itself. Latter day Schumpeterians of a liberal persuasion were left in an intellectual vacuum. As is the case with Lester Thurow, the evils of capitalism were recited as a litany: inflation, instability, moral venality, political conservatism; but at the end of the day, it was the end of communism that had to be explained.[8] For, totalitarianism as a category did not exist in the post-Schumpeterian world. Instead, communism was reduced to a "social system" that failed to meet the challenges. The drain of warfare, structural inefficiencies in factory management, the absence of overseas markets, and the usual suspects were dragged out once again in an effort to explain what could only be understood by a sense of the political, a sense of state power unbridled by popular will.

The Schumpeterian view not only bequeathed a legacy that sowed doubt and confusion among the liberal and left-intelligentsia, it also served up a dilemma to conservatism from which it has yet to escape, much less resolve—namely, the relationship between profit making and public virtue. It has been the conservative inheritance to feel uneasy about considering capitalism only as a growth system, not only for its own capacity to innovate, but also for its capacity to ward off the impact of totalitarian statism. It was this element that disturbed members of the Austrian School of economics, right and left. Across the political spectrum they shared a deep mistrust for democracy, however they felt about capitalism. And for those who saw the lock-step way in which the two seemed to be marching—if not in the past, then certainly in the present, this symbiotic relationship remained a haunting reminder that state power did not translate into socialist power, but into varieties of liberal and populist express unsuited to the temperaments if not the ends of the Austrian School. The rather tame celebration and cheering about the moral capacity of capitalism comes upon its historical incapacity to live up to such claims of systemic virtue. And in this, Schumpeter's caution may be understood as a problem in private enterprise, and not just a weakness in his analytic scheme.

Modern capitalism, for Schumpeter, as for Weber earlier, was not only the search for *profitability*, but also the search for *rationality*. Western capitalism is a prominent example of institutions, modes of domination, and cultural opening—but it is not the unique institution of Western society as claimed by Marxists. The uniqueness resides in the political opening to the masses—the conversion of a pure economic theory into an impure or mixed political economy of life chances. The dilemma became how the State, through its planning mechanisms and guided policies, created conditions for capitalist survival and, curiously, democratic growth at the same time. It is not for anything that the Austrian School is better united in what it opposed than in what it supported—in a standing animus for the open society as a product of the entrepreneurial spirit.

In this sense, Weber better understood the energies of capitalism than did Schumpeter. Unlike Schumpeter, he knew that subjective longings are as important as objective conditions; ideals are equal to materials. In practice the city is not simply a consequence of proletarianization, but a search for cosmopolitanism. In practice, the rise of Protestantism was not simply a reflection of present wars in Germany but an aspiration for new horizons and worlds to conquer in the name of truth. Weber was close to the American spirit because he forced individuals to examine psychological longings and political legitimization, no less than economic sources. Perhaps that is why he stands out so much from all other twentieth-century German figures who influenced American social science: the optimism of the forward thrust underlining the pessimism of the backward glance.

The most important aspect of Weber with respect to the politics of ideology is the relativizing of capitalism and socialism. Both economic systems were subsumed under the category of bureaucracy. The rationalizing, legitimating role of the state, its implicit admission not only of a new class, but a new political ruling class, moved American analysis under the influence of Weber to a study of totalitarianism—not abstractly, not with a reforming zeal, but as a conserving zeal, i.e., the preservation of the democratic polity. Quite beyond specifics, therefore, Weber had an impact on American social science equal or greater to his impact on his native Germany. The Americanization of European *Sozialpolitik* became a transformation from political economy to political sociology.

The Austrian tradition came to a crashing halt with what

Hartman once called the victory of the Hegelian ideal over the Hegelian dialectic; whereas, its more radical wing was frustrated by the hollow victory of the Marxian dialectic over Marxian ideals. In plain words, social welfare was the technique by means of which the capitalist system survived and thrived. And the state—not the bourgeois state but the autonomous state, became the instrument of this outcome— one that at the same time proved to be benevolent and diabolical. This was the defeat of Schumpeterian prognosis in the real world. To this must be added his own self-deceits: Schumpeter's absorption in imposed abstractions and an all too-ready acquiescence in nationalism and anti-Semitism. Abstracted visions themselves became suspect. Schumpeter became one of the victims of his own supplications of the impact of modernization on the industrial world.

The Austro-German impact on American culture, beyond its obviously selective, and at times myopic nature, is a testament to the pluralism of American democracy in search less of its capitalist roots than of its appropriate, if tailored, affluent destiny. Its ability or lack better measures the strength of capitalism in the United States thereof, to fend off the power of the state welfare system than by any purely economic indicator of growth.

In a broad ranging review of Schumpeter's *Capitalism, Socialism and Democracy,* Seymour Martin Lipset properly cautions us not to be too dismissive too quickly about the death of socialism as a consequence of the post-Soviet debacle. Indeed, arguing from Schumpeterian premises, Lipset notes that the continuing sense of self-interest (or greed) coupled with the absence of any utopian fervor in the goals of capitalism, serves to keep socialist appeals alive in advanced countries. "The struggle between the left, understood as the party of greater equality, and the right, understood as the defender of the status-quo, is not over" writes Lipset in his prophetic mode.[9] Indeed, the murmurs of discontent among the conservatives who share with many radicals' contempt for capitalism at its very moment of triumph, beckons to a continuing struggle between capitalist and socialist systems. That said, the embrace of advanced capitalism of modes of benevolence and the use of state power for enlarging the bases of social equity, changes the name of the political contest. The state as giver of welfare and succor may well negate the pessimistic stance of Schumpeter. But at the same time, it does so by changing the parameters between state and society as such.

The problem for the conservatism bequeathed by Schumpeter, and the Austrian School generally, is whether to send up cheers or huzzahs for capitalism. Clearly, much depends on whether capitalism is perceived as friendly to personal liberty and innovation or as a system grinding down such ambitions. In the long tradition from Edmund Burke to Russell Kirk, the hostility to capitalism is barely disguised, and not much different in its consequences from that displayed by the Marxists—although stemming from different intellectual sources. The sense that capitalism frustrates individual initiative and self- reliance and annihilates moral probity and religious observance alike, is strong in this tradition. The fact too that the family comes into disarray is laid at the footsteps of capitalism as a heartless system. In this way, older ideologies forged in an era of low- level technology find themselves at a loss to explain major shifts. They are reduced to volcanic and apocalyptic ex-post-facto modes of explanation.

On the other side, with scholars like Berger, Kristol and Novak, capitalism comes under reconsideration, but in a one-sided way. Post-industrial capitalism is seen as the great bulwark against totalitarianism, and in its innovative essence, as the carrier of democratic civilization as a whole. The issues of "paleo-" and "neo-" conservatism have been well described elsewhere and by others, but it is evidence that the unresolved attitude toward state power and capitalist economy is an essential source of the present conservative crack-up. If classical liberalism disintegrated under the impact of the need to incarnate government, or the state to adjudicate the needs and claims of the outsider classes, then classical conservatism seems to have done likewise by its incapacity to understand, much less approve of, the moral order that capitalism has engendered. Schumpeter's common sense spared him a manifest support for National Socialism, or for a creeping socialism with a capitalist core. But this was not a function of his theoretical framework. While good judgment may have preserved the reputation of the greatest Austrian economist of them all, the problem of the relationship between state and society not only failed to disappear, it became far more intense precisely because of his labors on imperialism, capitalism, entrepreneurialism, and social classes.

Notes

1. Robert Loring Allen, *Opening Doors: The Life and Work of Joseph Schumpeter, Vol. 2.* New Brunswick and London: Transaction Publishers, 1991. p. 255.
2. Joseph A. Schumpeter, *Essays on Entrepreneurs, Innovations, Business Cycles, and the Evolution of Capitalism* (1951). New Brunswick and London: Transaction Publishers, 1989. pp.71–72.
3. Ibid., p. 269.
4. Joseph A. Schumpeter, *Social Classes and Imperialism: Two Essays.* New York: Meridian Books (1919, 1927), New York: Meridian Books, 1955, esp. pp. 54–63; and 134–158.
5. Joseph A. Schumpeter, *History of Economic Analysis.* New York and London: Oxford University Press, 1954, esp. pp. 781–799; 1153–1159.
6. Joseph A. Schumpeter, "Can Capitalism Survive?" in *The Economics and Sociology of Capitalism,* edited by Richard Swedberg. Princeton: Princeton University Press, 1991 (originally written in 1936), p. 307.
7. Joseph A. Schumpeter, *Capitalism, Socialism and Democracy* (third edition). New York: Harper Brothers, 1947, pp.145–155.
8. Lester C. Thurow, *The Future of Capitalism: How Today's Economic Forces Shape Tomorrow's World.* New York: William Morrow & Co., 1996. Esp. 43–62, 242–278.
9. Seymour Martin Lipset, "Reflections on Capitalism, Socialism and Democracy". *Journal of Democracy.* Volume 4, Number 2, April 1993. pp. 54–55.

12

State, Military, Business:
The Trinity of Power: Mills

"C. Wright Mills' *The Power Elite* has become almost a Bible for a younger generation of "new Leftists" who have a deep-seated need to attack a society which they fail to understand. Mills' serious scholarship means little to them; it is his Marxist-Populist image of American society which captivates them."

—Arnold M. Rose[1]

The Power Elite is a work that was addressed to dangerous power tendencies at a time when few seriously thought it worthwhile to fuse sociology with moral commitment. The United States was emerging from a crippling cultural repressive period amidst a world of material plenty. One effect was to create a facade of government power that was unmistakably consensual. The critical evaluation of a great American celebration of its own power after the Second World War was needed. Mills's work attempted to throw cold water on national conceit and provide a warning that the possibilities of such power could lead to a reversal of the best democratic traditions in the American past.

Mills was less concerned with criticizing or defending specific agencies of power or institutions of repression than with holding the leadership of the United States answerable to its proclaimed democratic values. Sociologists who took this position looked to the classic tradition as necessary to the creation of important scientific literature. Mills emerged as a leading proponent of this point of view, which he and others believed, would restore to sociology great historical perspectives and contemporary relevance. This sentiment of the mid-1950s was best captured by the young Tom Bottomore, who clearly bore the traces of someone influenced by Mills's efforts to hold class divisions historically accountable to class actors:

> The principal fault in many recent studies of social classes has been that they lack an historical sense. Some sociologists have accepted that there was an historical development of classes and of class conflicts in the early period of industrial capitalism, but that this has ceased in the hilly evolved industrial societies in which the working class has escaped from poverty and has attained industrial and political citizenship. But this assumption is made without any real study of the evolution of social classes in recent times, or of the social movements at the present time which reveal the possibilities of future social change.[2]

Disheartened by the decline in significant concern about power issues, and by a style of small-range research that stood in perennial danger of becoming sterile and trivial unless its advocates moved on to larger generalizations, Mills and other sociologists, such as Robert Lynd and David Riesman, felt strongly that sociology should follow in the humanistic tradition that places science at the disposal of popular welfare. Their writings, and symposia of various kinds, upheld the significance of the uses of technology and power as a compelling subject for sociological attention. Arthur Kornhauser's anthology *Problems of Power in American Democracy*, which included a contribution by Mills, reflected an array of monumental social science options.[3] *Class, Status and Power*, edited by Reinhard Bendix and Seymour Martin Lipset, collected past and present social science studies and opinions on stratification and power, their nature and exercise.[4]

Two orientations developed among post-Second World War sociologists concerned with power analysis: they could be distinguished as consensus notions versus "veto-effect" notions. Mills represented the former position, and Riesman best expressed the latter. The idea of power consensus is based on a conception of power involving groups of individuals who see in their command positions a source of common interest and who collectively guard their power, regardless of other differences, against the vast majority. The sources of their power may derive from economic wealth, personal or professional prestige, or control of political machinery, and may be practiced democratically or not. The fact that some individuals control vast power creates constraints on behavior, whatever the origins and sources of that power might be. In this, Mills remained true to his empirical approach to stratification at its upper reaches.

The Power Elite helped formulate essential questions of power and liberty and restore them to sociological inquiry.[5] Social definitions of power and stratification for Mills derived basically from the European tradition in sociology. He used Max Weber and his linkage of class, status, and power to define the chief stratifying elements in group life; he was influenced by Gaetano Mosca, especially his political definition of power (rather than the Marxist economic emphasis); and he was made strongly "status conscious" through the early influence of Thorstein Veblen on his thinking. Mills conceived *The Power Elite* as a practical application of these notions to the present American scene. With a vigorous journalistic imagination, he "exposed" the issue in a manner not unlike American muckrakers of the early part of this century.

On the other side of the issue, and not necessarily completely distinct from Mills and his colleagues, were the veto-effect notions best exemplified in the sociological literature by David Riesman's *The Lonely Crowd*.[6] Riesman and Mills were considered the leading sociological "power theorists" of the decade of the fifties. Other voices engaged in the dialogue; Lipset[7] and Parsons[8] added vital contributions to the debate. But Mills and Riesman had a brilliant gift for summation and for formulation of fresh terms in which to express social experience. Not surprisingly, the language and jargon of both men became widely popularized, and they are often considered archetypes of their respective points of view.

David Riesman's notion of veto effect was a theory of power which differed from a power-elite approach by viewing influential groups as interest elements whose power is limited by either psychologically felt or socially imposed limitations to power concentration. Riesman emphasized the high risks in the constant use of power. Like energy, power can run down (something Mills failed to note); hence the relationships of powerful groups are diffuse, distant, and limited. To see that a group has power is not the same as to predict accurately how and to what ends such power will be employed.

Despite their differences, the positions of Mills and Riesman reflect strong starting points in common.[9] Powerful persons are no longer highly individualized characters. The vast majority of American society—comprising a "mass," a "public," or the "other-directed" middle-class consumer— is a vague amalgam that has surrendered active defense of its own interests or active participation in serious political dialogue and organization. Both positions see in the people anomie, and the in powerful who guide or dominate their lives anonymity. The powerful may be a cohesive elite for Mills, or an amorphous collection of small, competitive groups making a unified "top stratum" impossible for Riesman, but neither characterizes the powerful as bearing any burdens of principle or responsibility. Both the power-elite and veto-group positions reflect the mood of the decade of the fifties. They reveal a utopian nostalgia for romantic individualism, courage, and the bearing of responsibility by a concerned and politically involved public. Both reflect a feeling of loss for the past and dissatisfaction with the bland and seemingly uncommitted decade of the fifties.

The earlier work of the Lynds had argued that power was institutionally located and had emphasized its inherent tendency to concentration.[10] They described this as the "energy" of a social order, and as such, inevitable. The environment in sociology supported the institutions of government and business as great power agencies and considered the small number of "chairs at the top" of these hierarchies as major repositories of power. Sociology saw the problem as how to "harness" power for socially humane purposes while maintaining the pluralist ideal of curbing its extension over an illegitimate range of purposes. In this context, Mills addressed himself to the social effects and desirability of power concentration per se and found that the dangerous anonymity of decision-making behavior inherently tended to create irresponsibility, secrecy, and unsavory manipulation.

Mills was attempting to fix responsibility, and hence provide a moral dimension, for the exercise of power in large-scale decision making. He employed "structural clues" to identify the positions and decisions involved in the exercise of power in the United States, basically an inferential method of establishing the existence and range of a power elite. Mills rejected a notion that one sector, such as the military or the economy, was a singular source of power, and upheld instead the interrelationship of polity, economy, and military, considering leadership in any of these sectors to yield power. The elite is one of power rather than of mere wealth or status alone, but it is enhanced by the abundant presence of the latter two factors.

Implicit in Mills's free-swinging critique of "mindlessness," of "crackpot realism," of "hard" decision makers, is an approach strongly flavored by the pragmatic style, as is his resort to "educated publics" as a countervailing force to ir-

responsible or secretive power administration and policy
making. But his division of the political order into a ruling
minority and a vast, basically fragmented mass is drawn from
the sociological thinking of the Franco-Italian school no less
than from the German-exiled Europeans. His decisive fusion of these European currents with pragmatic orientations,
in combination, made a new sociology possible.

Mills saw liberals emanating only from the pragmatic tradition as powerless and nostalgic people, grown tired and
acquiescent with age. As professional philosophers they were
attracted to logical positivism with its love for technical and
linguistic analysis and were led away from a passion for applied research on social questions. But pragmatism had a
popular dimension, the "journalistic" tradition of exposing
social inequity designed to stimulate public action, and this
was the liberalism which Mills looked for among his fellow
academicians.

For Mills, the "muckrakers" set a radical liberal style.
Upton Sinclair, Ida Tarbell, and Lincoln Steffens were not
concerned with the overthrow or even an analysis, of the
capitalist system. They were issue-oriented, concerned with
moral advertisement of the unjust or corrupt practices of a
given industry, not of industrialism in general. They pressed
for reform of certain social practices, not of the social system. These were, in a sense, pragmatic sociologists, and their
theoretical energies were directed at the immediate, the
practical, and the reformable. But Mills aimed not only at
"exposure," but also at the study of essential characteristics.
His attention was directed primarily to social groups and
secondarily to overtly political battles. Weber, Michels,
Veblen, even Freud, became pragmatically useful rather than
intellectually enticing. Mills searched various intellectual
systems in order to make their many parts "operate" on the
stuff of the social world, which is one reason his legacy may
seem so dubious on methodological grounds.

To counter the dangerous possibilities of an unchecked

power elite, Mills sought to restore and protect, activate, and even lead an educated public to self-assertion. He consciously believed in the potential of reason, information, and public criticism as an answer to the updated Machiavellianism of James Burnham. Mills saw the "brake" on elite power as stemming from the political awareness of educated publics, which, tragically, became increasingly amorphous as the great stratification trilogy came to a climax.

The Power Elite seeks to demonstrate that a locally based scatter of power pockets, based largely on property ownership and solidified by upper-class families as property-owning units, has given way to a solidly compact and widespread network of power that resides in nameless, safely entrenched "top strata." Property ownership perpetuated through family inheritance has given way to the systematized management of corporate wealth, marking a great change in the exercise and maintenance of power in the United States. Starting from the romantic pluralism of Jeffersonian America, Mills sees fragmentation and dispersion of power reaching its climax and initial stages of deterioration in the nineteenth century. *The Power Elite* is a study of national patterns of power over a one-hundred-year span of American history. In this, Mills's work differs from kindred works like Floyd Hunter's *Community Power Structure*,[11] which never get beyond local or regional considerations.

The concentration of power occurred as a consequence of changes in the technological machinery for producing material wealth, which allowed for rationalization of social relations in the form of centralized management and control of social wealth. Locally based elites, when given holdings that made it logically in their interest to do so, entered into new combinations or allowed them to merge with large economic institutions and monopolies. This pattern of absorption and displacement dominated the life of the country until all competitive power groups were bypassed, absorbed, or crushed by a cohesive power elite.

Critics have said that Mills's power coherence scheme illustrates a highly exceptional circumstance; that in the main,
powerful groups compete with, fragment, defeat, or coun-
tervail one another and limit their spheres of influence. It is
also said that Mills's exposé is little more than a naive discovery that power is not always and everywhere wielded
democratically, even in a democracy. The nature of politics
requires that the powerful exercise a certain amount of secrecy and manipulation since that is the only ways to keep
power and use it. But Mills does not argue with either of
these premises. Without denying the validity of the criticisms, it must be said that Mills's examination of a power
elite does identify a worrisome trend in United States power
patterns over half a century.

Despite the competitive groups that make up a power alliance at any given time, centralization of authority, as part
of its rationalization around modern technology, has vested
increasing power in heads of vast bureaucratic organizations,
and in the informal and non-elected top strata of advisers
surrounding the executive of the federal government. Mills
emphasizes the increasing importance of the non-elected,
appointed, powerful experts who back up executive decisions. Simply stated, whatever the competitive status of powerful and prestigious groups with respect to each other, all
are losing a sense of responsibility to the public for whom
they ostensibly make decisions; all are unable or unwilling
to be subject to a popular will; all operate anonymously without the mandate of election and without being obliged to
give candid and publicly stated explanations for their acts.

The power elite is not a monolithic bloc, but rather a
nameless non-elected, and hence non-responsible body acting without the support and knowledge of a vast public.
The absence of enlightened public opinion and inquiry, jeal-
ously guarding its rights and exerting its influence, makes
such an elite possible. For Mills, the power elite is made
cohesive by its ability to manage public affairs in a relatively

uncontested manner. Its consensus is not conspiratorial but arises out of a need for a coherent policy despite certain class antagonisms. Mills seeks to restore public responsibility on the part of top decision-makers, to restore the tension between an enlightened public and their elected officials. Beyond this lies a plea for restoration of an interest-bound public concerned with issues, rather than a gradual development of a frightened, nameless, and acquiescent "mass."

The Marxist position on power, aside from taking as its fundamental premise a class society dominated by an economic ruling class, is based on a concept of social battle or class struggle. This struggle, which is carried out by classes characteristic of a given mode of social production, is sometimes conscious, as, for example, in revolutionary periods. For Mills, power "stratifies" into a hierarchy. At each level in the hierarchy, power or interest groups may compete, but "upper" and "lower" levels are not set in combat against each other; one does not overcome the other in order to maintain and exercise power. There is a "rise" through the acquisition of wealth and prestige. Groups concentrate around the "means of production" and crystallize into status hierarchies, manifesting power differences. Social competition rather than class struggle is the norm—competition is within the power elite and not between the masses and their rulers.

Once the social means of power are concentrated, competition for control begins to manifest itself in possession, delegation, and display of authority. Since such power inheres in the decision-making positions themselves, struggle for power replaces class struggles. Passage to the ranks of the powerful, accomplished initially through acquisition of strategic wealth, is a passage into a realm removed from the "people," the "public," or the "masses." The struggle for power is not consciously carried on to subdue and dominate mass society, but is waged in order to rise into another level of existence entirely, which is responsive only to a mobilized challenge "from below."

The looseness in Mills's use of the phrase "power elite" has made him vulnerable to his critics. The concept fails to account for the property-distribution patterns and political character of a capitalist system as differentiated from a socialist or other system. Some critics have argued that the implied universality of the power-elite scheme lacks specificity about the social system in which elite groups operate and by which they are determined. For sociologists like Lynd, this was a failing in all analyses of elites, and he found political science distasteful because it held such analyses in high regard.

In *The Power Elite,* Mills set himself a clear task: concern with general conditions of "modernity" rather than with "capitalism." His approach blurred capitalism's line of continuity with the past as well as the characteristics peculiar to capitalism. Mills believed that modern technological rationalization and the concomitant centralization of authority were more significant than the uniqueness of any system; they were, in fact, destroying such uniqueness. His unpublished writings attest to his belief that economic "systems" were giving way increasingly to a universal technological style. "Power elites" marked the Soviet Union as well as the United States; their differences were increasingly ideological, and decreasingly economic.

In preliminary drafts and studies for unpublished works, Mills showed his fascination with characteristics of the twentieth century that were reflected on a worldwide scale. Influenced by the work of Isaac Deutscher and Edward H. Carr, Mills searched out shared characteristics of the United States and the Soviet Union which were the result of their convergent status as competitive giants, industrial complexes, and mass societies. He saw their patterns of stratification and social goals as providing a base for comparing similarities, especially because few saw these comparisons as valid.

Mills's intellectual energies were increasingly directed toward creating historically relevant political sociology which would get beyond a liberal rhetoric inherited from the "bourgeois" revolutions of 1789 and 1848, and a Marxology which was also useful only between 1848 and 1918. For Mills, liberalism disintegrated after the revolutions of 1848 because the middle classes could not deliver on their promises. Universal truth, free conscience, unfettered choice, all became disguised supports for capitalist systems and colonialist expansions. Likewise, official communism, while culminating in the deliverance of the Russian masses from capitalism, at the same time outflanked Marx's humanism and transformed proletarian rule into bureaucratic rule, political association into party life, and voluntary association into terrorist cliques. Just as Anglo-American liberalism collapsed when socialism became a world-rallying cry, so too did Russian Bolshevism collapse, intellectually at least. In his unpublished writings Mills treats socialism as larger than American or Russian nationalism. *The Power Elite* carries the ever-present implication that industrialism overrides systematic political differences to a sufficient extent to enable us to look for "global developments" as well as unique national differences.

His scientific "looseness" was intentional. He discarded traditional notions of ruling class domination, defining the powerful as those "who are able to realize their will even if others resist it." He was influenced by, but did not adopt, traditional Socialist approaches. For him, there were no impersonal "laws" of social movement; social movements created "laws." He departed strongly from the heavily felt influence of Pareto. For Pareto, there are clusters of elites around goods and values and, therefore, many kinds of elites. But Mills holds that the interrelationship of these groups yields a new unity, and a coherent concentration, which creates a passage from quantity to quality. Under new technological conditions, smaller and plural elites are transformed into a single elite, growing smaller in number as they acquire greater decision-making power.

Mills explicitly rejects a notion of a ruling political elite after the model of Mosca. He considers this concept of a "creative" or "tightly organized" minority to be tautological since it says nothing of the character of such an elite and does not deal with sources of power. Even when it throws light on the craft of ruling, it is not applicable to present conditions in the United States, which is always Mills's first concern.

Mills specifically disowns conspiratorial notions of power manipulation, although he has been criticized on such grounds. Daniel Bell's critique is a case in point. However, though Mills's analysis does verge on conspiratorial implications, these chiefly derive from his resentment of anonymous or non-responsible authority. He does not ascribe to the prevailing elite either a conscious or a malicious determination to rule behind the backs of the people. Mills is concerned with the issue of which groups have how much power at the present time, rather than how such power has been acquired.

Mills begins *The Power Elite* with a broad look at the "Higher Circles," intended to capture the present power atmosphere. He distinguishes the upper power levels from the "ordinary" activities of most people. The crystallization of big power groups is based upon their social location. From this follows their other distinctions and ultimately their elite status. Appearance, education, and other "achievement" items separate people into various levels of prestige, but power underlies and upholds these differences and determines their level of importance. Such power involves the heaviest and farthest-ranging decision making in history. Command posts are at the head of the three major hierarchies: state, corporation, and military. Their interdependence in the present century has blurred the lines of authority amongst them, but has not resulted in any lessening of the concentration of power as a whole. The acquisition of wealth now occurs within these sectors, since nothing of import exists outside of them. And acquisition of wealth within their ranks is the first step to power.

Mills builds structures by means of architectural metaphors: top level, middle level, and public, mass level (which remains basically dormant). The powers of the last-named may or may not be exerted. The masses may exhibit a high state of powerlessness, even if it derives from unthinking surrender rather than imposed domination. Society, once led by competitive families and politicians at various levels of government office, now confines these to a middle level of power. To acquire great wealth it is necessary to combine moneymaking with entry into a national elite, since its organs and instruments are necessary to such wealth because conventional avenues have been blocked off.

Despite their secure positions as heads of corporations, the state and the military, the power elite is not socially visible in the same way that older aristocratic elites were in Europe. The United States has never passed through a feudal period, and there is consequently less emphasis on conspicuous displays of power than in societies with a feudal heritage. This is all the more the case because middle-class technicians are being raised to new heights of power in a society that is increasingly complex. What is more, a decrease of wealth in the hands of individuals makes the display of power more difficult to appreciate. This is not the case with state, military, and corporate leaders living in a democracy; institutions have no problems with egoism. Continuing this implicit critique of Veblen, Mills notes that their posts concentrate more power in the hands of a few than wealth could command—more than any individual could possibly amass in his or her own person.

Far from being "alienated," this relatively impersonal stratum comes to believe in its own worthiness and begins to live an approximation of the qualities others impute to it. But, contrary to the beliefs of a conservative and romantic humanism, the new power elite does not rise from people

with superior personal qualities. Top positions shape
personality, creating people equipped to serve their needs,
which may not necessarily be those of leadership and
intelligence.

Mills claims three major keys to understanding the cohe-
siveness of the elite. First, there is the psychological identity
of elites with one another through a community of education, similar social origins, sharing the prestige that accrues
to them, and social and political intermingling. Second, these
psychological factors are backed up by the structure and mechanics of institutional hierarchies, in which organizational
similarities and the fact of occupying command positions
further shapes a conscious community of interest and personal similarities. Third, the mechanics of these hierarchies,
the fact of intermingling, will produce a need for stricter co-
ordination. This coordination intensifies the above features
but is initially produced by the pressures for efficiency.

Prior to the shift of wealth and power to the metropolis,
local control in America was what counted. The United States
was a "scatter" of locally powerful elites in whose hands lay
the wealth of the country. The class, status, and power systems of local societies were relatively equally weighted. The
professional politician, whatever he was or was not in other
respects, represented a powerful voice for these elite interests. The "new technology" brought into being a new group
whose wealth no longer derived from property or "raw" goods
but rather from technology, manufacturing, and industrial
investment, and eventually monopoly empires were built.

Before that point was reached these new industrializing
classes successfully engaged the "old local families" in battles
for social eminence, wealth, and industrial potency. Manufacturing, the strategic source of wealth and power, soon
overcame the old local society prestige and power system.
The "old family" was overcome by "new money" derived
from enterprises with which it had little or no connection.
The "pedigrees" and status old families had acquired still

lingered, but they no longer represented real power. The new manufacturing middle classes became national in the scope of their wealth; political representation, and hence power and prestige, were underwritten by the growth of the industrial metropolis. A great American fiction and nonfiction literature exists to illustrate this nineteenth-century social drama.

In the pre-Civil War years the big-city upper classes were a stable and close group, living on riches derived from landed wealth, inheritance, and speculative investments. After the post-Civil War boom in the industrializing North, these classes were overwhelmed with new money. The *Social Register* was, and remains, their chief source of socially recognized status. Graduates of those university institutions that keep the "top" supplied are likely to be intimate with this "Four Hundred," and through this association new wealth may acquire a certain distinction. Hence the Four Hundred are connected to, but not decidedly in, the power elite. Like local elites, they are the living reflection of another era, but their location and great wealth have given them the possibility of "hanging on."

The celebrity system creates another sphere of influence or means of acquiring it. Celebrities are loosely speaking, "names" that need no further identification. They are not people of power, but they are people of wealth and considerable prestige. They are surrounded by prestigious accoutrements and are identified in the popular imagination with power and influence. They are more a reflection of than a part of a power elite.

Mills never makes his discussion of the celebrity explicitly relevant to *The Power Elite.* He seems to be interested in accounting for various patterns of success in an affluent society. However, he does not elaborate on, or solidly establish, connections between the "celebrity" and the "power elite" except to point out the new celebrity style of symbolic prestige. The very rich and, consequently, the very power-

ful of today rose from the ranks of big business. Their wealth
came not out of their adventurousness (though this was a
trait of some) nor out of greed or guile (though this, too,
may explain certain fortunes) but rather out of what Mills
calls the "structure of opportunities." No single person could
have built, out of his or her own achievement orientation,
the vast business empires and combines that manage and
constitute today's industry. At one time America was a domain of untapped wealth to which millions of people migrated. Its population steadily rose, its land values increased,
and its markets developed. Through the use or violation of
existing legal statutes, and the passage of new ones protect-
ing the rights of property in the form of the corporation,
fortunes were accumulated. The state provided guarantees
for the property-owning rights of great fortunes and in various ways protected the corporation. The corporation became a means to manipulate existing law to the advantage
of industrial enterprises.

Behind corporate wealth, individuals continue to collect
personal fortunes of unprecedented size. This class of people
is called "the very rich." These people are not necessarily
managers or caretakers of wealth, but they are recipients of
the corporation's greatest monetary rewards. They hold its
top seats and are its chief investors. Those who enter the corporate ranks without already possessing a considerable fortune find it almost impossible to acquire enough to climb to
the top. The propertied family and the wealthy continue to
supply the top ranks of corporate life, which in turn operate
through a host of legal technicians and agents to protect their
wealth. The corporation has made the very rich less visible
than they once were, but no less powerful and no less wealthy.

Chief executives of the corporation are another component of the power elite. These new industrial captains are
quite different from the entrepreneur of past epochs. They
are not owners of corporate properties, yet they manage
these complexes. They are not clearly distinguishable from

the "very rich" who actually own the corporations, yet they constitute a distinctly twentieth-century group produced by the centralization and rationalization of private property. Corporate ownership breeds loyalties to industry as a whole rather than to the individual firm. Despite such corporate realities, Mills claims that the illusion of personal ownership in corporations is widespread. In reality, individual ownership is restricted, and management even more so. The top corporations are knit together by associations within their respective industries and regions, and by their common interests. This intricate machinery—that is, the technology of corporate management organized into profit-making centers—lends itself to central control. Management is increasingly becoming management of automated machines rather than people, and social problems are placed within an entirely manipulated context, one that emphasizes psychological rather than economic issues.

The executives in these top corporation posts are drawn from urban, upper-middle-class, Protestant, and entrepreneurial circles. Mills finds that in type and background, the factors that bind those chief executives are stronger than those that divide. "Free markets," "free competition," the fragmenting tendencies of the past, have given way to corporate consolidation. In this fact Mills sees the potential and the dangers of central control.

The rise of military commanders to the top strata of power is connected to the rise of the United States to international political preeminence. Military power in a big nation brings about the "return of the warlord" and a new military ascendancy. The national state has monopolized the "means of violence," and the new military is head of a heavily centralized organization that is increasingly vocal in national affairs. Formerly, armies in the employ of kings and nobles fought or conquered each other, but violence was limited and local, and power tended to re-create itself in localized areas and in multiple centers. Revolutionary periods may have created temporary "people's militias," but the "standing army" is the product of the modern nation-state. The military establishment is a thing apart.

In the nineteenth century the United States was preoccupied with making money and producing goods. Its middle class defended individual freedom, and the Constitution discouraged military preeminence in government. The early American elites were not a military caste or of a military temper. However, the increasing involvement of the United States government in the military and political life of foreign countries, the fact of recurring warfare, and the increasing United States involvement in colonial acts, in acts of "official violence," all demanded the maintenance and increase of military forces. As the American means of violence enlarged and became increasingly centralized, crystallizing into a major bureaucratic hierarchy, those in top military positions found themselves automatically in command of enormous centers of power. Increasingly, a military elite has informed presidential policy, particularly by a non-elected Joint Chiefs of Staff. And immediately below them is a high-ranking circle of generals and admirals exercising control over the far-flung military apparatus.

Mills traces the careers of military chiefs, establishing the overlapping training, religious affiliation, and psychological similarities of this new elite. Due to its honorable reputation, based on patriotic defense of the nation-state unit, the military is absorbed into the same status system that honors the corporate rich. The military tends to rely on industrial interests to produce its wares and weaponry. It underwrites, through funds granted by Congress, research employing industrial help and carried out in geographic locales of its own choosing. Just as industry has become bureaucratized, so the military person's managerial skill in a bureaucracy has become highly valued in industry. Hence military personnel have become a source for top industrial and corporate posts.

Because of the complexity of weaponry, the new types of military encounters, and the terrible dangers of modern means of violence, foreign policy is in genuine need of military expertise. The "middle levels" of power—Congress, special-interest groups, and so on—cannot provide adequate information for policy purposes, or are so fragmented as to be periodically incapable of influencing policy or counteracting undue military influence. Thus, the military fills a void rather than competes for power. Popular will or elections do not check military commanders; only executive resistance potentially checks military power. Because the military can act with fewer restrictions than other government agencies, its power is enhanced, and with it its conscious will and ability to press power to the limit.

Mills believed that America had never cultivated the art of diplomacy. It drew from both business and political circles, but it did not have a solid core of diplomatic professionals. The military, therefore, had the "space" to move into the higher councils of diplomacy. Production contracts between the military and corporate industry, overlapping directorates between the two, mutual absorption in the status system—all of these brought industry and the military into a top-echelon consensus. Thus, they became increasingly necessary for one another's policies and plans, and they are now enmeshed in a network of interdependent personnel and interests.

Like the other major hierarchies, the state has become enlarged and the scope of its activities has reached unprecedented domains. For information and such influence as professional politicians are able to exert, they, too, have become dependent on the welter of government agencies. Their chief arena, Congress, is so swollen, complicated, and bound by local and state pressures that politicians can barely consider issues of national (much less international) import. Their prestige has always been insecure in a country suspicious of politics, and the party that brings them forward is increasingly like its rival. The big issues of war and peace are largely outside the sphere of influence of party politicians. The need for efficient solving of issues of national and international importance has forced a greater role on the executive, which surrounds itself by advisory bodies drawn from the military and corporate elites.

Professional politicians have given way to "higher politicians," individuals with policy concerns who may be drawn to their task through idealistic or opportunistic motives. The money received in such a policy-making capacity is of little consequence; but the power and status that accrue to these politicians are tremendous. In direct concert with the executive, and over the heads of Congress—the leading cadre of policy makers makes the nation's most important decisions the old politicians' battleground—. There is little check on such decision-making power, and the freedom of operation the higher politicians enjoy is not matched elsewhere in political life.

The new "political outsiders" have superseded political institutions and politicians below the higher politicians. Party politicians in Congress are limited by responsibility to their constituencies and the political party sponsoring their career. "Bureaucratic politicians" are lodged in administrative agencies where they can work with or against the party politicians, but the limits of bureaucratic mobility and a semi-organized array of agency organs bind them. Political outsiders are neither party politicians nor bureaucratic politicians. They come straight to the top from military and corporate headquarters to advise the executive. They may cultivate helpful relations with elected officials, but they are freer than the elected officials to make policy, exert influence, and extract prestige. The party politician and the party bureaucrat are essentially the middle level of power. The non-elected, presidential appointed advisory official is an adjunct to the higher politician. In this way the policy process is brought inside the power elite.

Mills maintains that the rise of the "expert" in the United States was secured by the relative absence of a well-trained, informed, prestigious, and meritorious bureaucracy. The expertise and far-reaching view of the political outsider exists, in fact, in lieu of an efficient civil service. Thus, Mills claims that the U.S. government has never maintained a genuine bureaucracy in whom authority, rather than being wielded personally, is vested in the offices the bureaucrats occupy. The check upon development of an administrative bureaucracy is held to be the patronage system of the parties, which pays off party workers and supporters.

The old model of power assumed a plurality of independent, conflictual groups that settled into an uneasy social balance. Yet these represent, for Mills, the middle levels of power in which plural groups are hopelessly stalemated, despite occasional overlapping interests, they are essentially disunited. The emphasis of social scientists working in policy contexts is positivistic. They focus on appearance to such an extent that, Mills claims, "unseen" larger connections are simply not considered subject to scrutiny. Consequently, the emphasis on middle-level interest or veto groups has obscured a view of the structure of power as a whole, especially the top and bottom levels. The political sociologist has become a student of isolated political acts, of election behavior, and has thus lost the big picture. Because social scientists are a product of the professional middle class, their political activities and contacts are likely to be limited to middle levels of power, and they universalize this experience. Sociologists thus tend to bless the status quo, for the balance of power implies equality of power. What the social science observer often forgets is that a balance reached at a given moment seems fair only to those it favors. Hence the critic of a balance-of-power theory is likely to see a given balance as unfavorable and look to the larger structure of power in order to evaluate the sources of inequity.

Federal checks and balances have made the centralization of power in this country difficult, if not impossible. But for Mills, they serve more to check popular pressure than to accommodate it. "Divide and rule" prevents total power from centering on an individual or office, but it offers no justification for denial of a power elite. It rests upon the point of harmony between interests. But disharmony of interest is chiefly applied, in perfect sincerity, to public challenge rather than to political representatives.

Increasingly, political representation is deriving from monied groups, and the country is close to a dangerous decline in middle-class representation at the middle-power levels. Factors diminishing the political power of the middle classes lessen the effectiveness of the theory of checks and balances. Mills sees power at the top as relatively unchecked except for the convenience it finds in maintaining a democratic facade. The existence of a power elite, of which the public is vaguely aware, anonymous and little restricted except by the pressures of competing strains within its ranks, overrides the traditional middle-class politics of America.

The 1950s produced a pronounced conservative mood that pervaded the United States. Mills considered American conservatism far from a distinctive philosophy, bereft of a genuine class base or the possession of a classic tradition. Conservatism in its classic form, he said, involves some "natural aristocracy" suited for rule. The traditions it embodies are taken to be the cohesive element of society, responsible for its cultivated leadership and careful decision making. European conservatism has a philosophic bias in favor of an irrational "natural order" that reason must always exert itself to defend. The European conservative believes that real change is impossible, and consequently those who seek it can only bring chaos.

But in America there was no solid pre-capitalist class base to support a natural aristocracy. What is more, the competitiveness of American capitalism encouraged the ideal of the self-made individual and represented a constant challenge to a natural aristocracy. The European feudal order, its traditions and mores, and the classes and viewpoints stemming from it, are prerequisites for a society wishing to bring conservatism forward as a political credo. Capitalism became clothed in the ideology of liberalism, and the official ideology of United States capitalism from the outset has been liberalism. By refusing to acknowledge the facts of present-day power, liberalism has become nostalgic. Its rhetoric is itself the chief form of a new American conservative policy.

Periodically, disgruntled middle-class elements respond to challenges to their prestige with a reactionary policy orientation. But the top levels of power rarely support this. American conservatism is actually pluralistic: liberalism turned rhetorical, even fanciful. As a result, no serious opposition to ideological liberalism has crystallized. It has never shed its pretensions and continues to repose in absolute safety. The celebration of American life as supremely virtuous is seen by Mills to be the unfolding of the liberal rhetoric. This newer liberalism—and here Mills seems to have had in mind the young Arthur M. Schlesinger, Jr.—has no critical edge and lives on in an America that was, creating a reality to suit itself.

Without a class base for classic conservatism, liberal conservatism sees the natural aristocracy of the United States in a scatter of morally superior persons corresponding to locally based elites and the quality of middle-level political leadership. While there is no aristocratic class, the aristocratic ethos settles upon the exemplars of an uncritical liberal rhetoric. The petty-bourgeois right has an appeal to status-frustrated individuals, but these political fragments cannot generally be lumped with the conservative mood. By implication it falls to the "political left" in any given period to support real change in America or at least to provide some measure of criticism of the status quo.

The New Deal consolidated, even adapted, liberalism for the present day. Its victory between 1933 and 1945 effected a solid public loyalty to liberalism. The end of the Depression, brought about by the shadows of world war, consolidated this victory. Problems shifted from mass unemployment to mass culture. Most people seek status diversions and emblems. Defenders of what Mills called "Machiavellianism for the little man" stifle political criticism on a public scale and challenge nothing and no one at the top power-levels of the society. The top leadership is thereby deprived of the most intelligent and sensitive elements, and a mindlessness afflicts those holding the top posts because there is no critical public pressure to ensure that the very best do rise to the top. The separation of knowledge and sensibility from the top command posts and even from the middle levels of power, as well as the disaffection of the public from its critical responsibility, are reflected in and are the essence of the higher immorality in mass society. The result is organized irresponsibility.

The Power Elite was the object of furious controversy that has hardly abated with time.[12] When an American social scientist produces a book that attempts to evaluate the whole of United States society, such an effort is impossible to ignore. What is more, Mills wrote in a morally charged tone of indictment that invited challenge. Writing in The American Journal of Sociology, Bell suggests that The Power Elite does not describe a specific instance of power allocation but a scheme for power analysis.[13] For him, Mills is dealing with one aspect of the "comedy of morals." He holds that Mills writes in "vivid metaphor" surrounded by statistics, that he appears guided by Balzac's moral that "behind every fortune there is a crime." Bell sees The Power Elite as static and ahistorical because of Mills's disregard for the influence of ideology on sociopolitical behavior. The Power Elite is a hierarchy of "orders," rather than power organization in time. It is a "model" rather than a historical analysis.

Bell holds that Mills improperly interchanges terms, e.g., "institutions" for "domains," which is also confused with sectors, or orders. Therefore, to speak of a priority of certain orders over others says little. It ignores how and why such a dominance of priorities is maintained, and also ignores the belief systems which perpetuate and influence its historical course. What is more, according to Bell, Mills lacks a working definition of power. For Mills it is nothing more than domination, but he fails to take up the norms, values, traditions, matters of legitimacy, and issues of leadership which would give the notion of power concrete substance.

For Bell the notion of a power elite at the command posts of institutions is a perfect example of argument by metaphor. These institutions, set up like granite blocks, with heads, have no identities or ideas. Even if their ideas and identities are not of primary value, their significance is still misunderstood. What people do and think gives them access to power, even within the major institutions. Locating a top stratum does not come to terms with the actual distribution of power. Bell complains that Mills is vague on what the "big decisions" constitute, or their meaning, and that he comes close to a conspiracy theory of history, and by implication, to the idea of perfect ruling class cohesion. Since he does not include or appreciate the role of ideas and issues, Mills cannot describe what unites or disunities the elite. And ideas and issues for Bell are the "stuff" of politics. Thus, Mills fails to see conflict of interests and does not explain how centralization withstands polarizing tendencies among elites.

Since Mills fails to distinguish prestige and honor from power and violence, he cannot trace how the former lead to the beliefs and patterns that produce the latter. As a result, the relationship between raw power and accepted status is all but eliminated. He does not tell us what constitutes honor or when power will spill over into violence. He merely indicates the sources of prestige within the institutional hierarchy, not how status actually works. He does not explain why some values are brutally fought over and others are limited to political gaming—even within the same elite cohorts.

Mills's "big decisions" reduce themselves, according to Bell, to foreign policy and war decisions, rather than policies applied to domestic institutions, where more levels of decision making are involved. Bell accuses Mills of failing to recognize that the American Constitution centers war decisions on the presidential office, checked by Congress precisely to prevent a military elite from dominating top decisions. Presidential reliance on expert military personnel is, hence, not the equivalent of "military ascendancy," especially since decisions on violence are grounded in a world situation and not merely on military expertise informing foreign-policy making. Mills converts the obvious fact that leaders are responsible for decisions into a sensational discovery to suit popular resentment of power. His general neglect of concrete American experience leads to "obsessive oversimplification."

According to Bell, "power elite" is a slippery phrase that allows the social scientist to ignore the basic character of a social system. Mills does not differentiate the United States and the Soviet Union. He ignores the role of the Supreme Court. In sum, Bell sees *The Power Elite* as merely a polemic against those who say that in the United States decisions are arrived at democratically.

Critics, of course, have points of view in common, and there is likely to be considerable overlap in criticism. Robert Lynd simply and clearly raises the question of where the book was intended to go and then proceeds to criticize Mills in some respects as does Bell—but without his vitriol.[14] Lynd had been developing a theory of power in democracy since the days of *Middletown*. For Lynd, power is a social resource absolutely necessary for the operation of society; like physical energy, it can be consciously harnessed for human welfare or corrupted by misuse. Determining democratic goals and tasks for a given social operation and figuring out whether such an operation enhances a democratic national life is therefore a responsibility for all power theorists. Lynd shares Mills's concern with the proper uses and elite groups abused applications of power, which he also found. Yet he chides Mills for failing to undertake an analysis of power that extends its meaning, especially for democracy. The chief task for the observer of power, says Lynd, is developing a theory of power for a given society. While Lynd is in basic sympathy with Mills's view of American institutional life, he is out of sympathy with what he sees as Mills's lack of commitment to a liberal democratic ethos. Consequently, he finds that Mills's ambiguous "exposé" lacks concrete ground as well as meaningful goals.

Lynd also finds elite analysis generally limited, if not distasteful, because it obscures or ignores the basic characteristics of a given nation and social system. It breeds a careless or superficial "hit and run" analysis that amounts to a way out of dealing with capitalism, socialism, and class structure. Mills's pragmatism was far less attractive for Lynd in the mid-1950s, when he saw it as a poor stand-in for Marxist analysis, than when, in the mid-1940s, he saw it as a robust extension of philosophic analysis to include political issues.

Because Mills concentrates exclusively on power, Lynd claims, he overlooks the important continuities between present-day and nineteenth-century American capitalism. By focusing on "great changes," he fails to account for property as a power base. He treats the capitalist character of United States economic institutions as if it were a mere entry to the elite rather than the defining quality of economic life in the United States from the very outset of the Revolution.

Talcott Parsons also raises meaningful criticisms of Mills, from a more conservative framework, although he grants considerable importance to *The Power Elite* because it attempts a major interpretation of the entire American society.[15] Parsons begins by taking issue with Mills's use of terms, such as the economic meaning ascribed to "class" and "higher immorality." He considers that Mills is vague on relations between the power elite and other elements in the elite structure. But his doubts are more fundamental than terminological.

Parsons questions whether additions to the category of the "very rich" have occurred more through inheritance or self-earning, and he thinks Mills ascribes to them too much decision-making influence. Parsons holds that Mills erroneously confuses the "very rich" and the "corporate rich," making it appear as if they constitute a solid corporate hierarchy, when in fact they are distinct groups. He also argues that Mills's treatment of the "political directorate" is weak since he makes it appear to be infiltrated by business, leaving it little or no policy-making independence. Mills does allow independence only to the military, but on grounds which could just as easily admit the autonomy of the polity.

Parsons claims that government influence is great and very real, and hence its influence has considerable autonomy. Business interests do not direct it. This governmental influence makes the political directorate highly independent precisely because of the position of the United States in world affairs and its corresponding industrial maturation at the national level. The growth of power concentration appears pronounced only because nonpolitical decentralized patterns historically prevailed in nineteenth-century America, enhanced by a cultural emphasis on economic values.

Mills is said to look too nostalgically at Jeffersonianism, a doctrine incompatible with industrialization. Perpetuating the power of the local family elite, even if it would have preserved the "scatter of power," and thus competitive values, would also have impeded advanced industrialization, because it does not allow for differentiation of economic production in specialized organizations. Development brings specialization and structural differentiation, and more specialized leadership. There is specialization at three levels: (1) in organizations of economic production; (2) in functions within the economy; and (3) in class differentiation within society. Concentration is linked to the need to administer efficient production units while allowing for the numerous special tasks and skills needed to carry on production in a mature industrial economy. Parsons insists that Mills should have questioned whether this concentration has gone too far because of factors extraneous to development. Parsons claims Mills has provided no evidence that concentration exceeds the needs of efficiency and has contented himself with noting the fact of concentration. He further notes that the relative share of profits for the largest firms has been stable for more than a generation, suggesting equilibrium rather than excess. Parsons questions whether the power of managerial and executive classes has increased inordinately, and challenges Mills to demonstrate this.

Unlike Mills, Parsons separates the fortune-holders (very rich) from the executives (corporate rich). For the most part executives do not acquire fortunes that raise their status and position from the corporation. They are, rather, advanced by promotion, and decision-making control is in their hands rather than centered in family ownership. The original "captains of industry" failed to consolidate control of their enterprises. Executive responsibility was linked with competence in such a way that the ascriptive rights of property ownership gave way to the occupational functions of "professionals." There are two ways in which Mills obscures this shift, according to Parsons. He continues to speak of power within the economy as based on property, which is not substantively true, and he fails to appreciate the goal-oriented nature of industrial tasks. In old-style family enterprise, still predominant in the small-business sector, functions of management and ownership are fused in the same people. In the larger enterprise such functions have by and large become differentiated, serving as a system of checks and balances upon one another. Bonuses and large executive salaries should not be taken to mean control through property ownership. The power structure in business has been altered through the specialization process, not through control of property.

Contrary to Mills's contention, recruitment into the upper reaches of the economy operates almost entirely through relatively structured appointment. Mills insists that qualifications have little to do with this process. But the absence of formal entry procedures does not prove his contention. Given the nature of industrial society, Parsons indicates that the well-defined elite or leadership in business should be expected to develop. Power cannot be diffused equally in small units, as small-business ideology would have it. However, Mills is right in showing that recruitment does derive largely from upper-class groups. The problem of an elite within the economy must be differentiated from that of an elite group ruling over the whole society. Parsons claims that Mills should have separated professions of high prestige within the upper classes from those who hold power.

In a complex society the main locus of power lies in its political system. The early United States power system lagged behind its economic system. Since the end of the nineteenth century the mechanisms of political control have grown to control the economic sector. Mills mistakenly implies the reverse. He fails to understand the role of political organizations like parties in the power structure, nor does he see that the presidential office is the prize of party politics. The executive branch has extraordinary prestige as well as great powers that enable it to achieve political integration at a national level.

Parsons also insists that Mills exaggerates the importance of the military. While Mills sees the military as filling a decision-making vacuum, he is said to ignore crucial instances when it has been overruled. This criticism is meant to illustrate Mills's tendency to generalize short-term trends into essential features of the society. Further, Mills misunderstands the role of the courts and lawyers in interpreting, legitimizing, and translating the legal embodiments of power into the terms by which the members of the community agree to live. His conception of power is a "zero-sum" game, in which it is winner take all. But in fact power is not simply a facility for the performance of a function, but a basic, goal-directed social resource.

As a result, inequities aside, Mills is insensitive to what binds people to their positions, to their leadership, to their tasks. He focuses exclusively on distributive aspects: who has power, what interests are served. He ignores how it comes to be generated and what communal functions are served. The result is a partial and selective treatment. Mills foreshortens social processes, and the outcome is that short-run effects are taken for long-term factors. He also tends to think of power as "preemptively" illegitimate. In addition, on the basis of Parsons's schema of three types of philosophical utopianism, Mills is said to exhibit a socialist mistrust of private interest and a utopian notion of public control.

Although criticisms of *The Power Elite* have had a wide hearing, empirically based studies have been conducted which implicitly or explicitly have sought to answer or broaden Mills's leading ideas. The most notable of these has been *Who Governs?* by Robert A. Dahl, an examination of power and influence patterns in New Haven, Connecticut.[16] This study not only implies that *The Power Elite* is oversimplified, but stands Mills on his head by reversing the conclusions reached in his work. Actually, neither Mills nor Dahl is specifically concerned with the nature of power and its relation to socioeconomic systems. Both focus on the distribution of power in a modern (rather than specifically socialist or capitalist) context. Both are concerned with the effect of restraining norms on the exercise of political power. Yet Dahl seems to have deliberately decided that if Mills is right in the larger context it will be borne out in any community study. However, this is precisely what Mills's premises do not require. To reach the "nodal point" where decision-making power passes into the hands of a power elite, the range must be directly national in scope and ramification. To isolate the parts of the larger system is to focus on what is marginal and not necessarily on what is essential to system maintenance.

Dahl draws richly and effectively on the history of the city and the backgrounds of its leading people. He begins with the premise that historically the exercise of power moved from a ruling oligarchy in a relatively simple and undifferentiated social context toward a pluralistic-democratic community in a complicated and highly specialized context. This movement occurred, first, as part of the growing complications and fragmentation imposed by an industrial society; and second, through yielding to pressures for dominance by advantaged ethnic, business, middle-class and lower-class groups. Specialization and mass pressure ensured the breakdown of oligarchy. The small, aristocratically oriented ruling group could not, and finally would not, resist these democratizing tendencies.

A proliferation of new claims was imposed on government by large masses, and a fragmentation of areas of influence ensued. Politics could no longer be confined or defined by the interests of narrow and small upper classes. While it may be the case that lower classes remain without adequate political resources or high motivation to press their true influence upon government, the transformation of American democracy has been substantial. Many middle-range groups whose various overlapping interests have brought about a political style of variously patterned coalitions involving larger numbers than ever now largely manipulate political machinery. What is more, power and influence are primarily, if not entirely, centered in politics. And the political apparatus, however imperfect, does not operate through a guiding or covert directorate outside of government machinery.

Due to the dispersion of advantage and resources for middle-class groups and disadvantage for lower-class groups, politics is an interaction system with pockets of intense influence, gradually shading off outward. Influence crystal-

lizes on issues rather than class lines, and the various interests an issue calls forth give a pragmatic coalition style to
politics. This takes place in a context in which widely believed in democratic norms impose limits on excessive concentration of power.

Dahl shares with Mills a feeling for the ambiguity of the
sources and intensity of power. But, aside from a few superficial resemblances, the similarity of their conceptions of
power ends there. Dahl develops an elaborate structure, replete with detailed charts, to explain the nature of the public. This public is definitely not excluded from major decisions, and its removal from major issues is virtually self-willed
rather than engineered "from above." From a set of interesting hypotheses, Dahl finds that this public is always courted
as an electorate, and its temper and different interests are
nurtured, appealed to, and cautiously accounted for in higher
policy. Insofar as the public is ignorant or disinterested, this
is a natural outcome of differences in leisure, resources,
advantages, education, motivation, and interests. Opportunities are presumably always available to the elites, but, as in
all societies, there are numerous other pursuits and interests that impose limits on, and attitudes toward, political
participation. Consequently it is only to be expected that a
concentration of political resources and influence will be in
the hands of those who fully apply themselves to political
practice, whether out of interest or personal suitability.

Dahl's shrewd analysis, in its community focus, is not
unlike sociological analyses of the forties, which also considered the problem of class definition from the standpoint
of pluralism. This is the crux of the matter—the area of focus. By exclusive concentration on political machinery and
the ideology and composition of one city, whether typical
or not, other matters are sacrificed. For example, a "Millsian"
approach would have pursued the obvious economic ties of
a middle-sized city like New Haven to its neighboring giants, New York City or Boston. Furthermore, Mills did not

deny popular effectiveness in local government concerned with local issues. His argument rested on the extent to which this unit of power can suffice for the larger national picture. For example, he would have attempted to gauge the extent to which any New Haven mayor could achieve a significant political voice outside of his immediate electorate. For Dahl, this is not a serious question, for he is examining fluid interaction in one of its "eddies"—New Haven.

For Mills, the size of the terrain studied is an all-important question, since access to power is based on acquisition of office in a hierarchy. Lower offices are stepping-stones to higher ones, entry into which are the achievements of significant power. Mills would not have examined New Haven, to gauge the mayor's power, but the "mayoralty" in a national context. Different starting points and not merely points of view account heavily for the widest differences between Dahl and Mills. Far from providing an "answer" to *The Power Elite,* the "community" point of view was simply evaluated as a special case limiting a "national" approach to political sociology.

Mills's *Power Elite* provided little in the way of theoretical innovation. Bottomore was right to note the absence of a coherent philosophical outlook.[17] But Mills did provide a sentiment which came to fruition a decade later in works like Christopher Lasch's *The Agony of the American Left,*[18] Gabriel Kolko's *Wealth and Power In America,*[19] and G. William Domhoff's *Who Rules America?*[20] It would hardly be news to say that these were perhaps sounder treatises than that of Mills. They are worked mightily to search for America through a coherent, but usually European theory. However, Mills with his wide-open pragmatism left his American passions on public display. His populism, sometimes ripening into nativism, generated trust. Many of his erstwhile acolytes stopped looking at the utopian prospects of an America growing in a wide-open universe, and buried their passions beneath a rubble of socialist pieties. Their "improvements"

upon Mills, tightening the vise of ideology, may have improved theory but lost an audience.

Weaknesses and shortcomings notwithstanding, *The Power
Elite* still looks and feels less dated than the efforts of Mills's
more sophisticated critics. While they are shrewd and knowing in their selective exposure of the nature, function, and
division of power at a given time or place, they do not explain the enduring character of *The Power Elite*. This durability has less to do with specific empirical illustrations of
the use and abuse of power than with the utter transformation, in the second half of the twentieth century, of the relationship between economics and politics. The previous one
hundred years, certainly 1848 to 1948, took for granted the
economic sources of human behavior. Whether the motive
was personal greed, corporate control, or military conquest,
the answers were sought and inevitably found in economic
drives. Nor was this economic explanation confined to the
Marxists. Hobson on imperialism, Beard on warfare, and
Keynes on monetary policy provided ample "bourgeois"
formulas of the economic sources of everything from crisis
to conflict.

In reviewing Mills one is tempted to draw the same distinction between conspiracy theory and real conspiracies.
There is power theory and real power. Mills drew our attention to the latter but was saddled with the former. He could
not escape the presumption that because a person or a group
holds power they must necessarily act in concert. He failed
to consider psychological as well as political allegiances that
would serve crosscutting or multiple purposes. Mills also
presumed that holders of power necessarily held common
interests, again, without considering conditions under which
real interests drive holders of power to move in different
directions. His single-minded dedication to power theory
made him an easy mark for a variety of critics, right and
left, who saw Mills as a primitive lacking in sophistication or
saw him as substituting sophistication for scientific analysis.[21]

But in the great pull of time. what Mills did best was cut away the debris of inherited doctrines by reversing the causal process. Power is not simply *sui generis*, but a response to political domination. It is this political element which determines the character of economic systems and even economic performance. Whatever the specific changes over time in Millsian formulas about who wields power and why, it has become an axiom of social science and public policy that the political process is the "base" and the economic network the "super-structure." Whether in the long run we are "dead or red" is of less consequence to Mills than the fact that in the short run the political process determines which of the two we become. It is not power but politics that is the source of the continuing fascination with Mills's work in this area, a fascination that has turned into a fixation as more and more decisions about economic matters are managed and manipulated by politicians—whether in the industrial or underdeveloped nations; whether by people of talent or just plain fools. This, then, explains the continuing passion for power: the realization by Mills that it has become a higher game than the struggle for wealth or status.

Notes

1. Arnold M. Rose, *The Power Structure: Political Process in American Society*. New York: Oxford University Press, 1967, p. xx.
2. Tom B. Bottomore, *Classes in Modern Society*. London: George Allen & Unwin, 1965, p. 77.
3. Arthur Kornhauser, ed. *Problems of Power in American Democracy*. Detroit: Wayne State University, 1957.
4. Reinhard Bendix and Seymour Martin Lipset, eds. *Class, Status, and Power: Social Stratification in Comparative Perspective*, rev. ed. New York: The Free Press/Macmillan Co., 1953, 1966.
5. C. Wright Mills, *The Power Elite*. New York: Oxford University Press, 1956. All references to Mills's work in this chapter will be to this book.
6. David Riesman, Nathan Glazer, and Reuel Denney, *The Lonely Crowd*. New Haven: Yale University Press, 1950, 1953.
7. Seymour Martin Lipset, *Political Man: The Social Bases of Politics*. Garden City, N.Y.: Doubleday & Co., 1960. esp. pp. 439–456.

8. Talcott Parsons, "The Destruction of Power in American Society." In *Structure and Process in Modern Societies.* Glencoe, Ill.: Free Press, 1960, pp. 199–225.
9. Todd Gitlin, "Local Pluralism as Theory and Ideology." *Studies on the Left* 5, no. 3 (Summer 1965): 21–45.
10. Robert S. Lynd and Helen M. Lynd, *Middletown: A Study in American Culture.* New York: Harcourt, Brace & Co., 1929, esp. pp. 478–502.
11. Floyd Hunter, *Community Power Structure: A Study of Decision Makers.* Chapel Hill: The University of North Carolina Press, 1953.
12. Bernard Rosenberg and Eugene V. Walter. "The Power Elite: Two Views." *Dissent* (Fall 1956): 390–398.
13. Daniel Bell, "The Power Elite Reconsidered." *American Journal of Sociology* 64, no. 3 (1958): 238–250.
14. Robert S. Lynd, "Power in the United States." *The Nation,* May 12, 1956, pp. 408–411.
15. Talcott Parsons, "The Destruction of Power in American Society," pp. 199–225.
16. Robert A. Dahl, *Who Governs? Democracy and Power in an American City.* New Haven: Yale University Press, 1961.
17. Tom B. Bottomore, *Critics of Society: Radical Thought in North America.* New York: Pantheon Books, 1968, pp. 63–64.
18. Christopher Lasch, *The Agony of the American Left.* New York: Vintage/Random House, 1969.
19. Gabriel Kolko, *Wealth and Power in America.* New York: Praeger Publishers, 1962.
20. G. William Domhoff, *Who Rules America?* Englewood Cliffs, NJ.: Prentice-Hall, 1967.
21. Irving Louis Horowitz, "Power as the Measure of Political Man," *Foundations of Political Sociology.* New York: Harper & Row, Publishers, 1972, pp. 475–495. I tried to provide a basic methodological critique of both the power elite and power diffusion schools of thought in this work. I am struck by the degree to which this division in opinion runs like a spinal cord throughout the evolution of political sociology in America.

13

Totalitarian Visions of the Good Society: Arendt

"Arendt made many small errors for which her critics will never forgive her. But she also got many of the big things right, and for that she deserves to be remembered."

—Amos Elon[1]

Hannah Arendt was born in Hanover, Germany, of German-Jewish parentage in 1906. She was educated in Koenigsberg and later in Heidelberg. After fleeing to France from Germany in the late 1930s, she immigrated to the United States in 1941. She was naturalized as an American citizen in 1950. Most of her life was spent in the academy: she was a Guggenheim fellow in 1952–1953; visiting professor at the University of California at Berkeley in 1955; the first woman appointed to a full professorship at Princeton University in 1959; and visiting professor of government at Columbia University in 1960; from 1963 to 1967 she was university professor at the University of Chicago; and from 1967 until her death in 1975, she served as university professor at the New School for Social Research. It is fair to say that Arendt was an intensely urban person, and that being proximate to San Francisco, Chicago and New York meant at least as much to her as did the university affiliations.

The publication of *The Origins of Totalitarianism* in 1951 established her as a major figure in post-war political theory. In this work she attempted to provide a unitary approach to totalitarianism, seeing differences between National Socialism and Communism as of lesser significance than the organizational and cultural linkages that such systems have with each other. Such systems have a common base in the leadership principle, in single party politics based on mass mobilization rather than individual voluntary participation, and not the least, in a near insatiable desire to expand from nation to empire—whether directly through military adventure or indirectly through political infiltration.[2]

Anti-Semitism functioned differently in Germany under Hitler and in Russia under Stalin, but they had the same common roots: the existence of disparities between social classes and the need for objectivifying an enemy responsible for all shortcomings and defeats suffered by nations and systems. Arendt's powerful critique of anti-Semitism was directly linked to her participation in Jewish affairs once she came to the United States. She served as Research Director of the Conference on Jewish Relations between 1944 and 1946 and then as executive director of Jewish Cultural Reconstruction in New York between 1949 and 1952 (or just prior to her fame and assumption of the round of university posts mentioned earlier).

Arendt's views on genocide extended far beyond her *Eichmann in Jerusalem* volume. Unconstrained by journalistic narrative, she developed a general theory of totalitarianism, in which the subject of genocide was thoroughly explored. In defining Nazism, she argued against the idea that it is simply a distorted extension of Western culture: "Nazism owes nothing to any part of the Western tradition, be it German or not, Catholic or Protestant, Christian, Greek or Roman.... On the contrary, Nazism is actually the breakdown of all German and European traditions, the good as well as the bad."[3]

Arendt, rather than view genocide as a special property of Germans or Austrians (or any other people), considered it as nihilism in action, "basing itself on the intoxication of destruction as an actual experience, dreaming the stupid dream of producing the void." Not a few of Arendt's critics consider this formulation as apologetics, a way in which she was able to reconcile personal relationships with politically conservative mentors and lovers like Martin Heidegger with a larger series of politically liberal, and sometimes radical, claims. But, whatever the truth of such strongly biographical analyses, her views on national types are well within the mainstream of twentieth-century social theory.

The single most important element in *The Origins of Totalitarianism* as it pertains to genocide is that prospects for mass murder and selective mayhem are embodied in the structure of totalitarianism as a system rather than the special national characteristics of any particular people. The forms of totalitarianism may vary—Nazi, Fascist, Communist—but the content allows for genocidal acts regardless of the ideological proclivities of the extremist regimes.

The ground for such genocidal actions is prepared by the denial of citizenship, of political and legal rights of the victim class. In a brilliant examination and support of Edmund Burke's critique of abstract arguments of human rights that are divested of concrete sentiments of those natural rights that spring from being part of a nation, Arendt notes: "The survivors of the extermination camps, the inmates of concentration and internment camps, and even the comparatively contented people could see without Burke's arguments that the abstract nakedness of being nothing but human was their greatest danger. Because of it they were regarded as savages and, afraid that they might end by being considered beasts, they insisted on their nationality, the last sign of their former citizenship, as their only remaining and recognized tie with humanity." And, in a stunning conclusion to the segment on imperialism, Arendt points out: "[A] man who is nothing but a man has lost the very qualities which make it possible for other people to treat him as a fellow man." And this stripping the Jews of legal rights through deprivation of the rights of citizens per se is the essential and necessary (if not sufficient) condition for the existence of genocide.

There is an ambiguity in her formulation in that, at times, it is the size and power of government that provides the seeds for totalitarian rule, while at other times, it is the cultural and psychological conditions that define prospects for totalitarian domination. So it turns out that totalitarianism depends on the assumption of power by the extremists at a point in time when state machinery is "frozen," or calcified and unable to remain a process. But it also turns out totalitarianism is made possible by the widespread installation of fear and what Arendt calls "total terror." And the totalitarians' system is one in which victims and executioners alike are selected without regard to personal conviction or sympathies, but only in terms of rigid "objective standards: i.e., who is a Jew. And who is an Aryan."

The Origins of Totalitarianism ends on a creative ambiguity, one hardly restricted to Arendt. A great deal of argument within political theory after World War Two focused on just such examination of the causes of extremism and the breakdown of law and democratic order. We need to know whether it is politics or culture that defines the limits of power; for, otherwise, not only are we limited in understanding or responding to such ultimate horrors as the Holocaust, but the nature of democratic options as such remain in precarious limbo. We need to determine whether totalitarianism is but an extension of the mobilization and massification of political processes or something quite different and antithetical to those processes.

Arendt attends to this ambiguity in a work that appeared a decade later. After *The Human Condition,* which might well be seen as an interlude rather than a continuation of the earlier arguments with her fine German mentor, Karl Jaspers, she returns squarely to the problem of totalitarian systems and political change in what may well be her most underrated effort, *On Revolution*.[4] Indeed, this work too is dedicated to Jaspers; she notes that, in *The Future of Mankind*, he "dared to face both the horrors of nuclear weapons and the threat of totalitarianism." *On Revolution* addressed the world one step further; with the nuclear powers at a stalemate, revolutions had become the principal political factor of the time. To understand revolution, for Arendt, became the key to unlocking the future.[5]

While *On Revolution* does not directly address issues of genocide, Arendt does illumine new directions, in coming to a psychological profile of political absolutism, a sense of how the "passions" and the "taste" for power lead to the emergence of the genocidal state. She takes Robespierre's theory of revolutionary dictatorship as the quintessential model of the European encounter with politics, an encounter that ends in *anti-politique*. "The thirst and will to power as such, regardless of any passion for distinction, although characteristic of the tyrannical man, is no longer a typically political vice, but rather that quality which tends to destroy all political life, its vices no less than virtues." With the appeal to the political as a framework for rational discourse, the sort of unique qualities that endeared American and British civilization to Arendt, there can be no democratic society, so that even in Revolutionary France from 1789 to 1794, the shouts of the day were "Long Live the Republic," and not "Up with Democracy."

Arendt remained in all her works the jurist, the legal analyst. Her concerns were to plumb the depths of legitimacy, not as an abstract discourse on nationalism, but as an effort to review the grounds that permit a people to survive even harsh and tyrannical conditions. In this, she was neither a conservative nor a liberal, at least in any conventional modes of those concepts. To be sure, this difficulty in easy characterization may be that property in Arendt that has proven most irritating as well as most elusive to critics.

For example, Arendt saw in modern conservatism (in contrast to the writings of ancient Greek philosophers) a profound two-hundred-year response to the French Revolution, seeing it as a polemic in the hands of Edmund Burke, Alexis de Tocqueville, Eric Voegelin, and their modern followers. While liberals, for their part, were doomed to provide an uneasy rationalization for a totalitarian Revolution they could neither quite understand, accept in full, nor reject. But the ambiguity of such formulations notwithstanding, in this way, she compelled a fresh reading of historical events of enormous magnitude.[6]

It is questionable, and not at all certain, that Arendt had her causal ducks in a row on this theme. It would seem that Jacob Talmon, who also wrote on *The Origins of Totalitarianism* with a different perspective, but with remarkably similar conclusions, was closer to the mark in suggesting that the radical segment of the French Revolution, and the French Enlightenment before that, were the real source of polemics—both as a style suited to ideological thinking and as a substantive way to treat political power. But that said, it may well be that conservatism for so many years did reveal reactive rather than pro-active tendencies. It did so until that point in time when it was once more linked to mass politics and political party life in America. But, of course, Arendt died just at that point in time when the transformation of conservatism from a class-based theory to a mass-based practice was commencing. But these are considerations within democratic cultures that were far removed from the monolithic world of totalitarianism that allows for genocide.

As someone steeped in classical Catholic thought and the German legal tradition, the juridical order of things was critical to Arendt throughout her career.[7] The legal system is that logical artifact that both makes possible and calls forth the loftiest aims of human beings, and at the other extreme, prevents or at least curbs the implementation of their most venal desires. These strongly ancient Jewish and classical Greek appeals to the legal as the logical were invoked by Arendt both to illustrate the survival of the human race and its function to limit and ultimately thwart the totalitarian temptation behind the genocidal invocation.

On Revolution is a continuation of discussions first broached in *The Human Condition* and in *The Origins of Totalitarianism*. Since this work is something less than social science and something more than mere speculation, perhaps a prosaic ordering of Arendt's materials is not only forgivable but necessary. Overlooking her contempt for the "modern debunking 'sciences' psychology and sociology," I shall state her position in proposition form and offer possible lines of disagreement and further inquiry.

War and revolution have violence as their common denominator. Conflict derives from fratricidal instincts, and political organization has its roots in crime. Crucial to revolution in the modern age is the concurrence of the idea of freedom and the experience of new social beginnings, of apocalypse.

Revolution gains a new significance as war, its partner in violence, becomes an implausible way to effect social change. Total annihilation has transformed the character of the military from protector of *civitas* into a futile avenger. Even prior to the nuclear age, wars had become politically, though not yet physically, a matter of national survival because of the widespread fear that the vanquished power would suffer the subjugation of its political organization. Non-technological factors in warfare have been eliminated so that the results of war may be calculated in advance with perfect precision. Foreknowledge of victory and defeat may well end a war that need never explode into reality. If we are to survive, this cannot become a century of warfare, but it most certainly will become a century of total revolutions. The universal goal of war is revolution. But even without the possibility of limited agreements, revolution will come to define the character of the modern uses of violence and the present impulse toward freedom and liberty.

Revolution in the modern age has been concerned with two distinct drives: liberation (absence of restraint and increase in social mobility) and freedom (political level of life). While liberation is consonant with various forms of government, freedom is possible only through a republican form of government, which explains why the American, French, and Russian revolutions all adopted this form of rule.

The two fundamental models of revolution are the American and French revolutions—though only the French Revolution became the basic model for Marxism. The American Revolution adhered to the original purpose of revolution—realizing freedom—while the French Revolution abdicated freedom in the name of historical necessity. The American Revolution was at one and the same time profoundly political and anti-historical and, no less, anti-political and quite historical.

The French revolutionary model, the model adopted by Marxism and which penetrated the ideological and organizational aspects of the Russian Revolution, was concerned with the social question—with problems of exploitation, mass alienation, and poverty. It was inspired by the idea of compassion but ended in a mindless passion. The American revolutionary model was concerned with the political question, with problems of politics and the predicaments that flowed from an elitist theory of mass human nature. Its revolutionary passion was mediated by norms and hence ended in compassion, or at least a sense of the worth of the process whatever the success of the policy.

The weaknesses of the classic French model are revealed in the abortive aspects of the major revolutions of the modern era—the Paris Commune, the Russian Revolution, and the Hungarian uprising. In each case there was the rise of two distinctive forces: the party, acting in the name of the people, and the voluntary associations (workers' councils, soviets, communes), or the people as a collective. In the betrayal of the revolution, the force of power over the people came through the consecration of political parties, whereas the council system because it failed to realize itself, as a new form of government (as in the American Revolution) tended to be short lived. It is this fact that accounts for the perfidy of modern revolutionary movements—the breakdown of voluntary association and its replacement by a swollen bureaucracy.

These propositions indicate Arendt's morphology of revolution. Although it is not possible to argue this book's thesis in terms of right and wrong, a number of questions arise. The key problem is the relative absence of evidence. How does one evaluate such speculations? The abundant confidence with which *On Revolution* is written is far from persuasive. The unsystematic prose style, which keeps the reader hopping about looking for the continuing threads, does not enhance a ready acceptance of her perspectives, even as one is drawn to her sentiments.

Arendt reveals little knowledge of modern warfare, that is, little about the ambiguities of modern conflict—counterinsurgency, paramilitary struggle, police action, guerrilla action—that would show that war is becoming obsolete. It might be correct to note that thermonuclear warfare would make total international conflict obsolete—since it is like a gun with two barrels pointing in opposite directions. But the absence of any distinction between war and annihilation throws all of the weight of her discussion on revolution into the questionable assumption that war is obsolete by reason of self-interest.

The absence of knowledge about problems of contemporary warfare is excusable—war and peace studies are dismal— but conceit is no reply. And when the author states that "the only discussion of the war question I know which dares to face the horrors of nuclear weapons and the threat of totali-

tarianism, and is therefore entirely free of mental reservation, is Karl Jaspers' *The Future of Mankind*," she is only revealing her ignorance of a widespread and valuable empirical literature that has just this relationship as its central
concern. Nor is the definition of revolution particularly en-
lightening. To see revolution as having everywhere a violent
quality is to fail to distinguish between change in social structure and strategies sometimes used in such changes. Even if
we generously assume that Arendt is speaking exclusively in
terms of political revolution, violence is not a necessary or
sufficient component.

Contradictory statements blemish her presentation: "The
part of the professional revolutionists usually consists not
in making a revolution but in rising to power after it has
broken out, and their great advantage in this power struggle
lies less in their theories and mental or organizational preparation than in the simple fact that their names are the only
ones which are publicly known." But elsewhere she says that
"without Lenin's slogan 'All power to the Soviets' there would
never have been an October Revolution in Russia." Which
cliché should be believed? Arendt's repeated assertion that
the consequence of revolution is always less freedom and
liberty than previously existed is belied by an appreciation
of the positive outcome of the American Revolution. Indeed, it is precisely her dislike for the revolutionary process
that causes her to search out special features in the American Revolution not found in Europe.

Arendt belongs in the unusual category of a revolutionary conservative. For, although she is bent on demonstrating the negative aspects of Thermidor and Robespierre and
the positive aspects of the *Federalist Papers* and the founders
of the American Republic, she nevertheless is seeking at the
deepest level for a way to make revolutionary movements
responsible to revolutionary men. Thus it is that councils of
workers, soviets, and so forth are held to be useful models
of voluntary control. The revolutionists constitute a "new

aristocracy" that would properly spell the end of general suffrage. As Arendt puts it: "only those who as voluntary members of an 'elementary republic' have demonstrated that they care for more than their private happiness and are concerned about the state of the world would have the right to be heard in the conduct of the business of the republic." The revolutionary elite would be guardian of the nation. How this differs from the betrayal of revolutions by political parties and how this guardianship could avoid becoming a political party is not discussed.

Arendt respects the "spirit of revolution" but scores its failures to find an "appropriate institution." She has located such an institution in the voluntary councils that accompany revolutions, but what is amazing is her unwillingness to support her theory with evidence: for example, there is no discussion of the actual strengths or shortcomings of the late, lamented Yugoslav worker councils or of the Israeli *Kibbutzim*. This is a result of her reticence to address the political revolution of freedom in relation to the social revolution of abundance. Her comments in this direction reveal awareness of the potential antagonism between economic development and political freedom, but not a consistent understanding of how and where state and society intersect, or toward what ends.

The big unanswered question of revolution is precisely the mix between economic rationalization and political reason. Polarization of these may make a stimulating treatise, but it cannot define the experimental character of most contemporary revolutions. For Arendt, the French and American revolutions were creative opposites. For peoples of revolutionary lands, both stand as selective options in search of the new. If massive revolution defines the century, it might be wiser to reach for new combinations of policy and publics rather than to look with nostalgia upon the Greek city-states and their prudent elitism for solutions to modern problems of caste and class.

The various strands in her thinking on law, revolution
and the social order come together in concrete form in her
"report" on the Nazi destruction of the Jewish people,
Eichmann in Jerusalem, to which we now turn. It is undoubtedly the most explosive statement on the trial of Adolf
Eichmann, held in Jerusalem in 1961 after his capture by
Israeli security forces in Argentina. The work originated in
a commission by *The New Yorker* magazine to cover the trial
and was finally written up in the summer and fall of 1962
while Arendt served as a fellow of the Center for Advanced
Studies at Wesleyan University. The book itself was published
in 1963, with a 1964 version that carried a postscript and
reply to critics.

The work has been subject to such repeated and withering assaults and no less fatuous praise from source remote
to Hannah Arendt's way of viewing and thinking that it is
not amiss to hearken back to the text itself. The biggest surprise is that the overwhelming burden of the book is a
straight, legal narrative of the trial of one man in one court-
room for specific crimes against one people—the Jewish
people. The Arendt volume shares the position of the Israeli judicial system: Eichmann was guilty of heinous war
crimes, and Israel, as the representative of the Jewish state
and its people, had every right to execute the culprit.

The largest portion of *Eichmann in Jerusalem* is taken up
with exposition and narrative: moving from the character
of the German judicial system and its corruption under
Nazism, to a biographical profile of Eichmann, onto the
stages in the development of the Nazi plan for the genocide
of the Jewish people leading up to the Wannsee Conference. The next large portion of the work is taken up with a
series of brilliant historical sketches of deportations. The
first wave came from Germany, Austria and the Protector-
ates, the second wave from Western Europe, France, Belgium, Holland, Denmark and Italy. This was followed by a
third wave of deportations, from Central Europe, especially

Hungary and Slovakia. At the level of historical sweep, the Arendt volume stands side by side with the works of Lucy Dawidowicz[8] and Raul Hilberg.[9]

The controversial elements are actually restricted to the Epilogue and Postscript. Indeed, even Arendt's description of the Nazi internment and killing centers at Auschwitz, Bergen-Belsen, and Theresienstadt, and recitation of the evidence and eyewitness accounts of the Holocaust follow a familiar path. There is no effort to dismiss, denigrate or become disingenuous about the existence of the Holocaust, or even that it was warfare aimed at the specific liquidation of the Jewish people. To be sure, it was the very specificity of the Nazi crimes against one sub-set of humanity that permits Arendt to reason that Israeli courts had full jurisdiction in the matter of the disposition of Eichmann, no less than the precedent set by the Allied courts after World War Two in the Nuremberg Trials.[10] So we must look at the ethical and psychological aspects of the Arendt volume for an answer as to why her work aroused such passions among scholars, politicians and Jewish communities the world over.

The problem inheres in the sub-title rather than the title: *A Report on the Banality of Evil.* The choice of words was not casual or accidental. Arendt was in search of the why of the Holocaust even more than operational details. She aimed to understand how this SS colonel could perform such a hideous role in modern history, show little remorse, yet also display keen analytical insight into the trial processes no less than the killing fields he helped organize and supervise. Arendt located the problem and her answer in terms of the nature of the bureaucratic mind—a world of operations without consequences, information without knowledge. In this strict sense, she felt that banality was the most appropriate single-word description of Adolf Eichmann.

While not even Arendt's most bitter opponents would accuse her of being a Holocaust denier, there is a problem with the word banality. It strongly implies the mundane, the ordinary, the everyday inconveniences experienced by all creatures—great and small. To use such a term to describe Eichmann thus appeared as a form of clever apologetics, making him into an everyday functionary—interchangeable with other unimportant people and their passive followers. At the same time, one might point out that for Arendt there is also a banality of goodness. In this category one might easily place Oskar Schindler—womanizer, profiteer, Nazi Party member, and savior of one thousand Jews from the ovens of Auschwitz. It was Arendt's special ability to appreciate the mixed motives from which human beings operate that accounts for good and evil alike. In this sense, her Kantian philosophical roots served her well as a student of the Holocaust.

The question thus arises, and Arendt admits to it, whether the trial was actually intended to punish a single person for his specific crimes, or whether it was a symbolic assault on the totalitarian regime that existed in Germany between 1933–1945. In response, Arendt argued that the use of the word banal meant nothing more or less than a factual description of an evil man, but not a deranged one, an ambitious bureaucrat rather than a dedicated ideologue. Arendt observed of the judges in the Eichmann trial, "a conspicuous helplessness they experienced when they were confronted with the task they could least escape, the task of understanding the criminal whom they had come to judge." As might be imagined, this only rubbed salt into a wound— one that still has not healed or even abated.

Arendt placed her finger on the soft underbelly of the trial, not only of Eichmann but of his likeness: to single out on the one hand the most monstrous of perverted sadists, and yet claim that he was intrinsically little else than a cog in the Nazi war machine, a figure representing the entire Nazi movement and anti-Semitism at large. While this might have passed with a disturbing nod, Arendt's further claim that it was the physical extermination of the Jewish people that was a crime against humanity, perpetrated upon the body of the Jewish people, and that this and not the nature of the crime against the people was what was subject to punishment. But again, the issue was joined between Arendt and her critics, since there was a subtle denial of the uniqueness of the Holocaust in the long history of human savagery.

Arendt's careful outline of how the decision is made at the Wannsee Conference to exterminate the Jews, to make Europe *judenrein,* or clear of Jews, is chilling and numbing. It is among the best writing she was able to muster.[11] And if there were strange elements, such as linking Eichmann to the Kantian precept of obedience to the law and a moral obligation, the actual savagery and fury of the Nazis and their more than willing helpers among the occupied nations can hardly fail to elicit a powerful response in readers even now.

The one element that did arouse additional anger was a subtle equation of the victims with the victimizer. The participation of Jews in all sorts of Jewish Councils and Zionist emissaries (exempt from the normal victimization) in bad bargaining and at times even in bad faith, efforts to save Jewish souls by trafficking into monetary and commodity bribes to the Nazis—which while not condemned by Arendt, are dealt with in less than sympathetic terms. That transport lists to concentration camps were often put together by Jews that sent many to their deaths and preserved the lives of some, has been well documented. But in Arendt's hands, such acts of complicity only deepened the notion of "banality" as a common feature of the tormentors and the tormented.

One can say that Arendt's book is a landmark in the psychology of the Holocaust. *Eichmann in Jerusalem* provides a foundation that makes possible a political psychology of Nazism far beyond earlier works—even of her own efforts to study the nature of totalitarian power and mass movements. If *Eichmann in Jerusalem* was found even by its admirers such as Stephen Spender as "brilliant and disturbing," and Hans

Morgenthau as "troubling our consciences," it is because
the psychological profile makes the Holocaust not a special
event but a common human failing of civility and decency,
induced by either an absence of or a breakdown in governance as a response to the human need for tranquillity.
Arendt wrote a work on Jews worthy of a German scholar
and a classical Greek humanist. Whether the work captured
the ultimate tragedy of the Jewish people in the twentieth
century, or even the imagination of the Israeli citizens at
the time, remain open issues. But whatever turns out to be
the ultimate judgment, this is clearly one of those rare works
in which the object of the discourse is of great significance
along with the subject of investigation.

The Life of the Mind represents a culminating philosophic
effort to understand the role of contemplation in the affairs
of human society. To be sure, it is not quite complete, but
leaves less than one-third unrevealed. Even stating the obvious is bound to create some misunderstanding since Arendt
disclaims being a philosopher or "professional thinker." Indeed, publication of a large part of the first volume on *Thinking* in *The New Yorker* magazine, not to mention that a widely
respected but thoroughly commercial publisher issued the
two volumes, might lend some weight to such a disclaimer.
But, in fact, the work is thoroughly philosophical in the
German classical tradition of Kant, Hegel, Nietzsche, and
Heidegger. It is a measure of Hannah Arendt's justifiable
fame as the author of such works as *The Origins of Totalitarianism, The Human Condition, On Revolution, Eichmann in
Jerusalem,* among others, that a work so demanding, so requiring intimacy with major figures of philosophical history,
would receive wide hearing. Under the circumstances, one
might well have anticipated commercial drivel from editor
or publisher. It is to their lasting credit that no such posthu-
mous exploitation is attempted. McCarthy's postscript is
entirely professional and pellucid. Everyone connected with
this project exhibited at least one central element of good

judgment ("judging" was to have constituted the final volume of this trilogy). That element is good taste.

The Life of the Mind picks up on themes first expressed two decades earlier in *The Human Condition.* The first two parts of the new work, offered as the Gifford Lectures for 1973 and 1974 respectively, seem to express polar opposites. The earlier work emphasized the active life—comprised of what we are doing—labor, work, and action. The new work involves the contemplative life—thinking, willing, and judging. But this triad is only superficially antithetical to the earlier one. Labor, work, and action are interconnected as biosocial activities, whereas thinking, willing, and judging occupy far more autonomous realms in the contemplative life. The triads remain, and the polarities remain, but the special nature of philosophical activities is in asking unanswerable questions and hence establishing human beings as question-asking beings. In this way Arendt sought to get beyond the atomism that afflicts the social sciences in particular—the search for the magical key word: *society* for sociology, *culture* for anthropology, *polity* for political science, *money* for economics, and *personality* for psychology. The magic key is less in the artifact, as stated in *The Human Condition,* than in the demystification of all artifacts, as in *The Life of the Mind.*

The temptation to review this work as if it is flawed by virtue of being incomplete is not simple to resist. But there are so many broad hints, fragments from lectures, and outright statements on judgment, that the work can be examined as a complete effort. The relationships between thinking, willing, and judging are set forth early in the first volume. And like a profoundly risky move in chess, the disallowance of any inter-translatability between the three categories drastically weakens the work. For, instead of searching out areas of analytic linkages (i.e., ways in which the act of thinking involves willing and judging), instead of considering each of these as aspects of a naturalistic theory of mind—perhaps along the lines of H.G. Mead or Y.H. Krikorian—we are required to see each aspect as a windowless monad. It is curious that this should be so since Arendt was so familiar with Aristotle and the remarkable way a sense of emergence created linkages—biological issues into social, social into political, and political into ethical. Indeed, these basic categories have survived 2,000 years, and if the contents of modern science are no longer Aristotelian, the twentieth-century impulse toward the unity of science remains inspired by the Greeks. This major dilemma notwithstanding, Arendt's work is such a thorough examination into basic concepts that it transcends its own checkmate. She can at least claim a draw between the idealistic and naturalistic traditions that propel her work.

These volumes consecrate Hannah Arendt's life's work, even if they do not effect a synthesis of epistemology and ontology. For the essential statement in *Thinking,* made many times over as variation on the theme of mind, is the quintessential point about twentieth-century existence: it is not the struggle between theory and action that is central but the struggle between theory and theory. Thinking is the hallmark of a free person living in a free society. To reduce action to behavior and then interpret behavior as if it were pure thought is for Arendt the shared fallacy of dialectical materialism and behavioral psychology. Whether in the language of revolutionary act or operand conditioning, the pure activist fails to understand that reducing thinking to doing is the end of the process of thought and the beginning of thought control or behavior modification.

In place of the casual slogan about theory and its issuance into practice, Arendt early on poses the question: "What are we 'doing' when we do nothing but think?" The totalitarian temptation is to assume that those not engaged in the collective will, in the process of bringing about progress, are doing nothing. This is the metaphysical equivalent of the theological fear that idle hands make for idle minds.

The reduction of metaphysics to a form of poetry by the positivist tradition is in fact a call for the repudiation of speculation as a human activity in itself. Arendt shrewdly notes that the crisis in philosophy, ontology, theology, social theory, etc., comes into being as a result of pronouncements by the intelligentsia itself. But what makes such premature deaths of disciplines so risky is that what begins as a disputation among intellectual elites, concludes with popular disbelief in the worthiness of thinking: "These modern 'deaths'—of God, metaphysics, philosophy, and, by implication, positivism—have become events of considerable historical consequence, since, with the beginning of our century, they have ceased to be the exclusive concern of an intellectual elite and instead are not so much the concern as the common unexamined assumption of nearly everybody. We are not concerned here with this political aspect of the matter. In our context, it may even be better to leave the issue, which actually is one of political authority, outside our considerations, and to insist, rather, on the simple fact that, however seriously our ways of thinking may be involved in this crisis, our *ability* to think is not at stake; we are what man has always been—thinking beings...men have an inclination, perhaps a need, to think beyond the limitations of knowledge, to do more with this ability than use it as an instrument for knowing and doing."[12]

Bridling the will is no small matter. Its subjugation to reason is more than an indication that in the hierarchy of thinking, willing, and judging, willing comes in a distant third. That this portion of *The Life of the Mind* was completed before only fragments of the portion on judging were done should not suggest that the will somehow mediate the claims of thought and taste. Arendt is the political philosopher par excellence and, unlike Kant, her sense of philosophic categories was filtered through twentieth-century awareness of totalitarianism. She sees will as a constant clash with thinking. In her words, "the will always wills to *do* something and thus implicitly holds in contempt sheer thinking."[13] But more, this impulse to will translates itself into the constant search for the *novus ordo seclorum*. The will remains the final resting-place of "men of action." Such activists demand forever new foundations, constantly destroying what was and is, in the name of the new and the yet to be. Perhaps in this Arendt's strong conservatism emerges, certainly her critique of the men of action would so vouchsafe: "There is something puzzling in the fact that men of action, whose sole intent and purpose was to change the whole structure of the future world and create a *novus ordo seclorum*, should have to go to that distant past of antiquity, for they did not deliberately [reverse] the time-axis and [bid] the young 'walk back into the pure radiance of the past'. They looked for a paradigm for a new form of government in their own 'enlightened' age and were hardly aware of the fact that they were looking backward. More puzzling, I think, than their actual ransacking of the archives of antiquity is that they did not rebel against antiquity when they discovered that the final and certainly profoundly Roman answer of 'ancient prudence' was that salvation always comes from the past, that the ancestors were *majores*, the 'greater ones' by definition."

I suspect that more than conservatism is at stake. For theorists of the act, of freedom, always had a way of terminating their freedom with their own visions of society. Since for Arendt the capacity of beginning is rooted in the human capacity for renewal, it requires no end point. Terminus is not freedom but death. In this sense, freedom as system is a doomsday called utopia. That is why judgment becomes so important for her; judgment makes transcendence of will possible without a denial of reason. The aesthetic sense is not an accouterment but a necessary faculty that tells people that what is perfect to one person or one ruler may be imperfect to another person or ruler and downright ugly to yet a third person and a third ruler. Arendt locates the source of democratic survival in the pluralism of judgment.

What has consistently infuriated neo-Platonists and Marxists alike about the Kantian view of aesthetic judgment is its
distinction between beauty and taste on one hand and applicability and moral purpose on the other. Arendt states
the Kantian argument quite bluntly: "If you say, 'What a
beautiful rose!' you don't arrive at this judgment by first
saying, all roses are beautiful, this flower is a rose, hence it
is beautiful. The other kind, dealt with in *the second part*, is
the impossibility to derive any particular product of nature
from general causes. Mechanical in Kant's terminology
means natural causes; its opposite is 'technical' by which he
means artificial."[14]

Judgment thus is concerned with that "enlargement of
mind" that derives from evaluating "something fabricated
with a purpose." But far from supporting an elitist vision of
aesthetics or culture, Arendt draws precisely the opposite,
namely a populist, conclusion. Taste is a community sense
(*gemeinschaftlicher Sinn*), and hence while not all people are
geniuses, all people are capable of rendering judgment. What
is so terribly important about this populist vision of judgment as both autonomous from thinking and willing is that
it provides the solution to the problem of democracy and
also that basis of unity amongst the *polis*.

Arendt still leaves us with a problem: the contradiction
between the idea of progress as the law of the human species and the idea of human dignity as an inalienable aspect
of individual human beings. This presumably would have
formed the nexus of the third volume on Judgment, *The Life
of the Mind*. For those to whom limitations on knowledge
are a fact to be overcome rather than celebrated, the problem bequeathed by Kant and now by Arendt is a challenge
of no small magnitude or light consequence.

Arendt suffered a dialectical passion, or at least a commitment to the reality of reification: the warfare between
thought and common sense, the Greek question and the
Roman answer, the gap between the past and the future,

thinking and doing, the active life and the contemplative life, the impotence of the will versus the omnipotence of the will. This gives her writings a tremendous tension, a dramaturgical sensibility that has virtually disappeared in the empirical tradition. Perhaps that is why she can so readily and categorically dismiss Hume's dictum on reason being the slave of the passions as "simple minded," while Locke does only a trifle better as a believer in "the old tacit assumption of an identity of soul and mind." Indeed, the British empiricists fare less well at Arendt's hands than at those of her master, Kant.

It is to Kant that the work is really consecrated, for her divisions of thinking, willing, and judging derive in great measure from Kant's great works—*Critique of Practical Reason, Foundations of the Metaphysics of Morals,* and *Critique of Judgment.* From the transcendental dialectic of the *Critique of Pure Reason* she drew the cardinal lesson: the insolubility of the nature of providence, freedom, and immortality by speculative thought. But what Arendt does, what is so unusual about her work, is that it infuses Kant's deadly logical prose with the excitement of Hegel's dialectical scaffold. Whether by intent or accident—and to know Hannah Arendt and her work is to know that scarcely a word, much less a concept, happens randomly—Kant is given the ultimate victory in the classical philosophic struggle. This is no cheap victory, but a victory over titans like Plato and Hegel. For Arendt, it is Kant who gives us conscience as a realm of freedom unto itself; it is Kant who understands that judgment is something that can be practiced but not taught; and it is Kant who sat astride the will, uniquely understanding it as neither freedom of choice nor sheer spontaneity of activity. Kant's will becomes Arendt's will, "delegated by reason to be its executive organ in all matters of conduct." Karl Popper's proponents of the closed society (Plato and Hegel) now meet their match in Arendt's proponent of the open society (Kant).

Arendt points to a great divide in modern scientific quests:

on the one hand is the positivist quest for truth, and on the other is the rationalist quest for meaning. For her, it is a basic fallacy to confound the two, a fallacy to which even such figures like Heidegger fall prey. The distinction between the urgent need to think and the desire to know is an operational way of distinguishing thinking from doing. And here, although the Greeks are called upon to bear witness to this distinction, I dare say it is Arendt's Jewishness that provides the missing link. For it is the historical role of the Jews to search and not find redemption and the redeemer, in contrast to the truth announced by Christianity of redemption through the Son of God, that really distinguishes Arendt's claims for thinking as the ultimate act.

There is a strange myopia in Arendt, an all-too-conventional vision of the history of philosophy as a movement from the Greeks to the Romans to the Christians to the Medieval Schoolmen, and finally to the Germans. But such a mechanical rendition of the history of philosophy fails to explain why Heidegger the existentialist falls prey to the same error as Carnap the positivist. Why does the metaphysical impulse to certainty take precedence over epistemological distinctions? Is not the answer at least in part located in a shared scientific vision of the age in which the quest for meaning is seen as less urgent than the delivery of truth, even the imposition of truth on nonbelievers, infidels, and heathens? Perhaps in the third volume on judgment such matters would have been addressed. I suspect otherwise. Having rejected the philosophic dialogue written by opponents of the open society, Arendt was powerless to cope with the betrayal of that life in its post-Kantian phase. The elementary forms of democratic expression are described as in mortal combat with the evolutionary Nazi and historical Bolshevik forms of anti-democracy. The allies of the demos are left disarmed, so to speak, wrecked by intellectuals announcing the death of intellect.

There was a point in time when one would have had to

shuffle in embarrassment for reviewing a metaphysical work. But these are not such times. With figures such as Marx, Durkheim and Weber anchoring major tendencies in current sociology, no apologetics for reading such a masterful treatise is required, nor need it be hidden under sociological pillows. To be sure, those who represent phenomenological, symbolic interactionist, and humanistic varieties of sociology will probably be far more attracted to these volumes than will advocates of behavioral, functional, or physicalist sociologies. But to disentangle a potential audience for such an undertaking is aptly evocative of what Arendt understands as the topsy-turvy world of action and theory: "The Marxian and existentialist notions, which play such a great role in twentieth-century thought and pretend that man is his own producer and maker, rest on these experiences, even though it is clear that nobody has 'made' himself or 'produced' his existence; this, I think, is the last of the metaphysical fallacies, corresponding to the modern age's emphasis on willing as a substitute for thinking.... And this is of some relevance to a whole set of problems by which modern thought is haunted, especially to the problem of theory and practice and to all attempts to arrive at a halfway plausible theory of ethics. Since Hegel and Marx, these questions have been treated in the perspective of History and on the assumption that there is such a thing as Progress of the human race. Finally we shall be left with the only alternative there is in these matters—we either can say with Hegel: *Die Weltgeschichte ist das Weltgericht,* leaving the ultimate judgment to Success, or we can maintain with Kant the autonomy of the minds of men and their possible independence of things as they are or as they have come into being."

As long as thinking, willing, and judging are viewed as three basic mental activities that "cannot be derived from each other" and that "cannot be reduced to a common denominator," the very edifice Arendt attempts is subject to the same criticism as any other absolutism. In twentieth-

century terms, her work consecrates the collapse of acceptable paradigms in social science and philosophy. Hence the
trinitarianism of thinking, willing, and judging can do no
more than confront each other in field after field, discipline
after discipline. But if Arendt did not effect the grand synthesis (nor does she claim at any point to be after such a
Holy Grail), she sheds a great light on what is ailing our
social and behavior disciplines. We at least know what the
sources of division are with a precision and a clarity that
makes possible new creativity. And that is ultimately what
the life of the free mind is all about.

It is ironic that the author of *Eichmann in Jerusalem* should
also be a supreme devotee of German high culture. For there
can be no mistaking that in philosophy, law, and politics,
Hannah Arendt was a complete product of the German
Aufklärung. The century has been rolled back with these volumes—as if Hitler and Nazism had not happened, as if German liberal thought were an unbroken chain of continuities.[15]
But this is not the case. And Arendt in her towering works
has been a prime mover in enabling us to understand the
essence of the totalitarian persuasion. But at the last, she remained true to the tradition of German liberalism. The French
language, which she loved, counted for little more than a
Cartesian footnote, and the English constitutional tradition,
which surely nourished her faith in compassionate justice over
and against impassioned (nonrational) vengeance, counted
more as sentiment than as structure. Russian democratic
thought from Herzen to Solzhenitsyn scarcely existed for her.
And perhaps most shattering to those who saw her primarily
as a Jewish writer, the Hebrew tradition was reduced to several hyphenated footnotes to Christian theology.[16] In the end,
in the long pull, this remarkable woman, scholar, critic, exile,
and teacher turned out to be not an avenging angel remorse-
lessly pursuing her totalitarian quarry but the last loving product of German Enlightenment: the keeper of a flame she her-
self had helped resurrect from the charnelhouse of postwar

Europe. The dialectical process is indeed mysterious and insoluble, as Kant insisted. It brought forth, fifty years late in a foreign language by an exile from Nazi repression, the last hurrah of Weimar democracy.

Notes

1. Amos Elon, "The Case of Hannah Arendt," in *The New York Review of Books* (November 6), 1997, pp.25–29.
2. Hannah Arendt, *The Origins of Totalitarianism*. New York: Harcourt. Brace & World, 1951 (new edition, 1966).
3. Hannah Arendt, *Eichmann in Jerusalem: A Report of the Banality of Evil* (revised edition). New York: Penguin Books, 1997.
4. Hannah Arendt, *The Human Condition*. Chicago: University of Chicago Press, 1950.
5. Hannah Arendt, *On Revolution*. New York: The Viking Press, 1963.
6. Hannah Arendt, *Between Past and Future: Eight Exercises in Political Thought*. New York: Penguin Books, 1968.
7. Hannah Arendt, *Love and Saint Augustine* (edited by Joanna Vecchiarelli-Scott and Judith Chelius Stark). Chicago: University of Chicago Press, 1996.
8. Lucy S. Dawidowicz, *The War Against the Jews, 1933–1945*. New York: Holt, Rinehart & Winston, 1975.
9. Raul Hilberg, *The Destruction of the European Jews*. New York: Quadrangle Books-New York Times Book Co., 1961.
10. Hannah Arendt, *Lectures on Kant's Political Philosophy* (edited by Ronald Beiner). Chicago: University of Chicago Press, 1982.
11. Nora Levin, *The Holocaust: The Destruction of European Jewry, 1933–1945*. New York: Schocken Books, 1973; and Isaiah Trunk, *Judenrat: The Jewish Councils in Eastern Europe Under Nazi Occupation*. New York: Stein & Day, Publishers, 1972.
12. Hannah Arendt, *The Life of the Mind, Volume One: Thinking*, edited with a Postface by Mary McCarthy (New York: Harcourt Brace Jovanovich, 1978), p. 258.
13. Hannah Arendt, *The Life of the Mind, Volume Two: Willing*, edited with a Postface by Mary McCarthy (New York: Harcourt Brace Jovanovich, 1978), p. 277.
14. Hannah Arendt, as edited in Steven E. Aschheim, *Culture and Catastrophe: German and Jewish Confrontations with National Socialism and Other Crises*. London: Macmillan, 1997.
15. Karl Dietrich Bracher, *The German Dictatorship: Origins, Structure, and Effects of National Socialism*. New York: Praeger Publishers, 1970.
16. Yechiam Weitz, "The Holocaust on Trial: The Impact of the Kasztner and Eichmann Trials on Israeli Society," *Israel Studies*, Volume 1, Number 2 (Fall 1996), pp. 1–26.

14

Beyond the State:
Civilization and Community:
Etzioni and Huntington

"Compassionate communities, as distinct from welfare states, exist only where there is a rich symbolic life, shared, and demanding of the self a hard line limiting the range of desires. The symbolic impoverishment of the Western communities cannot be corrected by analysis, or by analyses of other analyses. Rather, the present correction of this impoverishment amounts to an effort to change the criteria of the impoverishment."

—Philip Rieff[1]

Since the start of the sociological revolution, with perhaps Franklin Giddings[2] and Pitirim Sorokin[3] being the last of the system builders, civilization has simply been discarded as being too gross a working concept with which to comprehend the modern world, and too general to provide policy relevance. Yet, a tradition has developed, persisted might be a better term, among the historians in particular, to maintain intact the core notion of civilization. It reached a metaphysical high point with Arnold Toynbee[4] and the notion of challenge and response as a source of civilizational birth, growth and death; Oswald Spengler[5] and the decline of

Western civilization under the impact of new and improved
barbarisms from points East and yet to be determined; and
culminating with Fernand Braudel[6] and the notion of a universal history operating under laws greater than those perceived by ordinary economic systems.

Into such a context of intellectual ancestry, and practical
exigencies, along came Francis Fukuyama[7] and Samuel
Huntington[8] to resurrect these presumably deceased European ideas of civilization and give them a political force
with policy consequence that has made many of the more
alert thinkers in the social and political sciences take note.
There is a category beyond the welfare state with which to
contend. Without going into the specific arguments of *The
Clash of Civilizations and the Remaking of World Order,* the
fact that we can seriously think in such terms, terms that
invoke such primordial identifications as religion, ethnicity,
language, and culture makes it evident that there are larger
matters at stake than state power. The huddling of various
states is not just a function of some new technology, or a
world without borders, but the reverse, an attempt to maintain borders—but along huge fault lines on a world systems
basis.

The boldness with which Huntington, in particular, offers up his thesis on the revival of the civilization level of
analysis merits a pause. He states his thesis plainly enough:
"Peoples and countries with similar cultures are coming together. Peoples and countries with different cultures are
coming apart. Alignments defined by ideology and superpower relations are giving way to alignments defined by
culture and civilization. Political boundaries increasingly are
redrawn to coincide with cultural ones: ethnic, religious,
and civilizational. Cultural communities are replacing Cold
War blocs, and the fault lines between civilizations are becoming the central lines of conflict in global politics."[9] This
is not a recent theory for Huntington. As early as 1962, in
his *Changing Patterns of Military Politics*, he put forth in bold

terms the linkage of newly developing areas with interstate warfare at one level and insurrectionary war at another level. The former is territorial and specific, while the latter is destructive and total.[10]

The ideological source of Huntington's belief in Western style democracy is linked not to popular sovereignty or personal expression of differences, but its ability to bridle violence. It is civic society that is uniquely democratic, and only in the West can one locate such a system intact. For the rest, for the remainder of the planet, it is military society that defines the behavior of people to each other. His sense of the social is related to issues of loyalty to the state or alienation from the state. Radicalism is seen as linked to national, progressive, authoritarian and developmental tendencies. For this reason, the civilizations less capable of satisfying civil requirements are the most likely to display patterns of revolutionary insurrection. This vision of the world as divided between those promulgating international tension and sponsoring domestic violence is deeply rooted in an international relations tradition that extends from Sir George Clark to Harold Lasswell. What is so fascinating is not the novelty of Huntington's approach but rather its remarkable consistency over time.[11]

It might be claimed that Huntington is actually arguing a subtext more forcefully than the text itself warrants an end to Western military and technological supremacy, and an exhausted West versus the "rest of them" mentality. It might also turn out that national rather than civilizational interests are involved in many of the current struggles, as exemplified by the Middle East, which pits not just Israelis against Palestinians, but a variety of Moslem Arab states against each other. All of that may be the case, but that the very restoration of civilization is not just a broad descriptive frame of reference, but potentially a policy-grounded way to conduct foreign affairs, makes the question of state power enter a new and smaller frame of reference.

Part of Huntington's subtext has always rested upon a moral inversion of Lasswell's theory of the Garrison State. Lasswell was fearful that the conjunction of military force and state power would have a disastrous impact on democratic tendencies worldwide and on civil liberties within an American context. Huntington is far less concerned with such niceties than with the conduct of foreign policy as such. His overriding fear is that the diminution of military prowess on the part of the West opens the flood gates not to democracy, but to a series of barbarisms that, while often inspired by theological edicts, have a far more parochial geopolitical goal. Huntington's struggle over civilizations is a concern that the West will fail not for want of democracy but for lack of will.

That which is taken for granted in Huntington is the verities of the democratic credo. The West as a civilization is said to embody liberal values, but these become absorbed in the larger concerns over survival. The forces of darkness are real for Huntington, and they are to be met by the darkness of force—the state and its military machinery. These lessons were deeply ingrained by Huntington from the time of his writings during the Vietnam War epoch, and rather than dissolve over time, seem to have deepened. But the nation state gives way to the international state. For when the notion of the West is made concrete, and is stripped of its cultural artifacts, what remains is a contest in which not even the United States as a superpower can hope to stand alone against the other contending civilizations. Hence, civilization is in effect for Huntington a mega-state, or the reverse of the Kantian premise of such a world state as being a pre-condition for universal peace and brotherhood.

A serious problem for civilizational analysis of the Huntington variety is the extent to which it has absorbed multinationals as myth no less than reality. It might be argued that in this epoch, the nation state has become more rather than less powerful. The capacities of the state to develop policy strategies and direct funding for the domestic market can hardly be ignored. Indeed, it has recently been claimed that the strength of external pressures is largely determined at the national rather than civilizational level, with the effect of such pressures varying with the strength of domestic institutions. The emergence of developmental oriented states in Asia, and increasingly in Latin America, parallel models used in earlier epochs in Europe and North America. But it might well be countered that such essentially economic integration at the international level takes place within civilizational blocs, and hence the state, rather than operating at cross purposes with the larger global context, actually serves to enhance transnational integration.

Another serious problem that Huntington's work faces is the slippage between the military and the state. There is a tendency to see force of arms as the overriding consideration in state power. But the problem with this formulation is that it omits any consideration of the military as a temporary mobilization of might for specific goals dictated by the state, with the state, and its ultimate monopoly on both power and protraction of the public. As a consequence, what Huntington leaves us with is a vision of might rather than a theory of the just society. The nuances of state power and its relationships to social claims are thus minimized, and at times even trivialized.

At the other end of the scale is the reemergence of units of measurement that are greater than the individual but far smaller than the society, not to mention civilization. Ideas about community and association, of voluntary groups and social organizations created for highly targeted purposes that seemingly can the State or the society perform neither have now once more appeared. Once again, whether in its Rousseauian or Thoreauian form, the cry of the heart can be heard. The state is too cruel, the society too soft, to provide the basis for a coherent order of things.[12]

Every piece of survey research available tends to establish

the existence of a deep suspicion of the rank and file in democratic societies for their states or societies alike. The tendency to find comfort in families, support in friendships, strength in clans and clubs, the huge mushrooming of voluntary associations, indicates that powerful forces are at work that may not confront, so much as undermine, the power of the state or the benevolence of the society. The emergence of the welfare state has seemingly made few people happy or content—or at least not the intellectual class that dispenses the federal largesse. Into this Owenite abyss steps Amitai Etzioni,[13] and the "movement" for communitarianism. It would appear that every movement worth its salt merits an "ism" behind it.

The rebellion against affirmative action, the resistance to taxation, the disbelief in the honor of those politicians who rule, the disaffection of left and right alike from the idea of the state as benefactor, indicates that something is afoot as we enter the new millennium.[14] It is not simply the rise of a new individualism, or retreat into familialism, which also has gained a hearing and which most certainly is taking place. But the key would appear to be the emergence of mid-level forms of human association, both benign as well as pathological, that are seen as protections against the state and society alike.

In this connection, as I have argued elsewhere, the decline in political participation, that is overt electoral participation, is less a function of indifference than of disaffection from the organs of power and welfare. We have become so involved with theories of direct resistance that the most obvious form of resistance, simple denial, has been underestimated, certainly understudied. What we see growing then is the voluntary sector, the informal linkage to events and movements that are not so much organized from the top, such as political rallies and conventions, as generated from below—from individuals who reveal an increasing suspicion of being managed by others.

In short, the behemoth in the form of civilization and the anarch in the form of individualism come back to haunt the twenty-first century. Far from doing away with the "non-rational" elements of state and society, the modern economic and industrial system has made it far easier to extend those elements. There is a sense in which the individual, sitting at his or her computer and accessing information and ideas from the world over, has a larger, if passive, investment in the course of events than was ever possible in the past. Symbolic politics of cyberspace has a way of reinvigorating real politics by providing every person with a sense of a stake in the social order.

In the new world of information technology, dreams of civilizational conquest intermingle with nightmares of individual impotence. Movements of an ephemeral sort emerge, uniting people in religious and chiliastic movements, while disuniting others in any sense of larger faiths and beliefs. The counter-utopian vision of Huxley,[15] Orwell,[16] and Kafka[17] come into play—as answers to the state and the society alike. It is not technology as such that is the alien object in this new world, but the struggle to counter or utilize technology for totalitarian ends that becomes decisive.

The nineteenth century produced a series of utopians and visionaries like Edward Bellamy[18] and Robert Owen,[19] who saw in the community some sort of organizing premise to make the whole greater than the parts. The twentieth century saw the rise of the counter-utopians, of Huxley and Orwell, who aimed to debunk that vision and revealed in the process how the state can readily co-opt such premises. But the twenty-first century will perhaps go beyond the utopian and counter-utopian alike, and grasp the capacity to enjoy life in terms of measurable units that are smaller than the state at one end, and larger than it at the other. In this enterprise, technology may prove the ally rather than enemy of elementary forms of democracy.

Admittedly, what is herein being framed is a speculative

view unto itself. I see no hope for the elimination of the
state, since the need to organize a system as a functional
whole to preserve and protect the political collectivity has
hardly abated much less dissolved. And I see no hope for
the elimination of the (welfare) society since the tendency
to rationalize the economic system so that the extremes of
wealth and poverty are muted also appear destined to continue well into the next century. Indeed, the most recent
empirical research indicates the emergence of a new equilibrium, the welfare state.

The collapse of the communist party state in Russia and
Eastern Europe gave rise to a wild transitional period of
economic speculation and movement to an unbridled "free
enterprise" marked by a rising tide of criminality, speculation, and deviance of all sorts. But this has been followed by
the push to ostensibly preserve the gains of socialism by an
evolving welfare net. Hence, the movement from party state
to welfare state in the East clearly parallels tendencies in the
West to move from the earlier state-society split of which we
have spoken to the welfare state. As Nicholas Spulber recently showed, there is a multidimensional quality to industrial systems: with movement away from State ownership and
control of economies to the deliverance of social goods on
one side, and followed by a consolidation and globalization
best viewed as a welfare state.[20]

There are, to be sure, differences between the operation
of the welfare state in Russia, Sweden, England, Germany
and the United States. These are not to be minimized, and
they warrant research in their own right. But in the larger
scheme of things, it is clear that a new equilibrium has been
reached on a massive scale, one in which the welfare state
displaces older forms of capitalism and communism alike,
to produce a new equilibrium. If this is not quite a synthesis, or even a positive outcome of two centuries of antagonism between the forces of political power and social policy,
it comes as close as modern civilization can to achieving

some sort of global consensus in the practice as well as theory of the state.

It is easier to postulate the decline of participatory or electoral politics, than it is to perceive its transformation in the hands of those hoisting the flag of civilization (or globalism) at one side and the smaller—in size at least—flag of communitarianism at the other. But having established a new equilibrium, social forces fueled by the new technology are also a vehicle for escaping the boundaries of national chauvinism at one end and partaking of the decision-making processes within the nation at the other. In short, the new synthesis called the welfare state must now confront antagonists more in cyberspace than on the streets, more in personal decisions than in mass demonstrations. Aiding in this transformation of institutions and ideologies alike is the egalitarian impulse that fueled many twentieth-century movements, now ingrained in both the state and society. It is also part of the psychic wealth of each individual. Hence, there will be a series of contradictions in individualism, just as there will be a series of contradictions in collectivism. Again survey research repeatedly supports all notions of egalitarianism, even as they reveal a population desperately unhappy with the idea of the State serving as the punitive instrument whereby the leveling tendencies are fulfilled.

What will maintain the force of state, however, is not just the quest for equality but the belief in Western superiority, if not always in a valuation sense then certainly in a material sense. The West is unlikely to capitulate to cultures that it deems less worthy or advanced than itself. The fear of Islam is less over doctrinal questions than the belief that its triumph over the West would reverse the order of progress established in the twentieth century. We know that the order can be reversed: we have seen educated women in Iran put on veils and leave public life; we have seen the most highly civilized populations resort to cannibalism and extreme violence as needed. So it should be clear that the state in its most profound essence, as a guardian of the individual, would not easily depart. It is simply a necessary evil with a price to be paid for its maintenance.

This is quite a different way of viewing the state than that of past centuries. It is not the earlier twentieth-century view of Albert Jay Nock, enemy and source of power and legitimacy.[21] Nor is it the late Twentieth-century State of Theda Skocpol, benefactor and source of welfare and fairness.[22] Huntington's state sheds its ideological dross and becomes a functional instrument in the survival of the nation, the economy and the culture. In this sense too it matters little to his broad-based thesis on the clash of civilizations which party is in power, since the mandate for parties in democratic societies within such an instrumental arrangement are essentially the same: to protect the civilization at one end and ensure the individual a right to exist—preferably without, but if necessary with coercion—at the other. In Huntington's world, we are left with a Hobbesian hard bargain rather than a Kantian world of universal tranquillity.

Americans in particular show the face of the future to the rest of the world: we have a people deeply interested in economy and psychology, in making money and wealth, and no less in findings ways of enjoying such a largesse. What Americans are less interested in is politics and sociology. Prospects of participating in the policy process are left to the specialists, whilst participating in the welfare process is viewed as simply a method of gaining one's due. The welfare system, like the social security system, becomes little else than the price extracted from a citizenry to gain social tranquillity, not a crusade for extending minority rights.

Amitai Etzioni in A Responsive Community develops one minimalist (that is, sub-statist approach) in contrast to a maximalist (that is supra-state approach). Expanding on the communitarian impulse developed by Philip Selznick in the *Moral Commonwealth*,[23] Etzioni took seriously the need to move beyond the welfare state in order to reconstruct a universe of communities, "a web of effect-laden relations among a group of individuals...and a community having a measure of commitment to a set of shared values, norms and meanings." Etzioni saw the answer to the growth of statist repression and societal imposition alike. Indeed, he views the task of communitarians precisely in such terms: whereas in order to resolve the main problem in totalitarian systems, one requires a far better anchoring of individual liberties, in the United States, the case is for more commitments to the common good.

Etzioni examines community in cultural no less than material terms. Thus a community does not require residential contiguities but may be simply predicated on allegiances: "a member of the gay community who moves to a different city is likely to know personally some individuals in the new city or at least to meet some who know people he knows personally." Etzioni wants a responsive rather than traditional community, one that encourages a free cultural domain. But the problem here is that the criteria for a notion of common good and shared value ends up resting on the shoulders of the community leaders. Thus, there comes into play good and bad propaganda, good and bad notions of values, good and bad personal preferences.

Amitai Etzioni may well be the last Weberian. There was always a part of Weber that was more moralist than sociologist, the figure who feared the bureaucratization of social life more than he concerned himself with examining the innards of this process. Perhaps that is why nearly every major figure in political sociology traces his or her origins to Weber, and can do so with a certain impunity. Thus it should be of little surprise that a figure like Amitai Etzioni, who cut his intellectual teeth on the study of formal organizations, should drift into broader considerations of American political life.

In a career which moved by steady progression from a study of organizations then to one of bureaucracy, and next of the actual operations of government, including its seamier side, and finally into a full-blown statement of the anti-statist position as a new communitarianism, Amitai Etzioni has served as a bellwether of the new post-industrial utopianism. Indeed, the Quixote-like effort at tilting bourgeois windmills should not blind one to the fact that whatever his professional "standing," he has sought a public role on the master debates of our time—from the peace movement in the 1960s to a top-down liberal movement of the 1990s.

There was and remains in all utopians a profound contradiction between the goals of egalitarianism and the means for reaching such goals. Etzioni has gone from a belief in an intellectual cadre that would serve as a set of philosopher kings to a view that each community would, in effect, appoint its own Platonic controllers. But the tension, the strain, remains; how could it be otherwise? The state, that implacable foe of all things anarchical, remains intact, indeed has grown exponentially, while the community remains an idea wrapped in local political mysteries. Now that the state has become the source of welfare, the utopians are driven from the temple of collectivism into a renewed consideration of individualism.

With Etzioni one witnesses the uneasy allegiance in overt terms to the canons of liberal orthodoxy—including a faith in democratic procedures and legislation, co-mingled with the impatient concern for community control. And in this swing, one finds Etzioni closer to the conservative verities of a Robert Nisbet than the liberal orthodoxy of an Arthur Schlesinger—a good example of a liberal who has remained firm to his principles in the very act of tasting power. So that the yin and yang of it all is a figure who is both desirous of the wonders of state power while being revolted by the spectacle of its actual execution in quotidian life.

It is hard to expect of someone like Etzioni, beating the drums loudly for communitarian causes, an intellectual self-analysis, or for that matter a consistency of doctrine. But that is true of utopianism in the past no less than the present. In an age that is suspicious of old-fashioned labels such as anarchism, socialism, and even liberalism, the efforts of Etzioni become symptomatic of a broad-scale effort to reposition normative thought, so that it both takes account of the struggles between state and society and seeks a way out of a perceived malaise—at least a way out other than the new synthesis of the welfare state. As a result, it is of deep consequence to review the efforts of a child of the Kibbutz grown to intellectual manhood in the universe of advanced industrial capitalism.

For all of its rhetoric of organic solidarity, spontaneity and traditionalism, modern communitarianism presupposes in the end a safely liberal baseline. That, the communities these partisans advocate are voluntary, open and functionally useful to liberal democracy at large. This implies certain value judgments about the nature of communities sought that are rarely spelled out, but which are practically impossible to achieve without either encouraging associations of an undesirable sort to be formed or exercising highly anti-democratic, elitist judgments about which sorts of social relations are legitimate. There is, in short, the potential for contradiction between communitarian goals. This creates problems that neither Etzioni at present, nor Nisbet a generation earlier, are able to cope with, much less resolve: what of the formation of illiberal hate groups, militias, fundamentalist communities, and so on? Can one be committed both to the conviction that group membership is an inherent good as well as a presupposition that these engagements will benefit the cause of liberal democratic institutions? At the margins, or better, in actual practice, these two distinct imperatives lead in different directions.

One recent argument against the communitarian view, and perhaps the most persuasive, since it emanates from a distinctly liberal perspective, argues that all we can essentially have in common within the context of an advanced

society "are certain shared *abstract* values and opinions regarding the kind of society in which we would like to live, as
opposed to opinions about the particular manifestations it
should assume. Commitment to such shared general values,
not the pursuit of common concrete purposes, constitutes
social cohesion in a great society."[24] It might be argued that
this dualism between the abstract and the concrete, the spiritual and the material, is drawn too tightly, but the broad
thrust of this position is to separate and distinguish a liberal order from a state-imposed order as to what constitutes
liberalism. And that is the great divide that separates Etzioni
from the liberal traditions of the past.

Problems in this formulation of the community are le-
gion and have been well articulated: the community con-
structed as an answer to the welfare state rests on volunteers
at one level and the coercion of the responsive group on the
other. Then there are questions as to whether the state is
actually confronted in this imagery of the community as a
cultural unit, or simply the retentive powerful force that remains untouched by this notion of community. Then there
is the problem of utopianism writ large: whether its advocates, either in the Comtean, Durkheimian, Sorelian or
Etzionian form really provides prescriptions that are removed
from descriptions, or at the least far weaker in economic
analysis than in cultural urgings. Whether a community is
something that enlightens, develops, and strengthens individuality, or represses personal control is by no means a
given. There is probably some truth to the view that communities or civic associations allow groups to achieve collective goals those individuals alone would be unable to attain. Along the way they develop skills and may grow as
human beings; however, the fact that groups and associations are often ascriptive, stultifying, restrictive and even
militant, calls attention to the valuation issues often begged
in this literature.

Moreover, this political effort at downsizing does little to overcome the emergence of counter-efforts to increase the size of the welfare state it seeks to displace. In particular, how does a "state"-led policy foster a "free society"? How does an advanced society encourage voluntarism or group life without constructing yet another massive bureaucracy? This is a problem that confounded presidential politics from Roosevelt's Conservation Corps to Clinton's American Corps volunteer work force. This points to the deeper dilemma of whether it is even possible to construct a national plan to reinvigorate civil society. Tocqueville counted on an well-articulated and well-understood traditional balance between political centralization and administrative decentralization. However, contemporary experiments with federalism, block grants, and returning government and welfare functions to the state and local levels, beg many questions of national standards, and beyond that, have a troubled legacy of local corruption and feeble administration. In this sense, a social science and social policy tradition of addressing such large-scale issues of a post-industrial world must replace the sociological tradition of solving problems by constructing utopias.

As far as our analysis is concerned, how a variety of critics, rather than the quality of such analysis have addressed the triumph of the welfare state merits consideration. The constant reference to moral virtues, to caring, commitment, discipline and self-transcendence by people like Selznick and Etzioni cut across the usual liberal-conservative divide. But this is more a moral imperative then a political agenda. Indeed, the communitarians are often drawn from liberal ranks, but then there are figures like Robert Nisbet,[25] which also have urged a similar standpoint in confronting the Goliath. The argument that the values being urged are spongy, and lack religious sources, often separate conservative and liberal varieties of communitarianism, but in the larger scheme of things the two ideologies stand together against the two major structures of state and society.

Perhaps the most serious charge is that modern states and societies already prove the cement of moral values. Indeed, the welfare state reveals a curious anomaly: on one hand, it does nothing better than guarantee the existence and growth of a large number of voluntary associations; while, on the other, it has rendered obsolete a great number of fraternal organizations, mutual self-help agencies, and private social services that served the same constituencies as the welfare state before its subsequent extension. Welfarism and the rise of federal bureaucracy breed a culture of dependency. At the same time, it seems to produce new varieties of non-sponsored associations. These can be predicated on professional or fraternal relations, and they may be beneficial—but they hardly represent a significant challenge to the welfare state. Indeed, Etzioni himself often boasted of his role as a White House advisor in the late seventies, i.e., in the Carter administration. In addition, there is a multitude of sub-societal units, from family to church. But these traditional institutions have remarkably little role in the world of the new communitarians. And this only fuels the suspicion that an ideological agenda rather than a personal association are the ground on which communitarianism walks.

The problem with communitarianism as a fall-back position, a way to end run the problem of participation in the modern welfare state while enjoying its benefits, comes upon the same problem we encountered early on with Rousseau in his *Discourses on Inequality*—namely, the growing disparity between the desires of the private person and the social control of the public functions. If this was clearly etched in the eighteenth century, how much more so is it the case at the start of the new millennium? Let us examine one simple fact—the introduction of electric power. If that power is cut off even for a few moments, the individual (and that I presume would include the most rabid individualist) takes to the telephone and demands a restoration of electrical power without delay. Other than lighting candles (if available), just about the last thing people do in emergencies is roll up their sleeves and dig in for a long haul without computers, radios, recorders, television, and refrigerators.[26]

What started with Rousseau as the devil's bargain of the social contract, more nearly a mythic contract between the person and the state, the presumed farming out of police, educational, and medical functions to a group called the specialist or the professional, grew into a vast network of public sector, tax-supported activities that served to alienate the individual from the sources of inspiration. As Allan Bloom reminded us, Rousseau's vision has now expanded not retracted under the impact of the modern state.[27] Even the Thoreauian ideal of the private life away from civilization has become a sham—with even the art of camping taking on aspects of a luxury hotel in terms of equipment and comfort. As a result, the argument about individualism is less a serious debate for the reduction of state power, and certainly not an anarchist cry against the state; rather it melds into a broad classical liberal type of argument of individualism as synergistic with a free conscience. And, as one must note, a free conscience can hardly be deprived even within the confines of a prison, much less in the larger confines of the benevolent state.

In some bizarre ways, the end of the twentieth century recreates the intellectual anxieties of the end of the nineteenth century—a radical revolt against rationalism. However, it does so in an era of mass communication rather than mass movements. As a consequence, the new revolt against reason is highly privatized rather than politicized. It gives added strength to the state, and even great confusion to the individual. In both cases, we witness a collapse of socialist prophecy, the displacement of socialist illusions with essentially liberal regimes; but such a displacement does not necessarily lead to a reconsideration much less an abandonment of such illusions. In the late nineteenth century, it led to demands for the *bourse du travail* or labor centers, and at

both epochs witnessed the conversion of the belief in socialism with a demand for the immediate realization of human
brotherhood, and now sisterhood.[28] At the global end, the
idea of a conflict between civilizations receives its ultimate
parody in caricature, in the idea of conflict between galax-
ies. Our earthly civilization is constantly at war with the dark
forces of civilizations from outer space—in science fiction
films and books at least. In short, at both ends of the ideological spectrum we have the creation and recreation of exaggeration and mannerism. At the microscopic end we witness the demand for instant affection through community,
while at the macroscopic end we witness the demand for
instant hegemony through global and now intergalactic
order.

At the end of the day, the extreme communitarianism
advocated by Etzioni, like the civilizational identification
claimed by Huntington, both reaches into all aspects of society. Like statism in general, totalitarianism becomes the
unwanted guest for each of these essentially liberal, democratic thinkers. Totalitarian ideologies, writ either small or
large, are relentless in collapsing intermediary social structures that permit behavior to depart from corporativist or
statist norms. Whether the emphasis is on the community
or the party, the results are the same: a displacement of
voluntarism by totalitarianism, and of law by order. It was
the great accomplishment of Montesquieu to break clear of
the Platonic State. It is the great tragedy of such fine talents
as Etzioni and Huntington that they end up by a return to
just such a stratified Republic so dearly embraced by Plato
and his many followers.

Notes

1. Philip Rieff, *The Triumph of the Therapeutic: Uses of Faith After Freud.*
   Chicago and London: The University of Chicago Press, 1966, p. 245.
2. Franklin H. Giddings, *Democracy and Empire: With Studies of Their*

Psychological, Economic and Moral Foundations. New York: Books For Libraries Press, 1902.

3. Pitirim A. Sorokin, *Crisis of Our Age: The Social and Cultural Outlook.* New York: E.P. Dutton, 1941; and his later text on *Social and Cultural Mobility.* New York: Macmillan Publishers, 1959.

4. Arnold J. Toynbee, *A Study of History* (abridgment in two volumes). New York and London: Oxford University Press, 1989.

5. Oswald Spengler, *Decline of the West* (in two volumes). New York: Random House, 1945.

6. Fernand Braudel, *A History of Civilizations.* New York: Penguin Books-Viking Press, 1995.

7. Francis Fukuyama, *The End of History and the Last Man.* New York: Macmillan: The Free Press, 1993, 418 pp.

8. Samuel P. Huntington, *The Clash of Civilizations and the Remaking of World Order.* New York: Simon & Schuster, 1996, p. 125.

9. Samuel P. Huntington, *Political Order in Changing Societies.* New Haven, CT: Yale University Press, 1969.

10. Samuel P. Huntington, *Changing Patterns of Military Politics.* New York: The Free Press of Glencoe (Crowell-Collier), 1962, p. 21.

11. Samuel P. Huntington, *Changing Patterns of Military Politics.* New York: The Free Press of Glencoe (Crowell-Collier), 1962, pp.41-44.

12. Samuel P. Huntington, *The Soldier and the State: The Theory and Politics of Civil Military Relations.* Cambridge: Harvard University Press, 1981.

13. Amitai Etzioni, *New Communitarian Thinking: Persons, Virtues, Institutions, and Communities.* Charlottesville, Virginia: University Press of Virginia, 1995. See also his foundation work in this area, *The Spirit of Community.* New York: Simon & Schuster, 1994.

14. Indicative of the broad sweep of anti-statist feelings on the left is the recent essay by Barbara Ehrenreich, "When Government Gets Mean: Confessions of Recovering Statist," *The Nation* (November 17) 1997, p.16. An earlier version of the same position was well articulated by William Kornhauser in *The Politics of Mass Society.* New York: The Free Press, 1959.

15. Aldous L. Huxley, *Brave New World.* New York and London: Harper Collins, 1989.

16. George Orwell, *1984.* New York: New American Library, 1990; and *Animal Farm.* New York: Harcourt Brace, 1990.

17. Franz Kafka, *The Castle.* New York: Schocken Books, 1995.

18. Edward Bellamy, *Looking Backward.* New York: New American Library, 1989. For a fine critique, see Arthur Lipow, *Authoritarian Socialism in America: Edward Bellamy and the Nationalist Movement.* Berkeley and Los Angeles: University of California Press, 1991.

19. Robert Owen, *A New View of Society and other Writings.* New York: Penguin Books-Viking Press, 1991.

20. Nicholas Spulber, *Redefining the State: Privatization and Welfare Reform in Historical and Transitional Economies.* Cambridge: Cambridge University Press, 1997, especially pp. 189-215.

21. Albert Jay Nock, *Our Enemy, the State*. New York: Morrow Publishers, 1935.
22. Theda Skocpol. *Bringing the State Back In*. New York: Cambridge University Press, 1985.
23. Philip Selznick, *The Moral Commonwealth: Social Theory and the Promise of Community*. Berkeley and Los Angeles: University of California Press, 1992.
24. Linda C. Rader, "Liberalism and the Common Good," *The Independent Review: A Journal of Political Economy*, Volume II, Number 4 (Spring 1998), p. 532.
25. Robert A. Nisbet, *Twilight of Authority*. New York and London: Oxford University Press, 1977; and *Quest for Community*. New York and London: Oxford University, 1962.
26. Daniel Bell, *Communitarianism and its Critics*. New York and London: Oxford University Press, 1993.
27. Allan Bloom, *The Closing of the American Mind*. New York: Simon & Schuster, 1987, pp. 189–190.
28. The spate of texts on community is well represented by a collection edited by Philip Nyden, Anne Figert, Mark Shibley, Darryl Burrows, *Building Community*. Thousand Oaks, California: Pine Forge Press, 1997.

15

Between Politics and Economics: Welfare State vs. Global Economy

---

"I just want to register a protest against the proposition expressed that anything, be it technology or be it economics, is the "ultimate" or "essential" cause of anything else. If we consider the chain of causation [we will find that] it runs sometimes from political to religious and then to economic matters, etc. At no point do we come to a resting place."

—Max Weber[1]

Where do we stand at the end of a two-hundred-fifty-year survey of statists, revolutionists and individualists? Starting with Montesquieu's *Spirit of the Laws* in 1749 until the present spate of political and legal scholars, there has been a deep concern with limiting the authority of the state and expanding the operational scope of the Individual. More precisely, we need to know the outcome of this protracted tension between the "repressive" state and the "benevolent" society. For, at this point, we are less concerned with two hundred and fifty years of history, or at least some key figures in the evolution of political sociology, than with how this dynamic process has played out on the threshold of the new millennium.

Those who have paid close attention to the evolution of political sociology in advanced systems will already know, or at least will guess at the answer: namely, the melding and blending, rather than triumph or elimination, of either or both state and society. Indeed, the fusion is now so thorough that we have come to live with a singular entity known by the familiar term welfare state. It has thoroughly eclipsed the older notion of the welfare society. The bitter controversies between communists and capitalists, statists and individualists, and at loftier professional levels, political scientists and sociologists, and loftier still, civil society and enterprise associations, are now part of history.

To be sure, this is not an insignificant slice of history, since we still need to know how the West evolved from a world of superordination and subordination to a rich—if at times stifling—blend in which we can hardly tell whether state or society is dominant at any given moment and in any specific context. While the shift from common law to law-making by the state has certainly taken place as Hayek and his followers predicted, I claim that the shift is less abrasive than absorptive, less a pre-empting of the former by the latter than an imperfect, even unpleasant amalgamation— one that heralds a new epoch in advanced nations and systems.[2] The source of discontent is not the downtrodden and disadvantaged, so much as the middle classes, who are asked to pay the freight for egalitarianism from above.

In a sense, the triumph belongs neither to the collectivism of the French Revolution nor the individualism of the American Revolution, as Hannah Arendt held, so much as to a belated triumph of the ideology of Wilhelmine Germany. The Kaiser's notion that the state should be all powerful, but benevolent, whilst the society should be responsive to national destinies gave us an early indication of how the issues between state and society would be resolved—to the everlasting frustration of revolutionists and reactionaries alike. To be sure, the late nineteenth-century German vision remained heavily weighted on the side of the state, with its organic ideology of the pre-eminence of personal obligations over political rights. Still, the seeds of the present are very much rooted in the German culture that reached its early pinnacle with Hegel in theory in the 1820s and Weimar in practice in the 1920s. Hans Mommsen has brilliantly argued that the aberration was National Socialism, not Social Democracy. To be sure, the totalitarian regime that seized power in 1933 and lasted through 1945 only served to interrupt a long-term secular process by means of which the antagonism between State and society was resolved by the establishment of the welfare state. The legacy of Weimar rather than Nazism lives on in the German social and economic system.[3]

That these earlier experiments in fusing the political state and the welfare society failed in their purpose had more to do with economic ineptitude, party divisions, and national character than any flaw in the overall design. Indeed, after each major war, Germany returned to the welfare state with a renewed vigor. Max Weber's concerns with the "iron cage" of bureaucracy were entirely appropriate.[4] Even in a political world of democratic norms, individualism remains a scarce commodity in German social life. This strange situation in which the Welfare State was tied to totalitarian rather than democratic modalities has been well documented in the post-war epoch by Karl Jaspers,[5] Ralf Dahrendorf,[6] and most recently, Hans-Georg Soeffner.[7] To be sure, the ease with which the welfare state can be detached from any semblance of democratic moorings is itself a source of deep concern for liberals as well as conservatives. There is an uneasy feeling that the uncontrollable urgings of the welfare state combine the worst features of the State, its repressive potentials, with the worst features of the Society, its unbridled utilitarianism. The flaws in German national character may be a factor in the special rise of Nazism, but it hardly explains the globalization of the welfare state.

At this point, one must allude to the putative causality between welfarism and totalitarianism first developed by Hayek. His *Road to Serfdom* was an early "post-modern" exploration of the ultimate domination of society by the state. For him, "welfarism" leads both logically and historically to totalitarianism, implying the ultimate inability of the state to limit its intrusion into just a single facet of social life. Beyond that, as Michael Polanyi later suggested, any overt attempt to remake all of society—its institutions, scientific organs, and social relationships at large—and not merely "welfarism" lay at the heart of totalitarianism. The means and nature of the state's domination of society has often been examined by the major figures in the history of political sociology, but a certain emotivism in past studies tends to obscure what the state is doing *for* society from what it is doing *to* society.

What obscures the tendency of state and society to blend their functions is the ever-widening separation of institutional boundaries from the private realm. There is a difference between state and society and public and private realms. The concerns of people like Michael Sandel and Alasdair MacIntyre are well grounded, but they fail to address a coalescence of *public* functions. In taking within its sphere ever-greater societal functions, such as welfare, education, children's services, health programs, etc., there is a blurring of the lines between society and the state rather than the annihilation of the former by the latter. Indeed, I would even argue that this coalescence of functions to form a welfare state is itself a source of alienation, of separation of the private realm from public aims and accountabilities.

What is so fascinating is less these national traits than the inexorable process of rationalization, the combination of state and society to form a welfare state in a nation so dedicated to individual rights such as the United States. If we take as our standard bearer the most pluralistic and diverse of these advanced nations, again, the United States, the extent to which we have a new combination and permutation that can be identified as the welfare state becomes clear. The portion of its gross domestic product absorbed by government spending rose from 3.9 percent in 1870 to 17 percent in 1920, to 27 percent in 1970, leveling off (if such a figures can be called level) to 33 percent in the 1990s. And these percentages are significantly higher in Western Europe. In addition, the portion of the gross domestic product that went to transfers and subsidies, that is to social welfare as such, rose from 15 percent in 1960 to 22 percent in 1990.[8] What this details is not a welfare society, but a welfare state. And the distinction is neither trivial nor easily dismissed. While the upper limits of the welfare state may be indicated by this leveling off rationalizing process—taking place in Western Europe at a 50 percent level and in the United States at a 35 percent level—it is evident that the fusion of what in past were viewed as antagonistic features of the political state and the social order—have now drawn tightly together. And, even if countervailing tendencies exist, the structure of the new welfare state is firmly etched in the body, if not the spirit, of advanced industrial societies.

The roots of the welfare state go deep into the technology no less than economy of Western culture. Indeed, no single essay better understood and anticipated this structural characteristic than Allen Schick's 1970 statement on "The Cybernetic State."[9] His essay merits a full citation: "In the post-industrial cybernetic state, government functions as a serving mechanism, concerning the polity the economy to achieve public objectives. As a result, government changes from a *doer* of public activities to a *distributor* of public benefits, and the kinds of programs it operates reflect this change." Schick goes on to point out how this blending takes place in operational, administrative terms: "Welfare has been one of the key programs of the bureaucratic state involving a large scale welfare bureaucracy with thousands of governments and millions of people. As welfare becomes cybernated, it shifts to some form of guaranteed income, adjusted automatically as the income of the recipient rise or falls." It matters little that economic movements are bullish or bearish, up or down, what matters is that state intervention is built into such flows. "Government writes the 'program,' monitors the system and activates the money disbursing machines. This is far different from the conventional welfare bureaucracy in which eligibility and benefits are determined by corps of case workers in accord with overall legislative and administrative rules." Indeed, this new structure is enshrined in new professional fields which give rise to new professional sub-classes: such as public budgeting and financing, that take off precisely in a new era in which state and society are melded and blended.

Despite the continuing broadside assaults on the State, for its inefficiency, interference, and utter disregard for innovation, the state continues to remain a viable institution—its potentials for authoritarian notwithstanding. However much one wants to approve of the tremendous effort by James C. Scott to bring the State to its knees, at least symbolically, by showing the operations and machinations of the State in a variety of contexts, from imposed rural settlements in Tanzania to equally imposed housing projects in America, the State has demonstrated a remarkable resilience.[10] I submit that a critical factor in this survival capacity of a seemingly repugnant structure is its ability to adapt to situations in the post-industrial world. The rise of the welfare state, of the benevolent state, has limited its capacity for evil, but also trimmed its excesses in the process. And as long as dominant economies continue to emphasize their capacities to make profits and create new frontiers of commerce, the hue and cry of the discontented and dispossessed for more rather than less state intervention will remain in force. The state like the leopard may change its spots, but it does not change its ferocious capacity to regulate and rule. And it certainly does not go quietly into the night.

There has been a considerable amount of recent theorizing about how the new technology impacts state power and social relations. The actual situation is perhaps less dramatic at the political level than had been anticipated. For while it is true that inexpensive modes of communication have internationalized channels of human contact, and states are no longer sealed off from each other at the whims of authoritarian leaders, the balance between the welfare state and the commercial society has hardly dissolved. Robert Keohane and Joseph Nye have provided the most sensible account of the current situation. "States are resilient, and some countries, especially large ones with democratic societies, are well placed to benefit from an information society. Although the coherence of government policies may diminish in these pluralistic and penetrated states, their institutions will be attractive and their pronouncements will be credible. They will be able to wield soft power to achieve many of their objectives. The future lies neither exclusively with the state nor with transnational relations. Geographically based states will continue to structure politics in an information age, but they will rely less on material resources and more on their ability to remain credible to a public with increasingly diverse sources of information."[11] The collusion of the political process and the cultural apparatus makes it abundantly clear that behind "soft power" remains the power of the state of earlier and simpler times. At the same time, this new technology is also a mighty phalanx of the business and commercial sector, and thus serves to fuel rather than resolve the antinomy which is the backbone of this concluding chapter: the equilibrium between the welfare state and the business society.

It is worth noting that this new condition, this resolution of the age-old dilemma of state and society, is not mandated in high or in advance by sharp thinkers, clever policy makers, or careful planning. It comes about as a part of the conflation of modern administrative functions and personal demands for equity. One might say this was an "accident" waiting to happen as a result of contradictory demands that could not be achieved by reaction or revolution. Hence, what is often identified as the "liberal" state or "open" society is in fact a welfare state that is essentially indifferent to ideological labeling, whilst becoming remarkably attuned to the demands of the political elite and the social mass at the same time.

From Machiavelli and Hobbes at the start of the process to MacIver,[12] Harold Laski,[13] and Oppenheimer[14] at the close of the process, many outstanding contributions have been made to political sociology, to an appreciation of how state and society intersect. What Schumpeter liked to call "the review of the troops" has been painfully incomplete on retrospect. Still, we can see how these earlier masters were bogged down in a primitive political psychology, in a world where states and societies alike were dominated by personalities, who in turn were part of dynastic ebbs and flows. The earlier masters of political science were better at understanding the force of military adventures and power distribution and gave little attention to administrative procedures. For their part, the earlier masters of sociology were so fascinated by divisions of class, religion and nationality that issues of welfare were paid short shrift in comparison to apocalyptic visions of social revolution. Indeed, welfare was such a dirty word that the field of social work and social welfare was shucked off like a bad ear of corn.

But there are more important issues at stake than a thoroughgoing intellectual review of past shortcomings and follies, specifically, the place of state and society as we enter a new millennium. Let me therefore turn our attention away from a review of the academic troops to present tendencies and future developments, in the belief that the historical examinations that have come before this warrant just such a contemporary projection.

In its synthetic unity as the welfare state, both state and

society remain viable concepts for years to come. But it is now evident that a genuine fusion has been forged, and that the welfare state is neither dissolving nor necessarily expanding. Arguments on this score are now well underway. But the level of fusion is at such an advanced stage of economic potency and political expansion that it has become a central modality of the turn of the twentieth century. It matters little whether the process is at the fortieth or fiftieth percentile, and it is beyond the scope of this effort to demonstrate whether the process of amalgamation of state and society has peaked. It suffices to identify the process and indicate the human forces that remain outside of the control of the welfare state. I speak here of an admittedly vague term like "human forces" for want of an adequate way to express the fusion of factors that resist the blandishments of the welfare sate. For, on either side of the state and society, or as we have now identified this fusion for shorthand purposes, the welfare state, is the resurrection of older forms of human social relationships that refused to disappear or go quietly into the night. On one side is the oft-discarded and discredited notion of civilization, whilst on the other, contemporary forms of utopias, or as the preferred lexicon of the day has it, community. A brief review of these options will indicate how serious is the sense of desperation among those less than thrilled by the new iron cage of the welfare state—and less pleasant to contemplate how limited these options appear at this time.

This brings us to the end—or the beginning, depending on whether we are looking backward or forward—of the "story" of the relationship of state and society. What happens once the two are fused—, as is now the case? Clearly, there is the no less powerful merger of business and technology. The wellsprings of innovation have taken on a vigorous anti-statist complex. This is the case for England, Western Europe, the Pacific Rim, Latin America, and certainly in the forefront, the United States. Even in places where totalitarian politics still obtains, such as China, the sense of wealth as determined by private sector growth and expansion remains or has become canonical. It might be argued that the abstract relationship of employer to employee dissolved the more grounded relationship of state and citizen. With the transcendence of the National State, and its displacement by the welfare state, whatever atavism remained of the pre-modern relationship of client and patron, seems finally to have given way to the pure logic of contract. Whether this anti-statist development actually improves the lot of the individual becomes itself a problematic for twenty-first century political sociology. As a recent work by Linda Weiss on *The Myth of the Powerless State*, points out: "There are now sufficient grounds to suggest that globalization tendencies have been exaggerated, and that we need to employ the language of internationalization to understand better the changes taking place in the world economy. In this kind of economy, the nation-state retains its importance as a political and economic actor. So rather than a uniformity of national responses producing convergence on a single neo-liberal model, we can expect to find a firming up of the different varieties of capitalism with their correspondingly varied state capacities for domestic adjustment."[15] I find this line of analysis as an essentially correct reading of the emerging polarities of state and economy as we enter the new millennium.

Thus, if government will not easily dissolve, it has an old adversary to contend with—the combined forces of business, commerce, and technology. One should note parenthetically, that labor too seems involved—at both ends—as recipient of government assurances of equity and business warnings that statist alignments and alliances with overseas forces imperil jobs and wages. When, as is now the case, multimillionaire interests are both supporting and supported by labor in their quest to prevent trade area expansions in the name of maintaining employment, some sense of the ironies of history merit being invoked.

A fascinating portent of things to come in the twenty-first century is the struggle between the United States government, Microsoft, and the limits of private initiative at one end and anti-trust legislation at the other. Without burdening ourselves with the specifics of the Justice Department's assault on the Windows operating system monopoly, or more specifically, to enforce a distinction between market for browsers of the Internet and a market for operating systems, the issue of state versus economy that first surfaced one hundred years ago in the Theodore Roosevelt versus John D. Rockefeller "trust-busting era," has now entered a mature period in the present era. The government's position is that a technology that in its design and nature disallows competition is in violation of the anti-trust provisions of restraint of trade. The Microsoft position is that by compelling it to sell the browser to a competing firm, the government is not maintaining competition but destroying any initiative to create property or products that cost a great deal. In the words of Bill Gates, the Microsoft opposition to the Justice department is "a defense of the right to innovate on behalf of consumers." He adds, "we simply do not think the government should get involved in product design."[16] Without judging specific settlements, lawsuits, and outcomes, it is evident that the great struggle of the state—whether in the realm of monopoly practices, labor-management relations, or taxation policies—has been against business and commerce. In this, the state has shifted ground from the oppressor of the people to the defender of the people—at least at the rhetorical level. At the reality level, the state has simply become a force unto itself, an end unto itself. The rivalry of state and business should remind classical theorists that issues of power and authority are a far cry from those of masses and elites. They are rather issues operative within elite domains.

In one sense, the epoch of open trade and laissez-faire business and industry that characterized the late nineteenth century has returned to face its old nemesis—the state. And it has done so in a far more formidable manner. For nearly a century the state has perceived itself as guardian of all equity considerations—a giant machine regulating what is maximal in terms of wealth and minimal in terms of survival. And while there remains general suspicion that business and commercial interests cannot be trusted to maintain the equity considerations of the broad masses, there is now a parallel mistrust precisely amongst these masses of the nature and character of large government. From the left as well as the right, cries that government is an enemy, not a friend, of the working man abound.

At the same time, as Daniel Yergin and Joseph Stanislaw have recently shown, the forces of marketplace, the new alliance of business and technology have not just grown nationally, but developed international linkages that are often more potent than the welfare state.[17] This is especially obvious in places such as The Netherlands, where the state remains guardian of social welfare and pomp and circumstance—but little else. In such a land, the force of the multinationals is evidence to the point of transparency. Royal Dutch Shell, Philips Electronics, and Elsevier symbolize a new condition, but also a new set of relationships in which the corporation itself becomes a source of social welfare and health benefits. The size of large nations masks this competition of state and corporation. It also makes the contest between them far more balanced. Nonetheless, the same processes are underway in the United States as in the Netherlands—only the outcome is in doubt.[18]

While the welfare state still can claim its preeminence in the past distribution of wealth (and here one would have to include Medicare and Medicaid, workplace safety and environmental regulations, laws against race and sex discrimination, cost of living increases in social security, etc., and a wide variety of measures related to justice in terms of race, gender and class), the technological economy, for want of an easier phrase, can now make the same claims outside the state. Indeed, in the management of taxation, social security, health and welfare benefits packages, etc., the technological economy comes with certain advantages over the welfare state, and it can do so without invoking the fears of a bullying and insensitive bureaucracy. Above all, transactions increasingly take place in a cyberspace environment. It is a situation in which globalization has compelled economies to develop frames of reference that have little correspondence to the older nation-state and even less to the contemporary welfare state. Just how these mazes of relations play out, and under whose domination, exceeds the boundaries of this work. But it is clear that a certain closure has been reached after 250 years to the functions of society and the structure of the state.

It is certainly the case that the entire twentieth century can be characterized as one in which the economists have attempted to convince the state to play the role of the helping hand. The Keynesian presumption was that one could, in this way, perform a good service, but also move more goods and services around the economy, and hence reduce the risk of state intervention to maintain harmony. Practitioners, from Lord Beveridge in England to David Lilienthal in the United States viewed this as a perfect corollary of political practice, and hence came to champion Keynes in all sectors of the advanced industrial empire. It seems as if Keynes has presented a blameless scenario, one in which incarceration or victimization by the state could little fit with a view of it as a benevolent source of grants to the intellectuals, tax benefits to the rich, and gifts and grants to the poor. The intermediary assumption of Keynes is that everyone would seek immediate gratification, and take this extra largesse and push outward into a sea of non-discriminate gift giving. Despite Keynes's obvious brilliance, he was unable to explain how this sudden burst of new wealth would translate into a new capitalism—since the raw energies of enterprise and innovation capitalism could themselves be harnessed or discarded.

Beyond the economy is the cultural transformation underway. Corporate systems now vie with state systems for creating the conditions for an equitable America. The new business literature, often following the pioneering works of Peter Drucker, emphasize the notion of service rather than profit, support of the family as well as individual employees, making work pleasurable, treating people as customers not members of an amorphous group, sharing decision making, and even expanding empowerment to employees. All of this is an effort by the technological economy and its advocates not just to compete with the state, but to usurp the conventional role of the benevolent society.[19]

As we enter the twenty-first century, the intimate structure no less than broad outlines of the new global condition begins to take shape. A communication and transportation system that makes great distances less relevant than ever cements the multinational corporation. The split screen can play out messages of domestic impeachment and global intervention by the state at the same instance. The capital of the new global economy is neatly tucked away in cyberspace rather than located in the counting houses of New York, Tokyo, London, Paris, Frankfurt, and now Moscow and Beijing. The level of economic rationalization exceeds anything envisioned by Weber less than a century ago. Whether such a congregation of economic forces can conjure up images of a manipulating elite is another matter. That the players in the game of international commerce know each other is obviously true. That they are thus able to collude toward ends apart from the general welfare is far less obvious. In the meanwhile, at the other end, the power of the state has scarcely diminished. Rather, the new concern is the super-state. In this, the European Union is a portent of things to come. The fusion of banking and business, and its new "capital" located in Brussels (but hardly responsive to the parochial whims of Belgium) gives the state in the new century an unparalleled force to set standards in wages, prices in goods, and rules for criminal prosecution. This development of the super-state also permits it to struggle on a level playing field with the impulse of huge capital formations to maximize profits and integrate products.

It might be argued that this sets up a Manichean future of the state versus commerce. I would not wish to conclude on such a sour note. Indeed, one might argue that competition between the multinationals and the super-state might actually be more beneficial to the imaginary "ordinary person" than would their collusion or cooperation. The size of the competition herein envisioned, while taking place on a global canvas, does at least provide maneuverability for new forces that come into existence to challenge either the multinational corporation or the supernational-state. Nor would I imply an H.G. Wells type "war of the worlds." What is taking place is well within this world. And if centrifugal forces are clearly at work in an overt and manifest form, so too are countervailing tendencies toward diminution and even dissolution of large structures. For example, the rise of secessionist and nationalist movements within the bowels of the new empires of state and commerce cannot be ignored, and must be reckoned with. Still, as we kick into a new millennium, the situation in political sociology has been radically altered by larger scale and often external forces that reveal a scale substantially beyond anything envisioned by Weber or Durkheim, much less Montesquieu or Tocqueville. If doomsday scenarios are entirely premature, so too are visions of a democratic future free of dictatorship or destitution. The human race will continue to muddle along in search of a more perfect political regime and social organization, but it will do so on scales hitherto unimagined and with consequences of error correspondingly enlarged.

Many older varieties of discourses in political sociology have become archaic in the process—not least the struggle between the bourgeois state and the proletarian society that dominated mid-nineteenth-century Europe. But other aspects of the traditional canon remain firmly intact—not least the place of the individual in this vast network and maze of institutional forms and structures. The struggle between the welfare state and the technological economy may profoundly reshape the forces that contend for power at the new millennium, but they do not necessarily alter the factors that comprise the moral foundations of human association; shaky though they may appear. So we can look forward to a different—but not necessarily better—world in which human beings must confront the artifacts of culture and technology they have created. It is a world in which big confronts big, no less than good confronts good—hardly a set of circumstances to give aid and comfort to those who believe that community will triumph over order, and good over evil. But it provides sufficient hope to go forward into a less than brave new epoch.

Notes

1. Max Weber, "Der Sinn der 'Wertfreiheit' der Soziologischen und okonomischen Wissenschaften," in *Gesammelte Aufsatze zur Wissenschaftslehre* (originally published in 1922). Quoted in Fritz Ringer, *Max Weber's Methodology: The Unification of the Cultural and Social Sciences.* Cambridge and London: Harvard University Press, 1997, pp. 151–152.
2. Charles K. Rowley, in an excellent survey article "On the Nature of Civil Society," in *The Independent Review,* Vol. 2, No. 3, Winter, 1998, pp. 401–419 provides a fine overview of the Hayek and Oakeschott line of reasoning concerning the shift from civil to statist ideologies. But the solution offered of going backward, or what he calls a "process of devolving power" strikes me as a failure to appreciate the ability of the state to absorb civic functions within its great bosom.
3. Hans Mommsen, *The Rise and Fall of Weimar Democracy.* Chapel Hill and London: The University of North Carolina Press, 1996. This is unquestionably the definitive work on the subject of Weimar social democracy. And whether one agrees or not with the primary thesis of the author on whether democracy or dictatorship is the true "interlude," the wealth of detailed information is unsurpassed in the English language.

4. Arthur Mitzman, *The Iron Cage: An Historical Interpretation of Max Weber*. New Brunswick and London: Transaction Publishers, 1984; and his important follow-up volume, *Sociology and Estrangement: Three Sociologists of Imperial Germany*. New Brunswick and London: Transaction Publishers, 1987.

5. Karl Jaspers, *The Question of German Guilt*. Westport, CT: Greenwood Publishers, 1978; and his classic text on *The Future of Mankind*. Chicago: University of Chicago Press, 1963.

6. Ralf Dahrendorf, *Society and Democracy in Germany*. Westport, CT: Greenwood Publishers, 1980 (reprint of 1956 edition).

7. Hans-Georg Soeffner, "Germany—Once Again 'Belated Nation'?," *Society*. Volume 31, Number 2 (January-February) 1994. pp.39–48. In this same tradition, see Jurgen Habermas, *A Berlin Republic: Writings on Germany*. Lincoln, NE: University of Nebraska Press, 1997, esp. pp.159–181.

8. Christopher C. DeMuth, "The New Wealth of Nations," *Commentary*. Vol. 104, No. 4 (October) 1997. I am deeply indebted to the letter by my friend William Petersen, who in a letter on "Work and Welfare," *Commentary*, Vol. 105, No. 1 (January) 1998, called attention to the remarkable strength and resilience of the welfare state.

9. Allen Schick, "The Cybernetic State" [1970], *Society*. Vol. 35, No. 2 (January-February) 1998, pp. 78–87.

10. James C. Scott, *Seeing Like a State: How Certain Schemes to Improve the Human Condition Have Failed*. New Haven and London: Yale University Press, 1998. 445 pp.

11. Robert Keohane and Joseph Nye, Jr., "States and the Information Revolution". *Foreign Affairs*. Volume 77. Number 5, 1998. Pp. 93–94.

12. Robert M. MacIver, *Web of Government*. New York: The Free Press, 1965.

13. Harold J. Laski, *The State in Theory and Practice*. New York: The Viking Press, 1935.

14. Franz Oppenheimer, *The State*. Toronto: University of Toronto Press, 1940.

15. Linda Weiss, *The Myth of the Powerless State*. Ithaca, NY: Cornell University Press, 1998, p. 212.

16. Bill Gates, "We Are Defending Our Right to Innovate," *The Wall Street Journal*. May 20, 1998. p.A14; and Holman W. Jenkins, Jr., ""On Microsoft, Standard Oil and Trustbusters," *The Wall Street Journal*, May 20, 1998, p.A15.

17. Daniel Yergin and Joseph Stanislaw, *The Commanding Heights: The Battle Between Government and the Marketplace that is Remaking the Modern World*. New York: Simon & Schuster, 1998.

18. Richard B. McKenzie and Dwight R. Lee, *Quicksilver Capital: How the Rapid Mountain of Wealth has Changed the World*. New York: The Free Press, 1991. This is a brilliant study of how the movement of capital has constrained the relevance of states.

19. A fine example of the new socially oriented corporate ethic is the work by C. William Pollard, *The Soul of the Firm.* Grand Rapids, Michigan: Zondervan-Harper Collins, 1996.

Index of Names and Titles